City of Parks

City of Parks

The Story of Minneapolis Parks

David C. Smith

Copyright © 2008 by The Foundation for Minneapolis Parks

All rights reserved. No part of this publication may be reproduced in any manner whatsoever without the prior written permission of the publisher.

To order a copy or for more information contact:
    The Foundation for Minneapolis Parks
    3954 Bryant Avenue South
    Minneapolis, MN 55409
    www.foundationforminneapolisparks.org
    info@mplsparkfoundation.org

Printed in Canada on acid-free paper.

ISBN: 978-0-615-19535-3

LCCN 2008923899

Photo page ii courtesy of the Minnesota Historical Society
Photo page iii courtesy of Peter Schmidt, Minneapolis Park and Recreation Board
Cover photos courtesy of Minnesota Department of Transportation, © David Larson;
    Minnesota Historical Society; Minneapolis Park and Recreation Board
Cover design by Kyle Hunter
Interior design by Rachel Holscher
Composition by BookMobile Design and Publishing Services

Contents

Acknowledgments vii
Preface ix

CHAPTER ONE
Three Extraordinary Men 1

CHAPTER TWO
Try, Try Again 11

CHAPTER THREE
Victory at Last 19

CHAPTER FOUR
A System Takes Shape 25

CHAPTER FIVE
A Turn to the Lakes 35

CHAPTER SIX
The Mythical Falls 43

CHAPTER SEVEN
Folwell Joins the Fray 47

CHAPTER EIGHT
Dreams Deferred 53

CHAPTER NINE
The Main Attraction 59

CHAPTER TEN
Let the Games Begin 65

CHAPTER ELEVEN
The Legacy of Horace Cleveland 71

CHAPTER TWELVE
Man of Action 73

CHAPTER THIRTEEN
Man of Structure 81

CHAPTER FOURTEEN
A Man of His Time 87

CHAPTER FIFTEEN
Earth Mover 105

CHAPTER SIXTEEN
The Rise of Recreation 121

CHAPTER SEVENTEEN
A Critical Evaluation 141

CHAPTER EIGHTEEN
Postwar Progress 151

CHAPTER NINETEEN
The Bigger City 163

CHAPTER TWENTY
A Man on a Mission 171

CHAPTER TWENTY-ONE
Freeways, Parkways and Public Action 183

CHAPTER TWENTY-TWO
Rise of Conservation 189

CHAPTER TWENTY-THREE
Return to the River 197

CHAPTER TWENTY-FOUR
Fragmentation 209

CHAPTER TWENTY-FIVE
What Endures 221

Park Commissioners and Superintendents 1883–2008 231
Selected Sources 235
Index 239

Acknowledgments

This book was financed by The Foundation for Minneapolis Parks to celebrate the 125th anniversary of the creation of the Minneapolis Board of Park Commissioners. All proceeds from the sale of this book will go to preserving and enhancing Minneapolis parks for present and future generations.

Thanks to Foundation president Frank Quilici and trustees Christine Hansen, Tom Nordyke, Don Siggelkow, Harriet Solomon, and Trent Tucker.

The completion of this book on a tight schedule would not have been possible without help from many people.

Bruce Benidt, the book's editor, contributed so much time to the project. His thoughtful advice, constant encouragement and deft editing are greatly valued.

The staff at the Minneapolis Park and Recreation Board were uniformly helpful and enthusiastic. Dawn Sommers provided countless hours of assistance. MaryLynn Pulscher and Michael Schmidt deserve special mention for their careful reading of the manuscript and many invaluable suggestions. Superintendent Jon Gurban provided unlimited access to park board archives and facilitated access to many people who contributed insights.

Thanks to park commissioners Walter Dziedzic, Bob Fine, Carol Kummer, Tracy Nordstrom, Mary Merrill Anderson, Tom Nordyke, Jon Olson, Scott Vreeland and Annie Young for their insights, as well as for their passion for Minneapolis parks.

Dozens of people provided assistance at many libraries, including the Library of Congress, Minnesota Historical Society, Minneapolis Public Library, Hennepin County Historical Society, Ramsey County Historical Society, University of Minnesota libraries, especially the University of Minnesota Archives and Northwest Architectural Archives, Minneapolis Municipal Library, and Riverside (California) Metropolitan Museum. These are amazing treasures; we must support and maintain them.

Paul Beck, the great-great-nephew of Louis Boeglin, the horticulturist for Minneapolis parks from 1906–40, provided valuable research assistance.

Thanks to my parents, Dick and Donna, for their love and support and to my wife and daughter, Nancy and Talia, for unfailing love, encouragement and patience.

To the many people named in this book—and thousands who aren't—who have devoted a part of their lives to creating and maintaining the parks, I give my thanks and admiration. Without their foresight and determination, life for me, my family, friends and neighbors would be much less than it is.

(Minnesota Historical Society)

Preface

A New England Picture in a Prairie Frame

In 1893, Charles M. Loring referred to a section of Minneapolis parks as "a New England picture set in a prairie frame." For Loring, who was already known then as the "father of Minneapolis parks," it was a statement of personal pride. Minneapolis was not yet the marketers' slogan—the "City of Lakes"—although under Loring's guidance for the better part of ten years, the Board of Park Commissioners had made considerable progress in securing the shores of the city's lakes for park use.

Loring's "New England picture" represented a personal objective for him and many city leaders at the time Minneapolis parks were created. The city was built largely by pioneers who had ventured west from New England. An astonishing number of the city's founders were, as was Loring, from Maine. As pioneers did everywhere, those early settlers attempted to re-create their new home in the image of the homes and towns they had left behind.

The personal vision of the creators of Minneapolis parks is significant because Minneapolis parks continue to be shaped and influenced by personal visions. Many residents of the city today have as intensely a personal view of the parks as did the New Englanders of 125 years ago.

Residents of the city, old and new, speak fondly of their experience and personal ownership of a bit of the park system. It is intense, passionate ownership. Those who have left it speak of it with longing. Those who enjoy it still claim it as a right and defend it as they would their homes. The personal connection with parks creates a sense of place and identity for many Minnesotans. This book was commissioned in part to relate how that passion came to be and how it has changed over the years.

This book is not a comprehensive account of every park or park feature that has been conceived, designed, created, used and loved. And it is not a social, cultural or political history of the city. That would be too much to ask of a single book or of many volumes. Instead, I have attempted to discover and relate the turning points that led to the creation and evolution of the park system, and the themes and values that are consistently reflected in the story of Minneapolis parks and recreation programs. I've looked at the visionaries who prodded development—and expansion—of a park system, and at their goals and their motives.

The Minneapolis park system today covers 6,400 acres in 182 properties, an amazing 16 percent of the city's total area. It encompasses twelve lakes, much of the banks of one mighty river and three significant tributary streams. The system is connected by nearly sixty miles of Grand Rounds parkways. In addition, the park system includes forty-nine recreation centers, seven golf courses, two ice arenas, a rose garden, a wildflower garden, a peace garden, two bird sanctuaries, a floating bog, four swimming pools, two water parks, six skate parks and much more. It costs about $60 million a year to operate. Moreover, the park board owns hundreds of thousands of trees, including those lining the streets of the city. It also continues to hold the deed for part of the Minneapolis–St. Paul International Airport, which the park board created.

Most important, perhaps, is that 125 years after its creation, the Minneapolis Park and Recreation Board remains an independent public entity that retains dedicated tax-supported funding. It is governed by an elected Board of Commissioners, one of the few park authorities in the country that has had, from the beginning, a single responsibility apart from other municipal authorities: owning and managing parks. Of course, that single purpose has expanded and shifted dramatically in the years since the Board of Park Commissioners was created in 1883. Those changes and shifts are the focus of this book.

Some names in this story are well-known, such as Charles Loring and Theodore Wirth. But many others who made immense contributions—Horace Cleveland, William Folwell, George Brackett, Maude Armatage, Francis Gross—are not so familiar. Their stories deserve telling too. In fact, many stories need telling that are not included here. What to leave out in such a tale is the hardest part. I have tried to touch on many, but far from all, of the important people and developments in the larger system of parks. This is a starting point. I hope others will take up where I have left off and tell what I have left out, perhaps even correct what I have gotten wrong.

The first thing most visitors notice about Minneapolis parks is one of the unique features of the city: nearly every foot of land that borders water, other than stretches of the Mississippi River banks north of Broadway, is owned by the park board. Truly extraordinary. Many times I have marveled that many of the grand homes of the city sit *across* a parkway from water.

This extraordinary fact of public life in Minneapolis, that the people own the waterways, is what intrigued me most about the story of parks in the city. Every city has its playgrounds and neighborhood parks, though few have as many so widely scattered as Minneapolis. But Minneapolis is unique in the number of bodies of water within its borders and in the fact that the public owns them. In fact, the city created some of them from wetlands long before wetlands were appreciated for the role they play in the ecosystem.

In today's world, Minneapolis probably would not have the park system as it is now. If the land had not been acquired when it was, no city could afford to buy it. And if the same park land were acquired today, some of it would not be dredged to form lakes. Knowing what we do now, parts of Lake of the Isles, Lake Calhoun, Lake Hiawatha, and Lake Nokomis might still be wetlands. They would still be enjoyed but used much differently.

The parks in Minneapolis cannot be termed "natural" in many respects, because early park designers and planners did not leave the land in its natural state. "Naturalistic" might be a better word. Lakes were dredged, swamps were filled, hills were shaved. As with much else in the land that was "tamed" from its Wild West past, the land was "improved." The belief in "improvement" was a cornerstone of the history of westward expansion in the United States in nearly every field. That we still have a Quaking Bog and an Eloise Butler Wildflower Garden in Theodore Wirth Park, a Thomas Sadler Roberts Bird Sanctuary at Lake Harriet and the magnificent glen from Minnehaha Falls to the Mississippi is especially noteworthy given the urge to "improve" landscapes.

This is but one example of questions that can be raised about and challenges that can be issued to the wisdom of early park planners. But hindsight is not nearly so rare nor so valuable as foresight. It is far easier to write history than to make it. To envision a land or a society that could be—or should be—

and bring that vision to life is the greater and nobler challenge.

William S. King, one of the great characters and visionaries in the early development of Minneapolis, said upon the approval of the park legislation by Minneapolis voters in 1883, "The intelligence, the pride, the public spirit and the humanity of our people have at last been vindicated. That mean, wicked and cruel spirit of selfishness and greed which for so many years has obstructed and defeated every effort to endow our city with public parks, has, at length, been overcome by the uprising and better sentiment and nobler spirit of our citizens."

The public spirit of those who envisioned the future also made sure Minneapolis was a city of trees. Often lost in consideration of the city's parks is that, from the very early days of the Minneapolis park board, it has been responsible for planting and maintaining street trees. Minneapolis wasn't always one of the greenest cities in the country, with a canopy of trees that shades much of the city. One writer noted that at the time the park board was created there was hardly a tree south of Franklin Avenue from the lake district to the Mississippi River, except for a few stands of oaks. What a different landscape that would be if not for the park board.

We can debate what should have been left as it was and what should have been changed, but the fact remains that the people of Minneapolis are now the stewards of considerable acreage of land and water. We are fortunate that we still get to argue over how we should manage and use those resources. We are fortunate that very long ago someone acquired those resources for us. Even as our dreams have changed, as our personal visions of the picture we want in this frame have evolved, we still have the land and lakes and river and creeks and trees. They are ours. We get to decide how they are used and in what state they will be passed to our children.

More pages in this account are devoted to the early years of park history than to later years because of the overriding importance of acquiring land and creating a vision of how parks would flow through the city. This was not my intention at the beginning of this project in January 2007. But the more I learned, the more I appreciated the incredible foresight of the early park heroes. Their far-reaching actions gave us the land for parks, but they also put in place the machinery for creating and sustaining recreation spaces. They truly did create a *system* of parks, both a series of parks centered on natural features and a method to address the demands for recreation, however those demands may have changed over the decades.

Few issues have emerged over the ensuing 125 years that the founders of the park system did not wrestle with at the beginning of this story. From recreation to transportation to health to finances, the issues have remained largely the same. The details of how we relax, draw inspiration, move about and take care of ourselves and others may have changed, but the basic issues haven't. That we can address those issues in an orderly, even if contentious, manner owes as much to the vision of park board founders as it does to the charms of the city's natural resources.

Over the ten months I have been immersed in this project, I have developed immense appreciation for the people who created the parks of the city and the opportunities they provide every day.

In the 1908 annual report, park board president Jesse Northrup wrote of the founders of Minneapolis parks:

> Their names will be forgotten, but unborn generations will thank them for all that they have done. "They may forget the singer, but they will not forget the song."

One hundred years later we know the song well. This book was written with the hope that we remember some of the singers too. And thank them. And add our voices to theirs.

DAVID C. SMITH
NOVEMBER 2007

Minneapolis looking west from St. Anthony in the early 1870s. The southern tip of Nicollet Island is in the center of the picture. The first suspension bridge across the Mississippi River, on Hennepin Avenue, can be seen center right. (Minnesota Historical Society)

Chapter One

Three Extraordinary Men

Minneapolis became a city the day Horace Cleveland arrived. History has made little note of his arrival on February 13, 1872, but it was his appearance in the northwestern outpost of urban America that set in motion a series of events that would eventually give Minneapolis its identity as the "City of Lakes." Cleveland was responsible more than any other for Minneapolis eventually being considered one of the greenest cities in the United States with one of the best park systems. He became the most eloquent and adamant proponent of preserving the city's natural features—the lakes on the outskirts of town and the mighty river at its core—for public enjoyment and enlightenment.

Cleveland's presence in the city did not seem noteworthy at the time. It would be another eleven years before he was asked to submit a plan for a park system and twenty more years after that before his basic plan was largely executed. Of far more immediate importance than Cleveland's arrival was the vote that day by the residents of the towns on each side of St. Anthony Falls—St. Anthony and Minneapolis—to unite into one city. By a margin of more than seven to one the voters declared, in the words of a columnist in the *St. Paul Pioneer,* "St. Anthony is no more—she is wiped out—extinguished—blotted from the face of nature and the map of Minnesota." What survived was Minneapolis, a city that Cleveland would help define.

An intensifying blizzard in the small river towns delayed Cleveland's debut in the place that would eventually owe him so much. As the snow swirled outside, the organizers of the "People's Course of Lectures" surveyed a meager crowd of a dozen or so hardy Minnesotans who had battled the elements and plunked down their twenty-five cents to hear Cleveland speak at the Pence Opera House on Washington Avenue. Hoping for a better turnout, the managers of the event decided to postpone Cleveland's lecture for two days.

Cleveland probably wouldn't have been a huge draw in the best of weather. He was an unknown from Chicago who had been a late replacement for a better-known speaker. And his topic, "Landscape Gardening as Applied to the Wants of the West," probably didn't generate much buzz in a town that, as of that February day in 1872, ended in rolling prairie a few blocks from the Opera House.

Cleveland could wait a day or two. At the age of fifty-eight, he needed work. The St. Paul newspaper speculated that wealthy citizens of the two towns might engage Cleveland to landscape the grounds of the estates their new wealth was building.

After the storm abated—the papers called it the

City of Parks

Pence Opera House about the time of Horace Cleveland's first lecture in Minneapolis. (Minnesota Historical Society)

most bitter day of the winter and were filled with reports of stranded settlers dying in snow drifts—Cleveland's address met with such enthusiasm in Minneapolis that he was invited to repeat it two nights later in St. Paul. There his lecture was greeted with a motion from Gen. Henry Sibley himself that the meeting give him a special vote of thanks for his message.

The seeds of Horace Cleveland's greatest successes were planted that week in Minneapolis and St. Paul. Out of those presentations grew a book, two enduring relationships and, eventually, a plan. The book, *Landscape Architecture as Applied to the Wants of the West,* was published the following year to very favorable reviews but had meager sales. Over the decades since, it has come to be recognized as one of the seminal works of landscape design, land use and preservation of natural resources. The relationships were with Charles Loring and William Folwell, the three of them linked in the creation of what is considered one of the great municipal park systems in the world. The plan, *Suggestions for a System of Parks and Parkways for the City of Minneapolis,* written in 1883, became the foundation of the park system that Minneapolis enjoys to this day.

We don't know if Charles Loring was in Cleveland's first audience. But it is likely that he was. Loring was one of a handful of people who had promoted parks and tree planting in the young town. Seven years earlier, in 1865, Loring had been the first president of the Minneapolis Floral Association, and he had planted some of the first trees on the prairie south of St. Anthony Falls. Loring had already profited handsomely three times by landscaping the grounds of his own homes and then selling those houses for sums he couldn't imagine—or refuse. Loring's love of plants and his appreciation for the economic benefits of landscaping probably would have put him in Pence Opera House for Cleveland's presentation. But whether they met that night or later, they established a bond that endures in Minneapolis's parks.

The third extraordinary man in the creation and development of Minneapolis parks was definitely not in the building the night of Cleveland's portentous lecture. William Watts Folwell, president of the University of Minnesota, was the scheduled speaker whom Cleveland replaced. Folwell had gone to Washington, D.C., for the first National Agricultural Convention. In fact, Folwell may have been the one who invited Cleveland to replace him at the podium that night. Their fruitful relationship continued for the rest of Cleveland's life.

The paths of these three men would cross and diverge many times in the next decades. Loring is the best known in Minneapolis because his name still graces the first park developed by the Minneapolis Board of Park Commissioners. He has been known for almost the entire history of Minneapolis as the "Father of Minneapolis Parks." As early as 1886 a cartoon appeared in a Minneapolis newspaper showing Loring "fathering" Minneapolis parks with a watering can. To Loring belongs the glory for his tenacious crusade to acquire park land, but to Cleveland belongs the credit for putting in Loring's hands the master plan and many of the ideas that compelled him.

Folwell brought the other two together and provided the consistent vision of the Minneapolis system of parks, especially during the difficult second decade of the Board of Park Commissioners. It was Folwell who, while urging the park board not to lose sight of Cleveland's original master plan, introduced in 1891 the name "Grand Rounds" for the system of parkways encircling the city. Folwell, along with Loring, founded the first civic improvement society in Minneapolis around the time of Cleveland's lecture. Folwell would also eventually become the first president of the Minneapolis Society of Fine Arts in 1883—with Loring as vice president—and become one of the founders of the Minnesota Historical Society. In addition to building the University of Minnesota from the ground up, he pushed for higher public education standards and public health systems and was an early advocate of a system of state parks in Minnesota. He envisioned a society he desired and was methodical and relentless in his pursuit of it.

Loring and Folwell left behind an impressive and clear vision for Minneapolis, largely achieved in their lifetimes, but that vision might not have been realized had it not been for Cleveland. With missionary zeal, the mesmerizing eloquence of an evangelist, and an immovable faith in the potent tonic of nature's beauty, Cleveland was the man Loring and Folwell needed. They were the thoughtful, immensely practical men who saw what needed doing and never lost sight of it. But Cleveland was a crusader. It was Cleveland who could incite a crowd to a "thunderous ovation" or a "cyclone of applause." And he was an artist. He understood how to create a pleasing natural environment, how to lay out a road, a path, a park, how to interpret the gifts of nature for the enjoyment of the eye, the heart and the soul. But most of all he was a lover of nature's beauty and its character-building beneficence.

As Cleveland paced offstage, waiting to deliver his talk, he could not have imagined that his subject for the night would presage a land preservation movement that over the next century would become a powerful force in society—or that this talk would lead to a park system that would stand as his greatest professional accomplishment. Least of all could he have imagined that he would have to wait another eleven years—years filled with disappointment and tragedy—to be asked at age sixty-nine, still looking for work, to design a system of parks for Minneapolis.

Minneapolis at the time was the very edge of the settled West. Railways west of Minneapolis were just being built. Flour milling was still a young industry yet to be transformed by Cadwallader Washburn's giant mill and processing techniques. The growing town was built not on flour mills but on sawmills that created lumber from the vast stands of pine forests that would soon be depleted along the Mississippi and its tributaries to the north. With the disappearance of the enormous white pines and the steady arrival of immigrants to bust up the prairie into plots of wheat, Minneapolis had channeled the power of St. Anthony Falls to turn massive stones to grind wheat, replacing massive blades to slice timber. The need for labor to supply and run the flour mills fueled the rapid growth of the towns that had voted to unite into Minneapolis earlier that day.

"This priceless opportunity may be lost forever for want of an appreciative eye to detect its value. The gem may be thrown aside as worthless, because no one is at hand to detect its lustre and arrange its setting."

HORACE WILLIAM SHALER CLEVELAND

According to the book that emerged from his lecture, Cleveland asked the leaders of the new towns of the frontier to consider "the raw material which is placed in our hands to be moulded into shape for the habitation of a nation, and such as we create, it must essentially remain for all future time." He went on to say,

> Year by year the advancing tide of civilization is forcing its way by new routes into this region of mystery and beauty. . . . We know that the health, and daily comfort and convenience of countless millions who inhabit the towns and cities which are to grow up through all this region may be affected for ages after we are forgotten, by the care or carelessness with which we perform our duty in designing their primary arrangement. . . . Yet this priceless opportunity may be lost forever for want of an appreciative eye to detect its value. The gem may be thrown aside as worthless, because no one is at hand to detect its lustre and arrange its setting.

Cleveland, with his appreciative eye, was at hand. He had arrived by a circuitous route.

Horace William Shaler Cleveland

Horace William Shaler Cleveland was born in 1814 in Massachusetts, the third son of a prosperous sea captain, Richard Cleveland, and Dorcas Hiller Cleveland, an innovative educator. Horace grew up in the rich intellectual and artistic world of Hawthorne and Emerson, and would bring their views of the transformative power of nature to Minneapolis decades later, where other transplanted Yankee civic leaders would recognize and welcome them.

Cleveland was educated at a Unitarian school in Lancaster, Massachusetts, founded by his mother. He was never encouraged to follow his father to the sea, a life his father had called, "a dog's life, at best."

From his earliest days he was immersed in the culture of books and ideas in the small towns around Boston. His early teachers included a future president of Harvard University and a cousin of Ralph Waldo Emerson. Both of his brothers attended Harvard, and one, Henry, became a writer and scholar of some note. Henry's book club, which Horace later joined, included Henry Wadsworth Longfellow and Charles Sumner, who would become a U.S. senator.

Cleveland later worked for Emerson and famous park builder Frederick Law Olmsted, with whom he established a lifelong friendship. Despite his repeated access to the salons of the elite, including many powerful financiers and industrialists who were clients in later years, Cleveland seemed never to enter those circles as a full member. Perhaps he never stayed in one place long enough to develop those potentially beneficial relationships—or perhaps he never stayed in one place because he didn't develop those relationships. For most of his life he was near greatness but never great himself, except perhaps to a few peers and colleagues.

Cleveland was a loner whose many letters, scat-

Horace William Shaler Cleveland, year unknown. (Ramsey County Historical Society)

tered among the papers of more famous people, give the impression that he might have been a difficult man to get along with. Cleveland revealed a good bit about himself when in later life he noted that his most regular correspondents were people he had never met or hadn't seen in decades. Cleveland was most at ease communicating from podium or paper.

While in his teens, Cleveland lived for a time in Havana, where his father held a diplomatic post. There Cleveland saw nature in a tropical setting and learned to work with quite different plants and soils than in his native New England. Attracted by the romance and the hope of the West and its uniquely American character, he made two trips there—which in the 1830s was Illinois. Working as a surveyor in the settling frontier, teaching school for awhile, he became an expert marksman and continued his education in the life of plants and the land they covered. He later called the region of the Mississippi north of the Missouri a "dreamland."

Returning from the West, riding on horseback from Illinois to New York, Cleveland lived with his older brother, Henry, near Boston. Cleveland regaled his brother's influential friends with his experiences on a frontier that held great fascination for them but with which they had little personal experience. Longfellow's epic poem *The Song of Hiawatha* was published in 1854 without Longfellow ever having seen Minnehaha Falls. The worldwide fame that the poem conferred on the falls would much later add impetus to the preservation of the falls and Minnehaha Creek as a Minneapolis park.

Shortly after marrying Maryann Dwinel of Maine in 1841, Cleveland bought a farm in New Jersey and became a "scientific farmer" in his thirties. He became active in the National Pomological Society (apple growers) and helped found the New Jersey Horticultural Society. Finding no satisfaction or income—it isn't clear which—in farming, Cleveland turned to the emerging field of landscape gardening. He moved back to Boston in 1854, at age forty, and entered into a partnership with Robert Copeland, a recent Harvard graduate who had studied under Longfellow, and they set out to sell their services to design gardens, cemeteries and parks.

Among their most prominent projects was a commission to lay out the grounds of Sleepy Hollow Cemetery in Concord, Massachusetts. The cemetery was the haunt in life and death of Ralph Waldo Emerson, who was a director of the cemetery and delivered an address on the dedication of the newly designed grounds in 1855. The design of the cemetery fit nicely with Emerson's notion that nature does not need artificial enhancement or decoration, merely interpretation through the eye of an artist. Nature without embellishment, to Emerson and his followers, was both ennobling in its beauty and humbling in its constant reminder of the finite footfalls of man. Nature could enlighten us and certainly would outlast us. Nature was unity and continuity. These were the scriptural texts of the sermons that Cleveland would preach to rapt audiences years later on the frontier.

Cleveland and Copeland's design of meandering walks and plantings among the gravestones provided the ideal walking and resting places for many notable American writers and thinkers, including Emerson, Henry David Thoreau, Nathaniel Hawthorne and Louisa May Alcott. Sleepy Hollow Cemetery was the first of several cemeteries designed by Cleveland, including Oakland Cemetery in St. Paul.

It was an opportunity to build a park that next occupied Cleveland and Copeland. Less than a year after the dedication of Sleepy Hollow Cemetery they published an essay, "A Few Words on Central Park," in which they advocated a comprehensive planning process for the entire New York City park. The next year a design competition was held for New York's sprawling park. Cleveland and Copeland's designs were topped by those submitted by Frederick Law Olmsted and Calvert Vaux.

Following the Civil War, which Cleveland spent teaching marksmanship—at forty-six he was too old to fight—he formed a lasting friendship with Olmsted. Cleveland had returned to landscape gardening but had little work. Two of his friends wrote to Olmsted in 1868, asking him to give Cleveland work in New York, which he did.

In 1869, at the age of fifty-five, Cleveland moved to Chicago to develop his practice near the frontier that he loved and the booming railroad towns the region's riches were spawning. It was while living in Chicago that Cleveland became an evangelist for preserving nature's beauty in the new cities growing up in the Midwest. He had seen the tremendous difficulty and cost that older cities in the East had faced in adding parks to built-up cities and warned the young cities to avoid making the same mistakes.

Although his concern was primarily with preserving natural beauty, particularly for the refreshment and edification of the poor who were crowded into urban squalor, he understood well the economic benefits of well-designed cities. "A distinct character to the city would have brought more wealth to it," he said of Chicago, "and what is better, more men and women of refined taste and culture." He encouraged city leaders not to allow opportunities to escape to obtain tracts of land "by the improvement of which the beauty and attractive interest of the city can be incalculably increased, while at the same time a lucrative return is secured in the form of increased valuation of taxable property."

He bolstered his argument by citing examples of increased property values and tax revenues around Central Park in New York, as well as the enormous cost to cities of delaying the purchase of land that "might once have been had for a song."

Cleveland's passion for planning great cities in advance of unfettered growth and preserving their natural characteristics did not lead to financial success or public acclaim at the time. He always stood in the shadow of the more famous Olmsted. Even today in Minneapolis, the names of Charles Loring and Theodore Wirth are far better known.

But Horace Cleveland, unheralded and already fifty-eight by the time he reached Minneapolis, found in the city an audience receptive to his message of planning and preservation.

Charles Morgridge Loring

By the time Cleveland arrived in Minneapolis, Charles Morgridge Loring had already resided in the city for nearly twelve years and had become a leader in civic and business circles.

Loring was born in Portland, Maine, in 1833. Like Cleveland, he was the son of a sea-faring family. Unlike Cleveland, however, his family and friends expected him to become a navigator like his father. Very little is known of Loring's childhood and youth, including his education.

While in his early twenties, Loring was put in command of a ship that sailed to Cuba. Life at sea did not suit him, however, and after marrying Emily Crossman, also of Portland, at the age of twenty-two, he set out for the West. He lived first in Chicago, where he worked in the wholesale grain business as a trader, an experience that would later be of use to him in Minneapolis, the city that would become the center of the nation's wheat trade.

Charles Morgridge Loring, around 1900, when he was in his late sixties. (Brush, Minnesota Historical Society)

After two years in Chicago, Loring's health forced him to seek a less rigorous climate. He moved first to Milwaukee and then in 1860 moved again with his wife and two-year-old son to Minneapolis. At the time, the Minnesota climate was considered beneficial to many people with respiratory problems.

Upon his arrival in the city, he took up residence at the Nicollet Hotel. In the room next to his in the hotel was another young man from Maine, who was the same age as Loring, Loren Fletcher. Fletcher at the time worked in the dry goods store of Dorilus Morrison, another Maine native, who had prospered in the lumber business. Loring soon joined Fletcher at Morrison's store. The store provided supplies to many of the lumbermen who had come to Minnesota, many from Maine, to float logs down the Mississippi to the sawmills at St. Anthony Falls. After working for Morrison for a year, Fletcher and Loring opened their own store, which would be a fixture on the Minneapolis retail scene for the next fifteen years.

Loring began buying property in the young city at an early age. He purchased a commercial building at the corner of Washington Avenue and Second Avenue in 1863, which he rented to the school board. He also bought three houses for himself and took some pains to landscape the grounds. Each time he did so, someone came along and bought it. His profit on one house, he claimed, was $24,000, an incredible sum in those days.

Loring's earliest recollection of a discussion of a park for the burgeoning city was from a social gathering at the offices of "Mac and Gene" in the early 1860s. Mac and Gene, William McNair and Eugene Wilson, were law partners whose offices served as a social club for the young businessmen of the city. Loring recalled that during a discussion there one evening of the great prospects for the young city, someone said if Minneapolis were going to be a great city, it would need a park. Another writer attributed that comment to Loring himself.

Loring demonstrated an early commitment to civic affairs and a passion for trees. In 1864 he was elected a road supervisor, and the following year he became president of the Minneapolis Floral Association. He later recalled the first flower show held in Minneapolis, which then had a population of just over two thousand. The 1865 show was held at Harrison Hall on the corner of Washington and Nicollet. At the time, he recollected, there was only one business west of Washington, and the woods began at Twelfth Street. The flower show was a huge success, generating $600 in gate receipts. Loring gave credit for the show's success primarily to the women of the city, including the wives of many men who would feature prominently in park history. With such a great success, the association held a second show the next year at the fairground built in south Minneapolis by William King. This time the show was a bust; the association lost the money it had earned a year earlier and consequently merged with the Minnesota Horticultural Society.

Loring's involvement in civic affairs continued with his election as secretary of the Athenaeum, a forerunner of the Minneapolis Public Library, in 1866. On the business front Loring and Fletcher were about to take a giant step into the fledgling milling trade. In 1867, together with another investor, they bought the Holly Mill. By the time Horace Cleveland came to town, Loring had also been elected to the city council in 1870 and was one of the founders of Lakewood Cemetery in 1871.

Twelve years after his arrival in Minneapolis, at the age of thirty-nine, Loring was at the center of business and civic life in the town and clearly a leader in both circles. Described as a man with a "sunny disposition" and as a "gentle and genial soul," he was very popular as well as an astute businessman. His many friends were among the most energetic and active boosters promoting the interests of the booming town that was making them rich.

William Watts Folwell

William Folwell did not choose Minneapolis, it chose him.

Folwell was from upstate New York, where he

William Watts Folwell, 1863, in uniform for his wedding, six years before he came to Minneapolis as the first president of the University of Minnesota. (Powelson, Minnesota Historical Society)

was born in 1833, the same year as Loring. As a boy he worked on a farm while attending school. He then attended Hobart College, where he established close friendships with other young intellectuals who would become prominent figures in the nation's leading universities.

After graduating from college and doing a stint as a professor of mathematics and languages at Hobart, Folwell pursued graduate studies in Germany. At the outbreak of the Civil War, he promptly returned home and joined the Union Army. As a member, then commander, of an engineering company, Folwell attained the rank of lieutenant colonel, the highest possible for volunteer engineers. Folwell was active in many of the largest campaigns of the war while commanding a force of 450 engineers. Both Cleveland and Loring later referred to the war in correspondence with Folwell, suggesting the importance of his military experience in shaping his worldview.

After the war, Folwell pursued a business career for a few years while he devoted time to the study of politics and economics. His greater interest in intellectual life, however, lured him away from business into teaching once again when he accepted an academic post at Kenyon College in Ohio, teaching mathematics and engineering

Encouraged by his friend and brother-in-law George Chase, who was rector at a church in St. Anthony, Folwell applied for a position on the new faculty at the University of Minnesota in 1869. But when it was offered to him, he turned it down. It was then that the Board of Regents made a decision that would have a lasting impact on the city of Minneapolis. The board contacted Folwell again and asked if he would consider coming to Minneapolis as president, instead of just a professor. That offer Folwell accepted, and in 1869 he became the first president of the University of Minnesota.

Through his position Folwell quickly got to know the elite of the city. Among the invitees to his house for get-acquainted dinners were such men as William McNair, the mayor of St. Anthony; John Pillsbury, president of the Board of Regents that hired him; and Samuel Gale, who was also on that board. All of these people would play important roles in the eventual creation of parks in Minneapolis.

His influence in the city was profound. Not only was he one of the founders of the university, but he helped create a secondary school system that would prepare students for university study. Folwell also took a position that put him in the minority in his day and made education at the university coeducational. When asked once by another college president what course of study the university offered specifically for women, Folwell replied that he presumed that a woman who applied to the university wanted a "college education." The university made no distinction between courses for men and women.

Folwell is also known for hiring Maria Sanford in 1880 as the first female professor at a public university in the United States. He would later call that hire one of his greatest contributions to the university.

In a foreshadowing of his later involvement in the creation of a park system, Folwell wrote in 1870 to the best-known landscape architect of the time, Frederick Law Olmsted, seeking advice for laying out the new campus of the university. In his reply, Olmsted tried to provide some helpful advice but demonstrated no interest in doing the work himself.

By the winter of 1871–72 Folwell had already earned such respect in the town that he was invited to be the concluding speaker in the "People's Course of Lectures" at Pence Opera House in February. But then, in one of the odd twists of fate in the history of Minneapolis parks, the secretary of agriculture in Washington organized a national agricultural conference. As the president of a state university that was created largely by land grants from the U.S. government to establish agricultural colleges, it was incumbent upon Folwell to attend. The organizers of the lecture series would have to find someone to replace him. On short notice, perhaps at the suggestion of Folwell, they did. Horace Cleveland would fill the vacancy.

Cleveland did acquire a significant amount of work from the wowed crowds in Minneapolis and St. Paul listening on those cold February nights in 1872, their receptivity to an image of landscaped greenery heightened by the annual late-winter longing for any landscape that wasn't white.

Ex-Minnesota Governor William Marshall hired Cleveland to lay out a tract of multi-acre estates in what would become the St. Anthony Park area of St. Paul. Bishop Whipple of the Episcopal school in Faribault, Minnesota, asked Cleveland to design the grounds of his school. The proprietors of St. Paul's Oakland Cemetery hired Cleveland to create a park-like setting for their grounds—part of a nationwide movement to create attractive burial grounds that predated the rage for park building that swept America later in the nineteenth century. Even Folwell, unsatisfied with his response from Olmsted about university grounds, sought Cleveland's advice on creating a plan for the nascent campus of the university. It was the beginning of a close friendship.

Despite the flurry of work for Cleveland, the creation of parks would have to wait. There was not yet the demand to spend money on parks. Cleveland's voice was still literally crying out in the wilderness. Minneapolis was still a frontier town. It would be another eleven years before he was formally asked for his recommendations for parks.

William Watts Folwell, in about 1920, then in his late eighties. (Minnesota Historical Society)

Lake Harriet in 1875 in one of the earliest photos of the lake. William King owned most of the lakeshore at the time. The double image was intended to be viewed through a stereopticon. (Minnesota Historical Society)

Chapter Two

Try, Try Again

Remember Nicollet Island! It would become a battle cry of park advocates for decades—and reemerge as a contentious issue more than one hundred years later. Loring, Folwell and Cleveland resorted to its painful memory often over the years to compel purchases of land for parks. The memory of the failed opportunity to acquire a park on prime land at the very heart of the city must have been especially galling for the leaders of Minneapolis on that 1872 day when Cleveland first spoke of the diminishing opportunities to acquire park land in cities. Union between Minneapolis and St. Anthony had that day been achieved, but the acquisition of park land was still far off.

And it might have been George Brackett's fault.

In 1866, a year *before* Minneapolis was formally organized for good, the Minnesota Legislature had approved the first attempt to unite Minneapolis and St. Anthony. The bill provided for a union of the two towns, with much of Nicollet Island—which sat in the river between them—to be purchased for municipal buildings. The north end of the island was slated to become a large park. The legislature mandated a referendum on the issue.

For many years the act was remembered not for the potential union of the two towns but for its park provision. The issue came down to the price to be paid for the land, which many citizens thought too high. Orlando Merriman, mayor of St. Anthony at the time (and who would years later be appointed one of the city's first park commissioners) later recalled ruefully that Nicollet Island, "which God Almighty intended as a park for us" was lost "just because someone was going to make some money out of it."

Minneapolis voters had first crack at the referendum, with St. Anthony voters scheduled to vote the following day. The citizens of St. Anthony never got their chance. March 19 found the town of Minneapolis "more excited than we ever remember seeing it," reported the *St. Paul Pioneer* the next day. In what it called "perhaps the most exciting election ever held in this State," the paper reported that "teams and vehicles of all kinds were busily engaged all day bringing voters up to the polls."

It is likely that some of those vehicles were under the command of one John J. Thompson. Brackett was so confident that the union and park vote would "carry handsomely" that he made a wager for $100—a huge sum in the day—that the people of Minneapolis would ratify the act. The man who took the bet was Thompson. As a result of the bet, Thompson "electioneered so forcefully," Charles Loring later recalled, that the measure was lost. It is not

George Bracket in 1916. George Brackett came to Minneapolis with his friend William Washburn from Maine in 1857 at the age of twenty-one. He was a man of many civic and business interests. He worked as a butcher, owned a meat packing company, owned a flour mill, and was the purchasing agent for the Northern Pacific Railway. He was the first engineer of the Minneapolis Fire Department and was the city's mayor in 1873. In 1880 he purchased what was then "Starvation Point" on Lake Minnetonka and renamed it "Orono Point" after his hometown in Maine. Brackett was one of the leaders in creating the first park board and served on the first board, in addition to founding several charities in the city. After the Panic of 1893 ruined him financially, he sought a new fortune in the gold fields of Alaska and attempted to build the first road over the Skagway Pass, a venture that failed. He named his seventh son, Karl Loring Brackett, after his close friend Charles Loring. (Lee Brothers, Minnesota Historical Society)

hard to imagine Thompson ferrying voters to the polls to secure his hundred bucks.

By fewer than one hundred votes, Minneapolis lost its first chance at a big central park. But park advocates had gained a rallying cry and had been made receptive to Cleveland's later dire warnings of opportunities lost. In the loss of Nicollet Island for a park perhaps were sown the seeds of success.

And perhaps not all of the blame should be placed on Brackett's head. Jessie Marcley, writing a history of Minneapolis's city charter in 1925, attributed the defeat ultimately to the "thrifty New England element" in the population of the towns.

The failure to secure Nicollet Island as a park was not the first nor would it be the last failed attempt to create a park in the growing town. But at least Minneapolis did have one park—although far from the city center.

In 1857, as the New York papers that reached Minneapolis told of the competition to design recently acquired land for a "Central Park," Edward Murphy was platting a section of land he owned southeast of downtown Minneapolis. In an extraordinary bit of foresight, he dedicated nearly two blocks of "Murphy's Addition" as a public park and deeded it to the city. That park, Murphy Square, still exists—although at first glance it appears now to be merely the central square of Augsburg College, which grew up around it. Murphy Square served as little more than a cow pasture for nearly twenty years.

The first real civic attempt to acquire a central park for the city occurred in 1865 as the region's growth was resuming at the conclusion of the Civil War. A special town meeting was called at the request of, among others, Dorilus Morrison, Loren Fletcher and William McNair. The meeting was to be held at Morrison's store to consider "the propriety and necessity of purchasing for the use of the town a lot of land for a Park or Public Square." Other issues on the agenda were grading Bridge Street, buying a steam fire engine, and employing a police officer.

At the meeting the citizens approved an offer from William Eastman to sell to the town a plot of land between Nicollet and Hennepin for $2,500. At the urging of his friend Charles Loring, Eastman offered to contribute $500 if others would kick in another $1,000 with the remaining $1,000 raised by taxes. It looked like the city had a centrally located park, even if it wasn't much larger than the duck pond it held. However, the lot was designated a few years later as the site of Minneapolis's first city hall and would eventually become the site of The Gateway, the most expensive failure in the history of Minneapolis parks.

In various accounts of the time, park opponents used arguments that Cleveland, through his experience in the East and in Chicago, knew were false. "Why do we need a park?" they asked. "There will never be a house south of Tenth Street," one opponent averred. Within a few years, the boundary had already moved out ten blocks. "The whole city south of Franklin *is* a park," was one claim.

Perhaps emboldened by their first small acquisition, park promoters hatched the plan to go to the legislature a few months later with the proposal to make Nicollet Island a park. When that attempt also failed, the agitation for parks diminished. It would be the history of park promotion in the early years of Minneapolis: a concerted effort for a park, failure, then a respite before trying something new. And it was always the same handful of wealthy men driving the issue.

One of them was Dorilus Morrison, among the wealthiest Minnesotans at the time, who was elected the first mayor of Minneapolis in 1867. Minneapolis was booming. The town of about eight thousand had seen the value of its taxable property nearly triple in the preceding three years to more than $2 million. In his inaugural speech, Morrison deplored the fact that the town had no public parks, which he called "the pride of almost all cities east and west."

By early 1869, park supporters were reenergized. With Morrison in the mayor's chair and Brackett as a leading councilman, the city council passed a resolution favoring the establishment of a city park. The renewed interest in a park caused Richard Mendenhall, banker and one-time president of the state horticultural society, to step forward with an offer to sell the city forty acres of land for a park for $25,000.

Brackett immediately presented a motion to the council to accept the offer and further moved that grounds be "at once selected and purchased" for

Dorilus Morrison in about 1870. Morrison came to Minnesota from Maine, like his cousin William Washburn, in the late 1850s and quickly became one of the state's wealthiest men, primarily through the lumber business. Charles Loring and Loren Fletcher got their first jobs in Minnesota in 1860 working at a dry goods store owned by Morrison. He was the first mayor of Minneapolis in 1867 and was a leading proponent of creating parks in the city. He was a commissioner on the first park board. He also helped create the first streetcar company in Minneapolis and hired Thomas Lowry to run the company. His estate and home on Twenty-fourth Street were later donated by his son, Clinton, to the park board as a site for the Minneapolis Institute of Arts. (Minneapolis Public Library, Minneapolis Collection, M0081)

parks in the First and Fourth Wards with a limit of $10,000 for each park. The land for those parks was to be selected by the council members of those wards. Offered the chance to acquire parks under its jurisdiction, and having earlier expressed itself in favor of acquiring parks, the council blew its chance. It came one vote short of the two-thirds majority needed to pass the resolution.

Some of the staunchest of park advocates in the city made one last try at preserving the land for parks. In 1871, Brackett, Morrison and William King each purchased from Mendenhall an *undivided* one-fourth interest in the land, with Mendenhall retaining a one-fourth interest, and they agreed to spend $1,000 dollars each to improve the land for eventual use as a city park. But when a more "aesthetic council" didn't materialize, the four men sold part of the land and built homes on the rest of it.

The land that Mendenhall offered eventually became the exclusive neighborhood where William Washburn, Morrison and John Pillsbury built lavish homes. Morrison's home and surrounding estate, which he built on his section of the land, was years later donated to the city for the site of the Minneapolis Institute of Arts. Washburn's home, Fair Oaks, was eventually purchased as the park that now fronts the art museum.

Unable to generate sufficient public support for parks, many of the leaders of the parks effort resorted instead to building what was, in essence, a privately owned park. In 1871, with King, Brackett, Morrison and Loring among the founders, Lakewood Cemetery was established near the shores of Lake Calhoun and Lake Harriet adjacent to King's farm.

Loring later claimed that the idea for the cemetery was his. He vowed to create a beautiful resting place for loved ones on the day in 1863 that he buried his infant daughter in Layman's Cemetery in south Minneapolis. He took the idea to King and together with others began to seek a plot of land where a cemetery could be located. Speculators got wind of their plan to buy land south of the present Loring Park and offered more for the land than the cemetery group was willing to pay. The plan then languished until King and Morrison resuscitated it in 1871, at which time the present site of Lakewood was selected and developed. The cemetery was used as a

William King in about 1878. King came to Minneapolis in 1858 at the age of thirty from his home in upstate New York. He was first a newspaperman and founded some of the city's first newspapers, including the *Minneapolis Tribune*. King served in Congress, representing Minnesota in 1875, and also served as Postmaster General for the House of Representatives for twelve years. King owned a 1,400-acre farm around Lake Harriet, where he raised prize cattle. He was often referred to as Colonel King, but the title was apparently an honorific. He built a hotel on the east shore of Lake Calhoun in 1877, but it was destroyed by fire. He was a vocal leader in park efforts and later donated most of the shore of Lake Harriet for a park, as well as part of his Lyndale Farm for Lyndale Park. King's Highway, named for him, ran past his farm east of Lake Harriet. (Minnesota Historical Society)

picnic ground by the public for many years until the people had parks of their own.

Horace Cleveland's first appearance in Minneapolis and St. Paul in February 1872 had an immediate, but short-lived, effect. With a history of failure behind them, the leaders of Minneapolis would not rise to Cleveland's challenge to obtain land before it was too late. They already knew it wasn't an easy task. But his sermon gave their notion of parks and possibilities a shape and face.

Within a week of his presentation in St. Paul, the St. Paul delegation to the Minnesota Legislature secured legislation that authorized the city to acquire land for a park. That legislation eventually led to the purchase of what is now Como Park in St. Paul. Moreover, the St. Paul City Council inquired of Cleveland his terms for providing an outline for improvements in the city, and that summer invited Cleveland to present his findings to the council. In that speech Cleveland provided a more detailed plan for the great metropolis he predicted St. Paul and Minneapolis would become. He especially urged preservation of the city's "jewel," the Mississippi River. No specific plans or work came from his speech for many years, but Cleveland's vision left a clear impression on civic leaders.

At a meeting of the recently formed Minneapolis Improvement Society, which was led by Folwell and Loring, Cleveland urged the audience to plat parks and construct boulevards at the earliest possible date. He recommended the appointment of a city forester and supported the city's supervision of all efforts for the beautifying of streets—the first mention of a notion that would much later distinguish Minneapolis. After the meeting, Cleveland's services were secured for the following day "for a drive about the city and such suggestions as he may give for future improvement."

Cleveland's urgings may have led to the grandest park proposal Minneapolis had yet heard. Around the time of Cleveland's speech, William King, who always thought big, made a proposal that dwarfed earlier schemes. King would sell to the city 250 acres of his farmland for a park around Lake Harriet for $50,000. The offer was met with derision. King was told to go back to Washington (where he resided much of the time since having represented Minnesota in Congress) and not try to "unload his farm on the city for so large a sum."

That was the end of park schemes in Minneapolis for awhile, other than a group of citizens participating—to no apparent effect—in a joint committee with St. Paul leaders. Their goal was to "consider the recommendation of Professor Cleveland," as the *Minneapolis Tribune* of July 20, 1872, put it, "relative to laying out a wide avenue between these two cities."

Fortunately for Minneapolis's future park system, Cleveland had acquired considerable private work—as well as the assignment of laying out a campus for the University of Minnesota—that kept him active in the region, further establishing his credentials with park enthusiasts.

Cleveland wrote to Olmsted after his first visit to Minneapolis of his optimism and gratification that perhaps people were finally listening to him. His future looked bright when, a few months later, he was selected as the landscape architect for Chicago's South Park Commission and put on an annual salary. Part of his work would be to rebuild parks in areas devastated by Chicago's fire and to adapt Olmsted and Vaux's plans for the park system. (Cleveland had lost out to Olmsted again for the work of creating the original plans.)

Cleveland's success was, however, short-lived. The depression of 1873 killed his business. By the fall of 1874, the Chicago park system was broke and quit paying his salary.

But Cleveland continued spreading his message. Of his frequent evangelizing Cleveland wrote, "I am always glad of a chance to tell people what they ought to do for the future good of their towns—which clears my conscience whether they do it or not." For the most part, they did not.

Cleveland wrote to Olmsted in 1875 that "no new business has come to us" and asked if Olmsted had any projects on which Cleveland could render assistance for "small remuneration" in order to prevent tapping into the little savings he had set aside for the "not distant day when my working days will be past." Then sixty-one, Cleveland was still eight years away from his signature success.

As Cleveland's fortunes swooned, Charles Loring's fortune continued to grow. With Loren Fletcher, he had expanded his milling interests, buying the Galaxy Mill in Minneapolis and Minnetonka Mill on Lake Minnetonka.

In 1873, as Loring was completing his term on the city council, Edward Murphy obtained approval from the council to spend $500 to plant trees in Murphy Square, the land he had donated to the city as a park in 1857. It is likely that Loring supervised the planting, as it was always claimed that he had planted the first public trees south of the river. Having spent the amount appropriated, Murphy submitted his bill, and a warrant was drawn on the city treasury to pay it. The mayor at the time refused to sign the warrant, however, and it was never paid.

By 1875 Loring was such an established figure on the Minneapolis business scene that he was elected president of the Board of Trade, an organization that functioned as a chamber of commerce in Minneapolis. Later that year, the Board of Trade proposed a park for St. Paul and Minneapolis at Minnehaha Falls and appointed a committee to consider the matter. The St. Paul Chamber of Commerce appointed a similar committee, but the St. Paul contingent decided that Minnehaha was not a proper place for such a park, and the matter died.

By 1876 Loring and Fletcher's fortune and interests had become so diversified that they closed the dry goods store—one of the most successful in the city, the papers said—that had been the source of their early wealth. Loring's ill health and good fortune resulted around this time in his annual winter departure from Minneapolis. For most of the rest of his life, he and his wife would leave each winter, at first for Europe and later for Riverside, California, where Loring also became a proponent of parks and tree planting.

In the winter of 1877, with Loring in Europe and the local economy recovering from the devastating panic of 1873, the Board of Trade decided to push the Minnesota Legislature again for park legislation. But this time it wasn't just one park they wanted.

The Board of Trade proposed a "system of parks to be located in different parts of the city." Acknowledging that such a network of parks would require many years of "careful thought and unusual taste," the board proposed granting extraordinary powers to an independent commission "created for that purpose." The proposed citywide Board of Park Commissioners would have authority to buy and condemn land and levy taxes for park purposes.

The Board of Trade went to great lengths through public hearings to obtain input into their radical piece of legislation. Editorials and letters to the papers ran heavily in support of the park measure. One editorial suggested that park promoters had had too many failures already and that another "could so discourage advocates that they won't try again." They didn't foresee one procedural problem with the plan.

The legislation was intended to circumvent the city council. To mollify the council, however, the bill gave the president of the council the power to appoint park commissioners. The Board of Trade made a significant strategic error, however. Intent on securing public approval for the park bill *before* sending it to the legislature, the proposal called for a public referendum on the issue. But who held the power to call that referendum? The city council.

On February 7, while the newspapers were exhorting people to get out and vote for parks, and with the president of the council on the verge of controlling a park commission through his proposed power to appoint commissioners, the council voted eleven to nine against calling the referendum. Another chance to create parks—and another opportunity for the city council to control them—was lost. The Board of Trade wouldn't make that mistake again.

As the economy of the Mill City continued to boom—the flour mills of Minneapolis becoming the most productive in the world—the small group of wealthy men that had concocted or supported all the park proposals turned their attention back to amassing fortunes. That was something they knew how to do—without seeking approval from city councils or voters.

In the next couple of years, the two men who would become most responsible for acquiring the waterfronts that would be the glory of Minneapolis, Loring and Cleveland, one rich, one not, suffered personal tragedies that may have deepened their bond when history threw them together.

The two New England–born sons of sea captains who had turned inland, who had both spent teen years in Cuba, had a love for trees and a talent to make them grow, had fate place in their care young grandchildren. In 1880, Loring's daughter-in-law, Ida Eastman, daughter of William Eastman, died of puerperal fever in Minneapolis at age twenty-one just two weeks after giving birth to her first child. Charles Loring and his wife assumed some responsibility for raising their grandson.

Only a few months earlier, Horace Cleveland's son had died in Colombia. His son's Colombian widow told Cleveland that in keeping with his son's dying wish she was bringing her two daughters, ages two and five, to the United States. Shortly after bringing the girls to the United States, she returned to Colombia alone, leaving the little girls in the care of Horace and his sickly wife, Maryann.

Loring and Cleveland's concern for children and their need of places to play and be exposed to the beauty of nature, so often repeated in their pleas for parks, may have been given urgency by their own experiences raising children as older men. Both would become advocates in later years for not just parks but children's playgrounds. And in Cleveland's case, the care and feeding of two little girls certainly added to the financial necessity that he keep working well past the age of retirement.

The population of Minneapolis had grown to more than forty-five thousand by 1880, and the city was on the eve of its most explosive period of growth before or since. More than eighty thousand new residents would stream into the city in the next five years, nearly tripling the city's population.

Loring remained active promoting his primary passion—trees—as president of the Minnesota Forestry Association. But in 1880 he provided evidence

The Minneapolis, Lyndale and Lake Calhoun railway in 1879. The train is headed north, just south of Thirty-first Street, which was still open prairie. (Minnesota Historical Society)

that a dream of boulevards and parks was still very much alive. In one of the first descriptions of how specific those dreams had become, Loring lobbied the Chicago, Minneapolis and St. Paul Railroad to change their right-of-way into the city. The railroad had proposed laying new track along the north shore of Lake Calhoun. Loring persuaded the railroad to locate their track farther from the shore. "The cordon of beautiful lakes encircling our city," he said, "has long been a pride of the city and our people have for many years cherished a hope which has lately developed into a full expectation that in the near future they would establish in the vicinity of the lakes . . . a grand system of parks with wide connecting boulevards extending around those lakes."

There is no indication of how "cherished hopes" had developed into a "full expectation," but park plans of some kind may have been in the works, because Cleveland and Loring met for some reason in October 1881. On October 22 of that year Cleveland inscribed a copy of his book on landscape architecture to Loring, and a few days later Cleveland wrote to his partner William French of the valued acquaintance of Charles M. Loring "who seemed a most estimable and agreeable man, and full of public spirit."

The "most estimable" man was about to get his comeuppance at the hands of Minneapolis voters, not for his stand on parks but on whiskey. In a campaign that the papers claimed was the least partisan in years, revolving only on the issue of "social order vs. social disorder," Loring was defeated for mayor of Minneapolis by a popular doctor and Democrat, Alfred Ames. In a vote split by the presence of a third party, the Temperance Party, "Law and Order Loring" lost despite enthusiastic endorsement by the Minneapolis papers and the endorsement of Ames by saloon keepers, who wanted less-strict enforcement of liquor regulations. Parks were never mentioned as an issue in the election.

Despite his defeat, Loring must have taken some hope from action by the city council that was voted into office the day he lost. One early act of the new council in 1882 was to acquire a park. The council voted to acquire land for a public square at what became Hawthorne Park, later renamed Wilson Park, just west of downtown. Of the total cost of $13,500, half was contributed by residents of the neighborhood.

Later that year, a second development gave park advocates more hope. The daughters of Franklin Steele, one the city's first European settlers, gave the city a plot of land for a park at Fifth Avenue South and Sixteenth Street, which still exists. They gave the land on a very specific condition: Charles Loring would be appointed to supervise improvements to the park.

Meanwhile, William Folwell was about to take the step he had wanted to take for years. Fed up with the politics of running a public university, he would resign from that post to pursue instead his love of teaching, writing and building a library. And now he would have time, when called, to devote his vision and leadership skills to keeping another public institution, the Minneapolis Board of Park Commissioners, from losing its way under a burden of debt.

Chapter Three

Victory at Last

Nearly ten miles apart, two meetings took place on the morning of January 2, 1883, that would have profound implications for Minneapolis parks, although neither meeting was called for that purpose. In St. Paul, the Minnesota Legislature convened for its biennial session. In one of its first actions it called for nominations for Speaker of the House. The Republican caucus immediately nominated a member of the Hennepin County delegation, Loren Fletcher. Without waiting for another nomination, the secretary called the roll. Ninety-five votes for Fletcher. Zero against. Fletcher held a firm grip on political power in Minnesota's lower house.

In downtown Minneapolis that morning, without the pomp and the buzz of an opening session of the state legislature, a dozen or so men gathered. They didn't have the power of elected office, although many in the group had been elected at one time or another. But the small group did hold considerable economic power. George Pillsbury, Charles Loring, George Brackett, Isaac Atwater, William King, Dorilus Morrison, Richard Chute, Samuel Gale and others were some of the heavy hitters in Minneapolis civic and commercial life.

"Some members of the hitherto moribund organization known as the Minneapolis Board of Trade have set themselves to the task of infusing new life into it," reported the *Minneapolis Journal* the next

Minneapolis City Hall in 1883 at the intersection of Hennepin and Nicollet. City Hall was built on the small triangle of land, once a duck pond, that William Eastman had partially donated to the city as a park in the 1860s. It would later become the site of The Gateway, a park created in 1915. (Minnesota Historical Society)

day. In derisive tones the *Journal* bid the board "God speed" in its quest to revive the organization.

Two days later the *Journal* reported that the Board of Trade had met again to discuss how to get James J. Hill's railroad, which would soon enter the city over the nearly completed Stone Arch Bridge, to commit to participating in a union depot. But the item was buried in a column of local news immediately followed by this earthshaker: "In the Crown Roller Mill yesterday, Hod Burke knocked J. R. James on the head with a club. The blow caused insensibility for a time." The Board of Trade still had work to do to reach the top of the paper.

It did within days. "The old Minneapolis Board of Trade reorganized this morning upon a basis that bids fair to make it a powerful instrument of good in forwarding the material interests of the city," the *Journal* reported. Col. William King, who had taken the initiative in reconstituting the board, was elected secretary. "If anything the board takes hold of doesn't boom now, it will be a wonder," wrote the *Journal*.

A week later the Board of Trade did indeed "take hold" of something. The board voted on January 14 to "take steps to secure a system of parks in this city with a view to such legislation as is necessary to authorize the inauguration of such a system."

With Loren Fletcher, a member of the Board of Trade's executive committee, installed as the Speaker of the House, such legislation would likely succeed. And James J. Hill did agree to bring his railroad into the Union Depot.

Action was swift. Almost too swift to believe that the proposed creation of a park system was not already on the drawing table before the Board of Trade is reported to have taken up the issue. Within two weeks the board passed resolutions that established the reasons and the method for establishing a park commission.

The board resolved, "That the rapid growth of our city has already been extended to some of the most natural and desirable locations for park purposes, warns us that the time has come when, if ever, steps should be taken to secure the necessary land for such a grand system of Parks and Boulevards as the natural situation offers and which if now secured will give to Minneapolis, not only the finest and most beautiful system of Public Parks and Boulevards of any city in America, but which, when secured and located as they now can be at comparatively small expense, will, in the near future, add many millions to the real estate value of our city."

Stilted language aside, the sense of the resolution could have flowed straight from Horace Cleveland's pen.

The board further resolved that for the "most speedy and efficient action," the Hennepin County

The Stone Arch Bridge nearing completion in 1883. The bridge was built by James J. Hill's Northern Pacific Railway. The "golden spike" that completed construction of the railroad to Seattle was driven later that year. (Burlington Northern Inc., Minnesota Historical Society)

delegates to the legislature were requested to secure "the passage of an act creating and establishing a park commission for the City of Minneapolis."

Finally, in what was either a futile—or carefully calculated—step in light of past actions, the board did request to confer with the city council to get their assistance in "carrying out this important matter." The president of council was duly notified—and the request was not answered. The Board of Trade forged ahead, perhaps relieved.

A first draft of the new park bill was circulated four days after the resolution by the Board of Trade. It was nearly identical to the bill drafted in 1877 that the City Council had refused to put to a referendum. This time the act didn't require a public vote.

Now weighing in, the city council protested nearly every detail of the bill, beginning with the fact that it had never been asked for by the people or taxpayers. The council also objected to the broad powers conferred on the Board of Park Commissioners: it gave the board control of a large sum of money in buying and selling lands, levying taxes and spending the money according to their own will without consulting the people; it gave the board the power to condemn private property without consulting the wishes of the owners, to sell lots, to increase the public debt, to borrow money, to issue bonds, to increase the burden of taxation; and ignored the rights of the people to be heard and allowed the people no voice in the selection of land for parks. All of which was true. But these were powers the council also already owned—and could have retained on park issues had they demonstrated over the years any inclination to act.

Other objections were raised as to whether parks were anywhere near the top of the list of priorities for the booming city. The city council passed a resolution that in its opinion "the city is more in need of effective sewers, a city hospital, water works extended to the city limits, bridges built over railroads, etc., than she is in need of spending money around Lake Calhoun."

Park proponents countered that all of those things, while needed, would not be made more difficult by the passage of time. A bridge can be built anytime, said one newspaper editorial, while the cost for park land could in a very short time triple or quadruple, pushing its price beyond any hope of public acquisition.

The issues raised by the council were debated at length by the Board of Trade, and several prominent lawyers on the board objected strongly to some provisions of the bill. Isaac Atwater led the opposition on the board, contesting most vehemently the power of the board to condemn land, or force its sale to the city at a price set by appraisers, a power now more commonly referred to as "eminent domain." Atwater and others thought that the power to condemn land for public use should reside only in the City Council.

The Board of Trade made numerous revisions to the original draft to accommodate concerns within the group, and, in a very clear attempt to circumvent the City Council further, it revised the power to appoint park commissioners. Instead of letting the council do it, and risk it never being done, the draft legislation provided for naming twelve commissioners who would comprise the first board. After one year, all commissioners would then be elected by popular vote in staggered terms. In a bone thrown to those who thought the city's elected officials should have more power on the proposed board, the mayor and two council committee chairs were added to the board as ex-officio members.

The would-be commissioners' names were inserted in the bill at the last minute and were subject to political wrangling to ensure equal representation on the board of both Republicans and Democrats. Those named were among the most active in civic and business affairs in the city: Charles Loring, Dorilus Morrison, George Brackett, John Pillsbury, Henry Wells, Orlando Merriman, Judson Cross, Daniel Bassett, William Eastman, Adin Austin, John Oswald and Andrew Haugan. The list included four former mayors of the city and one ex-governor of the state as well as others who had been elected to the city council or the school board. One last-minute provision was added by opponents of the measure in hopes of killing the bill: the legislation, if passed, would be put to a referendum at the municipal elections on April 3.

The "perfected draft," as one newspaper called it—another said it had been emasculated—was rushed to the house of representatives in St. Paul. Under a suspension of the rules, meaning it was not sent to a committee for hearings, it was passed immediately without a dissenting vote. The senate promptly passed it too, and Governor Lucius Hubbard signed the bill into law on February 27, 1883. All that remained was the referendum.

In later years, Charles Loring would credit William King with managing the passage of the bill in the legislature. Loring himself was, as during the 1877 park push, out of town. But Loring kept track of the park debate through Minneapolis papers and sent occasional advice to his friend George Brackett on how to manage the referendum effort. "It does look to me as though the long wished for time was near when the people of our city are to have a system of parks. . . . Yet there is work to be done. It strikes me that the commission should not agitate the question of location of a system of parks but that the election should be carried without exciting localities."

> "The bill presented for our consideration is by no means perfect, but its defects are small compared with the public misfortune of its defeat."
>
> EUGENE WILSON

Loring also mused whether he was the right man for the park commission. He asked Brackett if William King wouldn't be a better man for the job and expressed his willingness to step aside if King's name on the commission would enhance the chances for public approval.

Dorilus Morrison, former mayor and prospective commissioner, who was also out of town, also wrote Brackett to encourage him not to overlook the matter. "Spend time," he wrote, "and if a little money is needed, I will respond."

The Board of Trade organized their campaign for a "Yes" vote by appointing George Brackett, Andrew Boardman, John West and William King to coordinate the campaign in the city's wards. All except West would later serve as park commissioners. At their nominating convention for candidates for city offices in the upcoming election, the Democrats endorsed a "No" vote on parks. The Republicans, at their convention, gave only tepid support for a "Yes."

The Knights of Labor, a growing association of labor guilds, issued bitter resolutions against the bill. It objected to "none but capitalists" being allowed to serve on the board. Further galling to the Knights was that "friends of the measure point to the fact that all the commissioners are rich men and therefore will not steal, and by inference declare that poor men must necessarily be dishonest." To the Knights the parks measure was "a cunningly devised scheme by which the rich are to be made richer and the poor, poorer."

Much has been made in some historical accounts of opposition from the Knights of Labor, and it has been repeatedly cited as evidence of opposition to parks. And although it makes a great story, it is not clear that there was a class divide on the park question. The papers of the day said attendance at the Knights of Labor meeting that passed the resolution was small and unenthusiastic. And although the Knights invited working men to turn out in force at a meeting Saturday evening, March 31, where they would be advised on the "iniquitous measures," newspaper accounts suggest the meeting was not well attended.

One leading Democrat, Eugene Wilson, wrote to a newspaper to correct the impression that he objected to the bill. "The bill presented for our consideration is by no means perfect," he wrote, "but its defects are small compared with the public misfortune of its defeat." He added that "the Republicans named are all good men for the place." He concluded by noting that Minneapolis was behind other cities her size, including St. Paul, in acquiring public grounds. While others have acted, "Minneapolis stands timidly doubting, waiting for the millennium that general perfection may insure against fraud and mistakes." Wilson would later become a staunch ally of Loring on the park board.

The newspapers of the day campaigned ardently for passage of the park act. They had run editorials for years on the need for parks and now ran letters to the editor mostly supportive of the measure, including one from a self-proclaimed working man who said four of every five working men he knew supported parks.

While the debate raged, Minneapolis Mayor Alfred Ames, an avowed opponent of the park act, nevertheless called a meeting on March 14 of the commissioners named in the act for the purposes of organizing the Board of Park Commissioners should the referendum pass. Charles Loring was unanimously voted president of the board. He was still in Washington, D.C., where he was spending the winter. The citizens of Minneapolis had not elected him as their mayor, but the elite of the city named him to a position of far greater power in shaping the future of the city.

The *Evening Journal* reported on the day of the referendum, April 3, that early indications pointed to the defeat of the park measure. "The opposition to it comes from the wealthy citizens among who may be named, W. W. McNair, H. G. Sidle and Judge Atwater." The next day the *Times* reported a far different result. Owing, it wrote, to the sunny afternoon, a large number of Republican voters turned out to pass the park referendum.

Fifty-eight percent of Minneapolis voters had approved the creation of a Board of Park Commissioners with sweeping powers. What the *Journal* had called the "obstructionists and reactionary old fogies who set their faces like flint against any innovations or improvements" had been defeated.

The new board did indeed have wide powers. The park act of 1883 gave the board the power to acquire, improve and maintain park land, issue city bonds, condemn land and raise park funds through a tax levy not to exceed one mill on the valuation of all land in the city. (A mill is one dollar of tax for each one thousand dollars of assessed property value.) These are powers the board has continued to hold throughout its history, although not always without a fight and not always in quite the same form. Important additions were also made over the years, but these core powers have always characterized the board. Although the first commissioners were appointed, the act also provided for the independent election of commissioners after that first year. That independence has also been maintained by the park board since its creation despite repeated efforts to transfer the powers of the board to the mayor or city council.

> *"The intelligence, the pride, the public spirit and humanity of our people have at last been vindicated."*
>
> WILLIAM KING

The park board also had a power previously conferred on the city council by the legislature for other city improvements: it could make special assessments on property that derived "benefits" from the creation of parks. Through this power the park board could levy special assessments to pay for acquiring parks in a neighborhood. This provision was based on the already well-anticipated likelihood that property values would increase significantly near land designated for parks. In effect, the provision made property owners who reaped that bounty pay much of the cost.

It was a provision that would be used for nearly a century by the park board and would become a source of great controversy. Property owners who were willing and financially able to pay those special assessments petitioned for parks in their neighborhoods.

It was easy for later park boards to accept those offers, especially when funds were short, which they almost always seemed to be. Instead of buying land with park board funds, they could acquire land based on the promises of nearby property owners to pay for them over time. The result, many would claim over the years, was that wealthy neighborhoods got more parks than poorer ones, whose property owners couldn't afford special assessments.

But in the first years of the park board, those fears of imbalance were unfounded. For, contrary to the grand plans of park promoters—and Horace Cleveland—the first park board, packed with the wealthy elite who had carriages ready to take them on pleasure drives over distant parkways, did not look first to the city's lakes and rivers.

Horace Cleveland had a plan, but the park board would not follow it for many years. And without William Folwell, they might never have.

Chapter Four

A System Takes Shape

When he was sixty-nine-years old, Horace Cleveland finally got paid by Minneapolis for the services he had been providing for years in shaping the thinking of its leaders and winning converts for park building. In late June 1883, after the commissioners had been on the job for only two months, Cleveland delivered a bill for $540.75 for "professional services" plus expenses.

The specific professional services Cleveland had provided, billed at $20 a day for twenty-four days, were creating and writing *Suggestions for a System of Parks and Parkways for the City of Minneapolis*. The commissioners were so impressed with the report he wrote, complete with a map of the city that showed the parks and parkways he proposed, that they immediately had twenty-five hundred copies printed for distribution around town. Cleveland's grand plan for a system of parks and parkways provided the blueprint Minneapolis park commissioners would try to follow for decades.

Cleveland's greatest contribution to Minneapolis was in the title of his report; he proposed a *system* for connecting sites of extraordinary beauty or "natural interest." He noted his preference for an extended system of boulevards rather than a series of detached open areas or public squares. Cleveland's suggestions proposed no specific parks other than Farview Park for its spectacular views, riverside parks on both east and west riverbanks as starting points for acquiring the entire river gorge, and a large "driving park" along the Mississippi on the northern boundary of the city. Even among the boulevards he proposed, only those around Lake Harriet, Lake Calhoun and the river were acquired and developed over many years and kept as boulevards.

In fact, most of Cleveland's suggestions were never followed exactly as he proposed. Yet, thanks to visionaries such as Loring and Folwell, who came to understand Cleveland's vision from his own lips, and Theodore Wirth, who inherited the rudiments of that system and worked his magic expanding it, the notion of a "system" never died. It is with us still as park advocates of the twenty-first century work to complete it by closing the "Missing Link" of parkways connecting northeast to southeast Minneapolis and extending park land north from downtown along the banks of the Mississippi.

Cleveland never proposed what became Lake of the Isles Parkway, Minnehaha Parkway, Cedar Lake Parkway, Theodore Wirth Parkway, Victory Memorial Drive or St. Anthony Parkway. But by other routes, he did propose similar links in all directions. The links in that chain of parkways, today's

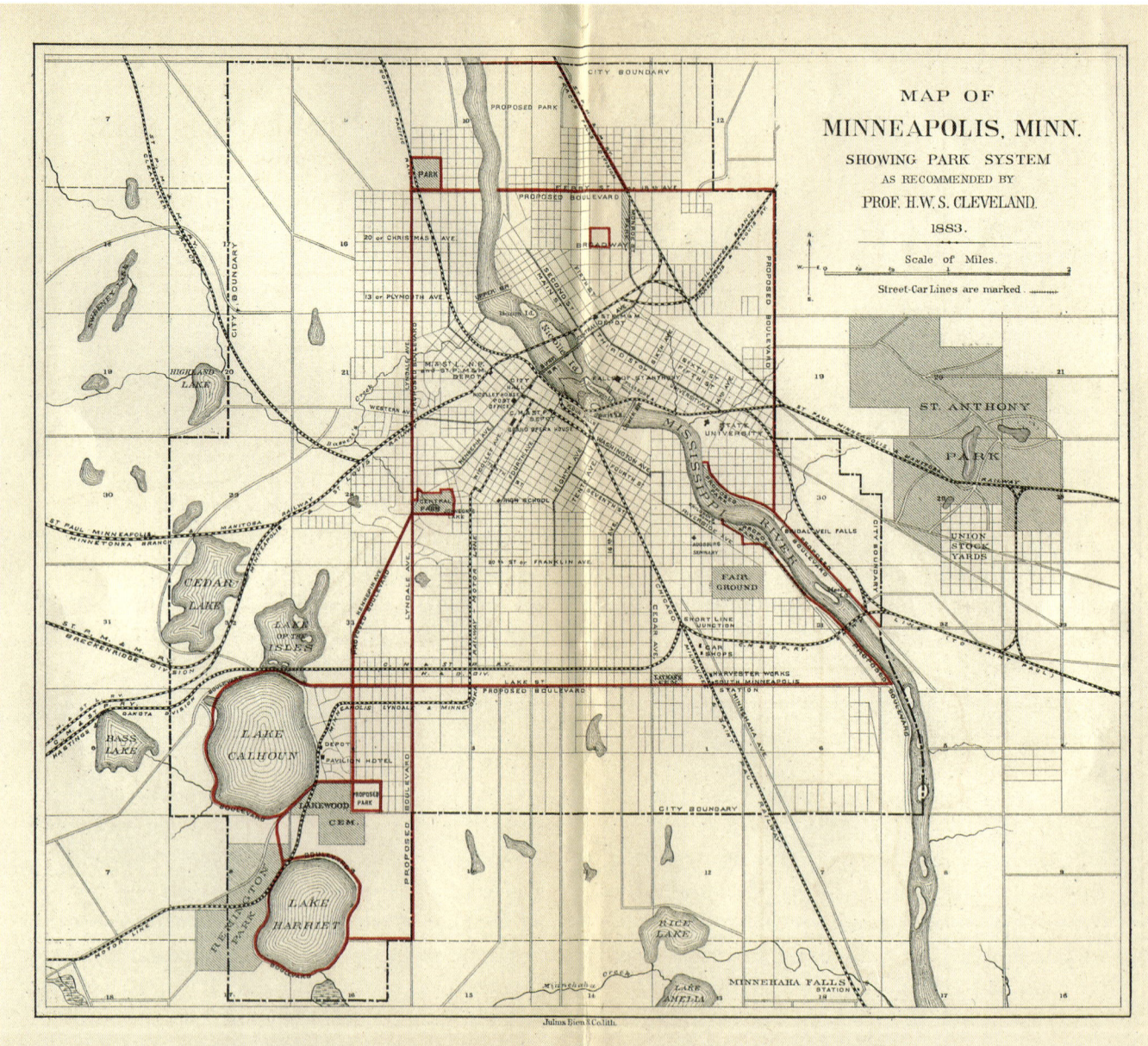

The map of the park system Horace Cleveland proposed in his *Suggestions for a System of Parks and Parkways for the City of Minneapolis* in 1883. His emphasis was on an encircling system of boulevards to connect features of natural beauty, especially the Mississippi River and the lakes, but extending into north Minneapolis at Farview Park and crossing the Mississippi to a large driving park in the northeast, then continuing to the river in southeast Minneapolis. The only park not connected by broad boulevards to the others was Logan Park in northeast, a park the board had already committed to purchasing by the time Cleveland submitted his suggestions. The large "driving park" along the Mississippi in northeast Minneapolis was the only suggestion never seriously pursued by the park board. The board tried to acquire land for the proposed east-west boulevard along Lake Street, but the land was too expensive. Of special interest is that Cleveland did not propose a parkway around Lake of the Isles and only on the west side of Lake Calhoun. Cleveland's vision of encircling parkways, later termed the "Grand Rounds" by William Folwell, was eventually achieved but much farther from the city center than Cleveland would have liked. The only section of parkway never acquired is the "missing link" through southeast Minneapolis to the east bank of the Mississippi. Although Cleveland always advocated acquiring Minnehaha Falls as a park, at the time of his suggestions the falls and Minnehaha Creek were well outside of the city limits. (Minneapolis Park and Recreation Board)

"Grand Rounds," changed over time, but its basic shape and purpose are much the same as Cleveland proposed in 1883.

The one important difference is that the parkways eventually created were much farther from the city center than Cleveland proposed. One of Cleveland's great criticisms of Chicago parks and boulevards—a central argument in his push for early planning and land acquisition in newer cities—was the distance of those parks from the people who needed them most: the workers and the poor who often lived in the central city. In his suggestions he had boasted that his encircling parkways were for the most part within two miles of central Minneapolis. By the time Minneapolis acquired the "Grand Rounds" of today, the linking parkways were pushed significantly farther from the city center.

That there is to this day no park named for Horace Cleveland in Minneapolis is understandable. He did not choose to concentrate his considerable powers of persuasion on individual parks. That there is no Horace Cleveland Parkway in Minneapolis, however, is an omission for which generations of park commissioners should not be easily forgiven.

The new Board of Park Commissioners held its first meeting, April 18, 1883, under the gavel of president Charles Loring. Within days, the city council that had fought the creation of the commission so bitterly turned over to the board the four existing Minneapolis Parks: Murphy Square, Market Square, and the two newest parks, not yet a year old, Hawthorne Park and Franklin Steele Square.

One of the board's first acts was to commission Cleveland to propose an overall plan for the city's parks. Without waiting for his completed plan, however, the board began acquiring land. The lesson of the long history of failed attempts to create parks in Minneapolis, reinforced by Cleveland's preaching, was to get land. Whatever the beneficial effects of parks might be—an issue being debated across the country—they required land. And what the early park commissioners, many of whom were wealthy landowners, did understand was the value of land. They pursued land in those first days with a single-minded sense of purpose. How that land would eventually be used was to be decided on much more egalitarian terms over the years: the people would use it how they wanted. Park commissioners would have to adapt.

> The motto of the Minneapolis Board of Park Commissioners adopted in 1883 was "Health and Beauty." The motto was chosen by a committee of commissioners chaired by Samuel Chute. "Health" referred to parks providing fresh air—they would be the "city's lungs," as Cleveland and later Loring often said—especially for the city's children. "Beauty" signified the board's commitment to creating beautiful places in which citizens could escape from the city. The effect of beauty on personal mental health—and social and economic health—was also considered an important benefit of parks.

The first acquisition was for a "central park" near the city center, which Cleveland treated as an accomplished fact in his suggestions. The ideal spot was then called Johnson's Lake. Charles Loring described Central Park, incorporating the lake later to be named for him, as "readily accessible by connecting streets and by horse cars and motor lines. It embraces Johnson Lake, fed by unfailing springs of pure water, a surrounding area of level land, and on its north and east side an undulating declivity covered with a fine growth of native deciduous trees and carpeted with an emerald turf which have long designated it in the public estimation for a park."

Loring had considered buying land overlooking the pond for his home, but his wife had decided that it was too far out in the country. Now it was not so remote. The lot Loring once considered buying had become the home of Henry Wells and would later become the site of St. Mark's Episcopal Church across the street from the park.

A later influential park commissioner, Andrew

Boardman, discovered fortuitously that land for Central Park had been acquired just up to the edge of his property. He now had a park-front address. Boardman was not a commissioner at the time, but he had helped manage the Board of Trade's campaign to get the park referendum passed.

Although many of the commissioners were significant landowners, few cases such as Boardman's can be identified that appear to show favoritism or other skullduggery in park land acquisitions. Several prominent Minneapolitans had land taken for Central Park, including three lots owned by Albert Loring, the son of the park board's president, who sold them to the commission at his cost.

The second acquisition was a park in the First Ward, on the east side of the river between Broadway and Jefferson (now Logan Park), selected primarily because it was then on the edge of an already populated neighborhood. The new commissioners were clearly intent on distributing parks among the city's wards. Newspaper accounts three years later claimed that the new wealth of city councilman Edgar Comstock, an ex-officio member of the first park board, was directly attributable to land owned by his wife being offered and taken as a part of First Ward Park. His remaining property in the neighborhood had appreciated considerably after the park was located there. It is unclear if Comstock's land ownership had any bearing on the board's decisions, but it is hard to imagine men of such wealth and influence as Morrison, Loring, Pillsbury and Brackett—who had fought so long for city parks—being bullied or bamboozled by a councilman once they acquired sweeping power to put parks where they chose. Cleveland claimed that he had purposely paid no heed to ownership of lands in creating his suggestions.

The view looking northwest over Johnson's Lake (Loring Pond) in the late 1870s. The building at left is the home of Henry Wells. It is now the site of St. Mark's Episcopal Cathedral. (Jacoby, Minnesota Historical Society)

The third new park was Third Ward Park, twenty acres of land on the north side of Minneapolis adjacent to Lyndale Avenue North. The new park included the highest point of land within city limits and was one of Cleveland's few specific park recommendations. The top of the hill in the center of the lot provided a complete view of the city and the Mississippi River for miles. First named Prospect Park, the name was later changed to Farview Park.

Also targeted for immediate acquisition was a park in the Sixth Ward along the west bank of the Mississippi a mile downstream from the falls. Riverside Park, as it would come to be known, comprised twenty-five acres of woods and meadow approaching the river. It was one of Cleveland's favorite places. Cleveland and the commissioners hoped it would be the beginning of a park that would extend downstream to the southern city limits at Thirty-eighth Street and eventually Minnehaha Falls and Fort Snelling a couple of miles beyond.

Each of the first four acquisitions is shown in the map Cleveland submitted with his suggestions, making it clear that the board had already made those decisions by the time he reported.

A fifth new park was added almost immediately to the growing inventory when Dr. Jacob Elliot, a onetime Minneapolis resident who had since moved to California, donated to the park board two acres of land that had once been his garden on Ninth Street. Elliot's donation was augmented by a purchase of adjoining land for $20,000 from the Homeopathic Hospital to create Elliot Park.

The time-consuming challenge of these first acquisitions was that they were located in portions of the city that were already partially built-up. Nearly all of the land had to be acquired by condemnation. A good bit of the park board's time was consumed in addressing challenges and appeals to the amounts awarded for land and in readjusting park boundaries when some land was appraised too high for their well-informed tastes. Adding to their challenge was the anticipated spiraling of real estate prices in the vicinity of parks. Property owners were reluctant to accept awards for their property based on appraisals that were outdated nearly as soon as they were written. Loring cited an example of two lots in Central Park that were valued at $25,000—an appraisal the board considered too high. Six months later those two lots, he wrote, were valued at more than $43,000 and were eventually acquired for the park.

The board assessed the full value of the lands

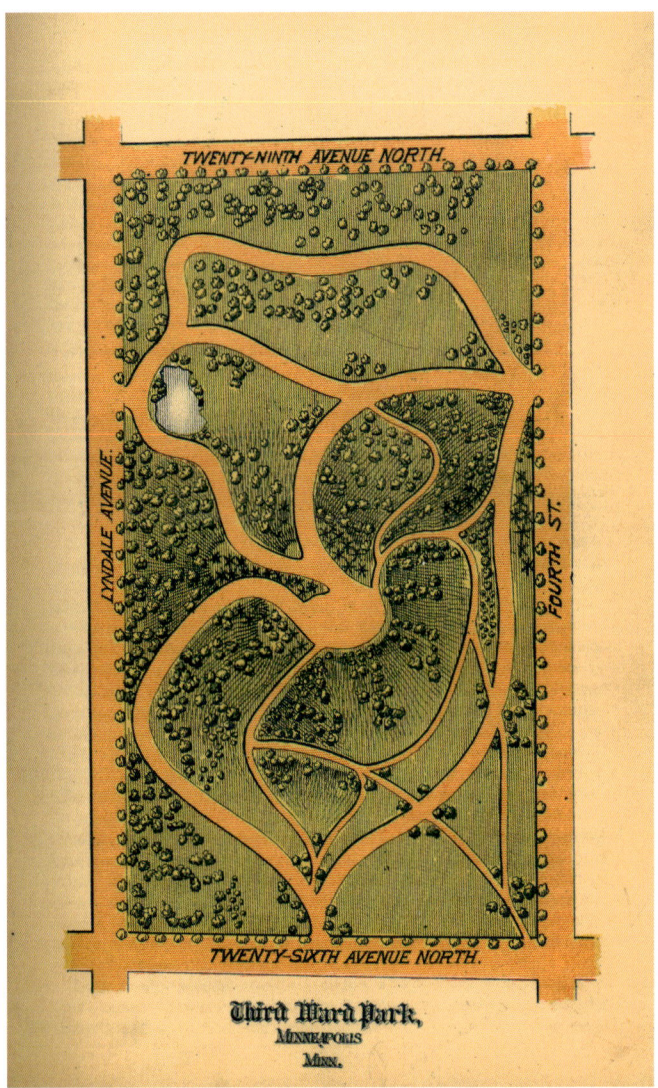

Cleveland's original design for Farview Park in 1883, then known as Third Ward Park. The park was later called Prospect Park for a time until the board settled on the name Farview Park. The park was valued by Cleveland for its views of the city and the river. It was the highest point of land in the city. (Minneapolis Park and Recreation Board)

acquired for Central (Loring), Logan, Farview and Riverside parks against the "benefited districts," which meant in effect that the land was acquired at very little cost to the city. The purchases did result, however, in using up much of the original bonding authority the park board had acquired by legislation. Central (Loring) Park with an initial acquisition cost of more than $150,000, and considerably more as it was expanded, would remain for decades the most expensive Minneapolis Park. The neighborhood would also soon become the center of the social life of the city's elite.

The board also charged ahead with acquiring for parkways Hennepin Avenue south from Central Park and Lyndale Avenue from Farview Park in the north to a proposed Lyndale Park adjacent to Lakewood Cemetery in the south. Cleveland had given these streets tepid endorsement in his suggestions as parkways that would be the connecting links from the lakes in the south to Farview Park in the north. Instead of the wide boulevard Cleveland wanted, however, the board recognized the limits of its purchasing power and chose to acquire a strip of Hennepin Avenue only eighty-eight feet wide.

Many years later Cleveland would claim that he always had doubts about those streets being able to be the boulevards he desired because they already carried too much traffic. The designation of those streets as parkways would prove over the years to be one of the park board's costliest mistakes.

The board also targeted three other areas for immediate land acquisition. One area was Cleveland's prized east riverbank south of the University to the city line with St. Paul. Cleveland had proposed a park on the east bank as a mirror of Riverside Park on the west bank, once again as the northern terminus of a drive that would extend downriver. Cleveland even proposed a bridge across the Mississippi to unite the parks. The board began acquiring land by condemnation for that parkway, but the cost proved higher than the board would tolerate. Nearly every appraisal was challenged in court. The project was abandoned even after the board had taken possession of several lots, which it would eventually put up for sale.

The failure to acquire the east riverbank was a bitter disappointment for Cleveland. Seven years later he urged Folwell to take other commissioners down to the riverbank to look at its park potential. "When once you take in the possibilities that are open it will drive you frantic to think of losing them," he wrote. "If all your committee could go it would do their souls good if they've got any."

The second targeted acquisition that failed, at first, was the entire shoreline of Lake Harriet. This, too, proved a more costly enterprise than the board anticipated, and it was abandoned for a short time, even though Cleveland had suggested that a strip of land only 100 feet wide was needed to provide the parkway he envisaged. Lake Harriet was the most desired of the lakes because it was the only one with a well-established shoreline nearly all the way around. Both Lake of the Isles and Lake Calhoun had considerable marshy areas on their shores.

The third failed acquisition in the park board's early years was the only one that would never be resurrected, despite Cleveland's impassioned plea for it and a concerted effort by early commissioners to secure it. In his suggestions, Cleveland had proposed a 200-foot-wide boulevard from Lake Calhoun to the Mississippi River via Lake Street. Cleveland described that area of the city, then "south of the thickly settled" neighborhoods, as "dead level, offering no natural features of interest."

To prevent that region from becoming "a weary and monotonous series of ordinary dwellings and shops," Cleveland recommended turning Lake Street into an ornamental avenue that would become "a rich and elegant quarter." To imagine what Cleveland had in mind for Lake Street, picture Summit Avenue in St. Paul from Lexington Avenue west to the river. The comparison is no stretch; Cleveland designed that segment of Summit Avenue for St. Paul a few years later, and it did indeed become a location for "rich and elegant" homes. The park board realized after a lot of wasted effort that Lake Street,

Lake Harriet in 1887. The lake was the most desirable of all city lakes for a park because it was the only one with a well-defined shoreline. Lake Harriet is the only city lake that has never been dredged. The first boat rentals on the lake, seen here, were operated privately under a concession from the park board. (Minnesota Historical Society)

too, would be too expensive to acquire, so it began considering alternatives. How about Thirty-fourth Street? The board made a very serious effort to stay true to Cleveland's suggestions.

With fewer businesses along Thirty-fourth Street, it might still be affordable, and it would meet at the river precisely with Summit Avenue on the St. Paul side and incorporate Powderhorn Lake. But even that land was too expensive, even after many property owners west of Bloomington Avenue had agreed to donate land.

Cleveland's grand east-west boulevard, which would have been an "intrinsic element of beauty," eventually died. What was lost in Cleveland's mind was not only beautiful open space, but also a firebreak and conduit of fresh air in what he correctly imagined would become a crowded neighborhood someday.

Apart from Cleveland's recommendations for a system of parks and parkways, the most important suggestion he offered may have been a bit difficult for the men of the park board to follow. Yet they did. Acquire the land while you can, Cleveland urged, then "we may take our own time before beginning its improvement." They avoided the temptation to spend their limited resources on improving and ornamenting parks.

Among the arguments made for parks over the years, in addition to providing for the health and happiness of its people by exposing them to fresh air and the character-building beauty of nature, was that a city of "great pretensions," as King once put it, must have parks to keep up with other great cities. Parks had become a point of pride. It was a checklist item—"we've got that"—for the well-traveled wealthy of the city to highlight in their argument that their frontier home was a first-class city.

Also, many of the new immigrants to Minneapolis—whether from New England, Sweden, Ireland or elsewhere—had the experience of parks or at least town squares in their older hometowns. They, like Loring, had a picture in their heads of what a city could or should be. In an article written by Loring in 1891, he credited those new immigrants for joining with the "small group" who had long agitated for parks to pass the park act.

Warning against too much pretension, however, in his "suggestions," Cleveland cautioned against the tendency to embellish and improve parks with ornamental gardening, statues, bridges and fountains. He warned against putting "cheap art" in parks "while so many demands exist for works of actual necessity." Cleveland compared parks so adorned to a person who puts on jewelry before he has comfortable clothing. For Cleveland and the board, the goal was to get land while they could.

In the introductory remarks of Cleveland's *Suggestions* he concluded with words that echo still across the city's lakes and down its river gorge:

> If you have faith in the future greatness of your city, do not shrink from securing while you may

such areas as will be adequate to the wants of such a city. Do not be appalled at the thought of appropriating lands which seem now too costly . . . that was precisely the feeling which prevented the purchase of Nicollet Island when it might have been had for a sum which now seems contemptible. Look forward for a century, to the time when the city has a population of a million, and think what will be their wants. They will have wealth enough to purchase all that money can buy, but all their wealth cannot purchase a lost opportunity, or restore natural features of grandeur and beauty, which would then possess priceless value, and which you can preserve if you will but say the word and save them from the destruction which certainly awaits them if you fail to utter it.

> *"Look forward for a century, to the time when the city has a population of a million, and think what will be their wants. They will have wealth enough to purchase all that money can buy, but all their wealth cannot purchase a lost opportunity, or restore natural features of grandeur and beauty. . . ."*
>
> **HORACE CLEVELAND**

The great city that Cleveland foresaw did happen; whether that city had—or has—the wealth to acquire all it desires remains a subject of debate.

The board failed to implement Cleveland's most favored projects, but it did give him more work, just not as much as he hoped. As early as 1881, Cleveland had considered moving to Minneapolis from Chicago. Now with the need for someone to design the new parks, that prospect was becoming even more attractive.

By December 1883, Cleveland submitted drawings and plans requested by the commissioners for the improvement of their first acquisitions. He provided detailed drawings for the original improvement of Central Park, Farview Park and Logan Park along with a lengthy explanation of the effects he intended. Cleveland planned for immediate plantings of trees and shrubs, knowing they would eventually have to be thinned, and for the grading of paths that would eventually need to be widened. He was intent on economy and speed—and hoped the board would employ him to supervise the work.

It did not. The board would leave that in the hands of Charles Loring. During his mayoral campaign the year before the park board was created, the *St. Paul Pioneer Press* had endorsed Loring for the office in part because "he had so far withdrawn from business cares as to have the leisure at his command for the conscientious discharge of the duties of this exacting office." With leisure at his command, Loring personally supervised much of the work on the new parks, including Central Park, which would eventually bear his name. His personal involvement would establish a precedent that would powerfully influence the creation of Minneapolis' future parks—and the diversion of attention to the chain of lakes from the river beloved by Cleveland.

By early 1884 the board realized that at a condemnation value of nearly $300,000, a Lake Harriet Parkway was out of reach. But near the end of the year Henry Beard called on Loring with the proposal that he, James Merritt and Charles Reeve, who had gained control of most of the land around Lake Harriet, would donate a strip of land 125 feet wide around nearly the whole of the lake for a parkway.

In 1885 the donation by Beard was, in Loring's words, "made ineffectual" by a court decree that William King was still rightful owner of the land. King's representative in managing his land around the lake, New York attorney Philo Remington (thus the name of Remington Park for much of the land west of the lake), had fraudulently sold off the land in cahoots with Louis Menage, an early developer of land west of the lakes. King, who had been selected to fill a vacant seat on the park board, confirmed title to the board of fifty-five acres of Lake Harriet shore once he regained ownership. As a result of what Loring called the "commendable and characteristic generosity" of King, the park board acquired the entire lake and its shores at practically no cost. The effort to acquire the southwestern lakes for parks, which would consume the park board for the next several years, was well under way.

And Henry Beard's initial generosity was not forgotten. (He was not implicated in the fraud around the lake, apparently buying the land from those who had stolen it from King.) The picnic area, tennis courts and wooded hillside on the west shore of Lake Harriet have long been named Beard's Plaisance. Beard also donated the land for Linden Hills Parkway, the original link between Lake Calhoun and Lake Harriet.

The other notable donation of land in those early days, a gift from James Stinson of a strip of land a mile long and 200 feet wide for a parkway in northeast Minneapolis, did not inspire the same expansion efforts as that of Beard, then King.

As the park board tried to find ways to acquire the land it wanted, it officially named Cleveland its landscape architect at a rate of $25 a day, a nice 25 percent increase in the rate he had charged for work on his *Suggestions*. (It was an act of generosity that proved a bit hollow as the board would contest several of Cleveland's bills in succeeding years, refusing to pay him for consultations with commissioners that were not authorized by the full board and refusing to pay his travel expenses.)

The members of the board did another nice thing for Cleveland in 1884. That summer, the trustees of Lakewood Cemetery, which included some of the same influential men who sat on the park board, replaced its original superintendent, A. B. Barton, with Ralph Cleveland, Horace's surviving son.

The results of that hire may have been profound for the park system of Minneapolis. In addition to exhorting the board to develop a system, Horace Cleveland had another invaluable service to provide to the future citizens of Minneapolis: he would play an important role in the park board's acquisition of Minnehaha Falls a few years later. If Ralph had not moved to Minneapolis, Horace and Maryann, challenged by raising two granddaughters, might not have moved to Minneapolis either. Who knows what the future of the falls would have been without Horace Cleveland agitating for acquisition of his land of myth and beauty.

After preparing plans for the improvement of Elliot Park, Murphy Park and Riverside Park in the fall and winter of 1884–85, and his consultations on Lake Harriet Parkway the next summer, Cleveland received almost no work from the park board for nearly five years. From the time Cleveland moved to Minneapolis in 1886 at the age of seventy-two until 1890, he was employed more by St. Paul than by Minneapolis.

In those years in which he did little work for the park board, he still made his influence felt and his voice heard, first, in the hire of a full-time superintendent of parks, William Berry, and second, in his continued exhortations to acquire vital park land.

As park improvements began beyond Loring Park, especially on parkways, it was apparent that the board needed a superintendent to supervise the work. Cleveland had someone in mind: William Morse Berry. Berry was the perfect fit for the job and the men who would employ him. Like so many of Minneapolis's leaders, Berry was from Maine, and like Cleveland and Loring, he had a seafaring background. He had actually been a shipbuilder at one time, but his shipbuilding days ended when one of his ships sank beneath him in the North

Atlantic. After his rescue, he turned to engineering and had eventually become superintendent for Chicago's South Park Commission, implementing designs Cleveland had created there. Cleveland knew that Berry could transfer designs from paper to land.

Berry remained park superintendent for twenty years through some of the most difficult times the park board has ever seen. He was on the job throughout the course of laying out the first parks and the rudimentary parkways around the lakes. His work included the thankless, and eventually hopeless, job of creating and maintaining as parkways both Lyndale Avenue North and Hennepin Avenue South.

With its initial land purchases made—nicely scattered throughout the city's political wards—and both a respected landscape architect and an experienced superintendent aboard, the people of Minneapolis probably thought that parks had been addressed adequately. The park board had met its initial obligations to provide parks in the city, and each section of the city had one. But Loring wasn't done. He wanted more. His goal was a "chain" of lakes that would eventually become one of the defining characteristics of the city.

William Morse Berry, holding the tree, helped park commissioners plant a tree in 1914 at Lake Calhoun. Berry was the first superintendent of Minneapolis parks, from 1885 to 1905. While Berry was superintendent, the state legislature granted the park board control of all trees planted along city streets as well as in parks. In this photo, Berry was already retired. His successor as superintendent, Theodore Wirth, is second from left. (Minneapolis Park and Recreation Board)

Chapter Five

A Turn to the Lakes

One of the enduring images from Charles Loring's scrapbooks is of Loring sitting on the floor of John Green's Kenwood home, going over plans for a park around Lake of the Isles. It is one of a series of Loring's recollections of his many meetings with Green and others to get them to donate land around the lake first for a park and then a boulevard in 1885 and 1886.

Loring had been intimately involved in the selection and improvement of park lands since the board was created. He had accompanied Cleveland on some of his investigations of Minneapolis, and diary extracts in his scrapbooks reveal his constant attention to the details of park improvements:

NOVEMBER 21, 1883. Made a contract with Foster Balch to excavate the lake of Central Park.

MONDAY NOVEMBER, 1883. Balch began work on the Lake at Central Park. Ice cut in blocks was hauled out by horses. The process is quite interesting.

JUNE 12, 1884. In grading the lake of Central Park the workmen left a piece in the center which I stopped them from taking out. I wrote to Mr. Cleveland that I should be pleased to leave it for a small island. He replied that would be alright. I only wish I had thought of it earlier so as to have had a larger island.

OCTOBER 1, 1884. Began cutting down the big hill on Hennepin Avenue and filling the street in the low ground.

OCTOBER 29, 1884. Today I planted the first tree in Central Park, a large elm. I saved it from the Hennepin Avenue which the men were grading.

The story of how Loring came to devote so much of his personal time to acquiring land around Lake of the Isles—an area not even mentioned in Cleveland's suggestions or in earlier proposals for parks—is not recorded. Its importance lies in the fact that Loring's success in acquiring this land likely was responsible for the extension of the "chain of lakes" concept that would eventually include Cedar Lake, all of Lake Calhoun, then Minnehaha Parkway to Lake Nokomis and Lake Hiawatha. (At this time Nokomis was named Lake Amelia, and Hiawatha was a shallow body of water and marsh—a widening of Minnehaha Creek—called Mud Lake. Both were well outside city limits in those days.) This shift in focus from the Mississippi River—where the park board had been stymied—to the lakes would dominate park board actions throughout the late 1880s.

Lake of the Isles from the north end in 1852 in a sketch by Adolph Hoeffler. (Adolph Hoeffler, Minnesota Historical Society)

Three factors probably turned the focus of Loring to the lakes. The first was that Loring and others realized very early on that Hennepin Avenue, despite considerable effort and cost in improving it and making it the primary parkway connection to Lake Harriet, was carrying too much business traffic. It appeared unlikely ever to be the parkway that Cleveland and the park board had hoped it would be. An alternative route to Harriet was likely encouraged by the offer of Thomas Lowry, a friend and business associate of Loring, to donate land for a lookout on part of his land, Lowry Hill, high above Loring Park to the southwest. Loring proposed a boulevard that would connect from Hennepin Avenue via Mount Curve Avenue to the proposed lookout park and then down to Lake of the Isles and around it to Calhoun and Harriet.

The second factor that probably influenced Loring was the nature of Lowry's offer: free land. The park board had experienced difficult negotiations to acquire land for a river boulevard and an east-west boulevard across south Minneapolis, and it was in the process of pulling the plug on both projects. It had already abandoned once, as well, the acquisition of Lake Harriet, although by 1885, thanks to Beard and then King, it looked as if that lake parkway was within reach. The board's money to acquire parks had been largely used up, and the only way to get more land was to have it donated.

It just happened that Loring's friends owned land in the vicinity. Thomas Lowry owned Lowry Hill and land in Kenwood, William McNair owned some of the shores of Cedar Lake, and William Washburn owned land along Minnehaha Creek that would later come into play. Loring had been involved with all of them in politics or business.

The nature of their holdings was also a factor in stimulating donations. All of these men were wealthy and owned land well beyond their own homesteads. Giving land to the park board would, as they all had seen happen at Loring Park, Lake Harriet and Hennepin Avenue, increase the value of the surrounding land they would still hold in the vicinity of new parks. This was often not the case along the east river and Lake Street (or for that matter at Loring Park), where more of the property owners lived or ran businesses on their land. Many of those people did not own adjacent property that would appreciate in value if they gave away or sold cheaply a bit of what they had. Naturally, these smaller landowners held out for higher prices.

The land around Lake of the Isles in particular was not highly valued. The lake was largely marsh, not an attractive site for home building. The grand residences of the day were being built in the vicinity of Central Park, Park Avenue and the land Richard Mendenhall had once offered to the city where the Minneapolis Institute of Arts is now located. The land around Lake of the Isles was unused and, perhaps, unusable.

One of Cleveland's arguments for years had been that many of the most beautiful sites for parks and parkways were those that would not hold much value for other development, such as riverbanks, ravines and hillsides. Loring saw in the land around Lake of the Isles what few others did: one of the most beauti-

The marshy southern shore of Lake of the Isles about 1908. The dotted white line was drawn in by someone of the time to show the location of the channel to Lake Calhoun. (Minnesota Historical Society)

ful spots in the city. "By dredging," he explained, "it could be in reality a lake of isles."

Whatever his vision for a beautiful lake of isles, Loring was following the path of least resistance in pursuing land around it. He was connecting Central Park with Lake Harriet through a direct course over unappealing tracts in a region where his friends owned much of the land or had influence with those who did, and were willing to give some of it to the park board. Loring later wrote in the 1887 annual report that property owners on Lake of the Isles had "uniformly dealt fairly with the Board, as had the Board with them." In the same report he contrasted the behavior of those landowners with the "narrow-minded avarice of a few property owners" who had prevented acquisitions elsewhere in the city.

The third factor in turning Loring's attention to Lake of the Isles was likely his success in securing Lake Harriet at almost no cost. He would repeat what had already worked. In an extract from his diary dated June 22, 1885, he noted the imminent success of acquiring the shores of Lake Harriet. "The work that has occupied my thoughts for many months is about to be accomplished," he wrote. "Long after my name has been forgotten the generations to come will see that this beautiful lake with its wooded banks was preserved for their use and its waters protected." Immortality is a powerful inducement.

Which is why a man of Loring's prestige and influence could be found sitting on the floor of the house of a prospective donor, going over plans and trying to convince him to give land. Loring noted, upon his eventual success, that he had met with John Green, who owned the land at the north end of Lake of the Isles, "probably 100 times" before Green gave in. Loring noted the turning point in their discussions: as they were debating the placement of survey stakes, Green's wife called him aside. Green returned from the discussion with his wife and said, "My wife is more liberal than I," and told Loring to put the stakes where he wanted, which he did. Loring was astonished a week later when he returned to the property and found that Green had moved the stakes again—giving the park board another fourteen feet of his property.

Acquiring for the city the shores of the lakes was Loring's personal mission. He noted in his diary in January 1885 that he would not go south that winter "for I am needed to aid in the securing of the land of Lake of the Isles and Lake Harriet."

In that acquisition he was tested not only by landowners but by fellow commissioners. In June 1885 he wrote in his diary that Daniel Bassett had made some "very unjust remarks" about the work already being done around Lake Harriet. "After saving over one hundred thousand dollars to the city and believing that we were doing the work on most

"Long after my name has been forgotten the generations to come will see that this beautiful lake with its wooded banks was preserved for their use and its waters protected."

CHARLES LORING

economical plans, I could not help resenting this," Loring wrote.

Just over a month later, Loring's resentment at criticism got to him. After a visit by the board to view improvements being made at Riverside Park, Commissioner Dorilus Morrison questioned a decision made on the ground. Considering Morrison's remarks "grossly insulting," Loring immediately resigned. The incident demonstrates the degree to which parks had become personal for Loring.

In a letter of advice to the board, along with his formal resignation, he gave highest priority to immediately securing land around Lake of the Isles and Lake Calhoun. He recommended the parkway linking Central Park through Lowry Hill to Lake of the Isles and also a parkway connecting Lake of the Isles to Lake Calhoun and Cedar Lake on land that he said Joseph Dean would donate (now Dean Parkway). He further urged acquiring land for two other parkways that its owners were willing to donate: William McNair had offered a strip of land two miles long through "the most picturesque portion of the lands adjacent to the city" on the west, and some landowners along Minnehaha Creek had proposed to give land for a parkway along the creek from Harriet to Minnehaha Falls. The only lands he recommended the board acquire that weren't offered free were the east and west Mississippi River banks, not willing to concede that they were unobtainable.

Loring's final recommendation was that the board ask the legislature for two additional powers: the power to police its parks and parkways, and control over the trees along the streets of the city.

Publications from near and far urged Loring to reconsider his resignation. "Hold on, Mr. Loring," said an editorial in the *St. Peter Tribune*, "That won't do. Minneapolis might perhaps spare the rest of the commission, although composed of good men, but it can't afford to spare so capable a man in that place as your modest self. Let your motto be 'pro bono publico,' and stick!"

Yielding to what the *St. Paul Pioneer Press* called "unanimous public demand," Loring withdrew his resignation in late September. He returned not only with his personal power on the board reconfirmed but with his agenda also implicitly given a stamp of approval. He would eventually get everything on his wish list.

By the end of 1886 the board had acquired the lakeshores and connecting links Loring wanted so much. Kenwood Parkway was acquired completely by donation, as was all but two small tracts of Lake of the Isles Boulevard, including Dean Parkway, which would connect Lake of the Isles, Lake Calhoun and Cedar Lake. The park board purchased the remaining two tracts and also initiated the purchase of the islands in Lake of the Isles to make its ownership of the lake complete. Dredging of the northern arm of Lake of the Isles

The east side of Lake Calhoun in the early 1890s. The fountain for watering horses is at the intersection with Thirty-sixth Street, which passes under the street railway tracks. A hedge separates the parkway from the lake. (Minnesota Historical Society)

was already under way to extend the lake and fill the marsh, plans for Kenwood Boulevard had been drawn up by Horace Cleveland, and Lake Harriet boulevard was completed.

The east side of Lake Calhoun from Lake Street south to Thirty-sixth Street was also acquired by condemnation. The valuation of the land by appraisers was, in the opinion of the board, "quite beyond the actual damages" but the land was considered essential, so the awards were paid. At a critical point in the debate over the Calhoun purchase, Loring and Eugene Wilson took fellow commissioner John Oswald out on Lake Calhoun in a rowboat to show him the beauty of the shoreline and won him over to buying the land.

Loring also got his wish on control of street trees and policing of the parks and parkways. In the next session of the Minnesota Legislature in 1887, it gave the park board what it wanted on both counts. The park board now controlled a separate police force for its property, and it was given broad authority to plant and care for trees along all city streets, not just on park property.

In the park board's annual report of 1885 Loring noted that the city in its natural condition was an "undulating prairie for the most part bare of trees. The only natural trees were clumps of black oak and scattered burr oak. These in the progress of improvement have largely disappeared." Loring expressed his hope "that no small part of the utility of the parks will be . . . the stimulus of a wider tree culture." To that end, the park board planted more than six thousand trees in 1885, including twenty-seven hundred elms. In an effort to gain authority over the trees it planned to plant and protect them from "hungry horses, stray cows and careless drivers," the park board had asked the legislature to transfer control of street trees from the city council to the park board. The Hennepin County delegation to the legislature refused to introduce the legislation, but, perhaps impressed by the progress of the park board's planting initiatives anyway, it reversed itself in 1887, and the park board gained full authority to plant and care for street trees—a power it has never relinquished.

That authority caused Loring to speculate that "in a very few years (Minneapolis) will be favorably compared with the shaded streets and avenues which so delight the visitor to the cities and villages of New England."

The importance of street tree powers went well beyond creating a green canopy over the prairie. It was one of the board's first actions that addressed issues in the life of the city outside the original scope of the park board. The park board looked beyond the narrow need for parks and at the larger needs of the community and said, "We can do that."

The park board employed the people and the expertise to plant, grow and care for trees. Why not use it? With the simple act of planting trees, the park board had expanded its role in city life. It was the first of many actions by park boards over the years to expand their scope, responsibilities and programs, gradually transforming a nineteenth-century Board of Park Commissioners into a twenty-first century Park and Recreation Board that today runs recreation programs, social programs and educational programs and has operated everything from golf courses and airports to day-care programs and employment programs for teenagers.

Did planting trees along the city streets lead to a park board that today has an annual budget of $60 million and has an office of environmental education and a youth programs coordinator who doesn't have anything to do with playing games? Not by itself. Skating rinks share some of the responsibility—and once again, we may have to give the blame—or the credit—to George Brackett.

One of Loring's earliest memories of Minneapolis was skating on a pond created by a depression between graded roads along Nicollet Avenue near the river in the winter of 1860. It was one of the only forms of amusement in his first winter in Minneapolis. Those fond memories led to his motion at a park board meeting in 1884 to maintain the newly expanded pond at Central Park as a skating rink. The pond had long been used by skaters in winter, but that year the park board cleared and planed about three acres of ice on the pond. The rink was a huge popular success.

The park board even put up lights around the Central Park rink in 1885. That's when George Brackett made a motion that expanded the scope of park board responsibilities. His motion seemed only fair. If we're going to maintain a rink at Central Park, he must have thought, the residents of other parts of the city should have rinks too. So Brackett suggested that rinks should also be established at Logan Park and at Murphy Park *or the vicinity.* With those words, Brackett acknowledged that it was the activity, not the park, that was central to his proposal. By adopting Brackett's resolution, the park board showed it was willing to step off park land to provide a service that it believed was needed and no one else was providing.

The creation of skating rinks was one of the first implicit actions by the board to address a question that hadn't been discussed much: What do we do with this land we're acquiring? The prevailing philosophy at the time was that parks were for passive, not active, use. They were naturalistic refuges shaped by an artist into tranquil and beautiful escapes from city life where, through communion with nature, people could find both relaxation and nourishment. They certainly weren't places to play and exercise. There was little thought of the need to exercise by people who worked six ten-hour days a week. The "Health" half of the park board's motto referred to the benefits of fresh air in crowded, filthy, smoky cities, not the cardiovascular benefits of raising one's heart rate.

Yet, as early as 1885, the park board voted to sponsor an *activity*—ice skating—instead of just improving or maintaining land. The philosophy guiding parks was starting to change. Over the next few years, the park board gradually increased the number of sanctioned activities on park land. In the winter of 1885 the park board gave permission for the first time to a private organization to use park facilities: the Thistle Curling Club was allowed to use a portion of the Central Park rink. In the summer of 1886 the board approved a bandstand at Central Park and concerts one night a week, paid for by the "liberality of residents in the vicinity." The next year the floodgates of active use were open: a tennis court at Central Park was petitioned for by residents, a horse racetrack on the ice of Lake Calhoun was permitted, and the Bicycle Club was allowed to use a parkway for its annual meeting. Not only were ice rinks maintained at several parks, but toboggan tracks were opened at Lake Calhoun as well as Farview and Riverside parks.

The uses of park land took another twist in 1887 when Charles Loring asked the park board to acquire the house of John Stevens, the first permanent home on the Minneapolis side of the river, and

Skaters on Loring Pond in 1884. The park board began providing a shelter for skaters and planing the ice on the pond in 1884. It was one of the first actions by the park board to provide an activity on park property. (Minnesota Historical Society)

move it to Riverside Park. Parks were now to be used to preserve history as well.

In a few short years, the park board had traveled quite a distance from simply acquiring and improving land. It was just beginning its slow transformation into an organization for the recreation and entertainment of citizens—beyond merely facilitating a stroll on, under, around and through greenery. It would take many years, however, for the park board to openly embrace that role.

The closer Loring got to achieving his personal vision for parks, the more his philosophy on parks emerged. Perhaps the legislative requirement to issue an annual report and write something of significance compelled him to express his views. Those reports at least gave him a platform. The annual reports of the Minneapolis park board to its citizens came to be highly sought after by libraries and park commissions around the country and were noted for their high quality in both content and design.

Loring's earliest expressions of his views on parks were limited to the beauty of trees and the value of beautifying the city. His arguments were rooted in aesthetics and economics, which in his mind were linked. His first mention of other benefits came in his speech to the Oak Lake Park Improvement Association in 1882 when he championed parks for "breathing places for the poor who cannot ride to the country for fresh air."

In his earliest annual reports he focused primarily on the economic imperative of acquiring land while it was affordable. Although throughout his life he would nearly always take the side of business interests in civic and park debates, by 1885 another more altruistic element would become a regular feature of his reports.

"The obvious rapid increase in values of property in the vicinity of parks . . . shows that the anticipations of the Board are likely to be realized," he wrote, referring to the assumption that parks would pay for themselves through higher tax revenues. "But," he concluded, "the greatest utility of park improvements does not appear in the assessment rolls and revenues. Prolongation of the term of human lives, capacity to earn and capacity to enjoy the fruits of earnings, are not less real though less tangible utilities."

By 1888 he had shifted his emphasis completely when he wrote in his diary after a walk in New York's Central Park: "The sight of these trees encourages me to fresh action in our own city where our citizens, especially the poor, can walk in the shade of fine trees without having to pay for the privilege of seeing a piece of natural woods." Perhaps Loring had spent enough time with Horace Cleveland by then that Cleveland's constant appeals for land for the poor to use and enjoy had converted him.

"I would make of the city itself such a work of art as may be the fitting abode of a race of men and women whose lives are devoted to a nobler end than money getting."

HORACE CLEVELAND

Cleveland wrote and spoke often not only of the need to provide for the poor but of his disdain for wealth. It was an attitude that may have contributed to his own difficulty at times in finding more clients—who were, of course, wealthy. Even Cleveland's words that would long adorn park board annual reports and city promotions were misappropriated. The Cleveland line so often quoted was, "I would make of the city itself a work of art." What Cleveland actually said in a 1888 speech to the elite of Minneapolis who belonged to the Society of Fine Arts was that he would make of the city itself "such a work of art as may be the fitting abode of a race of men and women whose lives are devoted to a nobler end than money getting."

The period of 1886–88 was a time of improvement and maintenance of the rapidly accumulated inventory of parks and parkways. The only park acquisition of the time was a ten-acre tract in northeast Minneapolis that became Windom Park. An initial attempt to acquire Powderhorn Park failed due to high valuations of the surrounding property. Residents in the Powderhorn area had petitioned for a park as early as 1883 when the park board was making its first park decisions, and it would have been a centerpiece in the failed plan to make a boulevard of Thirty-fourth Street.

One of the reasons for the inactivity was that along with granting the park board the power of policing and planting street trees, the 1887 legislature had changed the rules on condemning property, tilting them in favor of landowners. The new rules made condemnation of land for parks nearly impossible.

But a coming boom in park acquisitions was presaged by several events in 1888. First, residents of north Minneapolis submitted a petition for the board to acquire the area around Glenwood and Inglewood springs. Second, Thomas Lowry, William Dunwoody and several others were considering donating land west of Central Park, including Spring Lake, a small pond at the foot of Lowry Hill along Groveland Avenue.

Negotiations for a third tract of land were also active: the land on both sides of Minnehaha Creek from Lake Harriet to Minnehaha Falls. Although much of that land was donated, the board still had to reach agreement with landowners on how much land they would part with. It was Loring's desire to create an east-west parkway in that pastoral setting in part to replace the southern connecting link between lakes and river that the park board had failed to create at Lake Street.

Curiously, the parkway was intended to link to a park at Minnehaha Falls that didn't yet exist. Perhaps the most important event in park history in 1888 had nothing to do with the park board. It may have been a speech given in April of that year by Horace Cleveland to the Minneapolis Society of Fine Arts. That speech helped to create the demand for a park at Minnehaha Falls that would lead to extraordinary action within a year by a handful of Minneapolitans, most of whom were not on the park board. Once again, George Brackett was in the middle of it, perhaps still atoning for his role in losing Nicollet Island.

Minnehaha Creek near Nicollet Avenue about 1900. (Minnesota Historical Society)

Chapter Six

The Mythical Falls

Attempts to acquire Minnehaha Falls for a park were nearly ancient in the short history of white settlement of the region. As early as 1868 the St. Paul Chamber of Commerce had passed a resolution to request Congress to permit St. Paul, St. Anthony and Minneapolis to purchase from Fort Snelling the land surrounding Minnehaha Falls for a park.

Interest in the possibilities were reinvigorated by Horace Cleveland's first speeches in St. Paul and Minneapolis in 1872, when for a brief time a joint committee was formed to look into acquiring the riverbanks and Minnehaha. Another joint effort to acquire the land around the falls for a park in 1875 failed when the representatives of St. Paul didn't consider it an appropriate site for a park.

Cleveland again urged acquisition of the falls in his *Suggestions* of 1883—calling it "exceedingly desirable"—but the park board did not focus on an acquisition so far from the city. Interest in the idea of a park at Minnehaha Falls never seemed to go away

"The Little Falls." Lithograph by Henry Lewis, 1854. Minnehaha Falls before it was named that. The "big falls" was St. Anthony Falls. (Henry Lewis, Minnesota Historical Society)

43

Minnehaha Falls, circa 1875, was already an attraction. (William H. Jacoby, Minnesota Historical Society)

completely. An editorial in a Minneapolis paper in December 1884 urged the creation of a "Union Park" at the falls.

Once again it was the Minneapolis Board of Trade that took up the cause for parks. In January 1885, the Board of Trade, not the park board, sponsored legislation to create a state park commission to select land for a park at the falls. The legislation was approved, and five commissioners were appointed to select land for the park: Charles Loring, who was president of the commission, George Brackett, William Yale of Winona (a former lieutenant governor who had once owned much of the land condemned for Central Park), William Van Slyke and Charles Strobeck of St. Paul.

Over the next year, while Loring was working so hard to acquire the city's lakeshores, the committee selected 173 acres for the park. But as the Minneapolis park board had already learned, it was never that easy. The appraisals were contested, and it was not until early 1888 that the state supreme court finally confirmed them. There was still plenty of time for the legislature to act at the next session. And they had to act because the authorizing legislation specified that the process had to be completed by the end of the 1889 session of the legislature. If the lands weren't acquired by then, all of the condemnation proceedings would be invalid.

Fortunately for the future of parks in Minnesota, the Minneapolis Society of Fine Arts had scheduled a presentation by Cleveland for the spring of 1888. The title of his lecture was "The Aesthetic Development of the United Cities of St. Paul and Minneapolis."

Cleveland, despite his age, could still move an audience. A year earlier, Cleveland—then seventy-three—had accompanied Charles Loring to Duluth for one of Loring's early speeches to promote parks.

A reporter for the Duluth paper quoted Cleveland calling on the Duluth leaders to "supplement the natural inheritance given to you by your own generous efforts so that future generations may rise up and call you blessed. Warehouses, stores, business blocks, elevators and coal docks are great things, but do not forget that there are other things also that add to the happiness of a people."

The reporter then commented: "The tremulous tones of age pleading for the health and joy of unborn generations was almost pathetic in its eloquence and the remarks of Mr. Cleveland were received with a cyclone of applause."

Such were the oratorical talents of the elderly man who stood before the influential Minneapolis crowd in Dyers Hall in April 1888. In his address he made an eloquent appeal for clothing cities in beauty to relieve "the sense of jarring friction, which grinds the nerves and constitutes the wear and tear of body and soul."

Then he got to his point, which was always his point: the Mississippi River and Minnehaha Falls. Cleveland knew his audience and its history, and for the first time he used what would be perhaps the

A painting of Minnehaha Falls by George Brackett, one of five commissioners named by the governor in 1885 to acquire land for a state park at Minnehaha Falls. Brackett helped secure the financing for the park that surrounds the falls. (Minnesota Historical Society)

clinching argument. He referred to St. Paul's recent acquisition of fifty acres on its side of the river opposite Minnehaha, today's Hidden Falls park. He played the rivalry card.

"It would be a standing and conspicuous reproach and stigma upon Minneapolis and one with which St. Paul might justly taunt her from its contrast with the superb development of her own side of the river," Cleveland astutely argued. He had been around long enough to know that those were fighting words to the leaders of the younger city upriver. He praised Minneapolis for its system of smaller parks and lakeshore drives and noted the substantial benefit the city had derived from the "prestige they have given her." But, he went on, St. Paul had made "a more decided demonstration of her recognition of future necessities" by beginning the construction of Como Park and creating Summit Avenue and a superb driveway down the riverbank with a park opposite the mouth of Minnehaha Creek.

The implication that despite her progress, Minneapolis was in danger of falling behind the one city that mattered more than any other, St. Paul, would have surely jarred any dozing arts patrons awake that night. These were powerful words not lost on the influential men and women in attendance. And they were needed.

In January 1889, the Minneapolis park board and the state park commission got a jolt: the legislature did not have the $92,000 it needed to purchase the condemned property around the falls. The four years it had taken to select land and gain approval from the courts for condemnation awards was about to be wasted. Without action by the legislature to buy the lands, the condemnations would soon be declared invalid. When would the chance come again?

A special meeting of the Minneapolis park board was called February 5, 1889, to consider its course of action. The board approved whatever measures were necessary to secure funding for the park, but it didn't have time to follow official bonding procedures. George Brackett, who was no longer a member of the city park board, only the state park commission, came up with a solution. He drafted a promissory note for $100,000 and signed it personally. He then took it to other influential men in town.

By the time he took it to Henry Brown, Loring's frequent partner in real estate investments, Brown recalled that Brackett had already secured the signatures of Thomas Lowry, Andrew Boardman, Eugene Wilson, Clinton Morrison, Samuel Gale, Dr. Hance and P. B. Winston to personally guarantee the loan. Brown signed it too, then went to his bank and withdrew $50,000 from his personal account, borrowed another $50,000 from the bank, and handed a certified check for $100,000 to Brackett. The next day the check was given to Governor Merriam, who deposited it in the treasury, and the legislature immediately approved payment of condemnation awards to landowners around Minnehaha Falls. Two months later, the personal note was redeemed when the park board issued $100,000 in bonds to repay it.

Fast action by Brackett had acquired for the city—and the state—Minnesota's first state park, and only the second state park in the nation. The men who had put their personal guarantees on a promissory note knew they weren't risking their fortunes, because Brackett had certainly worked out with the board and the city the means of repaying it. Yet the episode demonstrated their willingness to get things done for the fledgling park system, especially when urged on by Cleveland's vision.

Cleveland still hadn't convinced his bosses to acquire the entire river gorge, but he was inching closer, down Minnehaha Creek on one side and up Summit Avenue on the other.

Chapter Seven

Folwell Joins the Fray

One of the newest members of the park board was an enthusiastic supporter of the flurry of activity to acquire Minnehaha Falls. William Watts Folwell's long history of participation in civic improvement efforts with Charles Loring may have been responsible for the knock on his door one night in the fall of 1888. It was his neighbor stopping by to inform him that at the Republican Party's nominating convention that night, Folwell's name had been placed on the ballot for Minneapolis park commissioner.

In the November election, Folwell was the second-leading vote-getter for the park board. Thus began the longest tenure of any park commissioner in the first forty years of the board. Folwell would serve three consecutive six-year terms. He would become the president of the board for eight years, its conscience for eighteen, and its visionary for, well, perhaps forever.

The year 1889 had started out on a high note with the acquisition of Minnehaha Falls, beginning two years of spectacular growth for the Minneapolis park system, which was already gaining praise around the country.

This was the year in which the state legislature, perhaps in gratitude for Minneapolis paying for the first state park, gave the park board the legislation it needed to expand its system. The legislature increased the bond limit for the park board and simplified condemnation procedures, which once again made them feasible. But most significantly, the legislature approved a new method of acquiring land. The park board could issue "certificates of indebtedness," in addition to city bonds. The park board could acquire land by issuing certificates payable with interest in ten equal annual payments. The beauty of the method was that over the ten years the park board had to make payments on the certificates, it would collect special assessments on the benefited neighborhoods. The special assessments would, in theory, provide the money to pay off the certificates. It was almost like getting free land. The arrangement had only two flaws, one of which would become obvious within a few years, the other not for decades.

In 1889 the park board acquired fifty-three acres of Saratoga Park, which, along with eleven adjoining acres in Golden Valley, was the foundation of what was soon named Glenwood Park and renamed many years later Theodore Wirth Park. The park, "irregular in shape and greatly diversified in scenery," included the highest land in Hennepin County, a six-acre lake and natural springs.

The board also purchased twenty-five lots for a parkway along Minnehaha Creek. Those purchases had been instigated by the donation of land adjoining the creek nearly all the way from Lake Harriet to Lyndale Avenue by Henry Butler and Joseph Fogg.

In addition, the park board designated thirty-eight and one-half acres of land to be acquired around Powderhorn Lake. The acquisition of that land was completed the following year even as the board was deciding whether to act on a neighborhood petition to acquire an additional twenty-five acres, which it eventually did.

Amid those acquisitions, Linden Hills Boulevard was built on land donated by Henry Beard to connect Lake Calhoun to Lake Harriet.

The pace of acquisitions didn't slow in 1890. Interlachen Park, now William Berry Park, was purchased in recognition of the fact that Linden Hills Boulevard was not an adequate connection between Calhoun and Harriet. Interlachen provided a park connection, not just a parkway.

And in a nod to the rest of the city away from the southwestern lakes, the board purchased its first park in southeast Minneapolis, Van Cleve Park, near the University of Minnesota. The park of nine acres was purchased for $75,000 after repeated petitions from residents of the neighborhood.

The costs of all these parks were assessed against the benefited property in the neighborhood, so, as the annual report of 1890 noted, they had been acquired at "no cost" to the city.

With Loring in the thick of it, the park board was also in the midst of negotiations during 1890 to acquire additional land at Lake Harriet. William King had offered to donate forty acres of his Lyndale Farm on the northeastern corner of Lake Harriet. According to the *Minneapolis Tribune* the "magnificent new park" was destined to become the "picnic ground par excellence" of the park system.

One of the conditions of King's donation was that Lakewood Cemetery would also donate some of its adjoining land to create an even larger park on the lake's northern shore. The donation of thirty-five acres by Lakewood Cemetery—its trustees still dominated by old park men—between the present cemetery and Lake Harriet was quickly completed.

King gave much of the credit for the transaction to Loring for his "constant and effective aid" in various negotiations. Many years later Loring claimed that it had been King's lifelong dream to have a park around Lake Harriet and that he had died "near a poor man" trying to make it happen. In honor of King, Loring even attempted at one point to have Lake Harriet renamed Lake Lyndale. (The name Lyndale had been derived from the name of King's father, Lyndon King, a fiery abolitionist preacher in upstate New York.) Loring's full involvement in the King donation wasn't revealed until thirty years later when Folwell wrote a letter to the park board revealing that at the time of King's donation he held only "nominal" equity in the land. The men who held the mortgage, the true donors of Lyndale Park, Folwell wrote, were Loring and Henry Brown.

With so many park acquisitions over the course

Lake Harriet streetcar line at Hennepin and Colfax Avenue South in 1895. The park board still owned Hennepin Avenue as a parkway but had granted the street railway permission to lay track in the center of the parkway. (Minnesota Historical Society)

of little more than a year, Folwell was troubled that the park board had lost sight of its goals. His concern was heightened by the board's decision to permit Thomas Lowry's streetcar company to lay tracks down the center of a parkway: Hennepin Avenue. Lowry's company offered to pay nothing for the privilege except for a promise to reimburse the park board for its expenses of repairing the street after tracks were laid.

The proposal was approved by the board after vigorous debate. Even after approval, Folwell, an outspoken opponent of the measure, moved that the railway pay an annual license fee *plus* the cost of re-grading the road. The motion lost—with Loring siding with the business interests of his friend, Lowry, on both votes. Loring had already acquired the parkway he wanted to the lakes by way of Kenwood Parkway and around Lake of the Isles. He no longer needed Hennepin Avenue.

Fortunately for the park board, it was the beginning of the end for Hennepin Avenue as a parkway, which had never been much of a parkway except in name. It had already become simply a little-wider-than-normal street that consumed an inordinate portion of the park board's limited resources.

In light of all the scattered acquisitions and its streetcar decision, Folwell proposed that a committee of the board be appointed to consider the matter of enlarging the park system and how that should be accomplished. The board agreed and appointed Folwell the chair of a three-man committee to take a close look at expansion. The assignment gave Folwell the opportunity to propose a strategy for park expansion and establish the direction of the board for the next decade and beyond.

In early 1891, Folwell made his report on park enlargement to the board after consulting with Cleveland, who pleaded once again for making parks of the riverbanks and encouraged Folwell to make a report that will "drown out the sound of an eighteen-pounder." Cleveland's reference to a Civil War–era cannon was intended to call up Folwell's fighting spirit.

Folwell's report was indeed loud. It was critical of the park board and its acquisitions as few had ever been up to that time. Referring to Cleveland, Folwell said, "It was not the expectation of the artist that (his) plan would be carried out with literal exactness. His purpose was to impress upon his clients the *idea of a plan*" (emphasis in the original). Folwell continued that not only had this plan been neglected, but that the board and the public "seem to have lost the idea of a plan." It was a delusion to think that the city had the park land it needs, and worse, he added, that, admirable as park acquisitions had been, they were mostly unrelated parks "scattered in a fortuitous and unequal manner."

It was the first time in recorded park board proceedings that anyone had raised an issue that persists more than one hundred years later: that the park board had focused its attention, energy and money on the southwestern portion of the city to the detriment of other neighborhoods.

Giving credit to Cleveland "justly and gladly" for the idea, Folwell then proposed a system of encircling boulevards—it could be called the "Grand Rounds," he suggested—that would not be limited to the southwestern part of the city. The Grand Rounds would connect large parks in the northwest and northeast through the university to the river and along its banks. In addition he recommended that the park board secure the land on both sides of the river well upstream of Camden Place to protect the city's water supply.

Folwell also recommended "neighborhood parks" for those parts of the city that didn't have any and encouraged "prosperous, public-minded citizens" to follow the example of Edward Murphy, Jacob Elliot and Franklin Steele's daughters in giving land for that purpose.

Finally, Folwell proposed that the park board be relieved of its maintenance of Lyndale and Hennepin avenues, especially the latter "since its abandonment to the Street Railway Company."

Peavey Fountain, at the intersection of Kenwood Parkway and Lake of the Isles Parkway, was donated to the park board by Frank Peavey in 1891. The fountain, which was originally a horse watering trough, still stands at the intersection. Despite its functional use, it was the first "art" in Minneapolis parks. (Minnesota Historical Society)

There must be a plan, he concluded, and we must spend liberally to achieve it. "Let Minneapolis aspire to be what it is now in her power to become," he said, "the beautiful city of the land."

In retrospect Folwell's report would seem to be a personal rebuke to Loring for the policies of the previous seven years, but that was not likely Folwell's intent. Only two weeks before his presentation he had offered a resolution to the board to change the name of Central Park to Loring Park, a motion that had passed over Loring's objection. (Loring proposed the name of Hennepin Park instead.) And Loring and Folwell remained friends and allies on park issues for decades on and off the park board. Many years later it would be Loring who proposed that a new administration building at the University of Minnesota be named Folwell Hall.

Loring was not in attendance at the park board meeting when Folwell delivered his report. The acknowledged "Father of Minneapolis Parks" had been defeated at the polls in the fall of 1890 in his bid for reelection as a park commissioner.

Loring's defeat was not a public comment on his management of park issues as much as a reflection of city politics at the time. Loring had polled far more votes than any other Republican candidate for city office, but a tide of Democratic votes had swept him out of office along with every other Republican.

Loring, in his farewell address to the board, claimed that his biggest regret in his years on the park board was not acquiring the east riverbank, which prompted a bitter I-told-you-so letter from Horace Cleveland to Folwell.

Cleveland's relationship with the park board had deteriorated. He had submitted designs for the new Windom Park and Barnes Park, which were both approved. He had also submitted a plan for Van Cleve Park that contained a revolutionary concept for parks at the time: his original plan dedicated a portion of the park to a playground for children. Folwell, not yet a believer in such use of parks, suggested substituting a pond for the playground in the design, which the board then also approved. But other efforts to engage Cleveland were held up over the cost of his services.

Cleveland, then in his late seventies, was having more trouble getting the work done in the field, too. Ralph Cleveland left Lakewood Cemetery in 1891 to assist his father.

Age may have been a factor in Cleveland's declining work in another way too. In his letters, Cleveland began to show an irascible and cantankerous side that wasn't as apparent in earlier writings. His comment to Folwell on the souls of park commissioners, "if they've got any," was only a taste. He had also written of his disgust that the park board was considering permitting a structure next to Minnehaha Falls where people could have their photos taken beside the cataract. "If erected," Cleveland complained, "it will be simply pandering to the tastes of the army of boobies who think to boost themselves into notoriety by connecting their own stupid features with the representation of one of the most beautiful of God's works."

Cleveland's growing grouchiness and disillusionment may have raised a few eyebrows on the board, but commissioners must have thought he was crazy for sure when he proposed that the board acquire the shores of distant Medicine Lake, miles northwest of the city.

Cleveland's despair might not have been alleviated even when finally, late in 1891, the board approved new efforts to acquire the east and west banks of the Mississippi River. He had heard that before. Offers had actually been made for land on the east bank, but half the property owners appealed the awards. As another year ended, the board was awaiting the outcome of the appeals.

While the riverbanks remained in private hands, the board did make an important new acquisition in 1892, prodded perhaps by Folwell's encouragement to acquire land in areas other than the southwestern section of the city. Owners of land in the vicinity of Sandy Lake in northeast Minneapolis had made a proposal, which the board accepted, to sell the shallow 40-acre lake and the surrounding 104 acres of land for just over $200,000. The owners were willing to be paid in ten equal installments without interest. Owners of adjacent property petitioned the board to buy the land and expressed their willingness to be assessed for its cost. To sweeten the deal, the owners of the land agreed to donate $20,000 for immediate improvement of the land as a park.

It seemed to be just what Folwell had urged in his report, a large northeastern park that could be an anchor for a parkway. The citizens of the area had even done exactly what he recommended when he urged them to "organize and agitate for securing a park in that ward." But he didn't like the deal. While he favored the project, he thought the price was too high by half and complained of "jobbery," implicating unnamed "wealthy capitalists." Other commissioners disagreed, saying that the land was reasonably priced based on other sales in the area. Folwell lost a vote to postpone the purchase by a two-vote margin, and the deal was done. The park was named Columbia Park.

Park activist and one-time commissioner Andrew Boardman would later write that the purchase of Columbia Park at the peak of the real estate boom in Minneapolis was one of the park board's biggest mistakes. But who knew then that the bottom was about to fall out of the city's real estate market?

Loring returned to the park board for one year in 1893 and once again served as its president. He stayed on the board just long enough to redress the biggest regret he had over his first tenure as president: finally the park board completed purchase of the east bank of the Mississippi River. Ten years after Cleveland had made his "suggestions" and twenty-one after he had first encouraged the citizens of Minneapolis and St. Paul to protect the river, Minneapolis became the owner of nearly two miles of the east riverbank from the University of Minnesota downstream to its border with St. Paul.

In what would be the last land acquisitions for years, the board also added eighteen acres to Columbia Park, acquired ten acres to go along with the land donated by Thomas Lowry and friends for a parkway to connect Loring Park with Kenwood Parkway, and acquired a few additional lots to straighten Minnehaha Parkway. Dredging on the east shore of Lake of the Isles had been completed, and the dredger was being prepared for a move to Powderhorn Lake, where it would work for the next few years.

In his final report as president of the board, Loring issued a plea to provide playgrounds for children. He recommended Lyndale Park as a suitable place for athletic sports and children's playgrounds, which reflected the changing view of parks from passive to active spaces. "In this, and in the parks generally, a small area (should) be laid out for the exclusive use of little children," Loring urged, "where piles of sand, swings, seesaws and other proper appliances of amusement and exercise shall be furnished by the board." Quoting an authority of the time, he said, "A city without playgrounds keeps its children growing

The first dredging of Lake of the Isles began in the 1880s on the north arm of the lake and the west shore. This photo of a dredge at the lake appeared in the park board's annual report in 1894. (Minneapolis Park and Recreation Board)

in straightjackets. Some become physically and morally deformed: all are deprived of a fair chance."

In the space of just over ten years the park board had acquired 1,476 acres of land and water. Beginning with just four little parks, the park board had amassed an inventory of land valued at nearly $4 million. The cost of that land, acquired in the park board's first decade, was about $2 million, but more than $1.5 million had been assessed against nearby property that benefited from the parks. By the park board's estimate that meant the land had been acquired at a cost of less than $2.50 per person in the city of approximately 200,000 people. Another $750,000 had been spent on improvements, maintenance, administration and interest on bonds.

Judging by the parting comments of its leader during that time, the park board had also reached a point where it was willing to address consciously the second issue in the creation of parks: how do we use this land? Loring had provided a clear picture of what he thought at least part of the answer should be. It is unlikely that he had a full grasp at the time of how hard it would be to follow that path and how long it would take. The park board was entering upon the most difficult decade of its existence.

The coming years would be no walk in the park for Cleveland either. As the year 1892 came to a close, William French, then the director of the prestigious Art Institute of Chicago, wrote to several friends of his old partner, including Frederick Law Olmsted, asking for contributions to a retirement fund for Cleveland, who was then seventy-nine and still prospecting for work. "I shall die with harness on," Cleveland wrote to Olmsted, "I am constantly trying to devise means to stave off the necessity of becoming dependent on others." Long an advocate of the open spaces for the poor, Cleveland was perilously close to joining their number. But very few people were to avoid financial difficulties in the coming years. Hard times would hit a lot of people, some of them surprising.

> *"A city without playgrounds keeps its children growing in straightjackets. Some become physically and morally deformed: all are deprived of a fair chance."*
>
> — CHARLES LORING

Chapter Eight

Dreams Deferred

The headline must have been a shock to most in Minneapolis as they picked up their newspapers on November 13, 1895: "Loring Failure, A Man Much Beloved." The Father of Minneapolis Parks had declared bankruptcy. The man who only two years earlier had been so warmly praised upon resigning the presidency of the park board, the man who had devoted so much time to making Minneapolis "beautiful and profitable," had clearly succeeded more at the former than the latter.

A Minneapolis paper, long Loring's ally in park building, noted that his "financial embarrassment will be learned with regret by his thousands of friends and admirers." It was not as if Loring would soon be joining the "poor," the beneficiaries he had come to cite so often in his park-building efforts. The papers listed his assets at about $775,000, a tidy sum in the day, and his liabilities at just over $400,000. Of those liabilities, more than half were for loans he had endorsed for friends. To put the value of Loring's assets and liabilities in context, the park board paid general laborers $1.75 for a ten-hour workday at the time, and Superintendent William Berry received an annual salary of $3,000.

Loring had provided a hint of impending financial trouble as early as 1888 in a letter to George Brackett from his winter home in Riverside, California. "It was rather foolish of me," he wrote, "to incur so much indebtedness when I was so near out of debt, but I guess it will be alright. Additional money and property is of no value after we have enough to pay our expenses. Three of my old friends have passed away since I left home and they followed the iron rule and left their money behind. We shall do the same."

Loring's nearly full-time work "fathering" parks instead of tending to business interests may also have contributed to his financial decline. In September 1890, he wrote to his friend and coinvestor in several business ventures, former senator and secretary of the treasury William Windom, "There does not seem to be another such place as Minneapolis for its constant demands upon the time of its citizens. Everyday there is something that must be done. I suppose, perhaps, this may be why we are a great city." He continued, "Cities seem to grow in a most

> *"There does not seem to be another such place as Minneapolis for its constant demands upon the time of its citizens. Every day there is something that must be done. I suppose, perhaps, this may be why we are a great city."*
>
> — CHARLES LORING

irregular way. The tide of prosperity seems to ebb and flow and our city has been no exception to the rule. I think we are now on the flood tide again."

Loring was wrong about the economy. The city was headed for a more serious ebb in the tide of prosperity than he had ever experienced. His personal bankruptcy in 1895, which wasn't resolved for another two years, coincided with a widespread decline in the Minneapolis economy. The effect on the Board of Park Commissioners and their newly acquired parks was dreadful.

George Brackett also experienced a considerable financial setback in the 1890s. Among other investments, his ownership of the stockyards in New Brighton was lost. He wrote to the governor of Minnesota in 1895 to resign his position on the Board of Charities and Corrections due to the financial troubles that required his full attention and recommended that William Folwell take his place. The governor followed his advice. Brackett left Minneapolis to attempt to recover his fortune in the goldfields of the Alaska Gold Rush. He abandoned his attempt to build a road over the treacherous Skagway Pass when investors failed to reimburse him for what he had already spent and he had nothing left. Unlike Loring, Brackett never recovered financially. At a tribute to Brackett as one of Minneapolis's most beloved "pioneers" in 1910, attended by more than five hundred of the city's elite, he was lauded as a man whose measure was not wealth but his immense heart and his contributions to the development of the city.

To indicate how hard times were, in 1896 Henry Brown, who had personally withdrawn $50,000 of his own money from a bank and borrowed another $50,000 for the purchase of Minnehaha Falls seven years earlier, asked the board to reimburse him for $542 he had paid in interest on that money before it was repaid by the city. The board voted not to reimburse Brown.

Bankruptcy did not ruin Loring's life. Following the death of Emily, his wife of thirty-nine years, in early 1894, at the age of sixty, he married Florence Barton, the forty-five-year-old daughter of his neighbor and sometimes business associate, A. B. Barton, another immigrant from Maine. With his wedding coming only two weeks after his declaration of bankruptcy, his new wife wouldn't be called a gold digger. She became and remained Loring's partner in philanthropy for the rest of his life. In her own right, Florence Barton Loring retains a place in Minneapolis history; a quilt she made is in the permanent collection of the Minneapolis Institute of Arts.

Loring immersed himself once again in new business ventures but remained a tireless advocate for parks in Minneapolis and around the country. He would return to the park board to fill another vacancy in 1904. Though he would remain on the board again for only a year, he would once again influence the future of Minneapolis parks, this time not by acquiring land but hiring the man to shape it. Loring would personally select Theodore Wirth to become the city's superintendent of parks. But before Wirth would arrive in 1906, Minneapolis parks were in for hard times.

How hard were those times? In the 1902 *Annual Report,* William Folwell noted how far property values in the city had fallen. He noted that one of two small park acquisitions for the year—a single house and lot—had been made to expand the southwestern corner of Loring Park. The asking price on the lot years earlier had been as high as $75,000, which the board had considered too high even when it had funds. With the decline in real estate values, the board had again inquired into the property, and it was offered for $30,000. The board countered with an offer of $15,000, which was refused, so the board initiated condemnation proceedings. After appeals, the price was settled at $13,000, a stunning drop of 83 percent from the asking price years earlier. Such was the change in mood—and the value of real estate—in Minneapolis from the 1880s into the early years of the next century.

The owner of the lot and house was Swan Turnblad, the publisher of an influential Swedish-language newspaper. The park board, long interested in the property, took action to acquire the lot when

American Swedish Institute, 1905. The American Swedish Institute was built as the home of Swan Turnblad in 1903 at Park Avenue and Twenty-sixth Street. He had intended to build his home on what is now the southwestern corner of Loring Park, but the park board learned of his plans and acquired the land through condemnation to add it to the park. (Minnesota Historical Society)

it learned in 1901 that Turnblad was making plans to build a large residence there, which would have closed off any hope of eventually adding the land to the park. When the Minnesota Supreme Court refused to hear Turnblad's appeal of the condemnation award, he built his new home at the corner of Park Avenue and Twenty-sixth Street instead. That palatial home is now the American Swedish Institute.

Upon the motion of Patrick Ryan, the man who defeated Loring for a seat on the Board of Park Commissioners, William Watts Folwell was unanimously elected president of the board in January 1895. Folwell's election may not have been a tribute solely to his leadership skills, however formidable they were. No one else may have wanted what appeared to be a thankless job.

Well before Folwell was elected president, the park board was operating close to its limits. In mid-1891 the board voted to curtail improvements in parks because it was out of money. Real trouble appeared in August 1893 when the board was once again informed that finances were tight. The board reduced park maintenance to the bare essentials. The park workforce was reduced, and pay was cut for remaining workers. The situation kept getting worse. By November all park employees, with the exception of Superintendent William Berry, eight policemen and the park keeper at Loring Park, had been laid off.

By then the collapsing economy, in Minneapolis and around the country, had a name: the "Panic of 1893." When the park board received its annual settlement of property taxes collected in the city that summer, receipts were $40,000 less than estimated.

The result was that no new park acquisitions were made, and improvements were held to a minimum. Park maintenance in 1893 required borrowing money from the "sinking fund" that had been established to pay off park bonds when they became due. Part of the reason given by board president Andrew Haugan for that bit of iffy financing was "to give employment to a large number of men then out of work, owing to the financial crisis."

The park board had fallen victim not only to a general economic depression but to the creative financing system that had been concocted in boom times. When the park board had devised in 1889 the method of acquiring park land by issuing certificates of indebtedness to landowners instead of selling bonds to raise the funds, it did not foresee the collapse of land values that began in 1893 and did not recover for almost a decade.

The plan to pay off those certificates with revenue from special assessments worked splendidly until the Panic of 1893. As the economy took a nosedive, many property owners could no longer afford the special assessments. Defaults became commonplace.

The board's revenues took a hit, but their expenses weren't reduced. The park board determined that a failure to make payments on the certificates of indebtedness could impair the city's credit rating. So the board continued to make payments on those certificates even as it was no longer collecting the full assessments that were intended to finance them. Certificate payments had to be made out of the general park fund, which was supposed to be used for maintenance and improvement.

So why not just raise taxes? The board had the authority, mandated by the legislature in the original park act, to levy a tax of one mill on the assessed value of city property. But the board had never asked for more than one-half that amount before the financial panic. In fact, the board was proud of its frugality in managing park affairs.

In his 1888 president's report, Loring noted that improvements to parks had not been rapid due to the desire of the board to avoid "a heavy call for taxes." In his annual report five years later, Loring boasted that Minneapolis was spending less on park maintenance than any other city with similar parks, about twenty-five cents per person.

In the 1890s, the board gradually increased its request for money from the Board of Tax Levy, but the mill rate it received never surpassed .85 mill until the turn of the century. In 1898 the board did request its full levy of one mill, but the Board of Tax Levy authorized only .75 mill.

Despite modest efforts to increase revenue from taxes, the board was largely resigned to its situation. In those difficult years of the 1890s, Folwell tried to keep hope alive for a fuller and better park system. In 1895, Folwell compared the park board to a ship that "lays to for better weather," but stressed "it should be understood by all that on the return of better times, much will remain to be done to complete and unify the park system."

That seemed wishful thinking when the next year the assessed valuation of property in the city plunged another 20 percent. The park board's Special Committee on Retrenchment scrounged for ways to cut costs. Lights on parks and parkways were turned off, skating rinks closed early—and in 1897 weren't opened at all. In 1900, the park board sold 150 tons of hay harvested at Columbia Park, Lake of the Isles and Minnehaha Parkway. That followed a motion at a board meeting earlier in the year to direct the superintendent to employ sufficient help to keep the grass mowed in parks. The motion was defeated.

Improvements came to a standstill for a decade after the panic of 1893, perhaps best illustrated by the fact that Cleveland's original 1892 design for Powderhorn Park was not implemented until 1903, although dredging of the lake did commence in 1894. As a colorful reminder of the times in which these debates took place, the board did approve in 1896 the purchase of a new horse for Superintendent William Berry.

The board was besieged by complaints, criticism of park maintenance and petitions for improvements. One of the problems was parkways. A high percentage of the park board's maintenance budget went to maintaining its inven-

Logan Park fountain, 1904. One of the few improvements to parks in this period of tight money was the installation of the fountain at Logan Park in 1897, which had been in Cleveland's original design for the park fourteen years earlier. (Sweet, Minnesota Historical Society)

tory of parkways. Throughout the 1890s and into the early 1900s the board spent between 10 and 20 percent of its annual maintenance budget on Hennepin Avenue South and Lyndale Avenue North alone. In the first twenty years of the park board, nearly 6 percent of its *total* expenditures—including the costs of acquiring *all* park land—went to improving and maintaining those two avenues.

Maintenance of parkways meant more than simply grading an existing road. The parkway around Lake of the Isles especially was a maintenance headache, as it had been built in places on fill dredged from the lake. As that fill settled, regular work was required to keep the parkway passable. The board also addressed such peripheral issues as selecting uniform hitching posts for Kenwood Parkway and having "well-rotted dairy stable manure" spread along parkways needing to have soil enriched. That resolution soon raised protests from residents near parkways.

Two of the only improvements undertaken in this period were finishing Minnehaha Parkway from Lake Amelia (later Lake Nokomis) to the falls, which was completed in 1899, and beginning improvements on the East River flats in the same year, seven years after the land was purchased.

The issue of spending on Hennepin and Lyndale was raised again in 1899 by Folwell, who often joined with Patrick Ryan in opposing better-represented business interests on the board in those days. He submitted draft language for a legislative bill that would return both avenues to the city. His proposal was defeated.

The board couldn't have imagined in the late 1890s that the issue of parkway maintenance was about to become more complicated. By the early 1900s, the board had to wrestle with a new issue: automobiles. In 1902 the board addressed for the first time the issue of cars on parkways. A year later it reported its first ordinance for cars, limiting speeds on parkways to fifteen miles per hour. The challenge of parkways, then freeways, would continue for the park board for another century and would contribute to the downfall of a later superintendent of parks.

Fortunately for the park board, the issue of maintaining Hennepin and Lyndale would be resolved in the early 1900s, but not before it had sapped resources from parks when resources were most scarce.

During the hard times of the 1890s, fewer trees were planted in parks. In 1891 Folwell had suggested that wise park management required a nursery for growing trees and shrubs for parks and city streets. So before its revenues took a dive in 1893, the board had already reserved a tract of land at Lyndale Park for a nursery, which resulted in significant cost savings. The cost of planting trees along streets was assessed against property owners—$5 per tree—so the board incurred little expense in that process.

The struggle of the park board to maintain the land and roads it owned in the 1890s was the first low point in many cycles of expansion and belt-tightening for the park board in the next one-hundred-plus years. It would become the norm for the park board to curb expenses in hard times, then expand to meet growing public demand in times of prosperity. For in good times and bad, public demand on parks steadily increased. In the 1890s while funds were slashed, demands on the young park system were skyrocketing. The board was the victim of its own success. People used the parks.

The greatest unbudgeted expense for the park board during these lean years was probably also the greatest surprise—and the most resisted: amusement and entertainment in the parks. From the modest beginning of a skating rink on Loring Pond, the park board gradually expanded its provision and accommodation for activities on the land it owned. If the board thought objections to spreading "well-rotted dairy manure" were a headache, it couldn't have begun to imagine the task of managing the hundreds of recreation centers and athletic fields—not to mention the dog parks—of today. The roots of a vast system of recreation were already growing.

The present Lake Harriet Pavilion, built in 1986 from a design by Milo Thompson, was the fifth pavilion built on the site, but the first that was oriented to provide lake views for the audience. (Steven Linder, Minneapolis Park and Recreation Board)

Chapter Nine

The Main Attraction

As early as 1880 a newspaper editorial had campaigned for a park for the primary purpose of providing a place for the newly created city band to perform. Music in parks would become over the years one of the issues that led the park board into management of buildings and programs, instead of just land and parkways. Along with ice skating, boating, bicycling and swimming, music helped to change the board's notion of its purpose and increased the public demand for services in the parks.

A major conflict between philosophy and practicality was brewing in the parks. Early park designers and commissioners believed that fresh air, respite from crowded city life and the beauty of nature were the primary benefits of parks, but people went to the parks for other reasons. They went to the first parks in the greatest numbers for what they could do there.

Lake Harriet boat rental in 1892. The park board began renting boats on Lake Harriet and Lake Calhoun through concessionaires in 1887. The board took over the business itself at Lake Harriet in 1889. The pavilion pictured was built in 1892 by Thomas Lowry's street railway company. (Minnesota Historical Society)

As great as the contributions of Horace Cleveland and Charles Loring had been in devising a park system and acquiring park land, they weren't prepared for what was happening to their notion of pristine parks. Writing to Frederick Law Olmsted in 1893, Cleveland described the conflict, "Mr. Loring is doing battle manfully in the effort to preserve our parks to their legitimate use and teach the people that they are not intended as mere places of amusement to attract crowds by spectacular exhibitions. The charm of the beautiful drive around Lake Harriet has been mainly destroyed by the work of the Electric R.R. Co. in providing amusements there that attract crowds of Sunday visitors. Now the same company is trying to repeat the process at Minnehaha by illuminating the falls by electricity, the result of which would be to draw crowds there as would be utterly subversive of its essential object as a Park."

Despite Cleveland's claims for Loring, Loring himself had recognized the inevitability of such attractions and crowds as early as 1887 when he wrote in the annual report, "The public sentiment . . . shows that in a very few years more accommodation must be provided for large crowds (at Lake Harriet). The day is not far distant when private grounds cannot be used for the overflow."

The desire to accommodate larger crowds at Lake Harriet was part of the justification for purchasing Interlachen Park between Harriet and Calhoun and accepting the donations of other land north of the lake by Lakewood Cemetery and William King in 1890.

By then, the crowds at Lake Harriet had grown significantly. In 1887, the park board embarked on its first endeavor to provide activities for people around the lakes in summer. Ice skating rinks were already well established, and the board had built toboggan slides at several parks in winter. But for the summer of 1887 the board sold the rights to rent boats and sell refreshments at Lake Harriet for $1,250. Loring said in the annual report that year that in the near future the board should "reap all the benefits, without the aid of third parties." He said the experience of other

After fire destroyed the first pavilion, the street railway obtained permission from the board to put a floating bandstand on Lake Harriet for the summer of 1891 while a new pavilion was under construction. (Minneapolis Public Library, Minneapolis Collection, M5645)

cities had been that "revenue from boating is quite large and the work easily managed."

The popularity of boating and picnicking at Lake Harriet encouraged Thomas Lowry's streetcar company to build a pavilion on private property across the parkway from the lake in 1888. The streetcar company wanted to increase ridership on its Lake Harriet line by offering entertainment at the pavilion.

After only one more year of granting a private boating concession, in 1889 the board bought sixty-eight boats from the concessionaire, added another fifty-four new boats, and from then on ran the boat business itself. The board still didn't own any facilities, but it was in business.

Although it took over the boating business on Lake Harriet, the board continued to sell the boating concession at Lake Calhoun—much less valuable than the one at Harriet—until 1900. One of the major differences in how the board treated the two lakes revolved around ownership of the lake: the board owned all the lakeshore of Lake Harriet in those days and therefore the entire lake, but it owned only the eastern shore of Lake Calhoun.

There was also a clear distinction in the public's and park board's thinking about the two lakes. Calhoun was the swimming lake, and Harriet was the boating lake. Swimmers had priority in the early management of parks. The only buildings the park board managed in the 1880s were a bandstand at Loring Park built in 1886, an observatory built on top of the hill at Farview Park in 1888, and the warming houses at skating rinks. The warming houses weren't permanent facilities, however, as they were hauled into storage by late January or early February most years.

Citing "public demand," however, the park board built a bathhouse at Lake Calhoun in 1890—for men only. The success of that facility and more public demand led the board to build a women's bathhouse the following year. By 1895 the bathhouses were so popular that the cash-strapped board bought ten ladies' and twenty-five gentlemen's bathing suits for use by swimmers there. Incrementally, the park board's role in recreation was expanding.

It took another leap that summer when the board granted a petition from Mabel Clark and Harry Feagles to give swimming lessons at the Lake Calhoun bathhouse. The board even accepted an offer from a Dr. Avery to offer free lessons for bathhouse employees on how to resuscitate drowning persons. Perhaps without realizing it, and certainly without paying for it, the board had approved the first recreation instruction and the first education courses on park land.

The people had demanded a facility and by their use of it had caused the park board to expand services attached to that facility. William Folwell acknowledged as much in the annual report of 1897: "The maintenance of bathing facilities seems to be more and more regarded as a proper object of municipal care." That became and would remain the pattern in the expansion of facilities and services throughout park board history.

Swimming never gained a similar foothold at Lake Harriet. One reason is found in a 1903 discussion of whether to build a bathhouse at Lake Harriet: swimming in such a large sheet of water as Harriet was considered unsanitary.

The combination of boating and entertainment at Lake Harriet led the board into new waters. When the streetcar company's private pavilion burned down in 1891, the board wasn't ready to get into the business of managing a building of that scope.

As the streetcar company and the board decided what to do with entertainment at the lake, the company suggested a temporary floating bandstand on

Lake Harriet pavilion in 1895 with streetcars in foreground. The pavilion, built in 1892, was designed by architect Harry Wild Jones, who became a park board commissioner in 1894. Jones also designed the "water closets" built on the site in 1892. The women's bathroom he designed still stands near the present Lake Harriet band shell. (Frederick E. Haynes, Minnesota Historical Society)

Lake Harriet until a new pavilion could be built. The board gave its approval but retained the right to approve the design of the bandstand.

Shortly after, instead of building a new facility at Lake Harriet, the park board approved the construction of a new pavilion on the water's edge to be built and paid for by the street railway.

One condition of the agreement was that the streetcar company would pay for the entertainment, which had become a significant draw for both the park and streetcars. The board, however, negotiated significant control over the entertainment. It required the streetcar company to spend a minimum amount on entertainment to ensure high quality. In return, the board would pay a portion of boat rental receipts to the company. The reasoning was that the bigger the crowds attracted by concerts, the more boats the park board would rent.

Although the board exercised control over events at the pavilion, it did sell the concession for refreshments and other amusements. Some amusements were not allowed, others were. The board vetoed billiards and moving pictures but approved the streetcar company's request to stage its first fireworks display over the lake in 1893 and charge twenty-five cents for seats on the pavilion roof.

Folwell joined with Cleveland in objecting to entertainment at Lake Harriet. In the 1895 annual report Folwell said the pavilion had "outlived its usefulness," suggesting that some of the performances were "not appropriate to the ends of a public park." "The variety show and vaudeville may have their place," he wrote, "but that place is not in a park maintained at the public expense." He urged the board to buy and own the pavilion and devote it to "uses appropriate to its location." What those uses should be, he didn't say.

In 1901 at the expiration of the original ten-year agreement with the streetcar company, the board negotiated a five-year extension for the use of the pavilion. As an inducement to the park board, the company gave the city what Folwell described as "a considerable piece of ground" adjacent to the streetcar tracks to expand Interlachen Park.

However, fire destroyed the pavilion in the spring of 1903. By then the streetcar company wasn't so thrilled with its returns on entertainment. The company decided not to rebuild the pavilion. Instead, it contributed the $15,000 it had collected on an insurance policy toward the construction of a new pavilion to be owned by the park board. The park board's decision to build and operate its own pavilion was made easier when an association of Minneapolis retailers, including George Dayton, offered to loan the board another $15,000 for a new pavilion.

Pony rides at Lake Harriet pavilion in the late 1890s. Pony rides at the pavilion were one of many attractions offered by the concessionaire who ran the pavilion for the park board. (Minnesota Historical Society)

The new Lake Harriet pavilion built in 1904 was also designed by Harry Wild Jones, but in a quite different style from his earlier creation. The new pavilion was built into the lake. Concerts were provided on the roof. The original bandstand shown here atop the pavilion was replaced after one year due to horrible acoustics. It was moved to the intersection of East Lake Harriet Boulevard and Forty-sixth Street as a lookout. The cost of moving it and building a foundation for it was paid by Charles Loring. (Minnesota Historical Society)

When the new pavilion opened in 1904 it had a dining room and rooftop garden and bandstand. The board contracted with the conductor of the Minneapolis Symphony, Emil Oberhoffer, to provide a forty-five-piece orchestra for nine weeks that summer. After considerable debate, the board decided it would be fair to charge for tickets at the new pavilion to defray expenses. An entrance fee of ten cents was charged, twenty-five cents if a seat was desired. And the debate over the safety of swimming in the larger lake was won by swimming advocates, because the west wing of the building was devoted to changing rooms.

With the construction of the new pavilion in 1904, the board was in full business mode as the owner and operator of an entertainment facility. It even hired an advertising and business manager for the concert season at Lake Harriet for twenty-five dollars a week. However, the board was unwilling to extend its business into the kitchen and continued to sell the refreshment and food service concession.

At the other end of Minnehaha Creek, the park board had also expanded its services to the public—and once again the people turned out.

While the park board had been unwilling to own a building at Lake Harriet when the streetcar company's private pavilion burned down, it didn't have the same reluctance at Minnehaha Park. Second only to the Calhoun bathhouse among park buildings was a refectory built in 1892 at Minnehaha. Crowds at the falls had surged shortly after the board acquired the site for the state in 1889. Loring noted that whereas five thousand to ten thousand people visited the falls per year before it was a park, that many people visited the falls on a single day after it became a park.

To accommodate the growing crowds at the falls, the board built a pavilion in 1903. Designed by Harry Wild Jones, the refectory there had a short life. It was destroyed by fire the next summer. By this time, the board had granted concessions for pony rides, a merry-go-round and refreshments, which were offered at a few points in the park. The board never did grant permission to build a shack or platform where

The zoo at Minnehaha Park included this buffalo as well as bears, a mountain lion, sea lions and many other animals. Most of the animals were sold to Robert "Fish" Jones in 1907, who established a private zoo near the falls in what is now Longfellow Meadow. The park board kept elk, deer and bear in the park until the 1920s. (Minnesota Historical Society)

Cleveland's "army of boobies" could have their pictures taken beside the falls.

One reason a pavilion was desired at the falls was the many smaller purchases by the park board for Minnehaha Park beginning in 1894. What began with the donation of two deer that year became a full-fledged zoo. As it became known that the park board was buying or taking donations of animals for its zoo, a policy that Folwell claimed had "silently developed," offers of animals poured in. Deer were followed by elk, eagles, moose and buffalo, prairie dogs and foxes, birds of all sorts, then bears, a mountain lion, an alligator and sea lions.

By the turn of the century, the board was running a zoo. Folwell reported that the zoo had become "a great ornament to a city and a most admirable adjunct to school education" and admitted that more people might be going to the park to see the animals than the falls itself. He urged, however, that the matter "ought not to go much further without a definite plan and a counting of the cost." The cost of the zoo was becoming significant for a board that had little money.

As in so much else that had developed in the city's new parks, the zoo just happened. No one sat down to consider the ramifications of buying a "tame fox," bathing suits for public use or boats to rent, just as George Brackett hadn't thought of what opening a skating rink in the "vicinity" of a park would mean.

The relatively small group of elite citizens who pushed for a park board was imperceptibly relinquishing control of parks to the people who used them.

An even more powerful force was gaining strength through this time: the demand for more active recreational opportunities not associated with the city's abundant water. In the park board's short history it had focused almost exclusively on land acquisition and then providing services near the lakes. But there was growing pressure to provide activities and facilities that were land-based—and could therefore be provided throughout the city beyond the water-blessed southern fringe.

Chapter Ten

Let the Games Begin

Early park leaders did not have a favorable view of sports, especially in comparison with the quiet allure of nature.

In 1884, Horace Cleveland wrote to William Folwell with obvious disgust, "There's no controlling the objects of men's worship or the means by which they attain them. A beautiful oak grove was sacrificed just before I left Minneapolis to make room for a baseball club."

According to Minnesota baseball historian Stew Thornley, the baseball park at Seventeenth Street between Portland and Chicago avenues was built for Minneapolis's first professional baseball team, the Minneapolis Browns, which had begun playing in the Northwestern League a year earlier. The grandstand of the new ballpark could seat thirteen hundred, but space in two adjacent pavilions could bring total attendance to more than three thousand. The ballpark also provided a parking lot of sorts: one hundred hitching posts for horses.

Although baseball was established enough in those early days to be able to pay players, football was in its real infancy. The University of Minnesota played its first football game, against Hamline University, in 1882.

There is no mention of team sports in park board records for nearly twenty years. Sports and parks existed in different universes. Parks were simply not envisaged as a proper place for such activities.

It was not until 1888 that even the faintest recognition was given to a more active use of parks when the board first requested the removal of the "Keep Off the Grass" signs that dotted the parks. They apparently were not removed, because, in a letter from Loring to Folwell ten years later, he was still pushing for the removal of those signs. "I believe the grass is so thoroughly established now that there is little danger of its being injured by the tramping of the children," he wrote.

This protection of the grass was not in keeping with Cleveland's view of parks. In explaining some of his earliest park designs, he said he had limited paths and roads so people could wander about the lawns and among the trees. Restrictions on wandering on the grass were more likely the work of William Berry, the superintendent of parks from 1885 to 1906.

Berry not only protected his grass from the tramping of children but also erected fences—of barbed wire—around some parks to prevent damage. The board was sued over those years by several women whose skirts had been torn when they brushed up against park fences. Berry was also not a proponent of children playing in the parks. As

Skaters at Van Cleve Park in 1901. The image was taken from a hand-colored, glass lantern slide typically used for presentations. (Minneapolis Park and Recreation Board)

an engineer committed to economy and as a tree planter and grower, Berry was widely praised—one of "nature's noblemen" Loring called him—but he apparently had a limited view of how parks should be enjoyed. In Berry's defense, he was given almost no money or employees in those years to maintain the parks. The simplest, most economical solution to maintenance may have been, in his eyes, those fences and signs.

The provision of dedicated athletic facilities in parks began in 1885 with a tennis court in Loring Park. A few years later, a tennis court was added at Farview Park and then at Glendale Park. A clay tennis court at Van Cleve Park was added in 1904 along with a second court at Loring Park. None of the courts was the idea of the park board; in each case residents near the parks petitioned for them.

Skating, of course, remained a significant park attraction in winter. Loring noted that it was not unusual to see five thousand skaters on Loring Pond at one time. The board did defray its costs somewhat by the rental of skates, blades strapped onto shoes, and by the selling of concession privileges. (In 1892, the popcorn concession at the Loring Park rink was sold for four dollars.)

The clearest case of the park board accommodating a new public demand for recreation was in its treatment of the bicycle. The board first approved use of its parkways in 1887 for a meeting of a bicycle club. But as the popularity of the bicycle grew, the board made extraordinary accommodation for cyclists. Permission for the first bicycle race around Lake Harriet was granted in 1894, and it became an annual event.

The increasing attention given bicyclists from 1895 on coincided with the election to the park board of architect Harry Wild Jones. Although the bicycle craze had captured the entire country, nearly every proposal to accommodate cyclists was introduced to the board by Jones. In 1895 the board not only agreed to build bicycle racks at Lake Harriet but decided to investigate the feasibility of constructing a dedicated bicycle path, separate from the carriage path, out Kenwood Parkway and around Lake Harriet. That path was built in 1896, and the result was quite similar to the arrangement of paths today: a walking path beside the lake, with a bicycle path between it and the parkway.

The next year, a bicycle path was also built along a portion of Minnehaha Parkway. The board even cut down a hill along the parkway near Lyndale Avenue to make the climb less strenuous for cyclists and added a bridge over the creek specifically for bicycles. The extent of the bicycle's popularity was clear when the board built an enclosure at Lake Harriet for checking bicycles—it was built to hold eight hundred bicycles. In 1897 the board also purchased two bicycles for use by the park police.

In 1900 the Western Cycle Company was given permission to maintain bicycle pumps along the parkways on the condition that it not charge more than a penny for each service. By the early 1900s when new bicycle paths were built along the creek from Lyndale to Lake Amelia and along the river bluff from Minnehaha Park to Lake Street, the cost was partially defrayed by contributions from the bicycle tag fund run by the city.

Accommodation in parks for cyclists, or "wheelmen" as they were called, was not universally approved, however. A letter to the *Minneapolis Journal* in 1900 revealed a growing debate over which activities should get priority in parks. Writing as someone who was especially interested in "the rights of those who can afford to own neither carriage nor bicycle," the writer protested opening Loring Park to "wheelmen and carriage people." "The only change some of us desire to see in Loring Park is . . . devoting more space to unrestricted playgrounds for children." The writer was Florence Barton Loring.

Her letter revealed the avid and growing interest in play and recreation that would in a short time fundamentally change—and vastly expand—the park board's mission.

The first mention of playgrounds in city parks was contained in Cleveland's 1890 plan for Van Cleve Park. Loring devoted considerable space in his 1893 annual report to arguing the need for playgrounds, but with the ensuing depression the issue received little more attention. In 1898, however, the city and the park board were forced to face the issue of playgrounds. What became a playground movement did not begin as such but was the result of another initiative by Folwell.

In his 1896 annual report Folwell recommended that the board correspond with park officials in other cities to see if they might be interested in a conference of park people.

The idea was met with enthusiastic responses from nearly every major city of the East and Midwest. Louisville replied, however, that it had entertained the same idea and hoped that the meeting could be held in that city as it was near Nashville, where a major exposition was being held. So it was that Louisville hosted the first meeting of the American Park and Outdoor Art Association, the first organization of park advocates in the United States. Harry Jones represented Minneapolis at the event and extended an invitation to the group to meet in Minneapolis the next summer.

When the group convened in Minneapolis in June 1898, the countrywide interest in playgrounds was evident. Folwell opened the meeting with a paper on "Playgrounds and Public Squares," and Cleveland's paper on the "Influence of Parks on the Character of Children" was read by Charles Loring.

The day after the meeting began the *Minneapolis Times* announced that it would "take the liberty" of calling a meeting of anyone interested in playgrounds. The paper noted that Loring promised to attend the meeting saying, "I will lend my best efforts to anything that will help on the movement. I have long thought that there was urgent need of playgrounds and have been agitating to that end for sometime." Also promising to attend the *Times*' playground meeting was Folwell.

The sense of the meeting was that an independent

The dedicated bicycle path around Lake Harriet in the 1890s was similar to the modern arrangement. (Minneapolis Park and Recreation Board)

organization should be created to promote playgrounds, even though Folwell, always the educator, expressed his preference for attaching playgrounds to schools. An organization was created, the Public Playgrounds Association, which worked in conjunction with the Minneapolis Improvement League. Playgrounds were not yet considered a natural fit with parks.

The convention of the American Park and Outdoor Art Association (APOAA) concluded with the election of Charles Loring as its president, and the group named two honorary members, Frederick Law Olmsted and Horace W. S. Cleveland. Both actions helped solidify Minneapolis's standing as a leader in park efforts nationally. But more importantly to the city, the meeting helped to create solid support among city leaders for playgrounds. However, just as with trying to secure land for parks decades earlier, the support of city leaders and the newspapers would not lead to immediate success.

At the end of his annual report that year, Folwell commented on the subject that had been "busily discussed." Demonstrating his constant willingness to adapt his views, Folwell wrote, "The sports of youth are admirable deterrents from vice and excellent means of educating both body and mind. As a mere source of happiness they are worth much. While the main burden for the grounds and apparatus for play will fall on school authorities, a part of it will rest on those in charge of park systems. While waiting for larger means and fuller knowledge may it not be well for this board to begin as soon as possible with a single experiment in one of the larger and most accessible parks?"

That experiment did not happen. When the park board considered setting aside land in parks for children's playgrounds, superintendent Berry objected: playgrounds were too noisy. In noting his "fear of the effect of playgrounds in smaller parks in thickly settled portions of the city," Berry missed the point of playground advocates that those were precisely the neighborhoods where playgrounds were most needed.

Playground champions continued their push for playgrounds independent of the park board. In a solicitation letter in 1899, Loring, Mayor Robert Pratt and others of the Public Playground Association announced that land had been donated for two small playgrounds and money was needed to employ supervisors and buy equipment. The letter requested a contribution of one dollar, asking, "What investment would insure better returns than providing a place where little children can have the benefit of pure air and sunshine and be free from the dangers and pernicious influence of the streets?"

In 1900, Florence Barton Lor-

Horse racing on the ice of Lake of the Isles was also an early activity permitted by the park board. Charles Loring remembered that in some of his first winters in Minneapolis in the 1860s, he watched horse races on the Mississippi River above the falls. The horse race pictured was in the early 1900s. (Minnesota Historical Society)

ing and Susan Brown, wife of Henry Brown, petitioned the board to put in sandboxes and maypoles for children in Loring, Farview and Riverside parks, but the request was turned down due to lack of funds. It was not until 1904 that Loring succeeded in getting the park board to place a dozen swings, a dozen "teeter boards" and "white sand courts" in Loring Park and Riverside Park. But Loring did not stop there. The next year he would make a decision, largely on his own, that would elevate play and recreation to a new level in Minneapolis parks. He would select a new park superintendent—Theodore Wirth—who shared his commitment to playgrounds.

Throughout the difficult decade of the 1890s and into the twentieth century, Folwell was the steadying influence on the park board. As its president he demonstrated little tolerance for schemes that he did not perceive to be in the public interest. His pattern of voting on park board matters shows no prejudice. He would as often side with the Patrick Ryans of the board, who were not of the moneyed elite, as he would with those such as Loring, who were.

He was a man of conscience and principle but not an ideologue. He was a loyal Republican but had little tolerance for partisan ideologies. In a speech written in the early 1900s entitled "Brains Built Minneapolis," he chided both capitalists and labor for their notions that each was solely responsible for the growth of the city. Neither capital nor labor had intrinsic value, he wrote, until brains were used by capitalists to determine what should be built and by labor to determine how it should be built.

Folwell was a vigorous defender of the park board and its prerogatives. He was active in defending parks when charter commissions considered abolishing the park board or limiting its authority. And he was equally protective of the parks the city had acquired.

Folwell was a vociferous opponent of a plan to do away with Loring Park in 1895. The Board of Trade proposed to steal the state capitol from St. Paul by urging the park board to offer Loring Park as the location for a new capitol. With only Patrick Ryan and Folwell objecting, the board voted to give the park to the state "without consideration." Ironically, the site eventually chosen for the capitol on the hill of Wabasha Avenue in St. Paul had been recommended twenty-three years earlier by Cleveland as a site the city should secure for the future location of a public building.

"The sports of youth are admirable deterrents from vice and excellent means of educating both body and mind. As a mere source of happiness they are worth much."

WILLIAM FOLWELL

Folwell encouraged the board to adjust to the strengthening economy of the city at the turn of the century. "For a period of seven or more lean years" he said, "the board has been forced to talk poor and sing small to such a degree that we hardly know how to change to the manner of discourse appropriate to good times. These are good times."

But Folwell's greatest service to the city as park board president was that he adapted his view of parks to the reality of how they were used. The annual reports he authored reveal a considerable degree of flexibility and adaptability in how parks, such a new feature of city life in Minneapolis and elsewhere, would be defined.

By 1902, his last year as president of the park board, Folwell had recognized that his original view of parks, influenced by Cleveland, was perhaps wrong. "We cannot expect many people to resort to the parks from pure love for the beauty of nature as heightened by art. Additional inducements need to be given, in the way of music, places of rest and refreshment,

> In 1890 the park board asked the Minnesota Fish Commission to stock fish in Lake Harriet, Lake Calhoun and Lake of the Isles. The commission agreed to stock the lakes with game fish and maintain the lakes as reserve fish hatcheries. The commission noted that the lake in Glenwood Park was especially good for bass and perch and Minnehaha Creek for trout. Loring Pond, however, was overrun with bullheads and the fish commission said it might have to dynamite them.

games and sports, baths when feasible, boating and the like. It is the fact that those of our parks which do offer attractions are the ones most frequented. . . . Might it not be a wise thing to select another park in which to make a splendid show of plants and flowers? I would consent to the temporary use of such floral monstrosities as gates-ajar, national flags, grizzly bears and elephants if they would call out a lot of people who otherwise would not see the parks. It seems to me immediately practicable to set apart some ground for ball games in one of the parks."

In one paragraph—floral monstrosities and ballparks!—he had committed heresy in the eyes of early park evangelists such as Cleveland. But Folwell had the benefit of hindsight, while Cleveland campaigned for urban parks in largely unexplored territory.

To Folwell's lasting credit he promoted a vision for parks in Minneapolis, equitably distributed throughout the city, however they might be used. For eight critical years as president of a foundering park board, he never stopped encouraging the board to create a park system that would meet the present and future needs and wants of the people.

Cleveland's vision of a great city that extended to the banks of the river well downstream from St. Anthony Falls was far ahead of real developments. This picture, taken in 1910 on the West River Parkway, shows how undeveloped the riverbanks were. The island visible in the river at left provides a glimpse of how different the river was before it was dammed and became a reservoir. (Minneapolis Public Library, Minneapolis Collection, M0129)

Chapter Eleven

The Legacy of Horace Cleveland

William Folwell never missed an opportunity to sing the praises during those hard times of Horace Cleveland and his vision for parks. In his annual report of 1898 Folwell said, "It was the great good fortune of Minneapolis to secure the services of one of the masters of American park designing, Mr. H. W. S. Cleveland, and to enjoy the advantages of his experience, taste and skill, until his powers were exhausted by age and disease."

As early as 1893, before the "panic" took hold, the board had directed board president Charles Loring to negotiate terms with Cleveland to create plans for the newly acquired Glenwood Park. It is the last mention of Cleveland in park board proceedings. Loring apparently never acted upon those instructions nor advised the board as to their outcome. Plans for improvement of Glenwood Park were begun that summer without Cleveland's input. Loring and Folwell already knew what others did not: Cleveland could no longer work.

Cleveland would not, as he had predicted to Olmsted, "die with harness on." In the summer of 1893 Cleveland's doctors prohibited him from working in the field anymore. He attended the Columbian Exposition in Chicago that summer in a wheelchair, overcoming his aversion to crowds in the hope that he could see Olmsted again.

In March 1894 Cleveland's wife, Maryann, died in Minneapolis and was buried at Lakewood Cemetery one month before Loring's first wife died. Cleveland's granddaughters had already gone to live elsewhere by then, one to Denver in the care of a family friend, and one to Chicago to study at William French's Art Institute.

It was not until January 1896 that Folwell informed the board that due to age and illness, Cleveland could no longer serve as the board's landscape architect. With his father unable to work, Ralph Cleveland did not pursue landscape architecture. He took a job near Chicago in 1896, and Horace Cleveland moved there with him.

When Charles Loring contacted Cleveland in 1898 to write a paper for the American Park and Outdoor Art Association meeting in Minneapolis, Cleveland is reported to have at first refused, saying, "I'm already dead," suggesting that no one knew who he was. But that was not true. In a paper on "Appreciation of Natural Beauty" at the APOAA meeting, respected landscape architect O. C. Simonds said that Cleveland had "taught us how to make cities."

Cleveland's last letter preserved in Folwell's papers is dated July 10, 1899. The letter included an article from a Chicago paper about Minneapolis parks.

Cleveland asked Folwell to show it to William Berry and perhaps get it published in Minneapolis papers to show people how their "good works" were appreciated by visitors. Cleveland closed his letter by writing, "I've seen nothing of Loring."

On December 5, 1900, Horace William Shaler Cleveland died. His body was returned to Minneapolis to be buried next to his wife in an unmarked grave in Lakewood Cemetery.

In his annual report for 1900, Folwell praised the "great wisdom" of the first park board when "they called to their aid a landscape artist, Mr. W. H. S. Cleveland [sic] at the time recognized as one of the leaders in his profession." His plans for the park system, said Folwell, "deserve to be studied carefully by all who are concerned officially or otherwise with parks. It was ever his aim to adapt his designs to the natural situation and contours, to conserve and emphasize natural beauties, and to subordinate and suppress all obtrusive artificial constructions." In a footnote in the annual report it was noted, "Mr. Cleveland died early last month. He is buried at Lakewood Cemetery."

Perhaps it was the final ignominy of a life often unappreciated that Cleveland's initials were wrong in the only park board document that acknowledged his death. To this day, few in Minneapolis know his name or what he did.

Cleveland had said in a speech in 1887 at the House of Representatives in St. Paul when addressing the issue of acquiring the banks of the Mississippi River, "If I can feel that I have been in any degree instrumental in securing for the future city, which in my mind's eye I so plainly see spread out over these hills and valleys, the inestimable boon which this possession will then be, I should deem it the crowning effort of my life, and that having achieved it, I had not lived in vain."

In its final meeting of 1901, the Minneapolis park board learned that its financial situation had improved to the point that it could issue $70,000 in new bonds for park acquisition. Years of parsimony and dedication to paying off its debt had reduced that debt to a level that was in Folwell's words "no longer alarming." With new money at hand and the local economy improving rapidly, the board immediately approved a resolution to purchase the west bank of the Mississippi River gorge.

On February 17, 1902, thirty years after Cleveland's first speech in Minneapolis, the west bank of the Mississippi River from Franklin Avenue to Minnehaha Park was purchased by the park board for the modest sum of $42,846.

He didn't know it when he died, but Horace Cleveland had not lived in vain.

The cover of the 1905 annual report suggests the importance of the river to the park board. The cover photo, with the mouth of Minnehaha Creek at left, shows the wilder river of the day.

Chapter Twelve

Man of Action

February 1906 was an unusually warm winter month in Minneapolis. A short man with a bushy mustache took full advantage of the early thaw and warm weather. He was seen all around the city that month inspecting landscapes. This month of visits to Minneapolis parks may have been the single most important month in Minneapolis park board history since April 1883 when the first park board hired Horace Cleveland and acquired its first park land.

The man was Theodore Wirth, who a month earlier had been hired to replace the retiring William Berry as superintendent of parks. He had come from Hartford, Connecticut, where for ten years he had been superintendent of the country's oldest municipal park system.

At his first board meeting in January, Wirth had served notice that he was going to have a different relationship with the board than Berry had had. His first request was that the superintendent's office be moved from the maintenance shed at Loring Park to an office adjacent to the board rooms at City Hall. Wirth planted himself symbolically at the center of park operations and decisions.

Wirth would remain a vital force at the center of Minneapolis parks for the next thirty years, and a revered figure in city history. Today, many Minneapolitans think of Wirth as the man who created the Minneapolis park system. In fact, he did not—but he greatly improved it. He inherited a park system that already included most of the shores of the city's lakes, creek and river. The lakeshores that were not yet owned by the park board were in various stages of acquisition or had been ardently promoted for more than a decade before his arrival. Land to expand Glenwood (Wirth) Park and build the Grand Rounds parkways in the northern half of the city had also been targeted for acquisition years before he came on the scene. Although Wirth is often given credit for this expansion of the park system, he was a reluctant supporter of some of the new acquisitions. Wirth said when he arrived in Minneapolis that the city already had enough park land.

Wirth's greatest accomplishment was that he developed the land that the board already owned or acquired soon after he arrived. He dredged the lakes, shaped the lakeshores, built the parkways and planted the gardens. And he was very good at it. Wirth enhanced the beauty of the major Minneapolis parks and made it easier for the public to have access to that inspirational beauty. But along with credit goes historical accountability—Wirth did this at the expense of creating a neighborhood park and playground system in Minneapolis, which by the time he retired was in some respects substandard, and the costs of catching up had skyrocketed. He was always an advocate of more playgrounds and recreation facilities, but judging him by his accomplishments instead of his words, it is evident that those facilities were not his highest priority.

While Wirth was superintendent, the park board developed the park system that Cleveland and Loring had envisioned forty years earlier, a vision that Folwell had kept alive through lean years. But it never replaced the earlier vision with a new vision of parks for 1930—or the *next* fifty years. Wirth's preference was to develop parks for immediate use and enjoyment. During his tenure, the park system did not keep up with the ever-increasing demand for a new type of park that provided more active recreation opportunities. As superintendent, Wirth didn't have a vote in park board decisions, but he exerted considerable influence on park commissioners. And he did from the very beginning.

The result of Wirth's February surveillance of Minneapolis parks was his report to the park board on March 5, 1906. In his heavy Swiss German accent, Wirth set the direction of the park board for the next three decades and, perhaps as importantly, established his firm and audacious personal control over anything and everything that had to do with Minneapolis parks. There was little doubt after his presentation that this was now his show.

The *Minneapolis Tribune* the next day ran a one-word headline over its story on the park board meeting. "Staggered," it proclaimed. "Members of the park board fairly bewildered by Supt. Wirth's many suggestions," the paper continued, claiming that the "little Napoleon" had caused the commissioners to "catch their breath and wipe their brows."

At the same meeting, the park board approved the purchase of a Buick for the new forty-two-year-old superintendent. Wirth never learned to drive the Buick; he would have a chauffeur for the next thirty-plus years, but he did know how to drive park policy.

Wirth stood before the board that day in marked contrast to the old Yankee, William Berry, whose

Theodore Wirth, superintendent of parks from 1906 to 1935. (Minneapolis Park and Recreation Board)

monthly reports to the board seldom ventured beyond how many arrests had been made by park police. Wirth presented a detailed list of requests—and he asked for action on them as they were presented.

Number one. Fences around parks are "unsightly and offensive," Wirth said. If needed, they should be attractive and inconspicuous. Barbed wire was out of the question. Permission requested to take down the fences as "the superintendent may suggest." Approved. The appearance and accessibility of parks was at the top of Wirth's list.

Number two. Establish two or more small playgrounds. Request a special appropriation of $2,500 for playground equipment for parks. Approved. Wirth accomplished in one presentation to the board what the board and its members independently had failed to do for years.

Number three. Park grounds and trees are in deplorable condition. Request a special appropriation of $5,000 to hire a competent forester and a force of eight to ten skilled men and necessary equipment to shift from park to park. Approved. Wirth began building the organization he would need to run a park system the right way. Foresters had been hired before, but the position had been pruned long ago.

Number four. Request a special appropriation of $1,750 to hire a competent nurseryman. Set aside Lyndale Farmstead for seed beds and young nursery stock. Approved. Flowers and plants were essential to Wirth, whose renown in the park world was partially due to having created the country's first municipal rose garden in Hartford. This was also the first step in making Lyndale Farmstead, part of William King's old farm bought at a foreclosure sale, the administrative center of the park system.

Number five. The refreshment shed and dock at Lake of the Isles on Twenty-eighth Street are unsightly. Request permission to move them, remove the "dangerous" curves in the roadway on the west side of the lake, and prepare plans to link Lake of the Isles with Lake Calhoun and Cedar Lake. Referred to committee. Wirth established his intention to shape the landscape to his liking—and to initiate the lake-linking project that had been discussed for years.

Number six. Appropriate $2,600 for proper tools and equipment. Wirth specified exactly what he wanted—from a horse buggy and typewriter to exact numbers and specific types of hand tools, precise down to the number of short- or long-handled shovels. Referred to committee with power to act. Wirth noted that he had already purchased some of the equipment with permission of the president. Wirth was precise and detailed and was not always inclined to wait for board approval.

Number seven. Request permission to allow the city engineer to use part of The Parade as a storage ground. Approved. Wirth's preliminary plan for one of the newest parks, The Parade, included space for a football field, but there was no money to improve the field at the time. Wirth had already decided what to do with the open land across from Loring Park recently donated by Thomas Lowry and others. Beyond his advocacy of playgrounds for children, recreation facilities were not at the top of Wirth's list of spending priorities. Shaping the landscape of parks and beautifying them were and would remain higher priorities.

Number eight. There are no funds for the care of trees along the city's streets or for park police to protect them. Request the assistance of the mayor and city police to enforce ordinances protecting street trees. Approved. Wirth was a strong believer in the authority of the park board to control street trees, but that is not where he focused his attention or his resources. In the later years of his superintendence, even before the depression of the 1930s, he would discontinue planting new street trees altogether.

By the time Wirth finished his presentation to the board, requesting highly detailed decisions, which he got on the spot, he and the commissioners must have all been out of breath. Nearly fifty years later, park board president Walter Quist would praise the park board for being a policy-making body, wisely leaving the detailed administration of park matters to its professional staff. That tradition began this day in 1906 when Wirth made it known that he was in charge of every minute detail of park work.

Charles Loring, who sat with other commissioners that day, must have realized that never again would a park board president have to sit on a floor as he had done, going over plat maps with potential land donors, or supervise tree planting. The superintendent would take care of everything. Loring had hired well.

Theodore Wirth

Theodore Wirth arrived in the United States from Switzerland in 1888 at the age of twenty-five. He had left his home in Winterthur for foreign adventures before. As a teenager he had served an apprenticeship for three years with a florist and landscape gardener and then took an engineering course at a

Theodore Wirth in the early 1900s. The plan on the wall is for a park in Hartford, Connecticut, where Wirth was park superintendent before he came to Minneapolis. (Minneapolis Park and Recreation Board)

technical college in his hometown. One of his first jobs was at the age of twenty working for the National Exhibition of Zurich in 1883, where he helped to lay out and maintain the exhibition grounds. He spent the next three years in London working for a florist and in Paris, where he worked for time at the Jardins des Plantes. Returning to Switzerland, he worked briefly for a private estate and for the city gardener of Zurich, but he clearly had plans to leave home again, because he began taking English courses in night school.

His first love was horticulture, as was true of so many others among the nation's first landscape architects. Wirth found his first work in the United States as a gardener, working for a private gardener and rose grower in New Jersey.

In 1889, he took a job as a gardener in the growing New York park system. The ambitious young man rose to the level of foreman of a park crew, but lost his job with a change in city administration and went into business for himself as a landscape gardener. He worked for a time on an estate on Long Island but eventually returned to park work in the state park at Niagara Falls.

He got his big break in 1896 when he was hired as the superintendent of parks for Hartford, Connecticut. When Wirth arrived in Hartford, new parks were then being laid out by Olmsted's sons—it was their father's hometown—so Wirth saw the heirs of the acknowledged master at work.

Wirth's view of landscape architecture was influenced by the "naturalistic" preferences of Olmsted, although Wirth's park designs in Minneapolis over the years would demonstrate a much greater tendency to reshape the land than did Olmsted's. For instance, Loring noted after Olmsted's visit to Minneapolis that Olmsted's preference was to leave the shore of Lake of the Isles in its natural state. Wirth's preference was to shape the shoreline and clear most vegetation from the water's edge, as well as from the water itself.

In his early years in Hartford, Wirth created a public rose garden in the city's largest park, which was the first of its kind in the United States and won him national acclaim. He replicated that garden in one of his first creations in the Minneapolis park system in 1907, the Rose Garden at Lyndale Park near Lake Harriet, which is still a favorite of park- and rose-lovers today.

Loring likely met Wirth through the American Park and Outdoor Art Association (APOAA) at a time that Loring was thinking about the future of Minneapolis parks when Berry would step down as superintendent. When Berry decided to retire in 1905, Loring was named the head of a special committee to find Berry's successor. He knew whom he wanted. Loring visited Hartford and persuaded a reluctant Wirth to at least visit Minneapolis to have a look at the parks he could manage. Wirth visited in the summer of 1905 and left convinced that he would remain in Hartford, which he loved.

On the long train ride back to Hartford, however, Wirth began to warm to the idea of managing the parks in Minneapolis. He realized the vast potential of an unkempt and long-underfunded park system that included so much picturesque scenery. After considerable correspondence with Loring, and a visit to Hartford by a group of Minneapolis park commissioners, Wirth finally took the job.

In Wirth, Minneapolis had acquired both a park manager and designer. In his later years in Hartford, Wirth had begun to create his own designs for parks instead of relying on the Olmsted firm. Wirth's abilities as a landscape architect would solve the problem of park design that had existed since Cleveland had become too old to work. Apart from brief consultations with noted landscape architect Warren Manning in 1899, Minneapolis had not had a landscape architect since 1892. For many years, none was needed. No new parks were acquired, and some of Cleveland's plans still sat on the shelf for parks that had never been improved.

But since 1902, when the board realized it finally had the money to buy more land and secured the west bank of the river, the board had made other important acquisitions. At the same time the board decided to buy the west riverbank, it also designated the entire shore of Lake Amelia (Nokomis) for a park, even though the purchase wouldn't be completed for five years.

The biggest park acquisition between the purchase of the riverbank and Wirth's arrival was a fifty-acre tract of open land near the heart of the city, which would eventually be named The Parade. Thomas Lowry and others, including William Dunwoody, donated about half the land in 1903 and succeeding years, and the park board purchased the rest. Lowry also gave the park board $19,000 for initial improvements to the new park.

Also in 1903, the board purchased a one-acre block of land near the old center of St. Anthony, Richard Chute Square, and nearly four acres of lowland in south Minneapolis for a neighborhood park, Bryant Square, at Thirty-first and Bryant. The next year it added to its small inventory of neighborhood parks by purchasing another two-plus acres of low-lying land known as Long John's Pond at Twenty-second Street Northeast and Jackson. The city lost its most colorful park name when the park board opted to call the park Jackson Square.

In addition to the land the park board had acquired, it had already committed to buying land at Camden Place (later Webber Park), and petitions were coming in from all over the city for more park acquisitions: Keegan's Lake (Wirth Lake) as an extension of Glenwood (Wirth) Park, Cedar Lake, and neighborhood parks throughout the city. Petitions for the linking of Lake Calhoun and Lake of the Isles were a staple of park board meetings.

Moreover, landowners around Lake Amelia (Nokomis), exasperated that the board had not followed up on its designation of the lake as a park, were offering to donate most of the lakeshore. Many landowners around the west shore of Lake Calhoun were also offering to donate a strip of land for a parkway.

Demand for new parks, bottled up by a decade of depression and limited park resources, was finally exploding. Added to the demand for new parks was

Lyndale Rose Garden near Lake Harriet was created in 1907 and remains today much as it was then. Here a 1950s photographer stretches for a better photo of the blooming garden. (Minneapolis Park and Recreation Board)

Merry-go-rounds were popular additions to the parks when playground equipment was installed. This merry-go-round at Logan Park was one of the first. (Minneapolis Park and Recreation Board)

the growing insistence of civic leaders that space be dedicated to playgrounds, for which original park designs were not suited. With the improving economic picture, the likelihood of more park acquisitions, and the need to reconfigure existing parks, the board needed a landscape architect as well as a superintendent. In Wirth, it got both.

It was a perfect time for a new man to arrive. In 1905 the park board had finally given Hennepin Avenue South and Lyndale Avenue North back to the city and also resolved its long dispute with the city council over which body would control the level of water in city lakes. The city council gave the park board that authority, and the board immediately lowered the lakes a foot to remove water from its soaked parkway around Lake of the Isles.

Wirth knew going in to his presentation to the board in March that he already had public opinion behind him. He had endeared himself to the children of the city, and therefore their parents, by immediately pulling up the "Keep Off the Grass" signs that Loring detested and actually encouraging children to sled on the hills of Farview Park. In early February, the *Minneapolis Journal* wrote, "If that man Wirth keeps on all parties will compromise on him for governor before he has voted in Minnesota."

Two days before his presentation, the newspaper carried a story about how Wirth had given six axes to a park foreman headed out with a crew of five laborers to clear brush at a park. When the foreman asked what the sixth axe was for, Wirth suggested that the foreman use one himself, which prompted the *Journal* to write that it was withdrawing its nomination of Wirth for governor. "If he can make a park foreman work," the paper wrote, "he should be elected president."

When spring arrived, Wirth gave Loring Park a complete makeover and immediately rearranged the entrance to Minnehaha Park to make it more attractive. And the new playgrounds at Riverside and Logan parks were a huge hit. Wirth also had telephones installed at six parks so he could be in instant contact with park keepers.

Wirth enjoyed huge popular approval and the immediate support of the board. At the end of his first wildly successful year in Minneapolis, Wirth's influence on park decisions was enhanced when the "Father of Minneapolis Parks," Charles Loring, left the park board for the last time.

Although their relationship was not documented by either man, Loring and Wirth had similar views on many park issues. It probably was not coincidence that Wirth's first actions when he arrived were to open parks to children and recommend buying playground equipment, issues that were important to Loring, the man who had hired him. His early emphasis on Lake of the Isles also reflected Loring's commitment to that lake. Wirth's first park makeover when he arrived was the park that carried Loring's name. Perhaps the greatest testimony to the nature of their relationship was that Wirth served as a pallbearer at Loring's funeral in 1922.

The two park pioneers did have differences, too. As a gift to Minneapolis parks when he left the park board at the end of 1906, Loring paid for a two-story shelter for Loring Park. In winter it would be a warming house, but it also included two rooms for kindergartens, and a bathroom. Wirth didn't like the Spanish-style design of the building, influenced by the architecture of Loring's winter home in Riverside, California, and told Loring so in the hope that he could prevent Loring from making a mistake he would "later regret." Mistake or not, the design was not changed.

At the last scheduled park board meeting of Loring's long tenure, William Folwell offered a resolution praising Loring's generosity and expressing official appreciation and affectionate regards to the man for whom Minneapolis parks would always be "next to his heart."

In what a newspaper called Loring's "felicitous reply" to Folwell's poignant resolution, Loring reminded the board that another veteran member of the board who had contributed so much was also retiring that day: Dr. W. W. Folwell.

The two men who had done so much to shape a city, who had worked together for more than thirty years to that end, now both seventy-three, retired together from a park board they had led for most of its existence. Loring already had a park named for him, and Folwell would later be given the same honor.

Loring Park shelter in 1907. Upon his retirement from the park board in 1906, Charles Loring donated a shelter and warming house beside Loring Pond. The building also included two kindergarten rooms and a bathroom. The original shelter remains a part of the greatly expanded art and recreation center in Loring Park. (Minnesota Historical Society)

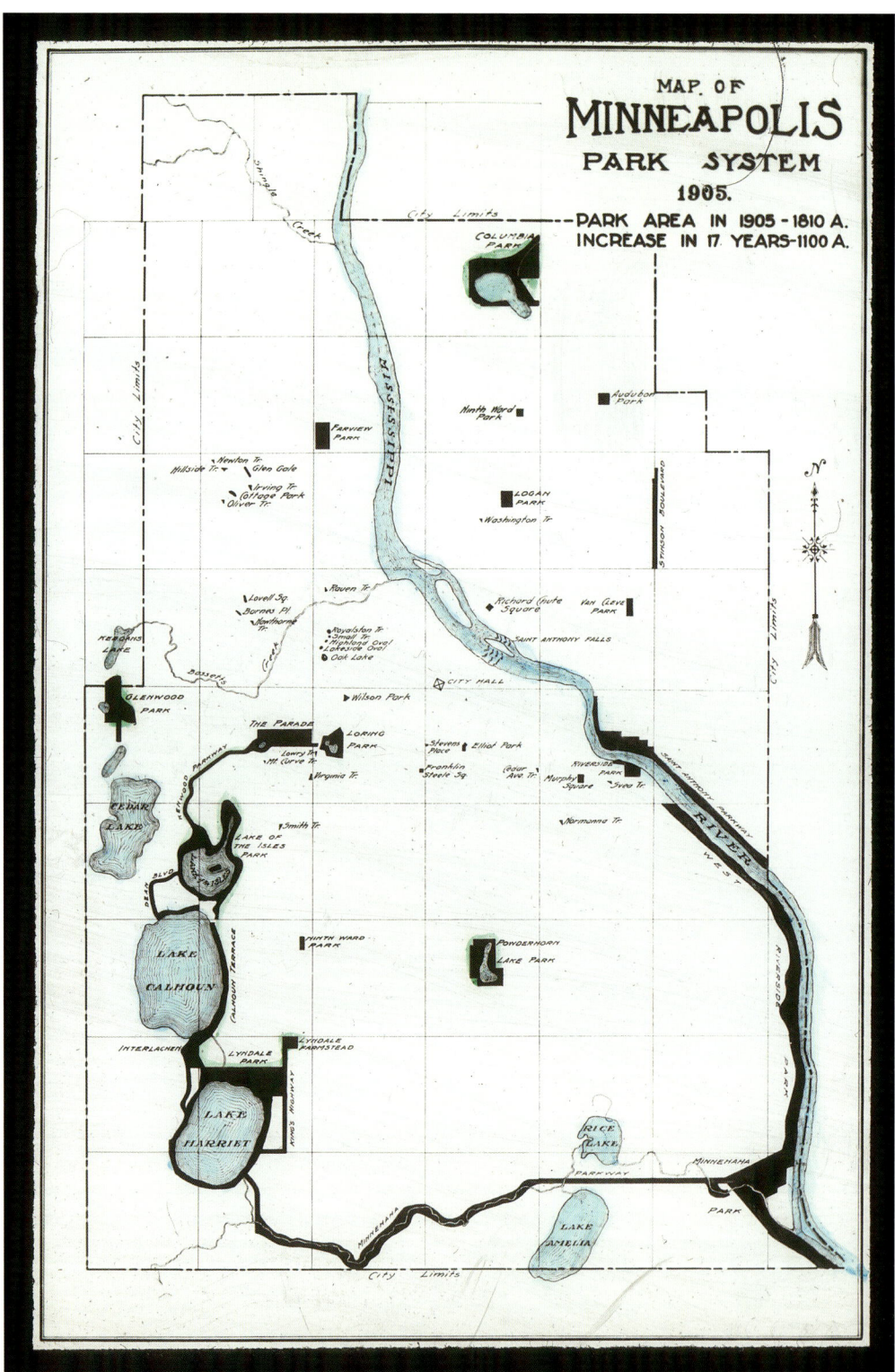

The Minneapolis park system in 1905 prior to Wirth's arrival. (Minneapolis Park and Recreation Board)

Chapter Thirteen

Man of Structure

Months before Wirth arrived in Minneapolis in January 1906, he had already begun to lay the foundation of a management system for Minneapolis parks. As soon as he agreed to take the job, he asked the board to send its secretary, J. Arthur Ridgway, to visit Hartford so Ridgway could see Wirth's bookkeeping methods. In those days the secretary of an organization acted as a chief administrative officer. Although Wirth tried to be diplomatic in his language, he was clearly telling the board that his bookkeeping methods were superior to those used in Minneapolis.

Not only did Wirth want his bookkeeping and accounting methods transferred to Minneapolis, he also wanted his clerk and bookkeeper in Hartford to come with him. So it was that Christian Bossen, his young clerk, arrived in the city with him. Bossen would remain Wirth's chief assistant for three decades and succeed Wirth as superintendent.

When Wirth called on Folwell to introduce himself and Bossen, Folwell asked, "Who's he?" When Wirth replied that Bossen was his clerk from Hartford, Folwell said, "Send him back." To which Wirth replied, "If he goes, I go." Wirth's son, Conrad, who was director of the National Park Service in the 1950s and 1960s, claimed that his father's success as a superintendent was due in part to Bossen's administrative skills, which complemented his father's creative skills.

With a clerk and bookkeeper already in place before he arrived, Wirth could devote his early days to creating the organization he would need. Of Wirth's eight proposals of March 1906 that "staggered" the board, six of them dealt with establishing the structure he felt he would need.

Before the summer of his first year, Wirth had acquired a supervisory staff: forester, nurseryman, florist and engineer. And within a year the board promoted Bossen to assistant superintendent. In 1907, the board also hired a supervisor of recreation for the three summer months, but that position would not be made a full-time job for several years.

Wirth explained his emphasis on horticulture in his memoirs. "It is the aspects of plant life which primarily inspire our desire for parks and gardens," he wrote. That belief formed the basis of his thirty-year administration—as well as his book. Wirth called horticulture, "an efficient promoter of civilization."

Wirth experienced rapid turnover in his horticultural (and engineering) staff in early years. The man who stayed was Louis Boeglin, who began as a florist in 1906 and rose to become head of all park horticulture in 1920, a job he held until his retirement in 1940. He lived for many years in a park board house adjacent to the park nursery across Keegan's (Wirth) Lake from the beach. Boeglin, who, like Wirth, emigrated from Europe, created and tended the Rose Garden, the Armory Garden, the chrysanthemum shows and, in 1929, the rock garden in Lyndale Park. He also managed more than two hundred gardens planted with nearly a hundred thousand flowers in parks across the city, nearly twenty thousand in Loring Park alone.

The most famous park board employee hired in Wirth's early years—and still the most revered—would never become part of his administrative staff. She worked independently in her growing garden.

Eloise Butler in the 1920s. Butler founded the Wild Botanic Garden in 1907. She established the garden as a volunteer until 1911, when she was hired by the park board. The garden was named for her in 1929. She tended the garden until her death in 1933 at the age of eighty-one. (Minneapolis Public Library, Minneapolis Collection, M2632B)

Eloise Butler was a Minneapolis high school botany teacher—from Maine, of course—who for years had taken her students to the unspoiled laboratory of bogs and glens in Glenwood (Wirth) Park to study plant life. In 1907, upon the request of Butler and others, the board set aside a small section of Glenwood Park for a botanical garden. For four years, working as a volunteer, she planted and tended wildflowers in the garden.

It wasn't until 1911 that the Woman's Club of Minneapolis petitioned to have a full-time curator appointed for the garden. The club recommended Butler and agreed to pay half her salary for the first year. When the Woman's Club sweetened the offer to a full year's salary, the board accepted. Butler became a park board employee at the unique wild garden later named for her.

Each spring she would plant new species and weed out unwanted invaders. During the summers she led visitors on personal tours of the garden. She also conducted botany classes, wrote a column on gardening for the *Tribune,* arranged demonstrations at the State Fair, and spoke to countless classes and clubs about the garden and the plants that grew there. She was also responsible for one of the only fences in the Minneapolis park system—erected to keep deer out of her garden. The garden was officially named in her honor in 1929. Butler remained on the job until she died at age eighty-one in 1933. A month later, on Arbor Day, the board met at the garden and planted a pin oak, her favorite tree, in her memory.

In his first years on the job, Wirth expanded his supervisory staff with two more hires. In 1909, the board stopped granting food concessions at its refectories and took over the management of food service itself. Wirth greatly disliked granting any concessions on park property. He argued that once the park board introduces any service in parks, "it becomes just as much the board's duty to see to it that

The park police force in 1912. Seated at center is the first park police chief, Burton Kingsley. He later became a park commissioner and was president of the park board from 1924 to 1927. The early motorcycles he wanted to replace with horses appear at far left and right. (Minneapolis Park and Recreation Board)

the public is served well and at the lowest possible costs, as it is the board's duty to keep up the lawns, roads, walks, woods or any other feature."

Charles O. Johnson resigned his elected position as a park commissioner to become the manager of all park refectories in 1910. He remained in that job until 1925 when a windstorm blew down the aging pavilion at Lake Harriet. With no more service at the board's most popular refectory, the manager position was reduced to a seasonal job, and Johnson resigned. Wirth's staff took on the job.

Another important expansion of the park board staff occurred in 1910, when the board hired a police chief at Wirth's urging. Until then the superintendent, going back to Berry's days, had managed the police force. Wirth attached great importance to police work in the parks and emphasized the unique role that park policemen must play. In Wirth's view, park police should not be enforcers so much as educators on proper park decorum, keeping park-goers in line with a friendly word of caution or advice instead of a club or a ticket.

In 1910 the board appointed Burton Kingsley as the first park police chief. Among Kingsley's endeavors to upgrade the police force, he argued that the park police's two motorcycles should be replaced by horses. His reasoning was that horses could be used in any weather, whereas motorcycles were useless for much of the year. He also believed that officers got more respect on a horse. Kingsley resigned from the post in 1913 despite the board buying its first police car that year. The board specified that the car have a top and a speedometer and cost less than $700.

Wirth noted in 1913 that the busiest time of year for park police was not, as one would expect, in summer, when crowds thronged to parks, but fall. The reason? Football and hunting. Rowdy crowds at football games, then being played at the original Longfellow Field and North Commons, required greater police presence. And the fall hunting season brought many hunters to the outlying parks, especially Lake Nokomis and Wirth Park. In the fall of 1913, police confiscated thirty weapons from hunters who couldn't resist the temptations of park land, where hunting was illegal. At that time, the board employed seventeen full-time officers and twelve seasonal men.

Kingsley's departure from the police force would not end his influence on parks. Kingsley was elected a park commissioner in 1917 and served until 1931 when he became a member of the legislature. Kingsley served as president of the board from 1924 to 1927 and would be among the first to warn the park board that it was perhaps overreaching in its spending spree in the mid-1920s. Perhaps it was to be expected from a man who knew you didn't have to have a motorcycle when a horse would do the job.

Wirth's transition into his new job was also aided by the only two other salaried officers of the board when Wirth arrived: the secretary, James Arthur Ridgway; and the board's attorney, a part-time position, Chelsea J. Rockwood. Both Ridgway and Rockwood had been park commissioners at one time and had been employed by the board since 1897 and 1889, respectively.

Ridgway was elected to the park board in 1889 and served as its president for a year between the terms of Loring and Folwell. He didn't seek reelection in 1894 but was appointed to a vacant seat, which he filled until 1897. He resigned as a commissioner to take the full-time paid position of secretary. He remained secretary of the board until his death in 1924. Ridgway was a real estate investor who knew land values in Minneapolis. Loring gave Ridgway much of the credit for obtaining extensive donations of land along Minnehaha Creek, and he did the same thing along the west bank of the Mississippi in the early 1900s.

Ridgway provided remarkable continuity to the park board over his thirty years as the board's secretary. He was also a music lover, who from the earliest days of the board's music program was responsible for securing musicians to perform in the parks. Wirth credited Ridgway for developing the idea of community sings in parks beginning in 1919, events that were among the highlights of park life for more than thirty years. In 1950, the board named the parkway from St. Anthony Boulevard to Francis Gross Golf Course Ridgway Parkway in his honor.

Rockwood was selected as the park board's attorney in 1889 and served until 1892, when he ran for election as a park commissioner. He only served until 1895, when he resigned his elective post to become the board's attorney once again. He remained in that position until he accepted appointment as a district court judge in 1917. His success as legal adviser to the board is remarkable in that none of the legislative powers acquired by the board while he was the board's attorney was ever overturned by the courts, despite frequent challenges to the board's power to condemn land or assess landowners for the costs of acquisitions or improvements.

Rockwood was a vigorous promoter of widely favored plans to expand Glenwood Park beyond its sixty-three acres at the time of Wirth's

The gardens next to the National Guard Armory at the corner of Kenwood Parkway and Lyndale Avenue were created in 1913. The Minneapolis Sculpture Garden now occupies that land. (Minneapolis Park and Recreation Board)

arrival. Rockwood lived near the park and, like Edmund Phelps, an influential park commissioner, was an ardent equestrian. Rockwood, along with Phelps, influenced Wirth's conversion of bicycle paths—unused when the bicycle craze finally petered out in the early 1900s—into bridle paths. The clout of the two horsemen also likely influenced Wirth's initial plan in 1915 to design Bryn Mawr Meadows as a polo ground. Rockwood deserves much of the credit for proposing and crafting the board's powers to control street trees, protecting them not only from horses and house-movers, but also the overhead electrical and phone wires that were sprouting along city streets at the time.

While the presidency of the park board changed hands every two or three years during Wirth's thirty years as superintendent, there was considerable continuity on the board. During the first twenty-three years of the board's existence only Folwell, Loring and two others had served more than ten years. During Wirth's years as superintendent fourteen commissioners served at least that long.

Continuity was matched by unanimity. Very few board decisions were contested. The remarkable lack of dissent on the expenditure of large sums of public money did not escape public notice. In defense of the board's lockstep tendency, president Wilbur Decker noted in his annual report of 1910 that "nature has blocked out our work so plainly that there is no room for doubt in the minds of reasonable men as to the proper course."

The city then owned 1,782 acres of land and water and had thirty-one miles of dirt parkways along lakeshores and river and creek banks. Although the core of the park system suggested by Horace Cleveland was in place—most of the lakeshores, the riverbanks below St. Anthony Falls, and Minnehaha Falls and Creek—Wirth would preside over a period of park growth that would more than triple park acreage and double the miles of parkway. At the same time, the park board would add significantly to the programs and services it offered.

But that phenomenal growth was neither Wirth's preference nor his doing. By the end of his first year on the job, Wirth assumed that with a staff to grow and care for trees and flowers the job of beautifying the parks was well in hand.

"With a few exceptions," Wirth reported in 1907, "the Minneapolis park system is as complete as it can be made and it is now simply a matter of developing same along lines of usefulness and beauty."

He was very wrong.

Over the next thirty years, the park system would expand dramatically, it would be almost completely reshaped, and a recreation program would be added. The next three chapters tell the stories of each of those developments, which although concurrent, really unfolded separately.

The third fairway at Theodore Wirth Golf Course overlooks the city. The golf course was made possible by the expansion of Glenwood (Wirth) Park in 1908, which made that park nearly as large as Central Park in New York. The large park provided Minneapolis the wild "scenic park" that Folwell had advocated for many years. The acquisition addressed the criticism that Minneapolis had "a park system without a park." (Minneapolis Park and Recreation Board)

Chapter Fourteen

A Man of His Time

"In submitting to your honorable body my first annual report I beg for same your indulgence," Wirth wrote to conclude his forty-two pages of recommendations after a year on the job. "It is my wish to put matters before you as I see them, and if I am wrong, I am willing to be corrected."

There is no record that anyone corrected Wirth at the time. If no one did protest Wirth's mistaken presumption that "with a few exceptions" the Minneapolis park system was "as complete as it could be made," it was only because nearly everyone in the city had his or her own list of a "few exceptions."

The people of Minneapolis wanted more parks—and they had for some time. As much as Wirth expected only to refine and develop the parks already in the system, the people of the city had completely different ideas.

The two ideas that Wirth agreed with—his exceptions—were a greatly expanded Glenwood Park, and more neighborhood parks and playgrounds. William Folwell had been the leading proponent for years of the one thing he believed was missing from the Minneapolis park system: "a great scenic park." Folwell and others wanted a great, wild, wooded park that would shut out the sights and sounds of the city, where tranquility and nature would reign. This was the most popular park conception of the time, espoused by Olmsted and his disciples.

Glenwood (Wirth) Park was the perfect place for such a park in Wirth's estimation and the only place, other than a bit of additional land along Minnehaha Creek, that "urgently calls for expansion." Wirth called the hilly land to the south and east of the original Glenwood Park "irresistibly attractive." In the wooded hills and meadows of "irregular outlines," Wirth may have seen something of his native Switzerland, much as Loring had seen New England along the banks of Minnehaha Creek. The notion is given credence by Wirth's suggestion that a flock of sheep be added to the park as well. There is "nothing prettier in a landscape effect," Wirth said, than a flock grazing on a hillside. (Wirth repeated the suggestion years later and finally convinced the board to give it a try in 1922. He argued that sheep would be self-sustaining; in addition to providing free mowing and fertilizing, mutton and wool could be sold. The experiment ended after a few months of the sheep grazing where they weren't wanted.)

Noteworthy in Wirth's recommendation for expanding Glenwood Park was that it did not include going as far north as Keegan's (Wirth) Lake, a proposal that had been promoted to the park board for many years by this time and that Wirth would later endorse.

Wirth's initial take on securing the west shore of Lake Calhoun was that it was more of what the park system already had and another shore drive there was "not pressing." In his view, although he favored protecting the wooded hillside of the lake, the city should improve the parkways it already owned instead of acquiring more and adding to the cost of maintenance.

His view of Lake Amelia (Nokomis) was much the same. "For scenery alone, the lake is not really needed," he wrote, although he did admit that if enough land were added for an extensive picnic and recreation ground, the acquisition could be a useful link in the chain-of-lakes park. In addition, he noted the long-held belief that Nokomis could serve as a reservoir to ensure a summertime flow of water over Minnehaha Falls.

Although in general Wirth was opposed to adding parkways, he did not specifically address plans that had been long favored for adding parkways for the northern half of the "Grand Rounds."

Many commissioners and park enthusiasts were already committed to a park system far larger than existed then, or than Wirth advised. Despite Wirth's opinion in 1907 that the city had all the parks it needed, in just the next three years the park board nearly doubled the acreage of Minneapolis parks.

In Wirth's first two years in Minneapolis, the park board addressed the long-standing demand for more neighborhood parks, which Wirth also favored. In 1906, the board acquired Tower Hill, nearly five acres of wooded land along University Avenue in the southeastern section of the city. (Tower Hill didn't yet have a water tower. It was named Tower Hill because it once had a lookout tower that one could climb for fifteen cents. The city council, not the park board, built the water tower—the Witch's Hat—on the hill in 1913.) In addition, another gift of land from Thomas Lowry and others extended The Parade to the south of the Armory, which sat along Lyndale Avenue. That land is now the Minneapolis Sculpture Garden.

In 1907, the board acquired three neighborhood parks: North Commons, twenty-five acres at Broadway and James Avenue North; Kenwood Park, thirty-three acres of low-lying land and surrounding hills extending north from the shore of Lake of the Isles; and Stevens Square, a two-and-a-half acre plot just south of downtown at Stevens and Eighteenth Street. North Commons and Stevens Square were developed in the next few years to meet the insistent demands of those crowded neighborhoods, but Kenwood Park would not be improved for more than a decade. The commissioners also acquired the southern and western

Sandboxes were among the first playing spaces added to parks for children in 1904. This photo of the sandbox at North Commons was taken in about 1920. North Commons quickly became one of the most heavily used playgrounds after the park land was purchased in 1907. (Minneapolis Park and Recreation Board)

shores of Lake Calhoun, in part out of consideration for the landowners who had already offered to donate their lake frontage. The park board then owned the entire lake.

The park board also acquired the land between Lake Calhoun and Lake of the Isles with the intention of digging a channel to connect the two lakes, a project that had been discussed since the 1880s.

In its final acquisition of the year, the board followed Wirth's suggestion to acquire several additional lots along Minnehaha Parkway so he could "correct" the streams banks where the creek "wandered" too much. By straightening the meandering stream, Wirth hoped to improve vistas, reduce parkway maintenance costs, and, by shortening the course of the stream, reduce the amount of water needed to produce a pleasing cascade at Minnehaha Falls.

Park commissioners had a rosy outlook for the economic future of the city, because they acquired almost all the land by issuing ten-year certificates of indebtedness that were to be paid off through assessments on nearby property. Relying once again on the financing method that had put the park board in such a deep hole in the 1890s must have set off alarms for park watchers who remembered those years. But the board at the time included only two commissioners who had been on the board in the late 1800s. And one of them, Jesse Northrup, who had teamed with William King's son, Preston, to create the seed giant Northrup King, was one of the board's biggest optimists, judging by his promotion of a new plan to "beautify by art the business portions of the city." He was referring to the proposed Gateway Park at the intersection of Nicollet and Hennepin avenues in downtown Minneapolis—a project that would generate a great deal of controversy.

Following the acquisitions of 1907, board president Northrup wrote that the park board was then entering a new era of improving parks. He praised past boards that had for twenty-five years "wisely adhered" to the policy of acquiring park land and leaving development for later. But now, he continued, the board "has secured so far as seems proper to anticipate, a sufficient park area." But just as Wirth had a year earlier, Northrup cited two "exceptions." One was enlarging Glenwood Park to provide more land for horse riding and, perhaps, for golfing. Northrup's other exception was the addition of neighborhood parks that should "largely be given over to children."

Wirth's 1907 report supported Northrup's view that the time for improving parks had arrived. He asked whether it was "better policy . . . to do everything for future generations and neglect the present one, or is it better to develop what we have for ourselves and our children and let the grandchildren and their children extend and build up with the means of their time as we have done with those of ours?"

Wirth said he preferred "to develop what we already have, before acquiring much more land." But he acknowledged that both policies may be correct and that both were desirable and asked "which shall we follow?"

The answer from the public and the park board was "both." In the next two years, while engaged in ambitious plans to reshape Lake of the Isles, the park board acquired all of Lake Nokomis, added nearly five hundred acres to Glenwood (Wirth) Park, including all of Keegan's (Wirth) Lake, and acquired a strip of land along the south and west shores of Cedar Lake.

The idea of acquiring Lake Nokomis for a park originated in early 1892. Loring proposed that the lake could serve as a reservoir to hold water to ensure a flow over Minnehaha Falls. Loring speculated that property owners around Mud Lake (Lake Hiawatha) would gladly pay to have Minnehaha Creek diverted through Lake Nokomis so they could drain their land.

When landowners offered to donate land around the lake in 1901, however, it was with the purposes of a park and parkway in mind. Landowners had seen the appreciation and development of land around the chain of lakes to the west and saw similar prospects for their land. The park board announced its intention to acquire the lake for a park in 1901 but delayed action due to a lack of money. Finally in 1908, while the offer of donated land was no longer on the table, residents in the area petitioned again for the park board to acquire the lake and agreed to pay for it themselves through assessments.

Part of the delay in acquiring Nokomis was due to the debate over how much land in the vicinity should be acquired. Should Mud Lake be included in the acquisition? Wirth notes that one of the opponents of buying Mud Lake was Folwell, who claimed that the worthless land around the lake could be acquired anytime. And he was right. His fear, based on his experience of the long recovery from the depression of 1893, was that a park board that relied too much on assessments to acquire land was playing dice with the economy. Landowners in the region would already be assessed for buying Nokomis, and Folwell feared that additional assessments to acquire what was essentially a swamp could overburden them.

So in 1908, the board purchased Lake Nokomis, 401 acres of land and water, for $63,000. Ridgway estimated at the time that the acquisition of Mud Lake would have added another $25,000 to $30,000 to the deal. Minnehaha Creek was not diverted into Nokomis and never would be. And the board did eventually buy Lake Hiawatha, with extra land for a golf course—for more than $500,000—fifteen years later. That lake and swamp were still useless and available as Folwell had predicted, but with the improvements to Lake Nokomis—on which the board would spend nearly $1 million—and subsequent development of that region, it was no longer worthless. The name of Lake Nokomis was officially adopted in 1910.

The addition of nearly five hundred acres to Glenwood (Wirth) Park had also been discussed for many years. The primary appeal of the land acquired was yet another lake, Keegan's (Wirth) Lake, that lay across the Minneapolis city boundary in Golden Valley. Residents of the north side had stepped up pressure on the park board to acquire the lake in 1905 in part to get rid of the many saloons and "resorts" that lined the lakeshore. The park board relied on the authority granted by the legislature twenty years earlier, precisely for this land, to acquire property outside its boundary. By this time Wirth was an advocate of expanding to the west the park that would later be named for him precisely because it was outside the city boundary and, therefore, wouldn't remove city land from tax rolls. The land acquired extended well north of Wirth Lake to include the picturesque valley of Bassett's Creek. After the acquisition, Minneapolitans proudly compared their park to New York's Central Park, which were then of similar size. Minneapolis had finally addressed the criticism that it had a "park system without a park."

The one remaining piece of land needed to connect the Lake District to the new large park was a parkway around Cedar Lake. While there was agitation to acquire the entire lake, the board settled for a strip of land from near Dean Parkway around the western shore to the railroad track beside little Brownie Lake at the southern edge of Glenwood Park.

And those were only the big purchases. The board condemned twenty-one acres along Shingle Creek for Camden (Webber) Park and assessed the cost against neighboring property amidst howls of protest. Petitions for and against the purchase were nearly evenly divided. Future park board presidents Thomas Voegeli and Francis Gross were northside businessmen who led the fight for the park to be acquired.

As divisive as the Camden acquisition was, it didn't approach the furor over the board's acquisition downtown of Gateway Park. The 1.2-acre triangle of land where Hennepin and Nicollet met just south of the river had once been the duck pond partially donated by William Eastman in 1865 where Minneapolis's first city hall had been built. With the removal of city offices to a grand new building on Third Street in the 1890s, however, the neighborhood was dominated by saloons.

Park commissioner Edmund Phelps noted that the neighborhood "was not one of which the city was especially proud." The neighborhood was a gathering place for the unemployed and for lumbermen waiting to head north on their next job. They hung out at Bridge Square at the southern end of the Hennepin Avenue Bridge and patronized the dozens of saloons in the area. Demolition for The Gateway eventually took out twenty-seven saloons in that small area—which was reason enough to support the project in the minds of some people.

Park board president Northrup proposed that perhaps the triangle should be the board's first venture into the business district. It would be Minneapolis's first attempt at urban renewal. Sitting as it did adjacent to the planned Union Depot, the triangle could be developed as an entrance to the city for arriving passengers, a "gateway" to the business and retail district.

Once proposed, the idea took off. The Publicity Club, the Commercial Club and the Minneapolis Real Estate Board thought it a splendid idea. But the city was soon bitterly divided over the issue, with heavyweights on both sides. Thomas Lowry was among the champions of the project, while his friend Charles Loring was among the opponents. Loring contended that it was not the park board's business to try to beautify downtown and that the park board shouldn't take property from businesses anyway. (Florence Barton Loring owned some of the property that would be taken for the park.) Loring thought the old city hall should be converted into a public bath house and warned that a park there would become simply a loafing ground for unemployed men.

The biggest objection, however, was to the price tag of $643,000, more than a half-million dollars an acre, just to acquire the land.

Ultimately, in early 1909, the board did approve the project, spreading a portion of the ten-year assessments over the entire city to cover the enormous cost. Because some of the buildings acquired had leases, some lucrative, that ran for several more years, the board did not initiate demolition of existing buildings for another four years. The income from those leases over a few years would cover the costs—about $100,000—of erecting a small pavilion with an information bureau and bathrooms.

The building finally opened to great fanfare in 1915. The pavilion was fronted by grounds designed by Wirth, including a fountain donated by Phelps. On the front of the shelter was etched, "More than

The Gateway. The park on the site of the first city hall, depicted on the cover of the park board's annual report, finally opened in 1915. The fountain, now located in Lyndale Park, was donated by park commissioner Edmund Phelps. (Minneapolis Park and Recreation Board)

her gates, the city opens her heart to you." The transient poor of the city appreciated the sentiment—and the pavilion's public bathrooms.

Wirth, who had supported the project from the start, noted with some alarm in his annual report for the year that "the building is too small for a place of prolonged rest for the army of unemployed that frequent this neighborhood. It was not intended as such. . . ." He estimated that eight to nine thousand people used the bathrooms there every day.

A newsstand in the pavilion generated some revenues for the board in its first years, but those revenues dissipated quickly. By 1925 the board was spending nearly 5 percent of its general park fund on maintaining the Gateway, a sum "out of proportion" to its small role in the park system, according to the annual report.

The Gateway pavilion was demolished in 1953 and a four-foot fence erected around the grounds to prevent loitering. A second urban renewal effort in the neighborhood began in the 1960s, which included the construction nearby of a new central library.

In the midst of the controversial acquisitions of Camden and Gateway in 1908, generous citizens and the city enlarged park land with three significant donations. The city turned over the old Maple Hill Cemetery, eight acres on Broadway Northeast and Fillmore, now Beltrami Park, to the board for conversion into a park. The city even gave the board $5,000 to develop the land, which included removing monuments. Wirth suggested turning part of the park into a school garden where children could learn to grow vegetables—at least on that portion of it where no one had been buried.

Anna B. Lewis donated a strip of land that was important to future lake-connection plans. She gave the board the wetlands that connected Cedar Lake to Lake of the Isles, which would eventually become Kenilworth Lagoon.

Finally, with Loring as intermediary, James J. Hill and Thomas Lowry donated eight acres of land to the south of William King's old barns for the expansion of Lyndale Farmstead. Hill and Lowry asked only that they be reimbursed for taxes they had paid on the land. Loring's involvement was likely due to what Wirth said was a verbal agreement he had with the park board through Loring that it would build a house for him to live in as a condition for accepting the job in Minneapolis. In Hartford he had lived in a house provided by the park board there and wanted the same in Minneapolis. The park board finally built that house in 1910 on the donated land.

The Gateway in 1937. As Loring predicted, The Gateway became a place where the unemployed gathered even before the Depression. The building was demolished in 1953, and the park became part of another urban renewal effort in the 1960s. (Minneapolis Star Journal, Minnesota Historical Society)

In the midst of this expansion binge, Wirth urged a "radical change" in thinking "in order to secure for the present generations some of the benefits for which those lands have been acquired." Despite Wirth's opinion, the park board added sixteen hundred acres to its park inventory, even though more than eight hundred of those acres were lake water.

Surprisingly, neighborhood parks and playgrounds—on everyone's list as an "exception" to the end of land acquisition—had been practically ignored. Of the huge acreage acquired, less than thirty acres were for neighborhood parks in two parcels of land: Maple Hill and Camden. Maple Hill had been donated, and Camden was partly a creek bed that was dammed to create a pond and skating rink. Everyone said they wanted neighborhood parks and playgrounds, but no one was buying them. In 1910, the board actually did acquire land for a neighborhood park when it purchased a little over five acres for Audubon Park on Twenty-ninth Avenue Northeast.

After a short breather, the board was back in the land business in 1911. With Camden Park (Webber) acquired in far north Minneapolis, the plan for a continuation of the "Grand Rounds" encircling the city and connecting the major parks was pursued once again. The park board purchased 170 aces of land north from Glenwood Park following the city's western boundary to Forty-fifth Street, then east to Camden Park. With that acquisition, which provided a boulevard one hundred to three hundred feet wide, the board had finally secured nearly every significant piece of land that had been contemplated in the 1880s and 1890s.

But there was still one old park failure left over from the 1870s that would be addressed in 1911 and would create a setting for one of the city's cultural landmarks. Clinton Morrison, the son and heir of Dorilus Morrison, approached the park board with a creative offer. After the city had declined in the early 1870s to make a park of the forty acres that Morrison, King, Brackett and Mendenhall held and developed

Maple Hill Cemetery became a park in 1908 and was eventually named Beltrami Park. In this undated photo, maintenance workers clean up the grounds among the tombstones. (Minneapolis Park and Recreation Board)

Minneapolis Institute of Arts in a 1915 postcard. The institute was built on the site of Dorilus Morrison's home. The land was donated to the park board in 1911 by Dorilus's son, Clinton, expressly as a site for an art museum. (Minnesota Historical Society)

as a park a block south of Franklin Avenue along Third Avenue, Dorilus Morrison had built his lavish home, Villa Rosa, on the southern eight-and-a-half acres of that land. Clinton Morrison offered to donate that land as a memorial to his father on the condition that it be used exclusively for an art museum.

Special legislation was written to allow the park board to accept the land and to levy a tax of one-eighth mill for a park museum fund to support the institution. The Minneapolis Society of Fine Arts had already raised nearly half a million dollars to construct the museum. The legislation was passed, the park board accepted the property, and to this day the Minneapolis park board collects the levy that is passed directly to the Minneapolis Institute of Arts.

But that's not where the story ends. Later that year William Washburn, another old park supporter, who had bought the land just north of Morrison's for his mansion, Fair Oaks, offered to sell the park board his estate. He would sell his estate for the value of the land alone, which was $200,000. At that price he was throwing in his mansion, which was valued at $400,000. The only condition of the sale was that Washburn and his wife would continue to live in the house until they died. The board accepted the offer, issued certificates of indebtedness, and assessed the cost to the neighborhood. With the death of Mrs. Washburn in 1915, the board acquired the land as well as the house, stables and greenhouses.

The greenhouses were immediately demolished. The park board never maintained the mansion. For a time the interior was renovated at the expense of the Women's Welfare League and was used by a number of women's organizations during and after World War I. The park board even considered establishing its headquarters in the mansion. But given its state of disrepair, the grand old house was demolished in 1924.

Despite the demise of two of the city's finest old homes, the park board finally acquired in 1911 a portion of the land that had first been offered to the city council as a park in 1869. The original offering price had been $625 an acre. For the portion it purchased, the park board finally paid nearly $27,000 an acre.

The land of another commissioner on the first park board was also acquired in 1911. The heirs of John Oswald sold the park board thirty-nine acres of Oswald's Bryn Mawr farm west of downtown along Bassett's Creek for just over $30,000. The board accepted the offer only after residents of the area agreed not to ask for immediate improvement of the land—which was a good thing, because the land sat idle for more than twenty years.

In addition to the acquisitions that all had a tinge of history to them, Glenwood (Wirth) Park, Columbia Park and Riverside Park were all enlarged. The Riverside acquisition was prompted in part by plans to open a dance hall across the street from the park. To forestall that unpleasantness on the edge of a park, the board bought the land. The remainder of the purchase extended board control of the west riverbank to Sixth Avenue South.

And finally, the board got around to providing some of the neighborhood parks and playgrounds it had been citing for years in its "exceptions" to curtailing further land purchases. The board purchased three acres for Sumner Field at Bryant

William Washburn's Fair Oaks mansion in 1917. Washburn sold his estate across the street from Morrison's home to the park board in 1911. It became Washburn Fair Oaks Park. Here the Girls Liberty League met in 1917. The park board never maintained the mansion, and it was demolished in 1924. (Minnesota Historical Society)

and Eighth Avenue North, just under three acres for Stewart Field at Twenty-sixth Street and Tenth Avenue South, and four acres at Minnehaha and Twenty-sixth Street for Longfellow Field.

Each of the parks had been requested by the neighborhoods. In the case of Longfellow Field, it was land that was already heavily used as a playing field. This was not the Longfellow Park that exists today, however, which is located about a mile farther south. Despite its popularity as a sporting field and extensive use by people from around the city, the first Longfellow Field was sold by the park board in 1917. The board purchased the present Longfellow Park at Thirty-sixth Avenue South and East Thirty-fourth Street, a much larger park at twelve-and-a-half acres, in 1918.

A change in the philosophy of funding park purchases showed up tentatively in 1911. Most of the land purchased that year was acquired by issuing certificates of indebtedness with the costs being assessed on property owners. The board made an exception, however, for each of the three playgrounds, recognizing that those neighborhoods couldn't foot the bill. The president of the park board at the time, Wilbur Decker, believed that all playgrounds should be paid for by bonds rather than assessments, because the neighborhoods that most needed them could least afford them. Each of the playgrounds was purchased with proceeds from a $150,000 city bond issue that was also used to pay a portion of the cost of the Riverside addition and the land for the Glenwood-Camden Parkway (later named Victory Memorial Drive).

Decker sounded a caution to the board at the end of the year. He praised the work of boards past in acquiring the features of natural beauty for parks, but, he added, "In days to come our proudest claim should not be that our natural park features are among the finest in the country, but that the people in every quarter of the city enjoy adequate park privileges. . . . Every citizen cannot have a beautiful lake or other great park feature opposite his residence, but it is quite possible for this Board to establish beauty spots and places of recreation within easy walking distance of every home."

Decker's message to "equalize" park privileges across the city, however, would take many, many years to accomplish. With a decades-old shopping list finally filled, the board slowed down its land acquisition. In the next eleven years, through 1922, the board added only 330 acres to its park inventory.

The largest single acquisition, accomplished over several years, was the land for St. Anthony Boulevard from Webber Park east across the river to Columbia Park, then south and east to meet Stinson Boulevard. With those acquisitions, about one quarter of it donated, the board came as close as it ever would to completing the "Grand Rounds." "The Missing Link" from Stinson Boulevard to the East River Road was missing then and is missing still.

Beginning in 1912 the board did begin to acquire neighborhood parks and playgrounds, slowly but surely.

1912: Prospect Park, now Luxton Park, 112 Williams Avenue SE. Five acres in southeast Minneapolis. ($15,100)

1914: Northeast Riverside Park, now Marshall Terrace. Just under eight acres between Marshall Avenue and the river. ($15,500)

1915: Bottineau Park, a six-acre playground on Second Street and Nineteenth Avenue Northeast. ($28,800)

1916: Nicollet Park, now Martin Luther King Park. Twenty-one acres were purchased on Nicollet Avenue and West Fortieth Street. ($72,000)

Cedar Avenue Field, just under two acres was donated for a playing field at Cedar Avenue and East Twenty-fifth Street by D. D. Stewart, who also donated land to expand Stewart Park, which was named for him.

1917: Folwell Park, thirty acres at Humboldt and Dowling in north Minneapolis. ($35,400)

Chicago Avenue Park, now Phelps Park. Nearly eight acres at Chicago Avenue and East Thirty-ninth Street. ($24,700)

1918: Longfellow Park, twelve-and-a-half acres at East Thirty-fourth Street and Thirty-ninth Avenue South to replace Longfellow Field, which was sold a year earlier. ($16,900)

1921: Linden Hills Park, eight acres west of Lake Harriet. ($31,000)

Lynnhurst Park, eight acres a few blocks south of Lake Harriet. ($24,800)

1922: Brackett Field, twelve acres at East Twenty-eighth Street and Thirty-sixth Avenue South. ($34,600)

Sibley Park, ten acres at East Thirty-ninth Street and Longfellow Avenue South. ($23,400)

1923: Pershing Park, ten acres at West Forty-eighth Street and Chowen Avenue South. ($27,200)

The park board did not follow for long Wilbur Decker's advice in 1911 to acquire land for playgrounds by issuing bonds. After the purchase of Luxton Park in southeast Minneapolis in 1912–13, and the purchase of the two parks in northeast Minneapolis in 1914 and 1915, all playgrounds were acquired by 100 percent assessment of the cost on the neighborhood—for both land and improvements. All, except Folwell Park, were also in the more prosperous and growing neighborhoods of south Minneapolis, some within easy walking distance of the lake and river parks that consumed so much of the park board's resources.

The competition for park board resources was just too great as the large areas acquired for parks and parkways surrounding bodies of water were developed and improved. Little was left for neighborhood parks and playgrounds, especially during 1917 and 1918 when the United States was at war in Europe.

With the nation at war, selling park bonds was out of the question. The greatest impact of the war was in reducing park maintenance and planned improvements to parks already owned. Postponing maintenance, of course, only increased the need and the expense after the war ended in 1918. The inflationary period after the war also dramatically increased the costs of maintaining and developing parks.

These were still days of transition in park philosophy. Nearly everyone was in favor of playgrounds and active recreation areas, but who should pay for them was still an issue. Was it the responsibility of the park board, the school board or charitable organizations? Could the park board provide neighborhood parks and still develop parks and parkways of natural beauty? Should it?

Decker had recognized that neighborhood parks were a complicated issue. He had found, as Cleveland had warned long ago, that acquiring land in built-up portions of the city was very expensive. Decker even recommended in 1911 that the park board consider leasing land for playgrounds with purchase options, so it could see over time which neighborhoods really needed and would use playgrounds.

One reason the park board may have been reticent to place playgrounds where residents did not offer to pay for them was its bad experience at Marshall Terrace on the river in northeast Minneapolis. Shortly after the board acquired the land, it built a small shelter there and graded playing fields, but no one used them. The shelter was eventually moved to Farview Park. The board intended to build a swimming beach at Marshall Terrace but found that the river currents there were treacherous.

Still there were large, crowded parts of the city, especially on the fringes of downtown in all directions, that did not have much in the way of parks. That problem was partially addressed in 1926 by the donation of land at Twenty-sixth and Clinton Avenue South for tiny Clinton Park which was later expanded by park board purchases, and by the donation the next year from Frank Peavey's grandchildren of the site of his home at Franklin and Park Avenue for Peavey Park.

In the densely populated center of residential Minneapolis for two miles south from downtown to Powderhorn Park, the only parks other than little Stevens Square, were on land that had been entirely or partially donated. Elliot Park was the first park donated to the park board. Washburn Fair Oaks and Dorilus Morrison parks, which contain the art museum and its approach, were acquired for little and nothing respectively and were never intended for active recreation. Peavey Field, Clinton Field, Stewart Field and Cedar Avenue Field were all either initiated or expanded by donations of land.

The unwillingness of the park board at the time to commit resources to playgrounds stood in stark contrast to the board's decision to spend $100,000 in 1923 on the purchase and improvement of two-acre Mt. Curve Triangle (Lowry Park) at the northeast entrance to posh Lowry Hill. Wirth abandoned his populist pronouncements in explaining that the expense was "justified" because it was "the entrance to one of the city's finest residential neighborhoods." Of course, as elsewhere in the city at the time, the cost was assessed to the neighborhood, but it nonetheless consumed scarce resources. Even where the park board assessed the cost of land and improvements, it was faced with immediate cash outlays that it would not recoup for ten years, and in some instances, twenty years through assessments.

Despite continued growth in park acreage, the park board also lost some park land. The largest single loss was nearly twenty-eight acres of river bottom that were flooded by the reservoir created by the "high dam" on the Mississippi. The dam would soon be named the Ford dam, when Ford built its car assembly plant on the St. Paul side of the river and acquired the rights to the electricity the dam generated. The park board was compensated with $15,000 and a few parcels of land owned by the federal government along the river.

The park board tried to insist on receiving half the power the dam would generate in return for granting the government flowage rights over park land. But that was a condition of transfer the U.S. government would not accept. The only other benefit of the "sale" of flowage rights to the federal government came when the park board donated to charity the timber rights on the largest island in the river. Neither the park board nor the federal government wanted a stand of dead wood in the middle of the reservoir.

The Ford Dam under construction in 1917. The dam created a reservoir in the river gorge downstream from St. Anthony Falls. (Minnesota Historical Society)

Park promoters had long touted the benefits of a two-mile-long "sheet of water" to replace the islands and rapids between St. Anthony Falls and the dam. Many thought the reservoir would become a park board asset as a premier course for water sports, especially rowing. Wirth saw great potential for Riverside Park, overlooking the reservoir. At various times he proposed a sports stadium and an outdoor concert theater on the land that sloped to the river. Wirth attributed the lack of enthusiasm for his plans to the sometimes "unbearable odor" that emanated from the river. Wirth wrote that damming the river had "transferred the living into dead waters" and called the reservoir a "decided detriment to the Twin Cities."

Until the mid-1930s, when an interconnecting system of sewers was built to transport and treat the city's sewage, it flowed directly into the river from most sections of the city. The reservoir for which people had such high hopes as a recreation area became a cesspool. The reservoir was at least 30 percent raw sewage, according to estimates of the time. As a result, the park board did not devote many resources to the riverfront—and no one wanted to row on it.

The other major sale of park land occurred in 1917 when the park board sold its popular Longfellow Field at Twenty-sixth and Minnehaha to a manufacturing company. The field was used for citywide athletic events at the time. The board's excuses were that the school board had decided to relocate the nearby neighborhood school first and that the athletic field was going to require significant investment for improvements anyway. The board did replace the field with a larger Longfellow Park a mile farther south, but it was much less accessible to the rest of the city than the old field. Moreover, the board didn't improve the new park right away, because the neighborhood was not yet heavily populated. The board did realize a substantial profit on the sale of the land it had held for six years, but it lost an important playing field in a neighborhood that would remain without recreational facilities until Matthews Park was developed a half mile away nearly fifty years later.

Park board decisions to give up land for public or private purposes would become one of the most significant issues it would face in the 1950s and 1960s as open land became scarce and freeways voraciously consumed land whether occupied or not.

In 1923, the park board finally closed the books on long-sought park areas. It purchased an initial 268 acres of land and water around what was then known as Rice Lake (previously called Mud Lake), soon to be renamed Lake Hiawatha. (The old name of Mud Lake had been dumped as too unappealing.) The total cost of $550,000, which included the banks of Minnehaha Creek from the lake to Minnehaha Falls, was assessed on benefited property over five years. The park board made no plans to develop the property for several years, because the assessment was so high that it couldn't add an assessment for improvement on top of the one for buying the land. By the time improvements would begin, the plans for the land would also change considerably. For by then, the park board had had its first taste of running golf courses, and the land acquired around Lake Hiawatha provided the only place the park board could build a golf course in the southern half of the city.

The next year, 1924, the park board entered into two creative agreements to acquire land specifically for golf. The success of the board's golf courses first in Glenwood (Wirth) Park, then Columbia Park, in 1916 and 1919, respectively, compelled the board to

> **The Unofficial City Rodent.** Wirth was not opposed to all animals in parks. In addition to his trial of a flock of sheep in Wirth Park, in 1907 he imported gray squirrels from Kansas to release in Loring Park. In 1919 Wirth reported that the gray squirrels had "extended their hunting ground over the entire city." While noting that some people complained about the gray squirrels, he added that "their friends outnumber their enemies."

seek other land that could be developed for the game that was rapidly becoming popular. Between the two new courses, Meadowbrook and Armour (Francis Gross), both outside Minneapolis city limits—one southwest and the other northeast of the city—the board added 360 acres of land.

The other acquisition arrangement made in 1924 would not actually provide park land for another several years. Robert "Fish" Jones was an eccentric fellow who ran a meat market in downtown Minneapolis at the turn of the century. Over time he acquired an impressive collection of exotic animals. As they were overrunning his downtown property, where the Basilica of St. Mary now stands, he was searching for a place to move them and expand his collection. Fortunately for Jones, Wirth detested the zoo that the park board was operating in Minnehaha Park from the time he arrived. To Wirth the zoo was unsightly and smelly. It ruined the views at the entrance to the park from the south. Moreover, Wirth pitied the poor animals cooped up in small cages. Not coincidentally, he also didn't want to keep storing animals all winter in the administrative buildings he had planned for Lyndale Farmstead.

The perfect solution was to sell all but the elk, deer and bear from the zoo to Jones. (The park board continued to provide pens for those animals in the park until 1923 when it removed them to expand the picnic grounds in the east glen.) Jones soon opened a zoo beside Minnehaha Creek near the entrance to Minnehaha Park at what is now Longfellow Glen. As a part of his entertainment complex Jones also constructed a replica of Henry Longfellow's house and raised money for a statue of Longfellow. Jones's property and his noisy and smelly animals, though very popular with visitors, did not please the neighbors. The park board addressed many complaints about Jones's facility next to park board property and at one point insisted that he build a high fence around his menagerie.

With extensive rehabilitation of Lake Nokomis and then the purchase of Lake Hiawatha as a park, it was clear that Minnehaha Creek was never going to be diverted to Nokomis as a reservoir for the falls. With that, the board decided it needed Jones's property beside the creek to create a smaller reservoir that it could augment with water from a deep well to provide a holding tank for a picturesque falls. The board began condemnation proceedings on Jones's land. Two sets of appraisals were completed, however, and neither was satisfactory to both Jones and the board.

Jones and Wirth finally came up with a better plan: Jones would donate the land to the park board on the condition that he could continue to operate

Robert "Fish" Jones created his zoo in Longfellow Meadow in 1907. He built a replica of Longfellow's Cambridge, Massachusetts, home and erected a statue to Longfellow on the grounds. The statue is visible in the center of this photo. Jones later donated the land to the park board. (Minnesota Historical Society)

his zoo for another ten years. That worked for everyone. The park board got the land (and the statue and the house), Jones kept his zoo, and park visitors could still see animals.

The Longfellow House was converted into the Longfellow Branch of the Minneapolis Public Library several years later. Today the house sits at a new location nearer the falls, where it serves as a scenic byway information center. No one has given the same care to Longfellow's statue, which stands in disrepair in the wild glen near the creek.

With golf courses to build and soaring debt from several years of building parkways, the board was in no position to buy more land by 1926. The park board did accept a donation from a real estate company owned by F. A. Clarke of sixteen acres between Diamond Lake and Pearl Lake west of Portland Avenue at Fifty-fourth Street as the first step in the eventual acquisition of all the shore of both lakes.

The donation was seen as a spur to land values in the vicinity. It was prompted in part by the impending action of Minneapolis in 1926 to annex about a mile of Richfield from Fort Snelling to the city's western limit with Edina. The annexation presented a significant challenge to the park board. It suddenly had many more neighborhoods to provide with parks and playgrounds. Initial discussions with residents of the annexed areas revealed little willingness to be assessed for local parks, which, given the policy of the park board at the time—if you really want it, you'll pay for it—was the end of discussions of locating neighborhood parks there anytime soon.

The park board realized that the only long-term solution was to work with the school board, which faced the same problem of expanding its services, to avoid duplicating facilities. In 1927 a joint committee of the park board and school board identified several tentative combination sites for new schools and parks in the annexed territory.

As early as 1911, the park and school boards had recognized their joint responsibility for recreation for children. They agreed at the time that the schools should have primary responsibility for younger children, and the parks for older children. In 1918, the park board's improvements of Audubon Park in northeast Minneapolis were coordinated with nearby Jefferson School. And in 1921 the expansion of Stewart Park was designed to accommodate shared use of the park's playground and the school's gym. In 1927, the two boards cooperated again in developing Keewaydin Field, four acres of land east of Lake Nokomis next to what was then Alexander Ramsey School (now Keewaydin).

Two years later, the park board delayed implementing Wirth's initial plans to develop Pershing

Maude Armatage in 1937. Armatage was the first woman elected to the park board. She served on the board from 1921 to 1951, the longest consecutive service on the board in its history. (Minneapolis Park and Recreation Board)

Park in the southwest corner of the city because the school board planned to build new Alexander Bell High School nearby. When the school board's plans were delayed the following year—and the proposed name for the school was abandoned (it was eventually named Southwest High School)—the park board proceeded with improvements to Pershing on scaled-back plans. Pershing Park had already sat idle for eight years since the park board purchased the land, and area residents were clamoring for improvements—and were willing to be assessed for them.

Many years later, after the Depression and World War II, the school and park boards picked up their long-neglected plans for schools and parks in the annexed portions of Richfield and developed several parks and schools together.

The driving force behind the increasing collaboration between parks and schools in the 1920s was Maude Armatage. Soon after becoming a park commissioner in 1921, Armatage became a staunch advocate for joint park-school projects. Armatage, who still holds the record for longest continuous service on the park board at thirty years, was honored by having named for her one of the first park and school projects planned together from the ground up. Armatage Park and Armatage School are located west of Penn Avenue at Fifty-sixth Street in south Minneapolis.

Armatage was the first woman to serve on the park board. She grew up in the nine-family "Colony" created in the 4600 block of Fremont Avenue just east of Lake Harriet by Charles Loring and Henry Brown. Loring and Brown gave lots to nine families in the wake of the 1893 depression on the condition that they build nice homes there. They hoped that the initial settlement of the area would attract more home owners, who would actually pay for land.

The nineteenth amendment to the U.S. Constitution, ratified in 1920, gave women the right to vote in the country for the first time. Women in Minneapolis had campaigned for the right to vote but had also vowed to do their share in running gov-

Maude Armatage on her ninetieth birthday in 1960 being presented flowers by park commissioners Inez Crimmins and Lorna Phillips, the second and third women to serve as park commissioners. (Minneapolis Park and Recreation Board)

ernment. In fulfillment of that promise, Armatage ran for park commissioner as an at-large candidate in the first citywide election in which women were permitted to vote, and she was elected for a six-year term. She was reelected four times before she retired at the age of eighty-one.

It would be decades after Armatage's first election before a second woman served on the park board. Lorna Phillips was chosen by the board to fill a vacancy created in 1957 when commissioner P. Kenneth Peterson was elected mayor. The following year Inez Crimmins was chosen to fill another vacant seat on the board, giving the park board two female commissioners for the first time. Although Phillips stood for election for her seat in 1961 and won, the second woman after Armatage to be elected to the board without the advantage of incumbency was Beverly Smerling in 1963. Phillips and Crimmins were joined by a third woman on the board when in 1962 city councilwoman Elsa Johnson served as an ex-officio member of the board. The first time there were three women elected as park commissioners was 1978, when Naomi Loper was elected to join Patricia Hillmeyer and Nancy Anderson.

Wirth's initial plans for the development of the lands donated at Diamond Lake and Pearl Lake showed one lake, Pearl, being filled to create playgrounds and the other being dredged to create a beach and swimming area. But by the time acquisition of both lakes was completed in 1936, no money was available for extensive improvement to the entire park system, so only the first part of the plan was implemented.

Luckily for those plans to fill Pearl Lake, more wetland than lake, the park board had a ready source of fill—the city's airport just south of Fort Snelling. The park board needed no one's permission to take dirt from the airport, which was undergoing extensive upgrades, because it had owned it since 1928.

An old Indianapolis-style speedway had been built on the flat land south of Fort Snelling in 1915. Several races were held there too, featuring the famous driver, soon to become World War I flying ace, Eddie Rickenbacker. But the racetrack proved unprofitable and folded. In its place arose a flying field using the long grass oval in the center of the paved track as a landing strip. The little airstrip grew in popularity, spurred in part by the heroics of the flying aces of World War I and in part by the novelty of flying machines, before anyone quite knew what to do with the amazing new technology.

Prompted in part by the decision of St. Paul to build its own airport closer to that city, Holman Field, the Minneapolis city council approached the park board in 1927 about the possibility of acquiring the airfield, named Wold-Chamberlain for two Minneapolis flying aces killed in the Great War. The park board was the only candidate to obtain the airport for the city because it was the only city agency that was permitted to own land outside city limits. Thrilled by the trans-Atlantic flight of Charles Lindbergh, which stoked interest in flying, the legislature passed a bill in 1927 that enabled St. Paul, Minneapolis and Duluth to use bonding authority to establish airports.

Minneapolis immediately used the maximum allowed bonding authority of $150,000 to purchase roughly three hundred acres of the airport land. Over the next sixteen years, the park board developed the airport into a first-class facility, the premier airport in the northwest. Through city bonds, and later through federal relief agency funds, the park board spent nearly $4 million developing and expanding the land.

The park board eventually turned over the six-hundred-acre airport to the Metropolitan Airport

A crowd gathers at the Minneapolis Municipal Airport to greet Charles Lindbergh after his trans-Atlantic flight in 1927. Part of the one-mile oval speedway is visible at the top of the photo. The airport used the grass infield of the former racetrack as its runway. The park board owned and developed the airport from 1927 until it was taken over by the Metropolitan Airport Commission in 1946. (Minnesota Historical Society)

The cover of the 1930 annual report of the park board celebrated the park board's ownership and development of the Minneapolis airport. (Minneapolis Park and Recreation Board)

Commission when it was created by the legislature in 1946. The legislature and the park board acknowledged that the operation of a modern airport was really beyond the scope of a municipal park authority. But the Minneapolis park board still owns the land under the heart of the airport.

While the creation and operation of a world-class airport has little bearing on the park system of Minneapolis today, it stands as a monument to the abilities and "can do" spirit of Theodore Wirth and his engineers.

Despite Wirth's tremendous influence on the creation and development of so much of the Minneapolis park system, it was in the airport project that his greatest skills were most clearly evident. He was a master of organization and detail. As much as he was at his core a gardener and as much as he advocated the creation of play areas in Minneapolis parks, he thrived especially on the details and precision of grading, filling and paving.

When Wirth arrived in Minneapolis in 1906, he wanted most of all to beautify parks, to shape the land, to the build the parkways, to improve the vistas. Minneapolis parks were, to his mind, a canvas quite large enough on which to paint his masterpiece. He didn't need more land to show what he could do; there was already enough of that. Not knowing when he arrived of the tremendous pent-up demand for more parks, and the long history of proposals to acquire this lake, that stream, or some other wooded hillside, he must have been taken aback at first. His dreams and plans for peninsulas in Lake Harriet, bays in Lake Calhoun, and a Spring Lake twice as large were never realized. Even many of his early plans for park layouts were not acted upon. His plan for a beautiful concourse at the top of Kenwood Park overlooking Lake of the Isles in the distance, for instance, never was used. Neither were his plans for amphitheaters at Washburn Fair Oaks and Riverside Park.

Wirth's immense skill was in having thousands of new acres of land and water thrown at him and molding them into the park system that park founders had dreamed of. It could never have happened without him. Build us a lake where a swamp stands. Carve us a parkway where a prairie lies. Turn that crumbling racetrack into a first-class airport. Wedge a golf course into that park. Give us a plan! He not only provided plans for the acres of land acquired, some against his better judgment, but he provided options a, b and c.

Wirth is often remembered for his rose garden and the floral displays he loved so much. They were great—but a dozen other men could have built them. Wirth is often praised for building playgrounds. It was the right thing to do—but dozens of other cities were doing the same, many in advance of Minneapolis. But who could have transformed the land as he did, making it usable, accessible and beautiful according to the tastes of his time? No one.

From 1906 to 1930 Minneapolis parks nearly tripled in size, but that was not Wirth's doing. What he did was pull all that land together and whip it into shape. More than anything else he was Theodore Wirth, Earth Mover.

The last park acquisition of this period of tremendous growth was an important one. In 1930, the park board completed acquisition of the banks of Minnehaha Creek west from Lake Harriet to Zenith Avenue, where today the creek emerges from private lawns to public wooded banks.

After that purchase, the Depression began, and budgets for land acquisition and improvement dwindled to nothing. The great days of park expansion were done. In subsequent years, acres would be added, but the challenges of park management would change. Gone were the days when park acreage was increased by a lake here, a golf course there, or a two-mile parkway on the other side of town.

Chapter Fifteen

Earth Mover

In Theodore Wirth's pivotal recommendations to the park board on March 5, 1906, he singled out only one park property for specific improvement: Lake of the Isles. Improvements there, which began with an innocuous recommendation for straightening some "dangerous curves" in the parkway, set the precedent for millions of dollars the park board would spend in the next three decades "improving" lakes and lakeshores.

In his superintendent's report at the end of his first year, Wirth wrote, "If not for the low swampy shore and shallow water in some places, [Lake of the Isles] would hardly have to be included in this improvement list." But because of those defects, "a dredge is needed from a sanitary standpoint more urgently than elsewhere," Wirth wrote.

In the next five years, dredging and filling at Lake of the Isles would transform 100 acres of shallow water, 67 acres of swamp and 33 acres of dry land into 120 acres of water and 80 acres of dry land. Land was made dry enough to drive on, and water deep enough to sail on, in MaryLynn Pulscher's words. It would become Wirth's signature.

In his memoirs published in 1945 Wirth wrote of his work at Lake of the Isles, "The transformation of those formerly mosquito-infested, malaria-breeding swamplands into clear, deep water surrounded by park lands of outstanding beauty naturally had beneficial results upon the city as a whole and *was a strong inducement for like operations in other areas offering similar opportunities for improvement*" (emphasis added). Wirth cited a real estate man of the time saying that lots facing the lake appreciated from 100 percent to 500 percent due to the dredging and filling operation.

Lake of the Isles exhibited the same strong pull on Wirth that it had on Charles Loring two decades earlier. Just as Loring had focused the board's

> The State Bird. Wirth's dredging and filling of marshes and wetlands did not eradicate mosquitoes, of course. Many references were made in early park history to "malarial swamps" before anyone knew that Minnesota mosquitoes, ferocious as they were, didn't carry the disease. In 1916, at the request of the Real Estate Board, the park board approved a mosquito-control campaign in parks. After a month, and an expenditure of $100, the board admitted that the problem was more extensive and expensive than it had anticipated and voted to discontinue the program. A metropolitan Mosquito Control District, which includes Minneapolis and still exists, was not created until 1958.

attention on the chain of lakes through his determination to acquire Lake of the Isles as a park, so Wirth's determination to remake the lake shifted the board's focus for many years to improving its lakes and surrounding shores.

Just as Loring had, Wirth turned his attention to Lake of the Isles after first focusing on Lake Harriet. Wirth's focus on Lake of the Isles came after his plans for improving Lake Harriet met with little enthusiasm. In his first annual report, Wirth provided detailed plans for altering the shoreline of Lake Harriet, which he found "regular and monotonous." To improve the lake's appeal he suggested building a peninsula on its western shore, a suggestion he would repeat several times. That plan attracted few supporters. Another plan submitted by Wirth in his first year would have doubled the size of Spring Lake, a swampy body of water on the western end of The Parade near downtown. That plan too was laid aside. So he turned to Lake of the Isles.

In ensuing years Wirth would take his success at Lake of the Isles to the other lakes in the system, already owned or newly acquired. By the end of his tenure there was hardly a marsh or bog left in the city. Lake of the Isles would remain, however, the only lake that got bigger. In every other instance, the lakes would be deepened, but their surface area reduced. The only other additions of water surface area came from the damming of Shingle Creek in 1909 shortly after the purchase of Camden Park (now Webber Park) to create a pond for swimming and skating, and the widening of the Mississippi River after completion of the Ford Dam. One Wirth proposed, the other he didn't.

Dredging was not new to the parks when Wirth arrived. Loring oversaw Horace Cleveland's plan to dredge part of the pond in Loring Park in the first year of the park board's existence. Then, under William Berry's supervision, the park board had dredged the east shore and northern arm of Lake of the Isles, creating nearly five acres of new land from 1889 to 1893. When the dredge was finished at Lake of the Isles, it was sent to Powderhorn Lake, where intermittent dredging occurred for the next ten years. (The dredge still sat there rusting when Wirth arrived.)

One of Wirth's favorite words in describing needed improvement projects was "unsightly." It applied equally in Wirth's mind to unkempt gardens, ramshackle facilities, steep slopes and swamps. For swampland, Wirth usually added "unsanitary" to the description.

Wirth's first concern, always, was with appearances. And he wasn't alone. It was the prevailing attitude of the day. Park land wasn't acquired to look like prairie or forest, and certainly not swamp. It was to be beautified.

In a prelude to Wirth's initial recommendations to the board in

The Camden Lagoon was created by damming Shingle Creek in 1907 shortly after the park was acquired. The John Deere Webber baths were created by diverting water from the lagoon into the pool behind the gray wall in this photo on a 1915 postcard. The money to construct the baths and the park building, which also housed a branch of the library, was donated by Charles and Mary Webber in memory of their son. (Minnesota Historical Society)

1906, he urged that all money previously budgeted for improvements be shifted into maintenance for the first year. To Wirth, and many others, the appearance of the parks after years of neglect was disgraceful. And a good bit of his success in earning the trust of the board and the public was making the parks more attractive. His first-year makeovers of Loring Park and the entrance to Minnehaha Park were crowd pleasers.

At the time, swamps were considered neither pleasing to look at nor very useful. And beyond beautiful, parks had to be useful to please Wirth. Reclaimed land and deepened water had an objective beyond making them pretty; they made parks more usable. This was long before any understanding of wetlands as filters for water running into lakes or purifiers for groundwater. Land wasn't overbuilt, so runoff to lakes wasn't an issue. Instead of worrying about land being overbuilt or overpaved, the concern was with land that was underbuilt.

Another way to make parks usable, of course, was to pave the roads and provide playing areas. Land that wasn't being reclaimed from swamp was being paved or converted to playing spaces. With the advent of automobiles, the old, narrow dirt parkways were no longer functional. They had to be widened, paved, and edged with curbs and sidewalks, in addition to being beautified with plantings of grass, trees and shrubs.

Wirth noted in his first report in 1906 that the most important improvement of the year was the construction of a permanent roadway on West River Road. He was an ardent supporter of permanence in everything he did, with the primary goal being to reduce maintenance costs. He was a student of road finishing and paving and oiling methods. The greatest single expenditure in his tenure as superintendent was not the dredging and filling of lakes and lakeshore, expensive as that was, but the grading and paving of parkways.

Finally, the park board devoted considerable attention to preparing parks for use as play fields. Although Wirth always championed playing spaces in parks, they received far less resources from the board during his tenure than other improvements.

But the type of land that was acquired for many neighborhood parks was certainly a factor in how—and how fast—playgrounds were developed. Many prospective parks and playgrounds were on low land that required filling. Jackson Square had been a pond. Bryant Square in south Minneapolis was so low that the neighborhood tried to bring it up to grade by dumping garbage there for a time. Linden Hills, Lynnhurst and Pershing in southwest Minneapolis were all on land that had to be drained or filled. To drain Linden Hills Park, Wirth constructed a 3,600-foot pipeline to Lake Calhoun. The city council paid part of the cost of that pipeline in order to drain the entire neighborhood.

The Webber Pool, built in 1908, was the only park board swimming facility other than the lakes until the 1960s. (Minneapolis Park and Recreation Board)

The other challenge was that athletic fields had to be level. Considerable grading was required to make them so. The amount of grading needed to create playing fields is evident today at many fields where steep banks surround playing fields or the fields are below street level. Bryant, Audubon, Jackson, Riverside, Keewaydin and Phelps are a few such fields that were created in the early years of park sculpting.

All of this earthmoving was accomplished during what remains the most complex period in park board history. Land was still being acquired in lots large and small throughout the city, lakes were being shaped and linked, parkways built and playgrounds created. At the same time, the park board was addressing constantly changing financing methods, complicated in part by Minneapolis finally adopting a city charter in 1920. The city charter was adopted after decades of attempts to write a Home Rule Charter that would remove most decision-making from the hands of the legislature. However, the board continued to rely on its status as a body created by the legislature to seek authority for some of its revenues.

In addition, the very notion of recreation continued to change—and expand. One reason Wirth is revered in park history, and given such wide credit for the Minneapolis park system that exists today, is that he had to manage so many factors in the growth of that system. He may not have fathered the park system, but he did raise it through the difficult, often exasperating years of its adolescence. Parks were growing fast and not quite sure what they would become.

Wirth's first dredging operation got off to a rocky start. The company hired to dredge the north arm of Lake of the Isles and extend the lake to the northwest quit dredging by the end of the summer of 1907. Even Wirth admitted that the dredging was more complicated than he had anticipated. A series of dikes had to be built on land to hold the lake-bottom muck until it dried out. With a new contractor hired for the next summer, the shape of Minneapolis lakes changed forever. For the next eleven years dredges would be continually at work somewhere in the park system.

The dredges remained at Lake of the Isles for five years. By the time they were done, the lake was deepened to an average depth of eight feet, and nearly fifty acres of dry land was created. A fifty-foot channel was dug between the north island and the shore to be sure it would remain an island, and the north island also doubled in size. Enough earth was moved to raise the level of the parkway around the lake between one and eleven feet. The total cost of the improvements to Lake of the Isles over those years was nearly $400,000.

When dredging at Lake of the Isles was nearing completion in 1911, the dredges moved across the lake to the southern shore to begin a project that had been suggested by Loring but had gained momentum in 1905. The dredges would create a channel between Isles and Lake Calhoun and later dig through the wetlands from Isles to Cedar Lake.

The linking of Lake of the Isles and Lake Calhoun was completed in July 1911. A week of festivities celebrated the grand achievement. A huge crowd of people witnessed the opening of the channel. The channel was progress, the channel was the future. Festivities included concerts in many parks, a historical pageant at Loring Park, and fireworks at Lake Harriet. A parade of decorated canoes followed the *Maid of the Isles* launch, carrying board members and dignitaries on its inaugural voyage through the channel.

The channel was much more modest than Wirth had originally proposed. Instead of the two lagoons Wirth proposed, one a boat harbor, only one was created. In the end, the lagoon was larger than planned due to the need for more fill to construct the approaches for the four bridges over the channel. Bridges presented the biggest challenge to Wirth in the lake-linking project. Railroad and street bridges had to be built—and built to suit Wirth's taste.

The great success of the Lake of the Isles work

and the channel led to immediate work on the other lakes in the chain. The dredges remained on Lake Calhoun for the next three years, working mainly on the east and north shores. On the east shore, the parkway was raised, and on the north shore dredges prepared the beach for the Calhoun Bath House that was built in 1912. Material from the Calhoun dredging was also used to raise the level of Dean Parkway, which was such low land that it had once been considered the best location for a channel to connect Isles with Calhoun.

Dredging also began at Cedar Lake in 1912, and with dredging there came a second lake link: a channel though the wetlands between Cedar and Isles that was named Kenilworth Lagoon. Most of the parkway around Cedar Lake was eventually built on earth dredged from the lake.

Wirth had more land to work with than the park board had originally acquired along the shore because when Cedar was linked to Lake of the Isles, its level dropped five feet. What was once an island near the western shore became a peninsula. Fill from the lake not only built up the roadway, but filled in much of the wetland near the southwest shore. Dredging on the lake continued until 1917 when Cedar Lake and Brownie Lake were also linked by a canal that could be navigated by rowboat. The level of Brownie Lake also dropped five feet when it was linked.

Before dredging was completed at either Calhoun or Cedar, another far bigger dredging project began. For seven years after its acquisition in 1907, Lake Nokomis had remained mostly in its natural state. In 1911, as the new Calhoun Bath House was being built, part of the old bathhouse was moved to the north shore of Lake Nokomis, which was accessible from Minnehaha Parkway. Wirth's original plans for a bathhouse on the east shore and a large island near the western shore were altered for a more modest plan with no island and the west shore designated as a beach. A beach in that location was more accessible to those who rode the streetcar out Cedar Avenue from town.

Over five years, from 1914 to 1918, Lake Nokomis was reduced in size from three hundred acres to two hundred acres, and its shallow waters were dredged to a depth of at least twelve feet. In several places where the dredges encountered sand pockets on the lake bottom, the sand was transported to the planned beach, and the lake reached depths of fifteen feet. The material dredged from the lake bottom was used to fill the seventy acres of swampy farmland at the northwest corner of the lake, which are now softball and soccer fields. Wirth proposed rerouting Cedar Avenue around the southwest bay of the lake to avoid the necessity of the bridge over the lake, but the Richfield City Council denied permission to do that. That section of Richfield was annexed by Minneapolis several years later.

The park board spent more than $250,000 on dredging alone at Nokomis over those five years. With

The linking of Lake Calhoun and Lake of the Isles by a channel in 1911 led to a weeklong celebration in July of that year. Here canoes pass under the new Lake Street bridge over the channel. (Minneapolis Park and Recreation Board)

A dredge at work creating a shoreline for Lake Nokomis in 1915. (Minneapolis Park and Recreation Board)

After the fill settled west of Lake Nokomis, the work of grading the land for playing fields began in 1921. (Charles J. Hibbard, Minnesota Historical Society)

additional improvements costing another $600,000 between 1914 and 1924, the park board spent $860,000 improving its $63,000 purchase, making it the most expensive of any lake makeover in park board history. Nearly the total cost of those improvements was assessed against property in the area.

While Lake Nokomis was getting its makeover, dredges were also put to work at Wirth Lake in 1916 and 1917. The goal there was not to reshape the lake, but to create a sandy beach on the eastern shore. The final layer of fine sand for the beach was not found at the lake bottom but was carted in. A section of the old Calhoun bathhouse was placed on the new beach of Wirth Lake.

As dredging was just getting started at Nokomis in 1914, the park board followed Wirth's recommendation to create another usable chunk of land from shallow water and marsh miles to the north. Wirth noted that the new storm sewer being installed in northeast Minneapolis made it unlikely that Sandy Lake in Columbia Park would ever regain its status as a real lake. Wirth claimed that Sandy Lake was really only a lake in wet years when runoff from surrounding land filled it. With the new storm sewer to drain city streets, that wouldn't happen anymore.

The drained lake eventually provided much of the land for Columbia Golf Course. Board president Burton Kingsley suggested in 1926 that perhaps the area could be restored to the boating and fishing lake he remembered from his childhood if a deep well were dug there, as Wirth had recently done to create Longfellow Lagoon above Minnehaha Falls.

A more ambitious dredging project than even Lake Nokomis was authorized before Nokomis was finished, but lawsuits stopped it. Although the suits were eventually decided in the park board's favor, court challenges delayed the project until the park board could no longer afford it.

In 1916, the park board had approved a plan first submitted by the Lake Harriet Commercial Club in 1910 to create an extensive "South Bay" on Lake Calhoun. The plan was to dredge the swampland from Lake Calhoun south to Forty-second Street between Upton and Xerxes. The idea of a waterway through the area had first been broached by Wirth in a set of alternatives the board requested in 1907 when considering the feasibility of linking Lake Calhoun with Lake Harriet. Although Wirth's preferred plan was to create a channel and lock adjacent to Lakewood Cemetery to navigate the seven-foot drop between the two lakes, he had presented the option of a canal and lock through Linden Hills and Dell Park (Thomas Avenue) to enter Lake Harriet at Beard's Plaisance. None of the plans was considered feasible.

When the city council refused a request from the neighborhood to fill the wetland between Xerxes and Upton, the group of merchants then went to the park board to ask that the land be dredged, rather than filled. The issue created division within the board as no other plan of that era.

A special committee appointed to investigate the issue in 1916 approved the project over the objections of an unusual minority report written by David Jones and Francis Gross. Gross, who would serve as park board president in the 1930s and 1940s, opposed the plan because it would give more park land to the southwestern lake district that was already receiving a disproportionate share of the board's attention and resources. Proponents of the plan argued that by assessing the improvements—estimated in 1914 to cost $450,000—to the neighborhood, more park land could be acquired at no cost to the city. The park board approved the plan in 1916 and again in 1917.

Some residents of the neighborhood, particularly those who lived near Lake Calhoun, however, were not willing to pay assessments for a lagoon and its encircling parkway on top of assessments for improving William Berry Park and building a parkway along the south and west shores of Calhoun. Many of those property owners had already been assessed for other lake district improvements. They'd had enough.

The lawsuits they filed over the right of the park board to assess those costs were finally decided in the park board's favor in 1922. By that time, however, the park board already had so many other improvement projects that it never took up the issue of "South Bay" again. Fixing the existing shores of Lake Calhoun was a big enough project.

The park board embarked on a three-year plan in 1923 to dredge the south and west shores of Calhoun and build a parkway there. The plan entailed dredging the lake near the shore to a navigable depth and using the fill to raise William Berry Park and the wetlands at the southwest corner of the lake. The low lands at the northwest corner of the lake were also brought up to dry-land standards, even though Wirth had once proposed dredging a boat harbor there.

The northern half of Powderhorn Lake, at left, was filled in 1925, and the southern half dredged. The filled land was used for playing fields. (Minnesota Historical Society)

By 1925 dredging and filling created another thirty-five acres of land out of shallow lake. The entire parkway on the south and west shores of Lake Calhoun was built on dredged soil. The remaking of the lakeshore and the wetlands were not universally applauded. Criticism of dredging and filling prompted William Bovey, the park board president in 1924, to defend the action in his annual report. "No one will deny that areas of swamp meadows and shallow water command great natural beauty," he wrote, "but it is also self-evident that such natural conditions cannot be maintained on park properties within residential districts." From the standpoint of "sanitation and utility," Bovey argued, the improvements were worth many times the cost of the transformation. The cost of dredging on the south and west shores of Calhoun was $185,000 over three years.

The final major dredging project of this period of lake reshaping took place at Powderhorn Lake in south Minneapolis. Noting that the lake level had dropped a few feet, Wirth recommended filling the northern half of the lake to create playing fields. In 1924 and 1925, the southern part of the lake was deepened, and the northern half filled.

The other filling project recommended by Wirth in these final years of land shaping was the creation of a meadow out of the marsh at the north end of Lake Harriet, which is now the Roberts Bird Sanctuary. With so many other major improvement projects at the time, however, the board didn't want another. Other than the bogs and swamps in Wirth Park and around Spring Lake, this was the only wetland of the time that was allowed to remain in its natural state.

The only other wetland still in the board's possession by then had remained wet only because of assessment burdens. Lake Hiawatha (still Rice Lake at the time) was not developed because that region of the city was still paying off the half-million-dollar assessment to acquire the lake and surrounding land in 1923—in addition to assessments for the extensive improvements at Lake Nokomis. Improvement of Lake Hiawatha was finally begun in 1929. In the next three years, the park board transformed another lake and its shoreline.

Wirth's original plan for Lake Hiawatha, like his first plan for Lake Nokomis, included an island, but once again the island was scrapped from the final plan. His initial plan to dredge the lake to a depth of ten feet was revised to create a uniform depth of fourteen feet, a depth that Wirth claimed was ideal and worth the additional expense. The dredged material was used to fill the swampy edges of the lake, including the rice fields that gave the lake its name, as well as to construct mounds along the western shore to make a more interesting golf course. When Hiawatha improvements were begun, the western half of the park had already been designated as a golf course.

By the time Lake Hiawatha's transformation was completed in 1931, Minneapolis's waterways were essentially in the form in which they have remained. The only two exceptions were projects made possible by President Roosevelt's New Deal relief programs during the 1930s. At that time Wirth's plans for creating lagoons out of the marshes along Bassett's Creek in Wirth Park were completed by the Civilian Conservation Corps. In addition, Pearl Lake was also filled with material generated by airport improvement projects funded primarily by another federal government program.

The only other body of water partially acquired by the park board of the time, Diamond Lake, would eventually be left in its natural state. It was

> A man-made waterfall, the Loring Cascade, was built on the shore of Wirth Lake in 1918. A gift from Charles Loring, the forty-foot cascade used water pumped from the lake. The design could not withstand Minnesota's climate extremes, however, and was dismantled in the 1940s.

the only water surface in Minneapolis other than Lake Harriet, little Spring Lake, and Birch Pond in Wirth Park that did not undergo a radical redesign.

Wirth was not responsible for the addition to the park system of any of the lakes acquired during his tenure, but he was responsible for the eventual shape of most lakes and the landscapes around them. To Wirth belongs the credit for making Minneapolis lakes so accessible to public use and for the recreational spaces and parkways on their widened shores. Without his monumental undertaking in shaping lakes, Minneapolis's lakes would be quite different recreational resources than they are today.

In the decades since, perception of lakes and wetlands has changed considerably. In the 1990s, the park board began to restore some lakeside wetlands that were originally filled. The southwest corners of Lake Calhoun, Lake Nokomis and Cedar Lake were all re-created as wetlands in an attempt to improve water quality in the lakes. With residential and commercial development in each area, and the paving of streets, polluted surface water running into the lakes became an issue that did not exist in Wirth's day. There is also a greater appreciation today for the biodiversity and floodwater storage provided by wetlands.

Over the time the dredges were at work in Minneapolis park waters—1908 to 1931— they handled more than six million cubic yards of material. That's enough muck and gravel to fill five football fields to the height of the IDS Center in downtown Minneapolis. However you picture it, Wirth moved a lot of earth around the city's lakes.

When Wirth arrived in Minneapolis, the park board owned thirty-one miles of parkway, none of them paved, although a few sections had been covered with gravel. By 1930, it owned more than fifty-five miles of parkway, and much of it was paved or ready to be paved.

Wirth's concern with the quality and safety of the parkway around Lake of the Isles is what led him to first look at improvements to that park property. It was an interest that led to the transformation of the lakeshore there and subsequently the shores of nearly every other lake in the city. Had Wirth not been so interested in what he considered proper road construction around Lake of the Isles, the shape of Minneapolis lakes might be dramatically different today.

Essentially, the first paving of roads followed the dredging of lakes, which created the fill needed for parkway construction. Wirth's first experiment in modern paving was the short section of parkway— The Mall—from Hennepin Avenue to the lagoon between Lake Calhoun and Lake of the Isles. Residents of the neighborhood had first proposed the short

---

The Engineers. A full-time engineer was among Wirth's first hires in 1906. At that time, Frank Nutter Jr. took over the work his father had performed as a contractor since 1883. A. C. Godward, who first worked in the department in 1906 while a student, became head of the division in 1911. Godward served until 1922 when he moved to the newly created city planning commission. Opponents of improvement projects at the time referred to Godward and Wirth as "Godless and Worthless." Godward was succeeded by his assistant, A. E. Berthe. The importance of the engineering function in those days of park building was illustrated by the rise of two young engineers on the park staff to positions of prominence. Charles Doell, who first worked on the engineering staff while a student at the University of Minnesota, was promoted to assistant secretary to the board in 1922 and eventually became superintendent in 1945. Harold Lathrop rose through the ranks of the engineering staff until he became the director of Minnesota State Parks.

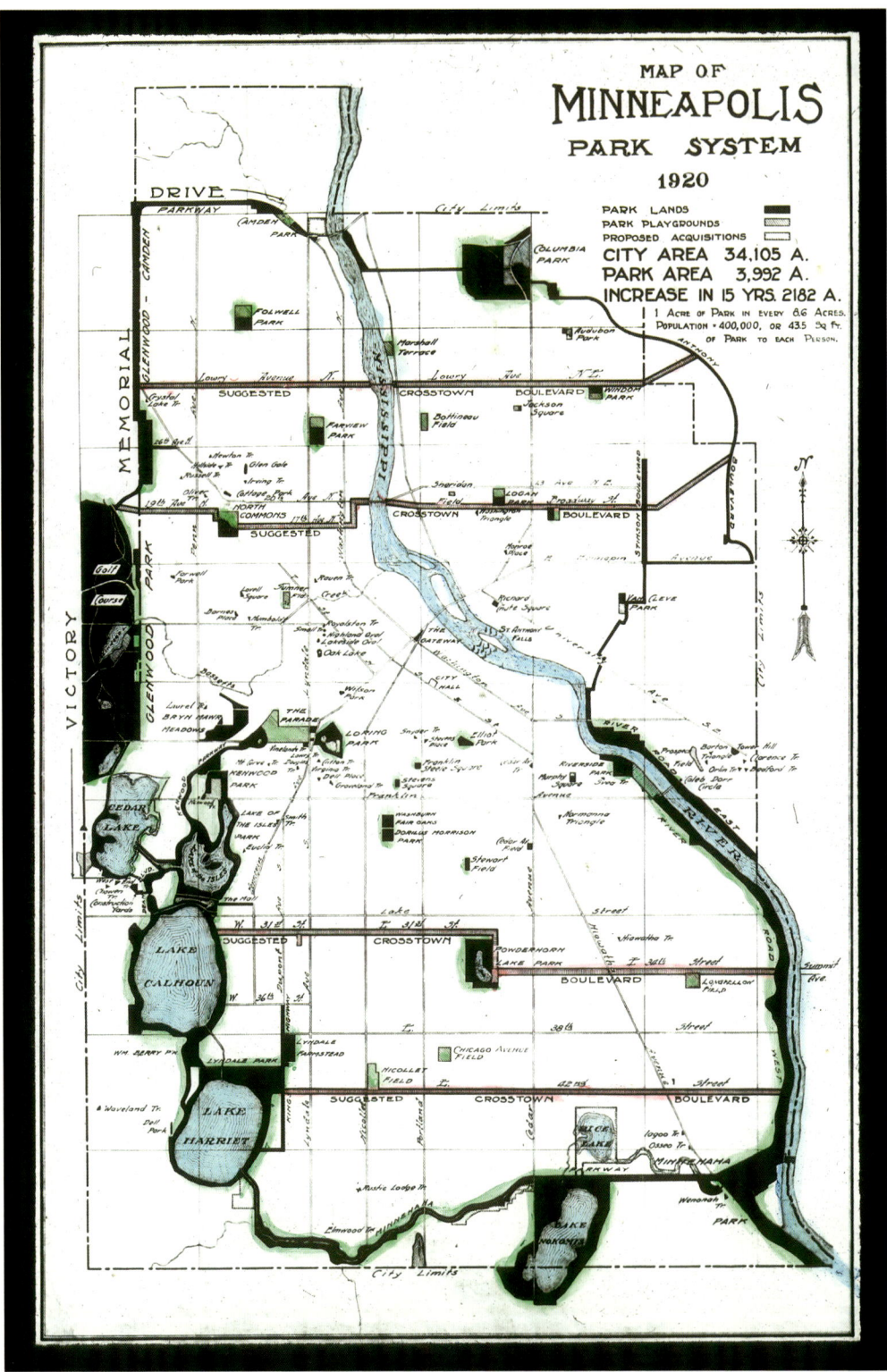

This 1920 map shows the growth of the park system since 1905 but also shows Theodore Wirth's suggestions for east-west parkways. He not only resurrected the old plan for a parkway across Thirty-fourth Street in south Minneapolis—to relieve traffic congestion on Lake Street—but added three more possibilities. None was implemented. (Minneapolis Park and Recreation Board)

parkway after the lakes were linked. There, in 1913, Wirth first used a two-course pavement, macadam over concrete. With the success of that roadway, the method was used on other sections of parkway: first the east drive of Lake Calhoun and King's Highway, then Dean Parkway.

Up to that point, the application of Wirth's growing expertise in paving methods and road construction was confined primarily to parkways beside water. The exception was Glenwood (Wirth) Park, where the addition of five hundred acres of park land required the creation of a road through the park. This was the first instance of Wirth designing the layout of a new parkway and building it from scratch. Due to a shortage of laborers at the time, Wirth hired a crew of forty Hungarian railroad laborers to do the work. They moved dirt along the roadway where grading or filling was required on railroad cars that traveled a temporary track installed for construction.

The experience of building that section of road north to Nineteenth Street North (Golden Valley Road) prepared Wirth for tackling the northern sections of the Grand Rounds. In 1917, Wirth presented his first plans for the construction of the Glenwood-Camden Parkway, which later was named Victory Memorial Parkway. The straight road north from Lowry Avenue, which passed through farmland that Wirth called "undeveloped and unattractive," was given a special treatment to dress it up. The parkway was flanked by wide stretches of open lawn and trees, with residential streets on the periphery.

The distinctive appeal of the parkway and its name, Victory Memorial Drive, grew out of Charles Loring's desire to create a memorial to American soldiers. In 1908, Loring commissioned Minneapolis architect William Gray Purcell to create a design for a veterans memorial arch. Purcell's files contain sketches for that memorial, which was never built, but there is no indication of where Loring intended to put it. According to Folwell, Loring later devised a plan for planting trees in honor of fallen soldiers and credits Wirth with suggesting that the trees be planted along the three-mile north-south section of

Victory Memorial Drive under construction in 1920. The parkway was an important step in achieving Cleveland and Folwell's vision of a "Grand Rounds" of parkways encircling the city. (Minnesota Historical Society)

Charles Loring and William Folwell in their eighties around 1915. It is appropriate that in one of the only photos of the two men together, they were photographed with young children. (Minnesota Historical Society)

the new parkway, instead of being scattered along other parkways.

Loring liked the idea and in 1919, shortly after World War I ended, suggested the name for the drive and donated the trees and $50,000 for a trust fund to provide for their perpetual care. It would be his last gift to the city. Wirth selected a special variety of Loring's favorite tree, the elm, to be planted along the new drive. The elms were planted along the drive in time for a grand dedication ceremony in 1921.

Then eighty-seven years old, Loring was too frail to attend the dedication ceremony, but earlier in the day William Folwell accompanied Loring on a drive over the newest parkway. As the two park visionaries viewed together the twelve hundred young elms that were growing tributes to fallen soldiers, they must have surely realized that this new parkway, even so adorned, was a tribute to them, too.

Loring died the next spring in his eighty-ninth year. He was buried in Lakewood Cemetery. His eulogist, Rev. Marion Shutter, said of Loring that "few men have been so loved and honored; none have more deserved such love and honor." Of Loring's dreams for Minneapolis's parks, Shutter said, "No longer a vision in the clouds, his work stands fair and firm upon the earth." The epitaph on Loring's granite memorial reads simply, "Father of the Parks."

The Loring family burial plot lies between those of Loring's friends, George Brackett and Loren Fletcher. A stone's throw away in the cemetery is a simpler monument that says only "Folwell." William Folwell died seven years after Loring, in 1929, at the age of ninety-six, shortly after completing a tribute to Loring for the last volume of his book *A History of Minnesota*.

Folwell had served on a special committee of the park board to write a tribute to Loring upon his death. That tribute concluded most succinctly, "He was a friend to us all." Those apt words apply to their author, Folwell, as well. Charles Loring and William Folwell, intimate friends themselves for fifty years: friends to us all. Friends to our grandparents as they stroll in steps no longer bold along a parkway. Friends to our sons as they splash carefree in the water of a city lake or pool. Friends to our daughters as they revel in play on city fields. Friends to our sisters rejuvenated by reflection on the emerald banks of the great river. Friends to our brothers who find solace under towering tress. Friends, as well, to city leaders of today and tomorrow to whom we entrust the preservation of their legacy. Friends to us all.

For the dedication of Victory Memorial Drive, white wood crosses and stars were placed beside many of the trees on the drive along with the names of soldiers who had died in war. Later in 1921, the parkway was visited by both General John Pershing and Field Marshal Ferdinand Foch, the commanders respectively of American and allied forces in World War I, who expressed their appreciation and admiration for the tribute. The original wood flagpole located at the northwest corner of the drive was replaced in 1923 by the American Legion with a bronze flag pole set in an ornamental base.

With the completion of Victory Memorial Drive in 1921, Wirth turned his attention to the last stage of the Grand Rounds to be completed: St. Anthony Boulevard from Webber Park to Stinson Boulevard. In the fall of 1924 the commercial clubs of northeast and southeast Minneapolis sponsored dedication festivities that marked the formal opening of the parkway across the northern neighborhoods of the city, skirting the southern edge of Columbia Park, extending through a portion of St. Anthony Village, reentering the city and heading south near today's Industrial Boulevard to East Hennepin Avenue.

The park board's extension of St. Anthony Boulevard outside the northeastern city limits was induced by the offer of Armour & Company in 1913 of free land and payment of construction costs through its land. When the parkway was finally completed in the mid-1920s, the company offered very favorable terms to the park board for the acquisition of much of the rest of the company's land adjacent to the parkway for the construction of Armour (Francis Gross) golf course. The Armour land was expendable after the company located its meat-packing plant in South St. Paul instead of outside northeast Minneapolis.

The southern part of that route, south of Francis Gross golf course, was abandoned in 1932 when Ridgway Parkway was built to connect St. Anthony Parkway and Stinson Boulevard. The change was made at the request of property owners who owned the land adjacent to the southern part of the boulevard, south of Broadway Road, and wanted the parkway land as a gravel pit. The landowners provided land for a new route and also paid the cost of constructing the new parkway, which was completed in 1935.

With these actions, the board once again demonstrated its sensitivity to business interests in the city, as it had in the sale of Longfellow Field. In both cases, alternative lands were still available, which made the transactions more palatable. Decades later, when park boards faced more demands for park land, few, if any, alternative sites remained.

As the northern boulevards were being finished, so were extensive road building projects in south Minneapolis. In the 1920s, the park board spent more money rebuilding and paving Minnehaha Parkway than it spent constructing either Victory Memorial Drive or St. Anthony Boulevard. The challenges of carving new roads and paving them along the banks of a wandering stream were far greater than cutting a new road across flat farmland. Even where the northern parkways encountered steep slopes, such as at Sunset Hill in the west and Deming Heights in the northeast—which still provide the most spectacular views in the entire park system—the engineering and construction challenges weren't as great as along the creek.

Simultaneously, the south and west shores of Lake Calhoun were filled, and the parkway there was constructed. To top off this era of road building, Lake

Victory Memorial Drive was dedicated in June 1921. This photo was taken at the northwestern corner of the drive, looking east. (Charles J. Hibbard, Minneapolis Park and Recreation Board)

of the Isles Parkway was given a modern pavement as well.

In the space of eight years, from 1917 to 1925, nearly the entire length of the Grand Rounds was either carved from farmland, filled from lake bottom, or completely rebuilt and partially paved. What was left unpaved during this road construction period was finished up mostly by the federal government through relief programs during the Depression.

With the alternating, sometimes overlapping, periods of dredging and road building, park board expenditures on improvements soared. In Wirth's first year as superintendent the park board spent $39,000 on improvements. With dredging at Lake of the Isles and Lake Calhoun and the linking of the lakes, improvement costs soared in 1911 to $213,000. And that was just the beginning.

From 1883 to 1905 the park board had spent a total of just over $1 million improving parks. From 1920 to 1925, when parkway construction was at its peak, the board's *average* annual expenditure on improvements was just under $900,000. The peak was reached in 1924 at $1.3 million.

Most of the costs of improvements were assessed to property owners in the benefited neighborhoods and across the city over ten years. The projects were funded through bonds issued by the city. From 1907 to 1922, the city issued more than $3 million in bonds for park work, with the city paying the interest on those bonds.

The park board was not alone in dramatic spending increases, however. Park board spending was increasing at a slower rate than that of the city government as a whole. Nonetheless, park and city spending were both increasing at a greater rate than the personal income of city residents.

The people of the city had so far been willing to shoulder the tax burden for improvements throughout the city. That willingness was demonstrated in the passage of two city charter amendments in 1921 raising the school board's maximum tax levy from sixteen to twenty-two mills and doubling the library board's tax levy from one mill to two mills. Both measures were approved by an astonishing 90 percent of voters.

But the voters did not approve tax increases indiscriminately. Another charter amendment, which would have raised the city council's tax levy a meager six-tenths of a mill from eleven mills, was defeated. The charter commission that put those measures on the ballot did not recommend an increase in the park board's levy. Despite being overlooked for a levy increase in charter revisions, the park board quietly succeeded in having the legislature increase the playground levy to three-eighths mill in 1923.

As early as 1923, park board president William Bovey began to sound spending alarms that hadn't been heard in more than twenty years. He warned the board that it was "moving too fast" to take on new projects, noting that the board had already approved twenty-two improvements projects that were in progress or to begin shortly at a projected cost of more than $5 million. And this was in addition to the $500,000 acquisition of Lake Hiawatha, which was just being finalized and would soon be assessed.

Although the park board and Wirth complained constantly of the shortage of resources to do all that was needed, even in days of vastly increased spending, Bovey recognized that revenue from levies and bonds was not likely to increase. He warned the board again in 1924 of the need to limit spending. He noted that a great many people of "limited means" in the city were struggling to pay for homes and found the mounting taxes a "real burden."

It was during these years of the board's highest spending that it decided it could not afford bond debt to acquire or improve neighborhood parks and playgrounds. The policy of the board from 1921 was that no future playgrounds or parks would be acquired or developed unless neighborhoods were willing to be assessed the costs.

This amplified the tax burden on the neighborhoods where people of "limited means" lived—if they wanted a neighborhood park. Because assessments for major dredging and road construction were assessed partly on neighboring districts and partly on the city as a whole, every property owner was bearing some of the cost. In essence, residents in neighborhoods without parks were already subsidizing those that did have parks nearby. And if they wanted a neighborhood park too, they had to pay the whole cost, without help from neighborhoods with lakes or parkways, which, as long predicted, had become the most affluent sections of town.

The method of assessing costs to property owners who received some direct benefit, a feature of Minneapolis city government from the time it was created in 1867, worked well in a city that was expanding. Buying land for parks in undeveloped areas was less expensive, so assessments were lower to begin with. In addition, the parks usually attracted development, which raised property values. Rising property values more than compensated owners for the relatively low assessments they paid. In areas that were already developed, however, land was already much more expensive, which meant assessments were higher and the prospects for dramatic appreciation in property values were lower. Neighborhoods that were already developed, including the poorest, received less financial benefit at higher cost.

Much the same was true for improvements. Adding a field house or a playing field to a neighborhood park was not going to increase property values as much as adding a parkway or sculpting a lakeshore.

The inequity of financing parks through local assessments was never fully appreciated by Wirth. He noted with pride that other cities copied the procedure developed in Minneapolis. Projects that were assessed 100 percent within a neighborhood did not have to be approved by the city council or the board of estimate and taxation. He asserted that it was a way for neighborhoods to acquire a park without waiting for funding from the park board, which might never happen. While that was true, the practice effectively ensured that some neighborhoods would not have parks for decades.

By the end of the 1920s, with the economy on the verge of collapse, revenue from assessments dried up as they were paid off, tax revenues dwindled as property valuations dropped, and the era of dredging and paving came to a close.

The large number of park improvements had put the board in a financial position where it could not have done much more for years, whether or not there was a Depression and whether or not there was more that needed doing. The board had no money. By 1935, when Wirth was required to retire at the age of seventy-two, park board spending on improvement projects had dwindled to $52,000 from the $1.3 million of 1924. In the four years from 1936 to 1939 the board spent a *total* of $65,000 on improvements.

By then the New Deal was pumping millions of dollars into the city to provide jobs for the unemployed—and that was the only way the park board could finance any of the improvements remaining, or even maintain the parks it had.

What is most surprising about the Minneapolis park system at the end of that time of explosive capital improvement is that it ended with a recreation system that was, by many measures, substandard. The city had a first-rate park system, but it had not adapted well to the ever-increasing demand for recreational opportunities or facilities. And that was not for lack of public demand or public participation when recreation opportunities were presented. Over the years, Minneapolis's children and adults showed up at the city's playgrounds and athletic fields millions of times. The people's demand for recreation was running far ahead of a park administration focused on physical park features.

The first playground equipment was installed at Logan Park, pictured here, and Riverside Park in 1906. Clifford Booth, physical director of the Minneapolis YMCA, volunteered to provide supervision and instruction, which led to the first recreation programs in the parks. (Minneapolis Park and Recreation Board)

Chapter Sixteen

The Rise of Recreation

The park board's recreation program began with a letter. Addressed to the "Honorable Board of Park Commissioners and Supt. Theodore Wirth," dated June 27, 1906, the letter began: "Dear Sir: I have been interested in the installment of playground apparatus in Logan and Riverside Parks, and have been much impressed with the need of supervision of the attendant children to such. In pursuance of a desire to be of help, I hereby offer to visit these parks as many times during this summer as I may conveniently arrange, to show the children such exercises and plays as could be advantageously used in the time I would be able to devote."

"Believing this may be one way of service, I offer it to you free, either for your approval or refusal," the letter concluded. It was signed, "C. T. Booth, Physical Director, Y.M.C.A." Park board action on the offer is noted at the bottom of the letter: "Proposition accepted with thanks."

Thus began the first program of supervision and instruction of recreational activity in Minneapolis parks. When Wirth presented the letter to the board and recommended that the board accept the offer, Minneapolis joined a recreation movement that was already well under way around the country. That summer, the Playground Association of America (PAA) was founded by, among others, Dr. Luther Gulick, the director of physical training for New York public schools, and Jane Addams, who had created Hull House, a settlement house in Chicago's

Clifford Booth, in suit and tie in the front row, was the first supervisor of recreation for Minneapolis parks. He initially enlisted people who worked for him at the YMCA, where he was director of physical training, to assist him in the parks. Frank Berry, Booth's successor as supervisor of recreation in 1912, is in the second row, far left. Karl Raymond, director of recreation from 1919 to 1946, is in the second row, second from right. (Minneapolis Park and Recreation Board)

Kids lined up to use the pommel horses at Logan Park about 1908. Playground equipment of the time required some gymnastic training and supervision. (Minneapolis Park and Recreation Board)

slums. The honorary president of the PAA was President Theodore Roosevelt, a living symbol of the movement toward vigorous exercise and outdoor activity that was taking hold across the nation.

At the time, forty-one American cities had supervised recreation programs. By 1900 Boston already had a comprehensive playground system with annual playground expenditures of a couple hundred thousand dollars. In 1901, Chicago had sold nearly eight million dollars in bonds to create thirty-one neighborhood recreation parks and more than ten facilities with athletic fields and field houses that would also serve as community centers. President Theodore Roosevelt called it the most significant municipal achievement of its day. In 1905 New York's municipal government took responsibility for providing all residents with recreational facilities. In the same year Los Angeles appointed a superintendent of recreation, followed soon after by Oakland and St. Louis. Cincinnati was on the verge of copying Chicago's success with a million-dollar bond issue of its own to create playgrounds and smaller-scale field houses.

Despite the advocacy of playgrounds by park commissioners and the designation of one of the newest parks, The Parade, as a "recreation park," Minneapolis already trailed many cities in the provision of recreation facilities. The appropriation of $2,500 for playground equipment in March 1906, on Wirth's recommendation, finally got the ball rolling. But it was Booth's offer of free supervision and instruction that really marked the beginning of park-sponsored recreation throughout the city.

Over the next twenty-five years the park board would develop a recreation system and implement programs that served millions of users. More playground parks were acquired, and The Parade became the hub of amateur sports in the city. Participation by men and women in sports leagues organized by the new recreation department mushroomed. Recreation on the city's lakes continued in popularity, reaching a peak in the early 1920s. Winter sports on park land also flourished. By 1930 the park board was operating fifty skating rinks, and hockey rinks were provided at thirty-eight of those facilities, sixteen of them lighted.

By 1930, the park board had also entered the burgeoning field of golf course operations with four eighteen-hole golf courses: Columbia, Wirth, Francis Gross and Meadowbrook. A fifth course, Hiawatha, was under construction.

From a single volunteer instructor at two playgrounds, the recreation department grew to six full-time employees and sixty-two seasonal supervisors at thirty playground locations. Combination warming houses for skaters and recreation shelters were built at most city parks. A phenomenally successful year-round community center that became the center of the city's recreation programs was built at Logan Park in 1912.

Yet despite the success of the Logan Park field house as a recreation facility and community center, it would be the only one built—and it was the only park that offered year-round recreation programs even in 1930. Although the recreation program grew tremendously, parts of the city remained without neighborhood parks, and nearly all lacked facilities. This was especially true in neighborhoods that could not or would not pay assessments required to obtain those services. In a period of significant and expensive improvement to the park system, the spending priorities of the park board and Theodore Wirth were the lakes and parkways, not the recreation system.

Caught by surprise by the demand for new, more-active recreational opportunities, especially from adults, the Minneapolis park system would scramble for years to correct the shortcomings of the recreation system it had built by 1930.

Clifford Booth was more than an interested observer offering to devote idle hours to working with a few kids. The Brooklyn native had come to Minneapolis in 1903 to be the physical director of the YMCA. He was a graduate of the YMCA's Training School in Springfield, Massachusetts, where he was a student and friend of Luther Gulick, the most influential advocate of public recreation in the country. Prior to working for New York schools, Gulick had been an instructor at the Y's Springfield school, where his students had invented both basketball and volleyball in the 1890s.

Booth was not only a recreation professional, but he already commanded a staff of instructors through the Y, some of whom had also been trained at the YMCA school. Booth not only donated his own time but the time of his staff to supervise and instruct children on Minneapolis's new playgrounds. Over the next several years, Y employees comprised the bulk of the volunteers who staffed the playgrounds. Two of those early Y "volunteers," Frank Berry and Karl Raymond, would follow Booth as directors of recreation for Minneapolis parks.

At the conclusion of 1906, Wirth commented positively on the first year of playground equipment and instruction. "A visit to the playgrounds by the unbelieving and skeptical is far superior to arguments in convincing them of the usefulness of the apparatus and benefits derived by the children," he wrote.

In June 1907, the board approved paying Booth three hundred dollars a month, June through August, to supervise the playgrounds. In effect, he was paid for a half-time, year-round position. Over that winter he had selected new playground equipment and supervised its installation at three new playgrounds. In his report on the second summer of activity, Booth claimed that nearly a hundred thousand children had participated in the summer programs at Farview, Powderhorn, Riverside, Logan and Van Cleve playgrounds.

The equipment installed was far more than swings and teeter-totters. It included gymnastic apparatus such as high bars, pommel horses and rings. The

A playground, probably North Commons, about 1910. Early playground equipment was not designed with smaller children in mind. The focus was on gymnastic training. Note the height of even the slide at left center. These were not the "tot lot" playgrounds of today. (Minnesota Historical Society)

instructors worked with children of both sexes by age groups and included a senior group for those seventeen and older. The instruction consisted mostly of gymnastics and calisthenics. Booth himself spent one afternoon and evening each week at each park.

Both Wirth and Booth emphasized from the beginning that proper supervision and instruction was essential to success. For the summer of 1908, the board hired six instructors, mostly schoolteachers, to each work at one park, and two kindergarten teachers for children's activities at four parks. North Commons was added to the list of equipped playgrounds and had the most complete set of apparatus. Children's swings were added to Minnehaha Park, and a merry-go-round, the kind kids push, was installed at Jackson Square.

Organized sports programs were introduced in parks in the summer of 1908. Basketball hoops were installed at five playgrounds, five baseball diamonds, without fences or backstops, were created at The Parade, and football goal posts were also installed there. Basketball leagues for boys, men and girls were created at some parks, as well as an early version of softball. Inter-park games were played in those sports, and in August a citywide track and field meet was held at The Parade featuring the best athletes from each park. The season was topped off by a festival at each playground. Booth estimated total attendance for the summer of five hundred thousand at the six supervised playgrounds.

That estimate did not include those who played or attended baseball games at The Parade. In the first year baseball fields were established at The Parade, Booth set up a system of issuing permits for use of the fields. Two adult baseball leagues, the Commercial League and the Flour City League, used the fields for their games and practices. In addition, many independent teams played there.

In three years, with a total expenditure of only $10,000 on equipment and instructors, the park board had provided services to eye-popping numbers of children and adults. In Booth's report on the year's activities, he cited a "pressing need" for expansion of the playground system and year-round programs.

Wirth responded to that demand by creating designs for a new layout of Logan Park that included a field house for indoor recreation programs and would also serve as a community social center. He recommended similar development at North Commons. He buttressed his presentation with a detailed look at similar facilities in Chicago and presented the case that Minneapolis should spend proportionally to its population on those facilities. He also recommended approval of a request from the city's high school principals to provide competitive fields at The Parade for the high schools.

The challenge in meeting that need for playground and athletic facilities was underscored in Wirth's annual report for 1908. No one, including Wirth, knew where the money should come from to ex-

A girls' basketball game at North Commons in the early 1900s. (Minneapolis Park and Recreation Board)

pand a recreation program. He called on schools and philanthropists to provide the funds, noting that the "park board alone cannot satisfy the needs . . . at least with its present means." He asked for a separate appropriation for playgrounds, using the same argument he had used for planting and caring for street trees.

If Wirth had a shortcoming as superintendent, it may have been his indefatigable energy and his wide-ranging interests. Only a fraction of the plans he submitted for park improvements over the years was implemented, including plans for recreation facilities. He knew dredging, paving, and road and bridge construction in great detail. He was a master of soils and plants. He even became an expert on golf courses and airports.

Wirth always kept before the board a list of projects that was perhaps too long. There were always improvements to be made within the old definition of parks. Perhaps Wirth never made the board focus. Perhaps he gave commissioners too much to digest and never required them to make the hard "either-or" decisions. Playgrounds were always one of many, many options he presented.

Nevertheless, in his own memoir, he devoted more pages to the history of lighting in Minneapolis parks than to the development of playgrounds and summertime athletic programs. The key is perhaps found in the 1909 annual report when, noting once again the huge popularity of the playgrounds and athletic fields, he urged supporters of the movement to "bestir themselves" to find the money to expand the program. It should be done, he would always say, but there was always at least the hint that it should be done outside of *his* budget.

Many others on and off the park board agreed. Playgrounds were being sponsored by others in the city. Unity House Settlement, led by Rev. Marion Shutter, an influential pastor and historian, had a playground program. The Minneapolis Improvement League and the Minneapolis Woman's Club were both active in raising money for playgrounds in the city. Clifford Booth at the YMCA was running a dynamic recreation program. And the city schools were still seen by many, including Wirth, like Folwell before him, as the organization that should take the lead in providing recreational opportunities for children.

Wirth and park commissioners saw their primary duty as creating and caring for parks under the traditional definition of parks as places of beauty and passive recreation. The exceptions, as always, were winter sports, especially skating, and boating and swimming, which had been accepted as the responsibility of the park board for many years.

From the time Booth was engaged as a volunteer and then paid part-time, the park board began to add to its playground inventory and improve those new grounds to provide more complete recreation programs.

North Commons, purchased in 1907, was intended from the beginning to be primarily a recreation park, as was the much smaller (and more expensive) Stevens Square just south of downtown. The other acquisition in 1907, Kenwood Park, was not seen as a playground as much as an addition to the Lake of the Isles park, although Wirth proposed creating playing fields on the flatter ground in the center of the park when it could be properly drained. (The neighborhood's new storm sewers often flooded the field.) The board made a distinction between playground parks and the more scenic parks around the lakes. Plans for Lake Nokomis and Lake Hiawatha included playgrounds and fields from their conception, but Lake of the Isles, Lake Calhoun and Lake Harriet did not have designated play spaces, with the exception of some swings at Lake Harriet near the pavilion. The cost of the three parks purchased in 1907 reveals property values at the time in the three sections of town: North Commons was purchased for roughly $2,000 an acre, Kenwood Park for nearly $5,000 an acre, and Stevens Square, in a more densely populated neighborhood, cost nearly $17,000 an acre.

A combination shelter and warming house was built beside Powderhorn Lake in 1908, the first of a series of new buildings constructed for recreational purposes. But like shelters built at North Commons, Jackson Square and Van Cleve parks in 1910, it was little more than a warming house for skaters and a bathroom.

Yet progress was being made. Tennis courts were added to Stevens Square in 1908 (although they weren't used and were torn out a few years later), playground equipment was added to Camden Park in 1909, and a new playground park was added to the northeast in 1910 when the initial four acres of land were purchased for $5,300 for Audubon Park.

In 1909, Booth's annual report on playgrounds provided a complete list of the city's recreational facilities in addition to the playground equipment that had been set out in eight parks other than The Parade: five volleyball courts, seven basketball courts, thirteen tennis courts and sixteen sandboxes.

The Parade had already become the city's recreation destination by then with seven baseball fields and a football field. The baseball diamonds were essentially just base paths laid out on uneven ground. Most of The Parade was former swamp land that had been filled. The fields didn't have fences, and the first backstops weren't constructed until 1911. (None of the tennis courts had fencing or backstops at the time either.) Still, having a field to play on was enough for the city's baseball players. Booth reported that the fields were used for practice every night and for games on Saturdays. No games were allowed on Sundays—even the playgrounds were closed Sundays—which was a bit inconvenient for most adults, as that was the only day they didn't have to work.

A staff of ten summertime playground instructors continued the work they began in 1908, still supplemented by YMCA staff and volunteers. Instructors were paid less than $100 dollars for the ten-week playground season. The estimated number of participants held steady at about five hundred thousand a year, and a little more than 40 percent were girls. Inter-park play continued in indoor baseball and basketball, including a successful girls' basketball league.

Wirth put great emphasis on expanding instruction at city playgrounds, recommending that hiring more instructors should take precedence even over more playgrounds. Booth advocated both—and higher pay for instructors.

Playgrounds were given a shot in the arm in 1911, when the legislature approved $800,000 in bonds for general use by the park board. Wirth finally had the special appropriation for playgrounds he had urged for several years, although he still wouldn't get the grandstand he envisioned for The Parade. He had pleaded for some wealthy citizen to donate the money for that. Once again, however, playgrounds were in competition with more glamorous and expensive dredging and road-building projects, and only a small part of the money was spent on playgrounds.

The park board did purchase three new park-playgrounds—Sumner Field, Stewart Field and Longfellow Field—which cost about $35,000 combined. The addition of Longfellow Field met park board president Wilbur Decker's plea for more space for baseball, the "Great American game" that was "well calculated to develop alertness and strength of mind and body." It also met Booth's request for

The field house at Logan Park shortly after it was built in 1912. (Charles J. Hibbard, Minnesota Historical Society)

a playground in south Minneapolis somewhere between Powderhorn and Riverside parks. The importance of that new field, the first Longfellow Field, as an athletic ground increased in 1912, when the park board closed The Parade fields for two years to grade and seed them.

In addition to acquiring three new parks, the park board used bond money to upgrade baseball fields and several tennis courts by installing backstops. Goalposts were also added to the field at North Commons, which along with Longfellow, became the city's football fields while The Parade was under construction.

The most important use of the remaining bond money devoted to playgrounds was the construction of a field house at Logan Park in 1912. For a total cost of $40,000, of which $8,000 was contributed by the Library Board, the city built its first athletic field house and community center. For the next four decades, the Logan Park field house would be the immensely successful center of park board recreation programs and play host to numerous community activities, as well as a branch library. For many years the facilities and activities at Logan Park would be highlighted in park board annual reports. The most amazing thing about Logan Park's field house, however, was that it would remain for nearly half a century the only one the park board built.

With a Playground Committee established for the first time in 1911 to oversee operations and improvements, the park board devoted more resources in 1912 to its playgrounds. Bryant Square was finally filled to an acceptable grade, Longfellow Field was graded and fields were laid out, North Commons was graded, and plans were made for improving the new Sumner and Stewart fields. The park board even added two new playgrounds at a cost of $22,000, one next to Sheridan School in northeast Minneapolis (which no longer exists), and the other in southeast Minneapolis, which became Luxton Park.

The board added five new instructors in 1912 to bring the total to fourteen, eight men and six women, who worked at nine playgrounds. Wirth noted at the time that he "fondly hoped" that year-round playgrounds would soon be possible. With the addition of the new parks, Booth estimated attendance at sponsored activities that summer at nearly 750,000. In the seven years after the first playground equipment was installed, the park board added several playing fields and playgrounds, but during that time, it spent a total of $33,229 on equipment, maintenance and supervision.

By that time, Booth had had enough. Whether worn out by holding two nearly full-time jobs or unhappy with low pay from both of them, Booth resigned at the end of 1912 from the parks and the YMCA and became an insurance salesman. One of Booth's assistants at the YMCA and a park instructor, Frank Berry, was chosen to succeed him as supervisor of recreation.

Amidst the new attention to playgrounds and active recreational facilities, traditions endured. Park commissioners accepted without question their duty to provide music and water-related sports, whether on liquid or frozen water.

Swimming got the lion's share of the money because it required facilities. The first expansion of the park board's swimming facilities since the early 1900s, however, cost the park board almost nothing. Shortly after the park board's acquisition of Camden Park in 1908, it received the type of offer Wirth had encouraged when he asked philanthropists to provide money for recreation facilities. Charles and Mary Webber offered to create a pool and recreation center at the new park in memory of their son. The pool, designed by Wirth, used water diverted from Shingle Creek. The pool was an immediate success, and the Webbers later contributed a community center that was also used as a branch library. Camden Park was renamed for the Webbers.

From its opening, the Webber Baths attracted nearly four hundred people a day, mostly boys. In 1910, the pool sponsored its first water carnival, featuring swimming and diving, as well as canoe races and log rolling on the small reservoir of the creek.

Following the acquisition of Wirth Lake, Lake Nokomis and the rest of Lake Calhoun, Wirth developed plans for new beaches and bathhouses at each. As the initial round of dredging at Lake Calhoun was concluding, the board built a new bathhouse on the north shore along Lake Street. The bathhouse, which cost $82,000 to build, featured changing rooms that accommodated 1,250 people. When it opened in 1912, lines of people waiting for a place to change clothes extended for blocks on the hottest days. To accommodate the crowds, the bathhouse was later renovated, replacing the changing rooms with lockers, which used less space. In its first year of operation, the bathhouse earned revenues of $5,000 from the rental of swimming suits.

No swimming facilities were provided at Nokomis during the years of dredging from 1914 to 1919, but in 1920 a new bathhouse was opened on the west shore and was within years the most patronized of all city beaches. A new bathhouse and beach were opened on Wirth Lake in 1919. With the opening of the new beaches, bathhouse attendance was estimated at four hundred thousand for 1920.

In the early days of the Calhoun bathhouse, the board noted a marked increase in the attendance of women and girls, which in the minds of commissioners created a new set of problems. Bathhouse employees were instructed to watch closely for improprieties and "looseness" and to enforce a high degree of moral conduct. The board even considered a rule that would require women's bathing suits to extend at least four to six inches below the knee. Wirth ended that discussion when he asked if he was supposed to take a tape measure onto the beach. The park board further addressed proper conduct on the beach when in 1915 it hired its first policewoman specifically to patrol the beach at Lake Calhoun.

By the mid-1920s, however, the attendance at beaches was influenced by a new trend of arriving at the beach, often by automobile, already in swimming suits. Because of that practice, which enabled many swimmers to use the lakes without going through the bathhouses, it was no longer possible to estimate the number of swimmers in city lakes, but Wirth guessed that the number exceeded one million.

The beach at the Lake Calhoun Bath House in the 1910s. (Minneapolis Park and Recreation Board)

The Lake Calhoun Bath House had no roof. The lockers were installed to accommodate more people than the changing rooms could. (Minneapolis Park and Recreation Board)

By 1930, the bathhouses suffered a sharp drop in usage, especially as more people used unsupervised beaches. From a peak in 1921 of more than three hundred thousand people paying to use the changing rooms and lockers (children were always free), paid attendance at all park board bathhouses had fallen to fifty thousand.

Residents of Minneapolis east of the Mississippi River never had a park swimming facility. Wirth proposed a year-round indoor swimming pool for Columbia Park in 1930, but with the coming of the Depression, those plans were not seriously considered.

The popularity of boating on the lakes followed a similar trajectory. A canoeing craze in the 1910s replaced the bicycle craze of twenty years earlier. Just as the park board had created a checking facility for eight hundred bicycles in the 1890s, Wirth proposed a boathouse at Lake Harriet that would hold more than eight hundred canoes and do away with "unsightly, vari-colored canoes" in racks along the shore.

Proper conduct in canoes was as much a concern of the board as proper conduct on beaches. In 1913, the board approved an ordinance that persons of opposite sex occupying the same portion of a canoe must sit facing each other, not side-by-side.

From a peak in 1922 of more than one thousand canoes licensed on city lakes and twenty thousand canoe rentals that year at Calhoun and Harriet, the park board's boating business on the lakes steadily declined. With the demise of the Lake Harriet pavilion due to a storm in 1925, the park board suffered its first loss from boat rentals. A new pavilion in 1927 brought a brief bounce in boating revenues, but Wirth noted that year that boating was "unable to cope with the lure of the automobile and other recreational attractions."

The park board also continued to devote money to providing winter sports, especially skating, the first recreational activity the park board had sponsored. Winter sports were not only a tradition in Minneapolis parks, but they had the enthusiastic support of Wirth, perhaps reflecting again his own upbringing in Switzerland, a winter sports paradise. Through the 1910s the park board spent more on

Water toboggans, built in 1924, were popular features at Lake Calhoun and Lake Nokomis. (Minnesota Historical Society)

Divers at Lake Calhoun beach in the 1920s. The bathhouse, built in 1912, is visible in the background. (Minnesota Historical Society)

Ski-jumping competitions at Glenwood (Wirth) Park, shown here in the 1920s, were a popular attraction. In 1924 the trials for the U.S. Winter Olympic team were held at Glenwood Park. The success of those trials prompted Theodore Wirth to speculate that Minneapolis could be the site of the 1928 or 1932 Winter Olympics. (Minneapolis Park and Recreation Board)

the maintenance of skating rinks than on combined maintenance and instruction at playgrounds. Most of the early shelters built on playgrounds were designed as warming houses for skaters.

The neighborhood parks designed by Wirth in that era always provided space for dual-use playing fields and skating rinks. With the addition of parks, the number of skating rinks expanded from eight in 1906 to seventeen by 1910. The next year the park board provided eleven skating rinks with warming houses, and eleven more without. It also maintained four hockey rinks. These were still days when park board employees cleared and planed the ice with horse-drawn implements. Skating rinks also provided some revenue to the park board to defray costs; in 1928, when total winter sports participation was estimated at 1.5 million people, the board reported a $5,000 profit from candy and popcorn sales and skate rentals at rinks.

Powderhorn Park still had its speed-skating rink, which remained one of the nation's finest. The park board also maintained toboggan slides—in 1930 it had ten of them, despite Wirth's concerns about liability—as well as tracks for ordinary sleds, and in the 1920s a "dog derby track" for sleds pulled by a single dog.

The city's first park hockey league played on a lighted rink at Lake Harriet in 1914. That league was the beginning of rapid growth in the popularity of hockey on park rinks. In the 1920s Wirth noted that demand for more hockey rinks was one of the "best-supported" in the city, and he called for every skating rink to have a hockey rink.

The Minneapolis winter sports scene also benefited from the expansion in 1908 of Glenwood (Wirth) Park. The hilly terrain of the park provided excellent opportunities for downhill and cross-country skiing. The conversion of much of the park to a golf course and the clearing of fairways in 1916 enhanced the park as a skiing mecca in the Twin Cities. With the addition of the Chalet in 1921 as a golf clubhouse, the park also had a skiing lodge. When a ski jump was also built that winter, Minneapolis had first-class facilities for nearly every winter sport. In 1922 the U.S. National Ski Tournament was held at Wirth Park, and two years later the park hosted the trials for the U.S. Winter Olympic team. The success of that event led Wirth to speculate that Minneapolis had a good chance to host the Winter Olympics in 1928 or 1932.

Winter sports were so popular, in years when there was sufficient snow and ice, that Wirth noted in 1927 they had grown as much as they could within the means of the park board. "The greatest task," he warned, "is to retain this useful public service within the sphere of our means and not to allow it to grow beyond our control."

The popularity of music at the Lake Harriet pavilion continued uninterrupted from the early 1900s. This was a program of public recreation that the park board would pay for even though it served fewer people than playground recreation programs. But it was a part of traditional service in parks—and boat rentals and refreshment sales at the Harriet refectory nearly paid for the music.

From 1906 all concerts were free, and they were expanded to other parks, including The Parade, Powderhorn, Farview, Logan, Riverside, Windom and North Commons. The park board had a portable bandstand that it pulled from park to park until 1919, when small permanent bandstands were installed in thirteen parks. Wirth explained that the bandstands were not "ornamental," meaning they weren't pretty, but they saved the time and expense of hauling around the portable band shell. The park board renovated the Lake Harriet band shell in 1914 and also reintroduced a floating bandstand. Throughout this era, the band at Lake Harriet featured many musicians of the Minneapolis Symphony Orchestra.

Park concerts soared in popularity in 1919 when a new wrinkle was added to the musical entertainment: community singing. Park board secretary J. A. Ridgway created the community sings along with Lucille Holiday, who had gained experience leading group singing at war rallies the year before. Seventy-three community sings were held in 1919, beginning a feature of summer life in Minneapolis that would last into the 1950s.

Part of the success of the community sings was due to the competition initiated in 1920 when the *Minneapolis Daily News* offered a banner to the community that sang the best. New community sing leader Harry Anderson led the singing in each park to full accompaniment and rated the audience on participation and quality. Riverside Park won the banner the first year. The second year, Logan Park won the honors and received a congratulatory letter from President Warren Harding. Average attendance at community sings was ten thousand, and some parks far exceeded that on some nights. In the summer of 1922, the park board sponsored more than two hundred concerts and community sings that were attended by an estimated six hundred thousand people.

By 1924, the board realized that the twenty-year-old pavilion at Lake Harriet would soon have to be replaced, but they never had to tear it down. The next summer a storm blew down the pavilion, killing two people. For the rest of that summer and the next, Lake Harriet didn't have a pavilion. The board built a new, more modest band shell and refectory in 1927. The same year it also built a band shell at Folwell Park.

Efforts to expand park board revenues in 1928 by charging ten cents for Lake Harriet concerts failed. Charles Doell, then the secretary of the board, noted that Minneapolis had too many other entertainment options. By this time, concerts at Lake Harriet were costing the park board more than ten thousand dollars a year, and Doell suggested using that money to pay for an amphitheater in Lyndale Park for concerts as well as the other great park board entertainment of the day, the playground pageant.

The first annual playground pageant, "The Cycle of the Seasons," was held at Lake Harriet Pavilion in 1916. The pageant featured children from every playground. By 1918, the pageant was attracting such large crowds for its two-night run that the event was moved to the hillside at Lyndale Park, where a giant

A community sing at Logan Park. The idea for community sings came from J. A. Ridgway in 1919. They continued at many parks into the 1950s. (Minneapolis Park and Recreation Board)

Playground pageants featured elaborately costumed children from every park. The pageants were written and directed by Alice Dietz. They were staged at Lyndale Park to crowds of forty thousand people during their two-night runs. Begun in 1916, the pageants were performed every year until 1941, with the exception of a year during the Depression. (Hennepin County Historical Society)

stage with elaborate sets was created for the performances. The pageants were originally directed by Julia Beckman, a teacher at North High School, but were soon taken over by Alice Dietz, a full-time park employee. The pageants eventually featured up to fifteen hundred children—each in an elaborate homemade costume—and attracted crowds of more than forty thousand. Dietz wrote and directed the productions. When she needed adults for parts, she recruited park commissioners but never allowed them speaking roles. The playground pageants, swan songs of playground summers, continued until 1941.

With Frank Berry's hiring as the new playground supervisor in 1913, he became the first full-time recreation employee of Minneapolis parks. In his first years he worked out of the new field house in Logan Park and began to offer year-round programs there. He continued Booth's emphasis on competitive sports at the playgrounds but also began to expand recreation offerings to include storytelling, folk dancing, sewing and plays. The wider array of activities was aided by a donation of a piano for Logan Park from a community group. The showers in the field house continued to be heavily used, particularly by men who stopped to shower on their way home from work.

Under Berry's direction the annual citywide athletic festivals grew, and for the first time playground children gave tumbling and pyramid-building exhibitions at the State Fair. A baseball league was created at North Commons for church-sponsored teams, and another league of business-sponsored teams played at Longfellow Field.

Total attendance at recreation activities in 1913 surpassed eight hundred thousand on the 44 acres of park land devoted to playgrounds—out of a total of just over 3,800 acres. Wirth noted in his report for 1914 that, with an expenditure of $43,000 over nine years, park board playground and athletic activities had served four million people. To help him make his case for more playgrounds and more money, Wirth brought in Liebert Weir, the field secretary of the Park and Recreation Association of America, to make a survey of Minneapolis's needs. Wirth and Weir put together a map that showed existing parks and playgrounds in the city and suggested which neighborhoods were not being served.

Armed with impressive attendance figures and Weir's map that showed gaps in service, the park board went to the 1915 legislature for permission to levy a one-eighth mill property tax to be used exclusively for playgrounds. The legislature granted that authority, along with authority for a one-twentieth mill levy to care for street trees, and for the first time the park board had a dedicated fund for playground activities. The levy provided about $20,000 a year for playgrounds, enough that the board could hire two full-time instructors to work under Berry the next year. The new taxing authority enabled Minneapolis to participate more fully in the national movement to provide recreation programming. Minneapolis's full-time recreation employees were three of the nearly twelve hundred then employed across the country. With the new funds, the board extended recreation programs to sixteen parks.

With new baseball fields at The Parade, Berry created the Minneapolis Amateur Baseball Association because he believed it was the park board's responsibility to not only provide fields but to organize play—a significant evolutionary step in park philosophy. Nearly three hundred teams that year obtained permits to play games at The Parade along with dozens more permits issued for other fields. Despite the many playground additions and improvements, Berry returned from attending a national recreation convention to inform the board that by the standards of that association, based on population, Minneapolis should have not the twelve baseball fields it had, but seventy-five.

The increasing popularity of baseball and football was matched by the growth in tennis. Over the years, the park board would build more than two hundred tennis courts around the city—sixty in 1916 alone—usually paved with concrete. In the early days, nets were not provided. Wirth proposed in 1915 that nets should be rented for use on the courts to help pay for them. Wirth was a believer in charges for services such as tennis nets and swimming suits because it was one way of getting people who used a particular service to pay for it and it provided an accurate gauge of the need for the service.

In 1915, Wirth recommended that the Elwell Law, which had created the modern authority in 1911 to

A women's kittenball team at The Parade in 1925. The most notable rise in sports participation in the late 1910s occurred in the game of kittenball, the forerunner of softball. Kittenball's growing popularity around the country—and the name—were attributed to Minneapolis fireman Lewis Rober. He had first seen the game played in Chicago in 1895 and thought that the game, with a bigger ball and much smaller field than baseball, was ideally suited as a diversion and means of exercise for Minneapolis firemen during idle moments. He laid out a field with a pitching distance of thirty-five feet next to a fire station. The first kittenball league was formed among Minneapolis fire stations and was named for Rober's team, the "Kittens." The game was also called "indoor baseball" even though it was usually played outside. Minneapolis changed the name from kittenball to the more masculine "diamond ball" in 1925, by which time there were one hundred men's and women's teams competing in park leagues. When the name elsewhere was changed to softball and the dimensions of fields increased slightly in 1926, Minneapolis refused to go along. Well into the 1930s Minneapolis kept the name diamond ball and played the game on slightly smaller fields than the rest of the country. (Minnesota Historical Society)

assess property owners for improvements of parkways, be specifically amended to allow assessments for the improvement of neighborhood parks and playgrounds, too. It was amended in 1917 and was used for almost all playground improvements into the 1960s.

In an effort to expand recreation opportunities, Wirth recommended in 1915 that Bryn Mawr be converted into a polo field. He noted that the new bridle paths through Glenwood and around Lake of the Isles, converted from bicycle paths, were not heavily used, but he speculated that was because there was not a bridle-path link to the city. He proposed that Bryn Mawr serve that purpose and be used by equestrians in general.

One of the park board's most notable hires in 1916 was Alice Dietz as an instructor at Bryant Square. Dietz would later become director of recreation for girls and then director of community programs. She would become best known for the playground pageants she directed, but her greatest accomplishment was the tremendous growth in playground and athletic activities for women and girls. Increased participation of girls in playground programs was one of the stated objectives of the park board in the year she was hired, and she, along with Dorothea Nelson, made it happen while working from her office at the Logan Park field house.

With the entry of the United States into the Great War in 1917, Americans became more concerned with recreational activities. Physical fitness took on aspects of national security as the poor physical condition of army recruits raised alarm. Inflationary costs after the war were alleviated partially for the park board when the state legislature granted an increase of a half mill to the general park levy. It was the fist time the general park levy had been increased since the board was created in 1883.

By the summer of 1918, playground instruction was provided by forty instructors, then more than half women, but they remained seasonal employees, and the parks still only offered programs during the summer. The recreation department's only full-time employees were the supervisor, Frank Berry, and separate directors of men's and women's programs. At the time, Minneapolis was spending six cents per capita on its recreation programs.

And then came that maddeningly attractive game—golf. The first mention of the possibility of the park board providing a public golf course was in Jesse Northrup's 1907 annual report. By 1915, Wirth was a strong advocate of creating a golf course at Glenwood (Wirth) Park, and so it was built. The first course was nine holes and featured sand greens. In its first year of operation, twelve thousand rounds were played, free of charge, and an instructor was hired. Early turnout was so good that Wirth recommended using money from the playground fund to keep the course open through October.

Golfing took flight. The next summer over fifty thousand rounds were played at the Wirth course, which exceeded all expectations. Theodore Wirth recommended that the course be extended to eighteen holes and that a clubhouse replace the two warming houses being used for the purpose. As for design, a Swiss chalet might be nice, Wirth suggested, still seeing his homeland on the grounds of the park. With no bond funding available, Wirth recommended paying for the clubhouse with general park funds.

The park board also recognized the need for another course, and in 1918 the former bed of Sandy Lake in Columbia Park was converted into a six-hole golf course, also with sand greens. By 1922, both the Wirth and Columbia courses were expanded to eighteen holes—although they still had sand greens. By then the park board realized it needed more courses and proposed that the land around Rice Lake (Hiawatha) provide a golf course for the southern half of the city.

Wirth and the board were convinced, based on

early experience, that golf courses would more than pay for themselves. Adding more courses would cost nothing, they thought.

Wirth finally got his Swiss chalet in Wirth Park in 1922. The building served a dual purpose as golf clubhouse and winter sports lodge. The Columbia course got its own clubhouse, which also served as a center for community meetings, in 1924. Both clubhouses were rented out by the park board for private parties, including meal service, but revenues generated by those activities did not meet expectations.

By then, the board had acquired the land for two new courses: Armour (later Gross) and Meadowbrook. Both courses were outside Minneapolis city limits, and both were acquired on very attractive terms. The board intended for the courses to pay for themselves through playing fees. The initial fee at Gross for 1925 was set at one dollar, considerably more than the forty cents being charged at Wirth and Columbia. But given the rough condition of the new course, fees were soon dropped to fifty cents.

In 1926, Meadowbrook opened too, but due to the flooding of the course by Minnehaha Creek, the course would only offer nine holes until 1930. To make all eighteen proposed holes playable, Wirth dredged a twenty-acre pond and used the fill to raise the fifty surrounding acres. In 1926 the board also committed to creating a fifth course on the land adjacent to Lake Hiawatha.

Interest in golf was given a boost in 1926 when eighteen-year-old Les Bolstad, who had learned the game on Minneapolis public courses, won the National Public Links Championship.

In 1927, 175,000 rounds of golf were played on the four courses, and a registration system was implemented to shorten the long waits to get on courses. But competition from courses in surrounding

The grand opening of Meadowbrook Golf Course in 1925. (Minneapolis Park and Recreation Board)

The Chalet at Glenwood (Wirth) Park was completed in 1922. The building served a dual purpose as golf clubhouse and warming house for winter sports at the park. (Minneapolis Park and Recreation Board)

communities was starting to cut into attendance. Still, in 1930, with a huge bounce in rounds played after five years of decline, the park board realized a $35,000 operating profit on its golf courses. But that was the end of operating profits for the park board's golf courses for many years. A 31 percent decline in rounds played in 1931 was a sure sign the Depression was setting in. In coming years, the golf courses wouldn't generate enough in fees to service the debt on the Meadowbrook and Gross courses, let alone pay for themselves.

In 1919 the park board secured legislative approval to double the playground levy, and the park board hired its first staff of year-round instructors, which in Wirth's words allowed recreation work to be more continuous instead of "spasmodical." To manage the new staff, five director positions were created to report to new recreation director Karl Raymond: B. G. Leighton, director of playgrounds; William Fox, director of municipal athletics (baseball, football and hockey); Alice Dietz, director of community center work, the Logan Park field house and the playground pageant; Dorothea Nelson, director of girls' municipal athletics; and, H. A. Johnson, director of recreation centers.

With the passage of a Home Rule Charter in 1920, Minneapolis had to rely much less on the state legislature, but it also had new limits on the debt it could take on. With these limitations, park improvements were restricted to those that could be assessed 100 percent on neighborhoods.

In 1921 North Commons was the most-used playground, and at both North Commons and Van Cleve parks girls and women participated in greater numbers than boys and men. Two hundred volunteers donated time to park programs, nearly three hundred businesses contributed in some way to support recreation programs, and nearly fifty neighborhood organizations participated in park activities. Petitions came in from around the city for expanded space, a shelter where none existed, or a larger field house where a shelter did exist.

With the expansion of recreation programs, the park board began to see something it hadn't anticipated: a dramatic increase in adult participation in park activities. Playground advocates had always focused on children, but once facilities and programs were provided, adults came out in huge numbers. Wirth noted in 1922 that 31 percent of participants in playground and athletic programs were adults. The park board now had to look at programs to "keep adults young" through "health- and mind-sustaining participation," Wirth said.

In another year, adult participation had increased to 45 percent, due primarily to sports leagues. Karl Raymond noted that one advantage of adult participation was that adult programs were self-sustaining through fees; they cost the park board almost nothing. The sports pages of the city's newspapers were filled with game reports and photos from dozens of sports leagues, women's as well as men's.

On its list of improvement projects for 1924, the board included more than $300,000 of its total improvement budget of $1.3 million for playgrounds. King, Phelps, Folwell, Brackett, Sibley, Linden Hills and Sumner all were prepared for full use as playgrounds and playing fields. Of course, all were paid for by residents, and none included more than a basic shelter, instead of a larger field house.

In these years, Wirth and the park board still paid close attention to the landscaping of the grounds around the playgrounds. They hadn't yet abandoned the notion that neighborhood parks should still meet the traditional definition as places of beauty and relaxation. In that sense park and playground existed nervously side-by-side. Wirth ac-

> The oldest, continuously operating club organized in Minneapolis parks was created in 1919 to generate interest in hiking. The *Minnehikers* club still operates and has a monthly newsletter.

knowledged the changing demands for parks in his plans for Lynnhurst playground in 1925; a larger percentage of the land was designed for "active service" and provided for less "ornamentation." It wouldn't be until the 1950s that park management gave in to the difficulty and expense of maintaining landscape effects in parks that served predominantly as playgrounds and de-emphasized landscaping and plantings in neighborhood parks. In Wirth's era, nearly every park property, including those that served primarily as playgrounds, was planted with flowers every year.

People's habits were changing as the automobile made life more mobile in the 1920s. Attendance at community playground festivals and Fourth of July celebrations diminished. They were no longer a novelty, Wirth noted, and so many people were leaving the city in their cars for vacations that there was less interest in community festivals.

Despite the popularity of athletic programs, the board was beginning again to worry about paying for them. In 1925, at the tail end of an unprecedented era of capital spending, principally on parkways, that increased the board's debt from $3 million to more than $7 million, Wirth wrote that in his opinion, "no really serious effort has been made by the Board to remedy these increasing (financial) difficulties." He said the park board should demand a greater levy for parks, playgrounds or both and put it to a vote.

Board Secretary Charles Doell wondered where additional money could come from for recreation, noting a rising protest against tax rates in the city. In 1926 the park board spent only $11,000 on new equipment despite an estimated active participation that had surpassed one million people. In 1927, the park board spent only $20,000 on playground improvements with all but $500 of that spent on nineteen new tennis courts and backstops, which gave the city a total of sixty-five concrete tennis courts.

> In 1921, Loring Park hosted the national horseshoe championships. Loring Park is the only place in the park system where one can still pitch horseshoes. The park still hosts an active league.

By 1928, with adults already comprising more than 40 percent of participants in recreation activities, recreation director Karl Raymond recognized a coming trend that would have a profound impact on recreation in public parks. He noted the possibility of more adult leisure time with the shortening of the work week to forty hours. Wirth said he did not look forward to that prospect, but the park board would do well to anticipate it.

The trend to greater female participation in recreation programs also continued, with total participation in activities nearly evenly divided between men and women. One of the people most responsible for the growth in women's sports, Dorothea

A football game at Bottineau Park in 1926. (*Minneapolis Journal*, Minnesota Historical Society)

Nelson, resigned from her post as director of girls' athletics during the year.

As for athletic trends, participation in diamond ball increased, while the numbers of people playing baseball decreased. Soccer participation also dropped, with only six teams in the park league that had once had sixteen. Wirth noted that as an amateur sport, soccer was dying out. At the same time he observed that it was almost impossible to provide enough tennis courts for those who wished to play.

Another park activity that was increasing sharply, for which estimates were not attempted, was picnicking. More families and groups were using the parks as settings for meals, and the park board added to the campfire cooking facilities in parks throughout the system.

Despite all this activity, in 1928 Wirth produced a report and map, based in part on a federal government survey of municipal parks, that noted a shortage of playing fields in Minneapolis. That deficiency would be hard to make up, given the coming crash of the economy.

In a sign of impending economic problems for the entire country, park board president Lucian Miller wrote in his annual report for 1930 that the park board faced a difficult choice. He echoed the sentiments of William Folwell in 1892 just before the depression of 1893 took hold of the economy. That difficult choice at a time of economic uncertainty and increasing unemployment was "between the urgent need to provide employment and the demand for relief from an already too-heavy tax burden." It was imperative, he said, that the park board absorb its proportionate share of a reduction in the city's tax revenues.

Playgrounds had come a long way since a brash young superintendent had proposed the purchase of the first playground equipment in 1906. From relying on the services of a lone volunteer instructor, the recreation staff had grown to seven full-time directors and more than sixty seasonal instructors at thirty playgrounds. Hundreds of thousands of people joined the recreation programs and actively used the parks. And it had been accomplished on a shoestring of a budget.

Despite the successes of the recreation program in Minneapolis parks, the park board had spent the vast majority of its money over the past twenty-five years not on the "new" recreation but on the "old" recreation of landscaped spaces and beautiful drives.

The money and focus of the era had provided Minneapolis with superb open spaces in picturesque places and the roads to connect them. The parks and parkways acquired and developed while Wirth was superintendent remain an invaluable and heavily used resource. No one can dispute their beauty. What was acquired and improved then has repaid Minneapolis many times in increased property valuations and the pure pleasure of open spaces and lakes, streams and greenery.

On the other hand, it is impossible not to wonder how the city would be different today if the some of the millions the board spent on dredging and paving had been spent on neighborhood parks and playgrounds instead. If Minneapolis parks had had a visionary leader in the first half of the twentieth century, someone with Cleveland's, Loring's, or Folwell's gift of seeing fifty or more years into the future, would the Minneapolis park system be different? Would it be better? Once the land and lakes and streams had been acquired, which was accomplished early in Wirth's tenure to meet long-standing demand, would it have been better for someone to say, "Good! Now we've achieved Cleveland's vision of forty years ago, but what will be the needs of the city forty years from now?" No one did.

It didn't require a visionary to see the future of city parks in the early years of the century. North Commons quickly became the city's most heavily used neighborhood park after its acquisition in 1907. The field house built at Logan Park in 1912 was clearly the most successful structure the park board had ever built. The evidence of those successes was constantly before the park board, yet they were not replicated throughout the city.

And it was not due to lack of funds, although Wirth and the board constantly pleaded poverty. Nearly $400,000 was spent reshaping Lake of the Isles in the four years before the Logan Park field house was built for $32,000 of park board money. (And millions of dollars have been spent since trying to fix the problems of the Lake of the Isles shores.) While neighborhoods in the central city couldn't get a park or a shelter built unless they paid for it, the board was spending nearly a million dollars to reconstruct the roadway along Minnehaha Creek, and nearly $200,000 more filling the wetlands beside Lake Calhoun, a project that has since been partially undone. While those projects were also paid for partly by assessments to nearby property owners, nearly a third of the costs were assessed to the whole city. If a man of Cleveland's vision had been around at the time, he might have said, "Leave it for now, we can do that later." Indeed, that was *always* Cleveland's argument.

Would Minneapolis's park system have suffered without the spending priorities of the Wirth era? The evidence of Lake Harriet suggests it wouldn't have. Lake Harriet's shores were not altered, and by the time Wirth wrote his memoirs in 1944, Lake Harriet Parkway still had not been paved. The only wetland near its shores is now a cherished bird sanctuary, and the neighborhoods surrounding the lake have always been among the city's most affluent. They were, after all, among the few city neighborhoods in Wirth's time that agreed to pay for their own neighborhood parks—Linden Hills, Lynnhurst and Pershing—despite their proximity to an unimproved lake.

When members of the park board gathered to bid Wirth "bon voyage" as he departed on a seven-month around-the-world vacation given to him as a gift for twenty-five years of service as superintendent in 1930, they were also bidding farewell to a period of expansion and nearly endless possibilities, some of which had not been seized. For the next fifteen years, including Wirth's last five years on the job, almost nothing would happen in Minneapolis parks without the help of the federal government.

Wirth had arrived in Minneapolis with the intention of perfecting a park system of eighteen hundred acres with many beautiful natural features. He was embarking on his celebratory voyage as developer and manager of a park system that included more than five thousand acres. While it was a park system that was highly praised for its natural features and its beauty, it was also a park system that would be criticized for its deficiencies in providing for the recreational needs of its citizens.

In the first thirty years of the century, Wirth and the park boards he served had created a fabulous park system by the standards of 1906. But the times had passed them by. Cleveland's vision of preserving natural beauty had been achieved. But no vision for a park system to meet the city's needs in 1930 or beyond had replaced it. At least no vision was put forward forcefully enough to mobilize park boards, civic leaders and the public to achieve it. And if anything, from his first months in the city when he "staggered" the park board with his take-charge proposals, Wirth would have to be described as a forceful man.

As much as Wirth deserves credit for developing many outstanding features of the Minneapolis park system, especially in its finer neighborhoods, he must be also bear some responsibility for neglecting to provide for the city's burgeoning recreational needs, especially in its poorer neighborhoods. He was enormously successful at moving earth but less successful at moving the city's parks into a new era of recreational opportunities for all its people.

The Minneapolis skyline over Loring Pond in the late 1930s. (Minnesota Historical Society)

Chapter Seventeen

A Critical Evaluation

Liebert Weir did not say many nice things about recreation in Minneapolis parks. And his opinion mattered.

From May to September 1944, while the nation was still at war, Weir surveyed the landscape much as Wirth had once done, but with a different objective. He was looking not at the physical condition of Minneapolis parks but at the recreational opportunities they offered.

He was invited to Minneapolis by the park board to assess the city's recreation needs and to recommend future action. The board got what it wanted from Weir—ambitious recommendations for improvement—as well as harsh criticism. The board had chosen for this recreation survey a man who knew park and recreation systems better than anyone in the country. Weir had been the national field secretary of the National Recreation Association (NRA) since 1910. He also knew Minneapolis parks well. In 1914 he had helped create a map of where the city might need new playgrounds. His report then had helped the park board get approval from the legislature for the first tax levy specifically for playgrounds. The park board was hoping to at least repeat that success.

Weir combed through detailed demographic data on the city, neighborhood by neighborhood, and looked at the land and recreation programs of nearly every public and private institution. His methodical analysis of Minneapolis parks and population was matched against "national standards" established by the NRA as guidelines for park and recreation development. Measured against those standards, Weir's conclusions about Minneapolis's recreation program were sharply critical.

Minneapolis was once a leader but has lost that leadership, concluded park superintendent Christian Bossen in summarizing Weir's assessment, "primarily because of its deficiencies in community and neighborhood facilities, that is, the lack of sufficient number of neighborhood parks and playgrounds in an inadequate all-year-round recreation program."

For fifteen years leading up to Weir's report, the park board had wrestled with its role in providing recreational opportunities. For twenty years after the report, the park board worked to implement Weir's recommendations. The report he issued was the pivotal event in thirty-five years of park board history.

From the onset of the Great Depression, park leaders had embarked on a journey of introspection. As tens of thousands of people in the city lost jobs and a great many more worked fewer hours as the work week was reduced to forty hours for everyone, "leisure" had taken on a new meaning. Recreation was no longer just child's play. In addition, the heartbreaking harshness of the Depression caused many leaders to examine closely the role of government in society.

Park commissioners and leaders expressed an increasing commitment to recreation as a vital component of a good life. In the 1933 annual report, board president Alfred Pillsbury wrote that recreation and relaxation were vital necessities, "just as vital as any function of government *not excluding* that of the apprehension and conviction of criminals and the education of our youth" (emphasis added). Director of recreation Karl Raymond quoted John Langdon Hughes to reinforce the point, "In our work we make a living, in our play we make a life."

Believing fervently in the critical role that recreation played in everyday life, the board hired Weir to give the voice of authority to the recreation needs of the city. He claimed that the city's recreation shortcomings were not the fault of the park board or its professional staff but were due to inadequate funding. He did not address the issue of how the park board had chosen to spend money in the past, but he pulled no punches when criticizing the recreation system that resulted.

Weir was critical of recreational opportunities in Minneapolis parks on three levels: land, facilities and programs.

First, he noted that Minneapolis parks were "markedly deficient" in playgrounds and neighborhood recreation parks. Minneapolis had only 23 percent of the playgrounds it should have based on NRA standards. To meet those standards, Minneapolis should have had 120 playgrounds supervised 310 days a year, instead of its 37 playgrounds supervised 52 days a year.

Weir recommended that instead of the twenty-nine neighborhood recreation parks or playfields it had, Minneapolis should have forty to meet the standard of one neighborhood recreation park for every square mile of residential area. He also observed that most of the space devoted to neighborhood recreation parks was concentrated in two large athletic facilities: The Parade and then-undeveloped Northeast Athletic Field. He also noted that "excessive" areas in neighborhood parks were "purely landscaped" spaces that had little recreational utility.

Alfred F. Pillsbury continued the legacy of his father and uncle in his dedication to city parks. His father, John S. Pillsbury, was one of the original twelve park commissioners, and George Pillsbury promoted parks as president of the Board of Trade in 1883 when the park act was created. In addition to serving nineteen years on the park board from 1925 to 1946, and as president from 1931 to 1934, Alfred holds a record as a University of Minnesota athlete that will stand forever: he was a seven-time letter winner on the Gopher football team—while an undergraduate and a law school student—before eligibility for university teams was limited. (Minneapolis Park and Recreation Board)

Weir also criticized the distribution of parks in the city, noting in particular that "the most socially needy parts of the city are without areas or facilities." He divided the city into seven geographic areas and noted serious deficiencies in each.

Weir's second criticism of Minneapolis parks addressed facilities, from playground equipment to indoor spaces. He noted that no playground should be without toilets and that Minneapolis had eleven without them. Swimming facilities were also in short supply, with more than 50 percent of the population more than two miles from a swimming facility; the northeast had none.

Finally, Weir observed that the parks did not offer activities throughout the year and that programs were unbalanced between indoor and outdoor activities. Both faults were due to Minneapolis having only one field house, the building at Logan Park. Weir concluded that there can never be a "satisfactory playground program" until it is conducted year-round. Weir criticized park shelters as "too large for merely shelter houses and too small for use as a general recreation building."

The failure to provide year-round programs and the facilities to house them also led to a shortage of non-sports programs. For Weir, recreation meant much more than sports. He wanted drama, music, arts, handcrafts and nature study. Finally, Weir noted that while an effort had been made to provide equal opportunities for males and females, at that time more emphasis was placed on activities for boys and men than for girls and women.

In Weir's conclusions he recommended strongly that in expanding services to fill the gaps he identified, the city should finance playgrounds through bonds, not neighborhood assessments.

On the positive side, Weir noted that Minneapolis had one of the best-organized and best-managed citywide sports programs in the country. He also had high praise for the community sings. Even the playground program was "excellently conceived," especially considering the inadequate number of instructors. He concluded that "informal individual activity" was one of the "most distinguishing features" of the city's parks. In essence, he was saying that the strength of the system was that it merely provided open spaces—the outdated goal of park planners of a half century earlier.

The deficiencies that Weir noted in the Minneapolis recreation system could not be blamed simply on population growth. The population of the city had surpassed 464,000 in 1930, but growth was slowing markedly. Minneapolis gained fewer than 30,000 inhabitants in the 1930s. Minneapolis population would peak in the mid-1950s at about 550,000 and then begin a sharp decline until about 1980 when population leveled off at about 370,000.

The Weir report was a clear signal for a hard turn in park board policy toward a greater emphasis on people and activities than on land and landscaping. The park board and superintendent Bossen must have known the hit they were going to take from Weir. Internal assessments of the recreation program had come to many of the same conclusions Weir did, and Weir noted that in his report. But the park board needed the criticism to move forward. It needed an expert like Weir to state what the board and staff already knew in order to present a credible shopping list to the city's postwar planning committee. That list eventually was compiled straight from Weir's report.

The park board's challenge was compounded by the paradox of Minneapolis parks during the Depression and war: the park board had no money,

> One of the longest-running sponsorships of park activities by a business began in 1936. Under president Chris Ellingsen, the Franklin Cooperative Creamery began underwriting the costs of many park recreation programs. In addition to paying for activities and awards, the creamery published a schedule of summer playground programs that was distributed through schools. From 1936 to 1963, the creamery spent an estimated quarter million dollars supporting park recreation programs.

but it ran the best recreation program in the history of the city. In that sense it was the worst of times and the best of times. Parks had subsisted on an infusion of federal money through work-relief programs. The recreation programs the board was able to offer with those federal dollars demonstrated the range of services that were possible in city parks.

Without relief programs, Weir would have seen a far worse park system. As the last dredging and paving projects were being completed in 1932, the park board had already received its first work-relief grants from the federal government. In 1931, an initial $11,000 paid for men to trim trees and restore lawns in parched parks.

That opened a spigot that would eventually pour more than $17 million into the park system—from federal, state and city government—until the work-relief programs ended in 1943. Most of that money paid salaries of people who would have otherwise been unemployed. (The federal government operated several programs to provide employment from 1930 to 1943. Most park programs during this period were administered under one of two iterations of the WPA—the Works Progress Administration and the Work Projects Administration. Essentially, the federal government paid workers' salaries, while state and local governments paid for supplies, materials and supervision.) The number of relief workers employed in the park system peaked at 3,100 in 1935 and remained at 3,000 for the next few years.

People employed under the federal programs performed an astonishing variety of jobs in city parks. They created the lagoons along Bassett's Creek in Wirth Park, paved 15 percent of the city's parkways, built retaining walls at Lake Harriet, Lake Calhoun, Powderhorn Lake and Lake of the Isles, poured sidewalks throughout the park system and constructed stairs to Minnehaha Creek below the falls as well as bridges over the creek. Also large sums of money went to upgrade the airport, which was still owned by the park board at that time. In park board offices they performed clerical and administrative tasks. In the park board shops they maintained equipment and built settees, tables and playground equipment.

Nowhere was the impact of federal work-relief programs greater than on the city's recreation services. As the Depression took hold, the park board's revenues dropped dramatically. From 1931 to 1933, park board revenues fell 62 percent, a reduction that Alfred Pillsbury noted was "far in excess" of any other unit of city government. The park board's levy for playgrounds was eliminated completely for 1934.

To cope with those cuts, the park board eliminated the positions of all seventy-five seasonal playground instructors. The American Legion tried to raise money for instructors but failed. Individual Legion posts succeeded in keeping eleven parks open with volunteers who were trained by Alice Dietz. The staff at Logan Park was down to Dietz alone, and with all the unemployment, Wirth noted that Logan Park was "overrun" with people. He added that without instructors there was an increase in rowdy behavior, vandalism and neighborhood gangs.

Even the park board's meager income from revenue-generating activities dried up. The golf courses operated at a loss. Revenue from boat rentals dropped by half, and Wirth said the service couldn't be sustained much longer. Refectory income dropped at all parks.

The park board eliminated music from its budget

> Even the influx of federal money to maintain parks couldn't save the profusion of flowers in the parks. In 1931, the park board maintained 215 flower beds in forty-nine parks. The next year those numbers dropped to 165 flower beds in thirty-five parks. By 1948, park board staff planted just 94 flower beds in nineteen parks. The annual Chrysanthemum Show at the Lyndale Farmstead greenhouse was canceled in 1933 but reinstated in 1937. The show was cancelled again in 1945 but resumed in 1946 and ran from then until 1978.

in 1932 and axed the playground pageant, too. The local utility companies and Holt Motor Company stepped in to keep community sings going, but the singing was accompanied only by an amplified piano instead of a band from 1932 to 1936. Wirth reported that by 1934, 64 percent of lights in parks were out of service.

Municipal sports leagues didn't suffer as much as playgrounds, because fees for adult leagues made them self-sustaining, although the condition of playing fields deteriorated. General Mills helped by sponsoring baseball leagues at Nicollet (King) Park. Many teams had been sponsored by employers who could no longer afford it—or had laid off their employees—but participation remained high. Still, Wirth noted that more people were participating in activities with low or no fees. Picnicking as a form of recreation saw huge increases.

In 1933, the recreation program received its first work-relief funds to maintain and supervise skating rinks. The next year, federal money for recreation really kicked in. For the first time ever, the park board offered year-round recreation programs at parks. In 1935, federal and state relief programs provided the city with 243 recreation workers.

The federal program in recreation was run by Alice Dietz, who organized training and supervision. The park board greatly expanded its array of programs, too. Programs in the arts, dance—a special interest of Dietz—music and handcrafts flourished. Federal funds even paid a troop of actors to perform in city parks, and musicians to play at Lake Harriet.

The bathhouses were staffed by workers paid by the federal government, and in 1935 the city beaches enjoyed their highest attendance ever. Swimming

> Operatic performances at Lake Harriet, which had drawn opposition in the 1890s, returned to the bandstand to huge crowds in 1935 when the Twin Cities Opera Association sponsored performances. The community sings were augmented in 1936 by a competition for choirs. The competition that year was won by the Minneapolis A Cappella society, which went on to win a national contest in Chicago.

was free if lockers weren't used, and practically no one used them.

Skating rinks continued to be supervised and maintained with federal money, although the number of rinks was reduced. Powderhorn Park remained the premier speed-skating track in the country. The trials for the 1936 Winter Olympic team were held at Powderhorn in the midst of what Wirth called the "best winter sports program ever."

By 1939, on the eve of World War II, the recreation program had become so reliant on federal money that board president Francis Gross warned that the difficult financial situation of the park board

Speed-skating competition at Powderhorn Park in mid-1930s. The 1936 Olympic speed-skating trials at Powderhorn Park were poorly attended due to subzero weather, but in other years skating meets at the park drew huge crowds. In 1936, Minneapolis men won four of the five events at the national championships. Five speed-skating clubs were active in the city, one of which, Maple Hill (Beltrami), produced the city's first Olympic team member, Charles Leighton. Ken Bartholomew of Powderhorn was national champion in 1940. When the Winter Olympic Trials were held again at Powderhorn in 1948, four of the nine U.S. team members were from Minneapolis, including Bartholomew, who won a silver medal in the Olympics that year at St. Moritz, Switzerland. (Minnesota Historical Society)

would be "shockingly multiplied" if the WPA program were discontinued. It was clear by 1942 that federal assistance was nearing an end when the WPA cut its program of recreation instructors from eighty-nine to sixteen. Early in 1943, Gross's fear was realized when the WPA officially ended and the park board was left to run a recreation program without federal assistance.

The park board recreation program for ten years had far surpassed anything offered before. And then it was over. Minneapolis had had a taste of what was possible, and the park board had to find a way to continue at least some of those services. Weir was hired, at least in part, to provide justification for getting that money.

The man who managed Minneapolis parks through the difficult years from 1935 to 1945 knew the park system well. Christian Bossen, who had arrived in the city with Wirth from Hartford in 1906, was named superintendent in 1935. Bossen took over a park system that no longer had money to maintain parks, let alone expand its recreation program.

It was a time, Charles Doell later wrote, when the park board became fully aware of the "extensive system of recreation facilities to be needed in the future." Playgrounds were no longer, he added, "subordinate to landscape and horticultural effects." Two years before Bossen took the reigns, Alfred Pillsbury wrote, "For years the annual doubling of enrollment of participants and number of spectators at our recreation activities was viewed with complacent satisfaction until its importance vied with the importance of the maintenance of physical properties."

Bossen stepped into the middle of that transition in the shadow of his predecessor and boss for nearly forty years, Theodore Wirth. When the beloved and acclaimed Wirth retired in 1935, the board named him superintendent emeritus. Stating that Wirth "had much more to give," the board gave Wirth office space and allowed him to continue living in the superintendent's house at Lyndale Farmstead. He was encouraged by the board to work on projects that interested him. In addition, Wirth devoted four years to writing his memoirs and history of Minneapolis parks. (Alfred Pillsbury paid for the book's publication.)

Wirth had received the prestigious Cornelius Amory Pugsley Award in 1933 from the American Scenic and Historic Preservation Society. But the greatest tribute to him came in 1938 when the park board changed the name of the city's largest park, then Glenwood Park, to Theodore Wirth Park. The parkway and lake in the park were also named for him. The idea of naming the park for him was not new. In 1913, shortly after the park was acquired, board president Edmund Phelps, had proposed several names for the new park, including "Wirthfield," to honor the dynamic superintendent.

Bossen took over after the worst of the Depression

Christian Bossen became superintendent of parks in 1935 when Theodore Wirth retired. He served as superintendent until he retired in 1945. (Minneapolis Park and Recreation Board)

had passed. The economy was starting to recover, and park board levies had been restored to pre-Depression levels. Those same tax rates yielded smaller revenues, however, as land values had dropped precipitously.

The park board, and every other branch of municipal government, tried to address revenue shortfalls in the summer of 1937 through charter amendments to increase tax levies. The referendum to increase the playground levy was defeated along with every other tax increase on the ballot. It was one of the only defeats the park board has ever suffered at the ballot box.

Despite defeat at the polls, Bossen and board president Gross argued eloquently for more recreation programs in city parks and a broader role for parks in city life. Bossen even suggested a study of the social and economic needs of neighborhoods to identify the role parks could play in meeting them. A park and recreation system, Bossen wrote, is "more a means to an end than an end in itself." He added that "leisure, and the opportunity for making proper use of it, are fundamental to the welfare of our nation" and concluded that "we have farther to go than we have come." Bossen considered recreation to be so integral to efforts to address city problems that the funding of parks should not be decided by assessments. "Where the congestion is great and the need is great," he argued, "then consideration must be given to a different method of financing."

Just as William Folwell had kept the park board of the 1890s focused on the park system it could acquire when better times came, so Bossen and Gross kept the focus on what the recreation system should become.

※ ※ ※ ※ ※

During the bittersweet years of running a better recreation program thanks to the largesse of the federal government, the park board did manage to add significant new parks at very little cost. The one exception was venturing again into downtown Minneapolis—despite the failure of the Gateway.

> One of the city's oldest parks, Oak Lake Park, disappeared in 1936 when the park board transferred ownership of the one-plus acres to the city for the creation of a municipal market. That's why today's outdoor market, with I-94 nearly overhead, is still bounded by Lakeside Avenue. The Oak Lake Park Association, the city's first neighborhood improvement association in the 1880s—in what was then an affluent neighborhood on the city's outskirts—was an early hotbed of park support. Oak Lake itself was filled by the park board at the request of the board of health in 1915.

In 1932, the park board purchased two-and-a-half acres on Marquette and Second Street South for Pioneers Square. This acquisition, at a cost of just under a half million dollars, wasn't the park board's idea. The federal government wanted a new post office in Minneapolis and asked the city to provide a landscaped park in front of the building. The city council asked the park board to acquire the land and develop it as a park. The city paid for most of it by issuing $300,000 in bonds. The rest of the cost was assessed to the entire city by the park board. The park was dedicated on the 103rd anniversary of Charles Loring's birth in the fall of 1936. Like the Gateway, the park failed to beautify downtown and was also a victim of redevelopment in the 1960s.

All other additions to the park system from the

> The centerpiece of Pioneers Square was a sculpture depicting the pioneers who arrived at St. Anthony Falls and built a city. The original proposal was for a grouping of people to include a Native American peering to the horizon, suggesting the coming of white settlers. The final version, however, depicted only three generations of white settlers. The sculpture was saved when Pioneers Square was demolished. It now stands on a tiny triangle of land at the intersection of Marshall Avenue and Fifth Street Northeast donated by the city specifically for the statue in 1966.

beginning of the Depression until 1947 came at little or no cost to the park board.

- Hiawatha School Playground. In 1931 the board of education gave the park board four acres of land at East Forty-third Street and Forty-fourth Avenue South adjacent to the grade school.
- Bassett's Creek Valley between Bryn Mawr and Wirth Park. The 1934 acquisition was sparked by the offer of Arthur Fruen, a city council member at the time, and the Glenwood-Inglewood Company to donate part of the land that still borders that company's offices. With the donation, all sixty acres were acquired for $14,000.
- The Armory site adjoining The Parade, now the Minneapolis Sculpture Garden. In 1934, the state gave the park board the land, and the Armory was finally demolished years after it had been condemned.
- Bohannon Park. The city council gave the park board the nine-acre site of the city's workhouse at Bryant and Forty-ninth Avenue North in 1935.
- Diamond Lake and Pearl Lake. The park board completed its acquisition of Diamond Lake and Pearl Lake (now Pearl Park) in 1936. At the same time it designated for acquisition the swampy land across Portland Avenue to the east of Diamond Lake, but that acquisition, which became Todd Park, was not completed until 1948. The 111 acres in that complex cost less than $3,000, and more than half of that value was donated. The cash cost to the park board was about $10 an acre.
- Elwell Field and Currie Park. The board initiated purchase in 1939 of two small playgrounds in south and southeast Minneapolis. Elwell Field, three acres at East Hennepin and Fifth Avenue Southeast, was purchased for $5,000 to be paid over ten years interest-free, but was later sold. (Another small playground also called Elwell Field was lost to the construction of I-35 in the 1960s.) Another acre was acquired at Fifteenth Avenue South and Fifth Street for what became Currie Park. The park board initially leased this land, for-

Martha Crone at Eloise Butler Wildflower Garden. When Eloise Butler died in 1933, she was replaced as the curator of the wildflower garden by her assistant Martha Crone, who would tend the garden and oversee its expansion until 1959. (A significant increase in attendance that year was attributed to the inauguration of mosquito-control measures.) The garden was expanded to the east in 1944, when Clinton Odell, once a high school student of Butler's, donated money to purchase an additional ten acres so the garden could include upland or prairie plants. Odell also founded the Friends of the Wild Flower Garden, Inc. in 1952, which continues to sponsor improvements to the garden. In 1969 that organization privately raised funds to construct a shelter at the garden that was named for Martha Crone. (Minneapolis Park and Recreation Board)

mer site of the Pillsbury Settlement House, for $1 a year, then purchased it in 1941 for $525 with a donation from Mary Howe. These two acquisitions broke with past park board practice of acquiring only land it could afford to maintain. "Faced with justified demands," Gross wrote, "we have not been able to deny them so long as a temporary solution can be found, even if they make more acute our future financial problems."

- Northeast Athletic Field Park. Most of the thirty-one acres at Johnson Avenue and Thirteenth Avenue Northeast were donated in 1941 by the city and the state, which had acquired the land through tax forfeiture.

Other than the assessments for Pioneers Square, the park board added nearly 220 acres to its neighborhood parks and playgrounds at a total cost of just over $20,000. Northeast Athletic Field Park would be the last park acquisition until after World War II.

With the entry of the United States into World War II in 1941, all plans for the expansion of a recreation system had to be shelved. As during World War I, war did not have a significant impact on park operations. Bossen noted at the outbreak of the war that a recreation system does not vary much in time of war or peace. The objectives remained the same, although Gross did stress the added responsibility of providing relief from the mental strains of war.

The park board did, however, lose 118 employees to military service. Others took higher-paying jobs in defense industries. One result of a shortage of male workers was that in 1943 the park board employed its first female life guards. Twelve of the thirty-five lifeguards at city beaches that summer were women.

As defense industries went into round-the-clock production, some baseball and diamond ball games were scheduled for 6:30 a.m. to accommodate players who worked night shifts. The park board also noted in 1943 that city lakes, even Loring Pond, were stocked with more pan fish to provide a supplement to rationed food.

The war also directed the park board's attention to longer-term goals and the city's needs after the

Minneapolis Celebrates Summer. The park board sponsored a float in the water parade during the first Aquatennial in 1940. The float, cosponsored by the WPA recreation program, is seen entering Lake Calhoun from the channel connecting to Lake of the Isles. The Aquatennial used mainly park property for activities. A rodeo, featuring Gene Autry, was held at The Parade, motorboat races and a sailing regatta were conducted on Lake Calhoun, and the first Aqua Follies were held on Cedar Lake. The Aqua Follies were later moved to a special pool constructed next to Wirth Lake. The playground pageant was moved to Aquatennial week in 1940 but was discontinued after the 1941 Aquatennial. (Minnesota Historical Society)

> **R**oberts Bird Sanctuary. In 1936, the wetlands north of Lake Harriet were designated as a bird sanctuary at the request of the Minnesota Audubon Society. The bird sanctuary was named after Thomas Sadler Roberts in 1947. Roberts, a retired doctor, was a professor of ornithology at the University of Minnesota and director of the university's museum of natural history.

war. Bossen noted in 1944 that the goal of postwar planning was full employment to avoid a depression and to pay off the huge national debt. Public agencies were, therefore, urged to prepare plans for "useful projects."

Gross provided the philosophical foundation for those plans. "The frontiers of human welfare, understanding and happiness," he wrote, "are today as close, as real and as of great a scope as ever were the physical frontiers that challenged past generations. In spite of our professed principles of human justice, we still do not have equal opportunities in all quarters. The most satisfying argument for equal recreation opportunities for all remains the simple one of human justice."

Bossen emphasized the integral role of the park system in life after war and depression. "Recreation is now accepted not only as the dominant factor in the scheme of a park system," he wrote, "but it is also accepted as a necessity to the well being of all people. To be intelligently managed, the department must necessarily take an important role in community matters in cooperation with many interests."

As for the recommendations of Liebert Weir, the blueprint for the future of parks and recreation in Minneapolis, Bossen worried that the "danger is that our sights may be set too low rather than too high."

Chapter Eighteen

Postwar Progress

Business Week magazine noted in 1945 that Minneapolis was one of the only cities that didn't have a war boom. There was no great influx of people either, although the population had finally topped five hundred thousand. Hubert Humphrey was the new mayor but would soon leave for higher office. The city faced a severe housing shortage that would be alleviated by a flight to the suburbs. In 1940, when Minneapolis had a population of just under five hundred thousand, its most populous suburb, St. Louis Park, had fewer than eight thousand people.

The park board's revenue had declined 20 percent since 1931. The value of all city real estate had dropped nearly 30 percent. Labor costs had increased 30 percent, and the buying power of the dollar had decreased 25 percent. Park staffing and maintenance for the previous decade had been paid for mostly by the federal government. The park board had a survey of its recreation needs on the table that cited numerous deficiencies. To accommodate the coming shift in population to the suburbs, which everyone knew would happen, highways were going to have to slice through the city—and its parks and parkways. City charter reform was being discussed that would eliminate the park board entirely.

Welcome to your new job, Mr. Doell.

To top off his list of challenges, Charles Doell, the new park superintendent in 1945, had not one, but two retired superintendents—Wirth and Bossen—looking over his shoulder. Fortunately for Doell, he knew them both well. He had worked for them for thirty years. Doell began working for the park board while he was still a student at South High School and joined the park staff full-time upon graduating with an engineering degree from the University of Minnesota. He was the first superintendent who was a native of the city.

Superintendent Charles Doell *(left)* with his predecessors Theodore Wirth *(center)* and Christian Bossen. (Minneapolis Park and Recreation Board)

Doell was meticulous and thorough. His first report for the park board in 1923, written when he was head of the auditing department, was a detailed ten-page report. Doell loved writing—publicity brochures, office manuals, policy papers—and he was a frequent contributor to professional journals. He wrote studies of airport operations, Minnehaha Creek and lake levels, and in later life wrote the standard textbook on park management used at many universities. He was the man to turn to for details. In a note to accompany several charts on park board revenues compared to other city agencies in the 1930s, he commented that the more you studied them, the more fascinating they became.

Doell took office two weeks after the surrender of Japan in 1945. His first responsibilities were to implement Weir's recommendations and to oversee park and recreation contributions to the plans of the city's postwar progress committee. He combined them into a single mission by assigning cost estimates to Weir's recommendations for park acquisitions and improvements neighborhood by neighborhood.

The result was a request for $11.7 million for new parks and improvements to be spread over ten years. With two-thirds of the total devoted to playgrounds, the plan reversed the priorities for bond funds thirty years earlier when park improvements had gotten most of the money. Doell emphasized that, in contrast to the earlier period, improvements would still be "pleasing to the eye" but were of a "utilitarian nature."

The park board's capitol improvement request was part of an estimated $150 million in improvement projects submitted by all city agencies. Over the fourteen years Doell was superintendent, from 1945 to 1959, while costs escalated rapidly, the park board received from the city just over $6 million in bonds, barely half of what it had originally requested in 1945 dollars. Liebert Weir's criticism of Minneapolis's park and recreation system had little effect on those in the city who allocated bond money.

A clear pattern was evident in the years of Doell's management of city parks—and it had deep historical roots. The park board had modest success convincing city authorities to fund acquisitions or improvements in the park system, but the board had repeated success going to the legislature and the public for higher tax levies. Since before the park board was created, the city government had not been friendly to the idea of spending public money on parks. Even the Park Act of 1883 had been approved by the legislature and the public over the objections of city government. Little had changed in more than sixty years, despite the acclaim earned by the parks—and the value placed on them by citizens.

At a time when the park board still expected to receive bond funding from the city for park acquisition and improvement, it had the first of several successes asking the state legislature for more operating funds. Before Bossen retired in 1945, the Minneapolis Parent-Teacher Association (PTA) asked the board to prepare a bill it could sponsor at the legislature to increase taxes for playgrounds. The board did so, asking for an increase of five times the existing playground levy. After an intense campaign by the PTA, the legislature authorized a smaller-than-requested one-mill increase to one-and-one-half mills. Still, the increase gave the park board an additional $240,000 a year to use for recreation beginning in 1946. The legislature also authorized the board to revive street-tree maintenance by assessing adjoining property owners.

The park board immediately put the increase in tax revenues to use for recreation programs. Year-round programs were started at Logan, Loring, Nicollet (King) and North Commons. Soon eleven other parks began to offer after-school programs.

The park board expanded its recreation programs, too, with the addition of a nature specialist. This was one of the last actions of Bossen before he retired, and reflected his keen interest in nature. One of his favorite places was the yet-to-be-named Roberts Bird Sanctuary, which he helped create. The path through the sanctuary, where Bossen's ashes were scattered upon his death in 1956, was named Bossen's Lane in 1957. After two years of operation as an experimental program run by the Minneapolis library's natural history museum, the naturalist position was expanded to full-time in 1948.

The park board also began a long collaboration with the University of Minnesota in 1945 to rebuild its summer playground programs and add after-school supervision at some playgrounds. Many of the instructors were students in the recreation department at the university. The relationship between the university's recreation department and the park board would continue for many years, and over that time many part-time student supervisors would join the park board staff after graduation.

One of the most dramatic changes that occurred in the city's recreation program over these years was a decrease in participation by women and girls. Weir had noted the disparity between the participation of males and females, both children and adults, in his report and questioned whether it was due to a greater emphasis on activities for males or whether they simply took greater advantage of park programs. After the war, boys and men outnumbered girls and women in recreation programs by nearly four to one. This had not always been true. In the early days of playground programs girls outnumbered boys at many parks, and women's sports programs in the 1920s were a huge success. By the early 1950s, the most popular activity sponsored by the park board for women was bowling at downtown lanes. When those lanes closed in the 1960s, women were even more poorly represented in park board activities. It would be many years before girls' participation in playground activities would increase again.

Doell and the park board got off to a good start implementing Weir's recommendations. The increase in the tax levy enabled the board to reinstate some playground programs of the WPA era. An initial bond issue of $400,000 for new acquisitions appeared promising, especially because the city also approved an additional $400,000 in bonds to purchase Meadowbrook and Gross golf courses. Due to the Depression and the unexpected expenses of running golf courses, those courses had not lived up to assurances that taxpayers would never have to pay for them. In fact, the board was in default on payments for both courses. With the prospect of the courses being sold for development, the board agreed to buy both on attractive terms, and the city authorized those purchases. In the decades since, as golf's popularity took off, the courses have been important sources of revenue for the park board.

When the Armour Golf Course was renamed for Francis Gross while he was still president of the park board in 1947, he claimed the action came as a complete surprise. The man known as "Mr. Park Board" declined to be reelected president of the board in 1948 after leading Minneapolis parks through thirteen years of dramatic change. Park commissioners created a new office, president emeritus, for Gross, which enabled him to continue to vote at all committee meetings.

Gross had been persistent in advocating a reevaluation of the role of parks in Minneapolis and in defending the park board's autonomy. A move to revise

Alice Dietz briefing recreation supervisors in 1947. A tax levy increase beginning in 1946 enabled the park board to provide supervision for more hours at more playgrounds. (Minneapolis Public Library, Minneapolis Collection, M0241)

the city charter gained strength after World War II, leading to a referendum in 1948 on a charter that would have ended the park board's independence as part of an effort to streamline city government. Gross wrote that the issue provoked on the board an "intense determination to survive and protect the city's beloved park system from the ravages of power politics." Just as in every other referendum since the 1890s that would have limited or eliminated park board authority, the public defeated the 1948 charter revisions. Attempts to limit park board authority through charter revisions were defeated again by voters in 1960 and 1963.

Gross continued in the unusual role of president emeritus until the park board election of 1949 when, as Charles Loring before him, he lost a bid for reelection to the board. Just as Loring had championed a park system that would serve all people, so Gross had championed a recreation system that operated on a foundation of "simple human justice." In quite different times and circumstances, they both helped to change the city.

The largest addition of park land immediately following the war, other than golf courses, was another patch of land that was not on Weir's acquisition list. Shingle Creek, north of Webber Park to the city line, was purchased by the park board with bond funds not because the park board wanted it, but because the city did. (There was a long history, however, of proposals to acquire the land along the creek as a park; the first was in 1905.) The city wanted to drain the wetland in the far north of the city so it could be developed for much-needed housing. The only way to do that was to lower the bed of Shingle Creek. So the city asked the park board to buy the creek. The park board obliged with some of the bond money it had hoped to use for playgrounds. From 1947 to 1949, the park board spent just over $200,000 acquiring fifty-nine acres along Shingle Creek.

The board also began an effort to acquire land targeted by Weir in the city's underserved neighborhoods. The board expanded Peavey Park east and south from the original donated park at Franklin and Park Avenue by nearly three acres at a cost of $200,000 in 1948. That would be the most expensive addition to neighborhood parks in the postwar years. The board noted that even though the adjacent grade school at Chicago and Twenty-fourth Street was being sold to a hospital, the area needed a playground so badly that a hospital and playground would have to coexist. (An attempt years earlier to convert Elliot Park to a playground was abandoned when nearby hospitals objected to the noise.)

Despite the park board's optimism for plans to acquire other parks in heavily populated neighborhoods with bond funds, almost every other piece of

Francis Gross, probably in the 1940s. Gross was a banker in the Camden neighborhood, who was first elected to the park board in 1910 at age forty. He served a total of thirty-three years on the board in four different stints until 1949. He was president of the board in 1917–19 and again in 1936–48. (Minneapolis Park and Recreation Board)

land added to the park system in the next twenty years would be acquired from another city agency or from the state. Park board staff routinely scanned lists of tax-delinquent property the state was putting up for sale and requested the state to withhold from sale land the board wanted. The personal pain of people unable to pay taxes on land during the Depression became the city's gain. Absent bond funds, the board acquired what land it could.

- McRae Park. Eight acres at Chicago Avenue South and Forty-sixth Street was acquired, half from the state's tax-delinquent list and half by condemnation at a total cost of $24,000.

- Perkins Hill Park. Four acres at Thirty-fourth Street and Fourth Avenue North were transferred from the state, and two additional lots were purchased for $276. More than an acre of Perkins Hill was eventually lost to construction of I-94 in the 1970s.

- Bossen Field. Originally named Airport Park, the thirty-nine acres of tax-delinquent land at Twenty-eighth Avenue South and Fifty-sixth Street were acquired from the state for $1 in 1948. Yet another tract of wetland, the field was filled by material from nearby airport construction projects and by making the north end of the field a garbage dump for a time.

- Dickman Park. Two acres at Main Street and Fifth Avenue Northeast were acquired in 1949 for $27,000. This was another of the areas targeted for a playground by Weir.

- Hi-View Park. Four acres at Main Street and Thirty-fifth Avenue Northeast were acquired mostly from the state. The total cost was $4,900. Children in this sparsely populated neighborhood between Columbia Park and the river were already using this land as a playfield. Although the area had not been targeted by Weir for a park, the board seized the opportunity in 1949 to acquire the land while it could.

- North Mississippi Park. The original twenty-five acres of riverfront north of the Camden Bridge was acquired in the early 1950s. Seventy-five percent of the land was acquired from the state, some was purchased for $17,000, and some was transferred from the city. The park was later expanded north to the city line, partly due to the park board's fight with the state over land for freeways.

Even without funding to acquire land in more crowded and expensive neighborhoods, the park board chipped away at the list of neighborhoods that Weir believed needed a park. Peavey Park, Bossen Field and McRae Park were in neighborhoods on Weir's list and met his criteria for suitable acreage. Dickman Park was in roughly the right location but was too small to meet Weir's standard of five acres for a neighborhood park.

The park board also followed another suggestion by Weir that it work more closely with the school board to develop programs and facilities. In the wake of the PTA's successful effort to increase the playground levy in 1945, the park board began experimental recreation programs at two junior high schools, Jordan near Folwell Park in north Minneapolis, and Bryant near Nicollet (Martin Luther King) Park in south Minneapolis.

Building on that collaboration, the school board and park board signed a joint declaration of cooperation in 1948 that led to the development of four school-and-park projects. The resolution, proposed by Maude Armatage, formalized efforts that had in the past led to cooperative developments at Keewaydin, Audubon and Stewart parks.

The joint agreement led to three projects that were planned from the ground up as schools and parks. The first was Waite Park at Ulysses and

Thirty-fourth Avenue Northeast, where the park board purchased just over eight acres of land adjacent to the school site for $11,400 in 1947. The school and park opened in 1950 and were named for juvenile court judge Edward Waite, who had long been active in the northeast community.

Shortly after the acquisition of Waite Park, the park board acquired two sites in the southern part of the city that had been annexed from Richfield in 1926. Nineteen acres were purchased at Penn Avenue South and Fifty-sixth Street for $11,400 in 1948 for what would eventually become a park and school named for Maude Armatage. The other site of ten acres was acquired about a mile west at Humboldt Avenue South and Fifty-seventh Street. The park board got half the land from the state and bought the rest for $11,600. The school and park, Kenny Park, were named for Sister Elizabeth Kenny, a revered polio fighter in Minneapolis.

The fourth joint development project was at a school that already existed, Cleveland School (named for Grover, not Horace) at Queen and Thirty-third Avenue North. There the park board purchased an acre and a half adjacent to the school for a playground in 1949 for $12,900.

All of these new parks were in areas targeted by Weir and, with the exception of Cleveland Park, were of a suitable size for a neighborhood park. Weir would have been pleased with the acquisitions and the cooperation of school and park boards, but he would not have been happy with how the park board paid for development of the parks. The park board returned to the assessment method Weir disliked for Armatage and Kenny parks. Acquiring the land was cheap compared to developing it for playing fields, especially at Armatage, where considerable grading was required to level the land. On land that cost less than $12,000, the park board spent more than $400,000 creating a recreation facility.

Over the next decade the park board and school board would also collaborate on joint projects at Bohannon, Shingle Creek and Hiawatha parks.

The initial excitement over the possibilities of an expanded recreation program dulled quickly in the late 1940s. By 1948, due to escalating costs, the board reduced the summer playground session by a week and reduced the after-school playground programs it had so proudly added just two years before. The park board was caught in a cycle that had existed from the beginning and has continued since. Operation and maintenance expenses constantly increased. The miles of parkway and acres of land of which the city was so proud consumed maintenance budgets, particularly because so little of it had been left in a natural state. Landscaped grounds and gardens and expanses of lawn do not look good untended. Beauty was expensive.

Even when bonding authority or assessments paid for initial improvements, operation and maintenance costs had to be paid from tax revenues. In time, costs escalated, increases in park levies were consumed, services were cut, and the park board would request more tax revenues. It was—and is—the board's primary source of income.

In 1951, the legislature came to the rescue once again by increasing the maximum tax the park board could collect. But this time the legislature made the increase temporary unless approved by Minneapolis voters. In September 1952, without organized opposition, voters agreed to the tax increase by nearly a four-to-one margin. The cycle started over.

> **P**olio was a frightening disease in the late 1940s. Dramatic increases in postwar playground attendance were cut short in 1946 by fears of a polio epidemic. The city's playgrounds and beaches were deserted the second half of the summer when parents wouldn't let their children play in public spaces for fear of catching the disease. No one went to park concerts either, which prompted radio station WDGY, with the *Minneapolis Tribune* as a sponsor, to broadcast the Lake Harriet concerts for the rest of the summer. Another polio scare in 1949 reduced beach attendance by 68 percent.

Theodore Wirth, Minneapolis Mayor Hubert Humphrey, Francis Gross and Charles Doell at the dedication of the Heffelfinger Fountain at Lyndale Park in 1947. The fountain, the third donated fountain in city parks, was a gift of Frank Heffelfinger. He had seen the bronze and marble fountain during a visit to Italy and had it shipped home. (Minneapolis Park and Recreation Board)

With the increase in revenue, the park board offered new programs, and the public responded. After-school programs were expanded, more skating rinks were opened, and more playgrounds were supervised in summer. Attendance at park programs jumped by a third.

That increase in attendance came without the benefit of indoor facilities. In 1952, the park board still did not have one up-to-date recreation center—instead of the six or seven Doell believed were needed—and they wouldn't get any soon. That year the city announced that it was trying to reduce its bonded debt and, therefore, would approve even fewer bonding requests than in the past. To assist in that process the mayor appointed a capital long-range improvement committee (CLIC) in 1953 to replace the postwar progress committee and prioritize all proposed city projects that required bond debt. Doell's analysis of the postwar progress committee many years later in an interview with Ben Wright was that the tangible results of the committee where parks were concerned had been "meager."

One of the successes of the committee, however, played an important role in the young lives of many baby boomers. For a generation of high school kids in Minneapolis, fall Friday nights were spent at Parade Stadium. In the 1950s and 1960s every Minneapolis public high school played football games at the stadium. It was a place of friendships, rivalries and courtships from across the city, a meeting place on neutral ground.

Parade Stadium was by far the most expensive item on the list submitted by the park board to the postwar progress committee—and it was one of the few things on the list that was built. Of the $6 million the park board received in bonding from the city during Doell's fourteen-year tenure, about $1 million went into building Parade Stadium. From 1950, when construction began, through 1952, the stadium received most of the bonds the city issued for the park board. Stadiums have always had an allure for policy makers.

The stadium was delayed by protests from Lowry Hill residents, which served only to increase costs at a time of rapid inflation. Construction had barely begun when the nation went to war in Korea and the National Production Authority banned the construction of all recreation facilities to conserve materials for war. Doell and Minneapolis mayor Eric Hoyer went to Washington to make their case, and the authority gave the go-ahead to continue with the stadium—Waite Park playground, too—because construction had begun before the ban was issued.

The result was a 17,000-seat, lighted stadium for football and a 2,500-seat stadium for baseball with off-street parking for six hundred cars. The planned basketball and ice arenas were put off for later construction. By the fall of 1951, the stadium was ready for business. It was inaugurated on a Sunday afternoon by a football game between two Minneapolis semi-pro teams before a near sell-out crowd. One of the players in that game was Walt Dziedzic, who forty-six years later would become a park commissioner. Later that fall a Catholic charity sponsored an exhibition pro football game at the new stadium between the Green Bay Packers and San Francisco Forty-Niners. More than twenty thousand fans packed the stadium for the game, the first demonstration of an appetite for pro football that would eventually bring Minneapolis its own team.

To make room for the stadium, the tennis center at The Parade was relocated to Nicollet (Martin Luther King) Park in 1952, and in 1953 the National Public Park Championship was played on the new courts. The Parade had been the hub of tennis life in the city for nearly forty years. In 1931, the National Public Parks Tennis Championship was played on new clay courts at The Parade. The men's doubles title was won by Minneapolis's William Schommer and Charles Britzius. The next year Bill Tilden played an exhibition on the new courts. The events helped give Minneapolis a national reputation in municipal tennis. The number of tennis courts in Minneapolis earned Weir's praise, although he noted that they weren't as useful as they might be because nets weren't provided; players had to bring their own. In 1968, General Mills donated money for permanent, all-weather nets at thirty courts.

The park board also updated many other facilities during the 1950s. The bathhouse at Lake Calhoun was rebuilt, and the one at Wirth Lake was replaced. The library branch in the Webber Park community center was so popular that in 1953 it expanded from its second-floor space to take over the whole building, and a separate warming house was constructed for skaters. The picnic shelter at Wirth Lake was remodeled and so was the Minnehaha Park refectory. Playground improvements were made at McRae, Audubon, Stewart, Peavey and Bohannon Parks, too.

The postwar progress committee's successor, the Capitol Long-range Improvement Commission (CLIC), was not much more inclined to recommend projects for funding by the city. In 1954, the committee responded to the park board's request for $1.3 million in bonds by approving $250,000, of which $200,000 was to improve the intersection between the river road and the Franklin Avenue bridge. The decision prompted board president Walter Quist to comment that depression and war had "dimmed our sensibility as to what cities can really be." He continued, "Do the sights need to be raised, or is there a lack of courage to attack the basic problem of taxation, or a deficiency of talent to compromise the diverse views of special interests?"

His answer from CLIC the next year was a return to neighborhood assessments for park development. CLIC recommended reinstating Elwell assessments for playground improvements under new terms: all new improvements would be paid by assessments split between the neighborhood and the whole city. CLIC would consider recommending 100 percent bond funding only for improvements in neighborhoods where financial need was demonstrated. For

The new Parade Stadium in 1952, looking east toward downtown. (Schreiber-Hager, Minnesota Historical Society)

the next decade, most playground improvements required 51 percent of neighborhood property owners to agree to the assessment before work to improve parks could begin. Improvements at parks were frugally designed in part to improve the chances that the neighborhood would approve assessments.

With the focus on developing existing park property in the 1950s, few acquisitions were made. Two small playground parks were added. In 1953, the board replaced the land sold at Elwell Field with the purchase of Holmes Park, less than three acres at Third Avenue and Fourth Street Southeast. And in 1956, the board purchased four acres at Fifty-ninth Avenue South and Thirty-sixth Street for Morris Park for $67,000.

Two other land acquisitions in the late 1950s culminated decades of petitions and plans. Between 1955 and 1960, the board acquired the remaining private property around the last significant body of water in the city that it didn't already own. The board purchased forty-two acres of shoreline on the north and east shores of Cedar Lake for $65,000 to give the board ownership of the entire lake. (Although part of the east shore of the lake appears to be private property, it is not.) In 1959, another goal of park planners for decades was achieved when the city added twenty-six acres of Fort Snelling to the southern boundary of Minnehaha Park.

A new player in park acquisition and development also appeared on the scene in 1959 when the park board acquired and developed Harrison Park at Fourth Avenue North and Knox on the near north side in conjunction with the Minneapolis Housing Authority. The Glenwood Housing Redevelopment, of which Harrison Park was a component, began in 1957 and opened in 1960 as the nation's largest housing renewal project at the time, encompassing 183 acres. The 7-acre park was acquired for $1,000 from the housing authority. This was the first collaboration between the park board and the city's housing and redevelopment agency, but many more would follow, from the redevelopment of Luxton Park as part of the Glendale housing project to Matthews Park in the Seward neighborhood to extensive efforts to develop the city's riverfront twenty years later.

Even before these last acquisitions, however, the park board had once again run out of money. The tax increase of 1951 had been consumed by spiraling prices and expanded programs. Again in 1957, the legislature stepped up by authorizing another bump in the tax levy, if voters would approve it. They did, but by a smaller margin than in 1952. Even with the increased revenues, superintendent Doell announced that it was no longer affordable to maintain all city parks as landscaped areas. The de-emphasis on

> *Si monumentum vis, circumspice.* During World War II, a record of Horace Cleveland's grave site was discovered at Lakewood Cemetery. A neighborhood historical association in a part of St. Paul that Cleveland had initially designed—St. Anthony Park—arranged a memorial service. On October 17, 1948, the man who provided the inspiration for Minneapolis parks was honored at the cemetery forty-eight years after his death. Theodore Blegen, dean of the graduate school at the University of Minnesota, delivered an address that summarized Cleveland's life and work. Blegen concluded with the Latin phrase that translates, "If you would see his monument, look about you."
>
> Four months later, the other giant of Minneapolis park landscape architecture was laid to rest a short distance away in Lakewood Cemetery. On a slope facing the superintendent's house at Lyndale Farmstead where he had lived for thirty-five years, Theodore Wirth was buried next to his wife on February 4, 1949. A resolution passed by the park board upon his death said, in part, "His life's work, always in harmony with nature, is finished, but those things of lasting beauty and benefit which our citizens continue to enjoy are memorials in his honor that will live on with Minneapolis for years to come."

> The board installed its first parking meters on park property in 1959 at Parade Stadium and at a new parking lot on the north shore of Lake Calhoun. The income from meters that year amounted to $5,000, and the park board predicted that its investment in meters would be retired in three years. Parking revenues at The Parade got a boost when the Guthrie Theater opened in 1963 and theater-goers parked in the lot.

landscaping in parks was underscored when Doell combined the horticulture division with the maintenance division in 1958.

With additional revenues from the levy increase, the park board created full-time, year-round programming at six recreation centers—Lynnhurst, Brackett, Pershing, Keewaydin, Powderhorn and Bryant. The first programs specifically for seniors, another recommendation of Liebert Weir, were also begun, and a supervisor of recreation for seniors was hired in 1959. The following year, the shelter that Charles Loring had donated for Loring Park, which had included kindergarten rooms, was remodeled as a senior center.

With the nation settling into an era of unprecedented prosperity in the late 1950s, the city loosened the purse strings a bit on bond funds, and many more neighborhood parks were improved. But even in years of more liberal funding, much of the bond money went into one project, an effort to raise water levels in the chain of lakes. Lake levels had been below normal since the 1930s and by the mid-1950s had dropped to levels never before seen—down nearly five feet from when Theodore Wirth had created the shorelines. Part of the problem was a drop in the water table caused by the sinking of so many new wells in the expanding suburbs. (All city lakes, except Lake Harriet, sit above the water table.) But Doell also concluded that when the lakes had been shaped, the levels that Wirth had considered normal were actually well above the historical norm. Even so, the level of the lakes had been lowered intentionally in 1935 when Lake of the Isles Parkway, created twenty-five years earlier on dredged soil, had settled so much that the parkway was often flooded.

Both high water and low water posed maintenance challenges at urban lakes that were the centerpieces of landscaped parks. Permanent facilities for swimming and boating required fairly constant water levels. In 1956, the lakes were so low that canoes couldn't pass through the channels between lakes, and the board's boat rental business lost $10,000. Not only were the lakes low in those years, but Minnehaha Creek was bone dry most of the time, which hurt refectory sales at Minnehaha Falls. No water over the falls meant fewer visitors to the park. With low water levels, shoreline deterioration and aquatic plants also became problems. The lakes were treated with sodium arsenite to kill plants, but that was viewed as a short-term solution.

One longer-term solution was to create a pumping system from Bassett's Creek to Brownie Lake. From Brownie Lake the water would run through the channels connecting to Cedar, Isles and Calhoun and from there seep into Harriet and beyond to Minnehaha Creek. (The first proposal to divert Bassett's Creek into the lakes had been made in the 1890s.)

In 1957, with the park board pumping city water into the lakes to raise them one and a half feet, the city approved the money to install the Bassett's Creek pump. Pumping began in 1958 but only raised the lake level four inches. By 1960, with increased rainfall and continuous pumping, the lakes were nearly back to normal levels, and canoes could once again pass from lake to lake.

Despite low lake levels, interest in sailing on city lakes increased dramatically in the 1950s. In 1958 the board increased the number of sailboat buoys at Lake Harriet from 100 to 130 but still couldn't accommodate demand. The Lake Harriet canoe racks were full after nearly being discontinued in previous years.

To address the lake level problem longer term, the board also hired a water-table expert in 1960 to look at subterranean water levels and propose a solution. His novel idea was to capture the water generated by the air conditioners at downtown buildings, which ran off into the storm sewers at the time, and pump that water to the lakes. The plan made perfect sense until downtown businesses realized they could achieve significant savings if they recycled the water in their buildings instead of dumping it down the drain.

Park board engineer Ed Braddock then proposed a more workable solution: pump water from the Mississippi River to the lakes. That pumping system was implemented in the 1960s. River water was pumped first to Bassett's Creek, then to the lakes. The plan's flaw was identified in 1970: the river water was polluted to a degree that no one wanted it in the city's lakes. By that time people had begun to understand that phosphates were not good for lake water quality and the river carried high levels of phosphates. Pumping water from the river to raise lake levels was discontinued in the late 1970s but was used again in the late 1980s during another dry period. The pumping station was dismantled in the 1990s.

Through the 1950s the park board had a mixed record measured by the goals it had established immediately following World War II. Its ambitious goal of adding neighborhood parks in underserved sections of the city had been partially met, but only on the periphery of the city through joint projects with the school board or by picking land off the state's tax-forfeiture list. It had not succeeded in adding parks to the older parts of the city, except by expanding Peavey Park and acquiring small Dickman Park. The board had built modest new recreation centers at several playgrounds, but it had built none of the larger community centers with gymnasiums that Weir had recommended. The board had expanded year-round programs from five parks in 1945 to twelve in 1959 and had expanded summer programming from thirty-eight to fifty-nine playgrounds. To do that, however, the board had to significantly reduce its horticulture and landscaping budget and defer maintenance on many properties.

> The once popular community sings finally passed from the park scene in 1957 when they were replaced with teen dances at several parks. In 1956, community sings were held at only three parks as attendance dwindled. The teen dances were poorly attended too. Most park board entertainment could no longer compete with the newest form of amusement: television.

The board had won three separate tax increases at the legislature to provide operating and programming funds, and two of those were approved by public referenda. On the other hand, the board had received little of the funding it had requested from the city. What bond funding the park board had received went mostly to buying two golf courses, draining the neighborhoods of far north Minneapolis by buying Shingle Creek and lowering the creek bed, building Parade Stadium, and creating a pumping system to maintain lake levels. Of those projects, only building the stadium had been a priority of the park board.

The 1950s were, in essence, a time of rebalancing park priorities and at the same time striking a balance between park interests and the interests of the rest of the city. The successes and the failures of the park board during those years were due, in part, to the personality of Doell. As much as Doell relished details—charts that were fascinating—he also saw the bigger picture of where parks fit among the competing interests in a growing metropolitan region. And it was in attempting to balance those interests, especially as they related to freeways and a metropolitan park system, that Doell left his biggest mark on the future of Minneapolis parks. On one issue, his approach didn't solve problems; on the other, it helped considerably.

The expansion of Highway 12 west of downtown in 1949 took land from Wirth Park. This photo was taken before the sale of land on the west side of Brownie Lake, at right, in 1952. (*Minneapolis Star Journal,* Minnesota Historical Society)

Chapter Nineteen

The Bigger City

Charles Doell was a quintessential leader of the 1950s, a team player, an organization man. That was reflected in his election to the presidency of American Institute of Park Executives in 1948. It was also evident in the park board's approach to the major challenges of its time.

Doell saw the bigger picture, parks in a "bigger" city. Not that he thought that Minneapolis itself would expand. In fact he cautioned the board early in his tenure that the city had seen the end of annexations; its borders were fixed. To Doell the bigger city meant a metropolitan area of competing interests and varied needs, from transportation to recreation.

Doell's way of addressing those emerging issues was to work behind the scenes to negotiate and accommodate conflicting plans. That attitude led to many cooperative ventures with other city agencies, from the school board to the housing authority to city engineers. Much of the expansion of the park system under Doell was arranged—cheaply—in cooperation with other agencies.

But Doell's quiet, cooperative style required some trade-offs, too. In his willingness to accommodate others' interests, the park system at times paid a price. For instance, in 1948, the park board abandoned an effort to expand Wirth Park to the west to include Sweeney Lake in Golden Valley. The board deferred to the Glenwood Hills Hospital, which wanted to build on that land. (That land, since the hospital's closing in the 1990s, was developed into high-priced homes and condos.) The next year the board leased the east river flats to the University of Minnesota for a parking lot in a section of town that was deficient in parks. (That lease was renewed through 1979.) In 1951, the board sold Elwell Field in southeast Minneapolis to a manufacturing company. The land was replaced nearby, but the board gave the impression, at least, that park land was fair game.

That impression led the next year to the biggest sale of land ever by the park board. In 1952, Prudential Insurance Company wanted to build its northwest regional headquarters in the city and identified the location it wanted: the southwest corner of Theodore Wirth Park south of Highway 12 just west of Brownie Lake. Intense pressure was put on the park board by business, civic and labor leaders to make the deal, and it finally did. Thirty acres of Wirth Park were sold to Prudential for a little less than $200,000. The park board even agreed to build a road from Wirth Parkway along the northern edge of Brownie Lake to the site of the new building.

Doell and the board defended the action by claiming it was in the best interests of the city. The sale delivered the "doubly desired" benefit of jobs and increased property taxes according to the board's 1954 annual report. The park board's attempt to do right by the city was not rewarded. In the three years immediately after the sale to Prudential, the city's capital improvement committee approved less than one-third of the board's requests for bond funds.

The park board under Doell's leadership was not the first to sell park land, and it wouldn't be the last, but it established a precedent for giving up precious land that would make defending parks more difficult in the years that followed as the construction of freeways began.

Christian Bossen had foreseen problems ahead with highways when he reported in 1940 that small encroachments on park land by highways had been settled satisfactorily but warned that "a decision as to what is more important to the public welfare, the highway or the recreation area, is a question which will soon need definite determination."

The park board had given up park land for city streets long before freeways were needed to transport the growing suburban population. As early as 1921 the park board had given up land at The Parade to accommodate traffic at the "bottleneck" of Hennepin and Lyndale avenues. "Park lands so effected," Theodore Wirth wrote at the time, "can well be sacrificed for this important service." His words were almost the same eleven years later when the city took another few acres of The Parade to improve street connections to Wayzata Boulevard (Highway 12). The same year, the park board diverted St. Anthony Boulevard so gravel could be quarried on the site of the original boulevard. Again in 1940, the board had accommodated business interests when it agreed to a land swap with the Soo Line Railroad adjacent to Columbia Park that was, the board said, to the mutual advantage of both parties. It had also reluctantly leased a block of park land between Loring Park and The Parade to a car dealer for $5,200 a year in 1940 simply as a way to raise money in difficult times.

In Doell's first annual report as superintendent in 1945 he called freeways "the first and most urgent" issue before the park board. But it was not until the mid-1950s that serious conflicts emerged. In 1955, the state and federal governments presented their first plans for a freeway system through Minneapolis. The park board immediately issued a memorandum that established its position. It stated first that "parks cannot stand reduction," and second, that the park board must be compensated for any park land taken.

In later statements, however, the park board sounded less insistent. The next year when Congress passed the Interstate Highway Act, which provided funding for freeways, the park board announced that it was encouraged to find that the state highway department was "inclined to accept" its suggestions. When the board restated its policy on freeways, it insisted on being informed of plans, retaining the "privilege" of making suggestions and being reimbursed for land taken. The board noted that it had "reason to believe this principle will be respected."

By the end of Doell's tenure as superintendent, the board had not suffered significant losses to freeway construction, but it had not demonstrated that it would put up much of a fight if it did. What Martin Friedman, director of the Walker Art Center, would later call the "urban lobotomy" of freeways in Minneapolis had not yet occurred. It would be left to later park boards and superintendents to change the terms of the fight to preserve park land from encroachment or to insist on adequate compensation.

Doell was much more successful in establishing the view of parks as a metropolitan, rather than just a city, resource. Doell's most enduring contribution to the Minneapolis park system may have been what he did to establish parks *outside* the city. His leadership in establishing a county park system—and metropolitan park mentality—paved the way for eventual creation of a regional park system and a way for Minneapolis to obtain money from the state to acquire and maintain parks that served the entire region.

City lakes and parks continued to be used extensively by people throughout the Twin Cities, even as Minneapolis's population peaked in the mid-1950s and began to drop in the 1960s. This photo was taken in 1960. Lake Harriet concerts were still being offered at the "temporary" bandstand built in 1926. It was not replaced until 1986. Opera at Lake Harriet made a comeback in 1951. Most performances were singing only and were free, but an admission was charged for a full-costumed version of *The Mikado* in 1952 by the Minneapolis Opera Association. More fully-staged operas were offered in 1953. But as in the 1930s, after a few summers attendance dwindled. In 1959, a jazz festival was held at Lake Harriet that drew overflow crowds. (Minneapolis Park and Recreation Board)

The challenge faced by the park board as population shifted to the suburbs was one that remains: suburbanites continued to use Minneapolis parks. The crux of the problem was that Minneapolis was providing a service to a lot of people who weren't paying for it through property taxes.

There were two solutions. One was to create more parks outside of the city that would relieve overuse of city parks and provide a type of park the city didn't have. Many thought Theodore Wirth Park would provide the "great scenic park" that William Folwell had advocated, but with the conversion of much of Wirth Park to a golf course, that land had been lost to wider and wilder use. Another solution was to secure revenues from the people who used the parks but weren't paying property taxes in the city. User fees were a way of doing that for some services, but for the use of the parks around the city's lakes in particular, that was not feasible.

Two concurrent and related developments would eventually help relieve the pressure on Minneapolis parks as the suburbs grew. Doell was a champion of both. The first was the creation of a mechanism of metropolitan government that could distribute resources more equitably across the region. Eventually that was accomplished when the legislature created the Metropolitan Council. The second was the creation of an independent park district that encompassed all of Hennepin County. Doell's contribution to creating that system was substantial and would lead to what he later called the "most rewarding" work he did.

Park advocates were among the first to propose cooperative efforts across city lines in the region. The leaders of Minneapolis and St. Paul had considered joint development of the Mississippi River as a park in 1872. Folwell was one of the first to propose a metropolitan park system when, in 1901, he suggested the creation of a system of parks that would stretch from White Bear Lake to Lake Minnetonka and embrace the "splendid valleys" of the Mississippi and Minnesota rivers. (A year earlier Folwell published an essay advocating a state park system, too.) In 1907, the park board appointed a special committee to investigate creating a metropolitan park system that would include Lake Minnetonka. "Let's do it and let's be magnificent about it," Folwell urged.

There was neither the political will nor the political machinery to accomplish such a goal then. City planning, let alone regional planning, was still in

"Let's begin to do it and let's be magnificent about it."

WILLIAM FOLWELL

its infancy. Still, the park board kept the issue alive, proposing a "Greater Grand Rounds" in 1912 to encompass the larger lakes of the region.

The park board and Wirth revived the issue of regional parks in the late 1920s after Minneapolis had finally created a city planning department in 1923 and the first regional planning association had been established in 1926. Wirth noted in 1928 that Hennepin County had expressed interest in controlling the flow of Minnehaha Creek from its source at Lake Minnetonka through the western suburbs and Minneapolis. Wirth advised assisting the county in its plans to improve Minnehaha Creek and later advocated similar plans for Shingle Creek. Shortly before his retirement in 1935, Wirth offered a detailed plan for a park system in the western half of the metro area.

By that time the first true intercity project led to a great cooperative success. Formed in 1933, the Minneapolis–St. Paul Sanitary District created the intercepting sanitary sewer system.

As park leaders began to contemplate life after depression and war, Francis Gross called for the creation of a county planning and zoning commission in 1941. Gross was a member of the second metro-wide agency, the Metropolitan Airports Commission (MAC), created in 1943 to manage the airport, which was transferred from the park board to the new agency. It was Doell who wrote the first comprehensive assessment for MAC of the airport's potential role in the growth of the metro area.

In the early 1950s Doell became a leading proponent of a metropolitan park system. Doell warned that the rapid development of open land in the suburbs was "endangering the recreation possibilities of a future generation." He even proposed a metro-wide park levy to finance the system. Heeding that warning, the state legislature created the authority for a metropolitan park system in 1955, but excluded Minneapolis and St. Paul. As always, Doell worked behind the scenes and kept a low profile to avoid the appearance that the Minneapolis park board was engineering a land grab in the suburbs.

An event that precipitated a functioning countywide park system was the donation to the Minneapolis park board of two hundred-plus acres on Lake Independence in rural Hennepin County in 1956 by the Morris Baker Foundation. The donation was made with the understanding that it would become part of a countywide park system when created. The next year the legislature created a new park district in Hennepin County, and the park board turned over what is now Baker Park to the new commission.

The Metropolitan Planning Commission was also created in 1957, which would eventually become the Metropolitan Council, through which the state would fund metropolitan parks. In 1958, Doell and the board's landscape architect, Felix Dhainin, wrote a basic plan for the new Hennepin County Park Reserve District.

In his last annual report in 1958, Doell wrote, "Seventy five years ago, Minneapolis could plan for its own potential population, and as far as parks were concerned, did so surprisingly well." But he added, Minneapolis could no longer stand alone. Upon his retirement as superintendent, Doell worked for several years as a consultant to the new park commission in creating a park system. Over the next twenty years, the Hennepin County Park Reserve District grew from the two hundred acres of Baker Park to twenty-two thousand acres. Doell deserves some of the credit.

Doell retired in 1959 with a solid record of achievement, but development of the parks recommended by Liebert Weir in 1944, the blueprint Doell had followed, was far from being achieved. The park board simply had never gotten the resources to implement the Weir plan. The high regard for Doell on a national level was indicated in 1957 when he became the second superintendent of Minneapolis parks—Wirth was the first—to receive the national Pugsley Award for service to parks in the United States.

When Doell retired in 1959, he was replaced by the secretary to the board, Howard Moore, who had also served as the board's attorney. Moore was chosen over Felix Dhainin. The park board was divided over whom to hire and did not give Moore a ringing endorsement. At the time Moore was given the top job, Dhainin was given a big pay raise and added responsibility.

Moore knew well the issues facing the park board because, like Doell, he had risen through the park board staff during the days of Wirth. Moore had worked for the park board his entire adult life except for military service during World War II.

The challenges of managing Minneapolis parks had gotten worse during Doell's tenure, despite tax increases. While per capita spending on Minneapolis parks rose from $1.19 in 1944 to $5.52 in 1960, most of that increase went to higher costs of labor and materials. Moore wrote in 1960 that the park board faced a backlog of $3 million in "deferred maintenance." And he, like his predecessor, faced the recommendation of a city charter commission that the park board be abolished. Doell's collaborative style ultimately had not convinced the city's political leaders of the value of an independent park administration. Still, the city's voters had a greater appreciation for the park system's existing structure and rejected a new charter at the ballot box in 1960.

Moore was a well-liked man who delegated authority to his staff but did not have an aggressive agenda for park expansion. He had lived through the frustration of the 1950s of not getting funds needed to achieve the goals of that era, and by his own admission, according to Ben Wright in an unpublished history of the period, he was coasting along to retirement. The only park land acquired during Moore's tenure from 1959 to 1965 was for Matthews Park in the Seward neighborhood. The ten acres at Twenty-eighth Avenue South and East Twenty-fourth Street were purchased for about $225,000 using money the board had been paid as compensation for land taken by freeways.

With continually rising costs, Moore made one

Howard Moore, superintendent of parks in 1959–65, helped launch a canoe in the channel between Lake Calhoun and Lake of the Isles in 1960. It was the first time the channel was navigable in two years due to low water levels. (Minneapolis Park and Recreation Board)

of his most important contributions to park management by using the mechanization of the time to reduce maintenance costs. Gas-powered lawn mowers, leaf blowers, tree booms and backhoes were all acquired to make park crews more efficient. Sump pumps were installed on golf courses to keep them playable, and the furnaces at park shelters were converted from coal to gas.

The park board's attempts to minimize the loss of land to highways, or at least receive fair compensation for land taken, appeared unsuccessful when in 1960 the park board identified more than three hundred acres that could be lost to highways, nearly 5 percent of city park land. The park board issued a policy statement once again that any park land taken

In 1962 the park board moved the speed-skating track from Powderhorn Park, which was experiencing record-low water levels, to Lake Harriet. The U.S. Olympic Trials were held on the Lake Harriet track in 1963, and Minneapolis skaters Tom Gray and Marie Lawler made the Olympic team.

should be replaced to keep the overall system up to "proper standards."

Finally in 1962, the board actually began losing land to freeways: a couple acres at Riverside Park and nearly twenty-one acres at The Parade, which eliminated seven softball fields. Board President Henry Rosacker noted the board's constant battle to avoid "nibbling" at park land by other agencies. The nibbling continued in 1963 with the loss of more than two acres at Nicollet (King) Park as construction of the Stevens Avenue Expressway—I-35—began.

The power of the park board's protests over losing land was diminished at the time by the board's own actions. In 1962 the board turned over part of Stinson Boulevard to the city council due to "functional changes" in traffic. The southern section of parkway was being heavily used for traffic in that industrialized portion of the city. The board also sold parcels of land next to Ridgway Parkway to Honeywell and Hillside Cemetery in 1963. Moreover, in 1962 Moore had compiled a list of properties the board could sell "without detriment" to the park system. Included were portions of Shingle Creek, Columbia and Hi-view Parks for homesites, and Murphy Square for apartment buildings. The compilation of such a list did not suggest that the park board would be a tenacious adversary in a land dispute.

However, the stance of the board began to shift at the urging of board attorney Edward Gearty. Gearty was elected to the park board in 1959 and served as board president from 1960 to 1963. Upon leaving the park board for the Minnesota legislature in 1963, Gearty was elected to be the board's attorney, a position he would hold through some of the board's most intense disputes with the state highway department later in the 1960s.

By 1964, in the face of increasing freeway encroachment on park land, Gearty recommended that the park board resist further land loss, or paltry compensation, by forcing land disputes with the highway department into court for condemnation proceedings. His position was that in condemnation proceedings the park board could state its case for much higher values for its park land than the highway department was willing to pay. Gearty's position would find a willing and pugnacious advocate in the man who took over as park superintendent after Moore.

One of the biggest changes in Minneapolis parks beginning in the late 1950s and continuing through Moore's superintendence was in the board itself. The control of the board by the city's old Republican elite was broken in the 1950s, and along with that control went the unanimity of action that had long characterized board actions. With the election in 1957 of Earl Arneson and George Todd,

Low water levels in city lakes and Minnehaha Creek were still a problem in 1964. When President Lyndon Johnson and his running mate, Senator Hubert Humphrey, made a campaign stop for Svenskarnasdag in Minnehaha Park that year, the city opened water mains into the creek to provide a flow of water over the falls. Governor Karl Rolvaag is at left. (Minneapolis Park and Recreation Board)

Each year a special flower bed was planted at the Kenwood Gardens, now the site of the Minneapolis Sculpture Garden, along Lyndale Avenue. Most years the flower message welcomed a convention held in the city, but in 1964 it paid tribute to Minneapolis's selection by *Look* magazine as the All-America City. (Minneapolis Park and Recreation Board)

both labor union agents, and the election of young Richard Kantorowicz to the board's presidency, came a level of contention and fragmentation on the board that was previously unknown. In the early 1960s, Arthur Naftalin, who as mayor was an ex-officio member of the board, commented on the lack of decorum at park board meetings. It had become a "jungle," he said. It was not a political environment in which a passive, hands-off superintendent, such as Moore, was likely to enjoy success. Moore was not the strong leader who could impose order or vision.

Near the end of Moore's superintendence, the board decided to revisit the issues raised by Weir in 1944. In 1964, the board voted to conduct a new study of the city's park system to measure its progress against the Weir report. Once again, the board chose for the task a man of impeccable credentials and wide respect, professor Charles Brightbill from the University of Illinois. Brightbill hired some of the leading authorities on park and recreation management in the country to assist him.

For much of 1964, Brightbill and his team poured over park assets and analyzed the city's recreation needs much as Weir had done twenty years earlier. Their conclusions were much the same.

- Despite the addition of a number of park shelters, the system had only two facilities, the recently built recreation centers at Longfellow and Powderhorn, that could accommodate modern recreation programs.

- The park board had never made the transition to parks *and* recreation. Park board expenditures on recreation were well below those of comparable cities, despite a 50 percent increase in attendance at park-sponsored activities through the 1950s. To refocus the board on its new mission of providing recreation, and to elevate recreation to a position of true equality, Brightbill recommended the name of the board be changed to the Park and Recreation Board.

- The recreation program was still too focused on competitive sports. Brightbill, however, took Weir's prescription of broader-based recreation programs to a new level. His goal was no longer simply to train people for leisure activities but to assist individuals in the process of "self-realization."

- The system was still plagued by a shortage of funds. One cause, as always, was the expense of simply maintaining the city's vast park holdings. Brightbill recommended an increase in the tax rate and turning over maintenance of parkways to the city.

- Another way to improve funding, said Brightbill, was to add to the staff's planning expertise, so that it could work more effectively with CLIC and other agencies in prioritizing park needs. Moreover, he suggested a relaxation of civil service rules that restricted who the board could hire. Brightbill believed that civil service rules rewarded longevity more than competence.

- Finally, Brightbill was critical of the board itself. He recommended reducing the size of the board to seven commissioners and improving coordination between commissioners and staff. In Brightbill's opinion, a divided park board no longer made policy but simply reacted to events in a haphazard fashion. There was no coherent policy to implement.

Brightbill concluded, much as Weir had twenty years earlier, that Minneapolis had lost its leadership in park issues. Neither the board nor the park system it ran was as respected as each had once been.

When Moore announced his intention to resign as park superintendent in 1964, it was the end of "Wirth men" managing the affairs of the Minneapolis park system. The world, the city and the demands on park management had changed considerably since the heyday of Wirth's management. The problem was that no one had been able to redefine park policy or management to meet the demands of a new time.

The task of defining a new vision and creating new structures to pursue that vision would fall to a new man, an outsider, who would step on some toes to get it done.

The number of golf rounds played at city courses reached an all-time high in 1963 at 255,000. The increase was due in part to the addition of a nine-hole course the previous summer at Wirth Park. Gross Golf Course was lengthened in 1963 in preparation for the 1964 National Amateur Public Links Championship. The clubhouse at Meadowbrook was also remodeled.

Chapter Twenty

A Man on a Mission

In 1970, the prestigious Cornelius Amory Pugsley Award for service to municipal parks in the United States was awarded to a third superintendent of Minneapolis parks, Robert Ruhe. In only four years on the job in Minneapolis, Ruhe had gained the national renown and acclaim that had accrued to Theodore Wirth and Charles Doell after decades of service.

A large, intimidating man—often brutally frank—Ruhe was brought to Minneapolis to replace Howard Moore in 1966 to shake things up, to break the cozy status quo. His attitude, according to Al Wittman, who became assistant superintendent for planning under him, was that Ruhe would rather be blamed for doing something rather than be blamed for doing nothing. The "something" he did in his first four years changed the direction of the park board. He transformed the administration of parks in Minneapolis, from staffing and funding to the structure of the board. He provided a new vision for leadership in recreation. And perhaps he was best known nationally for his defense of park land against highway encroachment.

Much like Wirth sixty years earlier, Ruhe was a brash newcomer who arrived at a time when there was both a pent-up demand for park improvements and the economic prosperity to do something about that demand after a long period of neglect. Wirth took advantage of the conditions of his time to change the physical makeup and the appearance of the park system. Ruhe, on the other hand, used those factors to expand neighborhood recreation facilities and broaden the scope of recreation activities.

Robert Ruhe *(center)*, superintendent of parks from 1966 to 1978, accepts a gift of thirty tennis nets in 1968 from General Mills, presented here by General Mills executive Sewall Andrews. Before this time nets were not provided on park tennis courts. The player at right is unidentified. (Minneapolis Park and Recreation Board)

Among the park board's first initiatives after Ruhe was hired was the creation of a "land policy" that had little of the accommodative language of the past. "A system of public parks and parkways has been acquired and developed to the city's everlasting credit and the immeasurable enhancement of said city and its environs," began the policy statement issued in July 1966. So far, so much the same as in the past. But from there the language was pure Ruhe: "Those who seek park lands for their own particular ends must look elsewhere to satiate their land hunger. Minneapolis park lands should not be looked upon as land banks upon which others may draw to satisfy a lack of foresightedness in properly anticipating their land requirements. The park system is still expanding and acquisitions will and must go on."

The policy also offered assistance to other agencies to find alternatives to taking park land. But, it warned, if the taking of park land is not in the public interest, the board "will take what action is necessary to resist."

Resistance began almost immediately. Over the next two years, the park board would dig in its heels over giving up park land, especially for freeways and highways. The board's OK Corral, where it would make its stand, was Minnehaha Park, where the board resisted state plans for Highway 55 (Hiawatha Avenue) through Minnehaha Park. (The issue is discussed more fully in the next chapter.) The board's showdown with the builders of highways gained national attention and made Ruhe a hero for park defenders and freeway opponents throughout the country.

The summer after the board's new land policy was announced, the board sponsored a city charter amendment that did two things: changed the name of the park board officially to the Minneapolis Park and Recreation Board and changed the composition of the board from sixteen members, including the mayor and two council members, to only nine elected members, six from park districts and three at-large. The six park districts were designed roughly along ward boundaries with just enough variation to provide what were considered then to be three "safe" districts for each political party. The park board at that time was evenly divided between Republicans and DFLers. The implicit agreement was that the parties would then fight for control of the park board in the three at-large, or citywide, seats.

The composition of the board was chosen to provide local representation while preventing the domination of parochial interests by having one-third of the board elected to represent the whole city. The new arrangement was facilitated by the fact that five of the six commissioners whose terms were to end in 1969 had already decided not to seek reelection, so no incumbents would have to face each other in an election. The charter amendment passed by a comfortable margin in 1967, with the changes to take effect in July 1969.

Even before those changes were implemented, however, the park board went to the state legislature in early 1969 with the most ambitious legislative program the board had ever proposed. The park board got nearly everything it wanted:

- A 25 percent increase in the maximum tax levy for the Park and Recreation Fund.

- A new fund for park improvements to address the problem of deferred maintenance. The board requested authority for a one mill levy and received six-tenths of a mill.

- Creation of a Tree Preservation and Reforestation Fund to consolidate five existing funds. The board requested three mills and received approval for two-point-three mills.

- Civil service exemptions for four assistant superintendents who would serve at the discretion of the superintendent.

With the legislative success, the board had increased park funding from taxes by more than $1.2 million a year. The park board not only had more money to work with, but Ruhe had the power to hire senior staff of his choosing.

The staffing exemption was particularly important to Ruhe. He had already reorganized the park board staff and worked with the Civil Service Commission to enlarge the pool of candidates for some positions. Ruhe had come to the conclusion early in his job that the park staff was one of his biggest problems. Ruhe was an activist who hated the status quo mentality of the staff when he took over. He said he wanted "proposers," not "reactors."

He brought in new people, replaced the old staff when he could, and if he couldn't replace them, he simply ignored them until they quit or retired, which in some cases took years.

In addition to the legislative success, Ruhe convinced the park board and the city council to stop using the Elwell Law to pay for improvements in neighborhood parks. From then on, the policy of assessing improvements to a benefited neighborhood was used only for parkway improvements, which was the same policy used by the city for street improvements. All neighborhood parks would be improved with bond funds.

The board rapidly built on those accomplishments with further success at the legislature in 1971. The park board received additional increases in levies for parks and recreation and forestry, and established new funds supported by levies for a Park Rehabilitation and Parkway Maintenance Fund and a Lake Pollution Control Fund. The board also received legislative approval to issue $4 million of its own bonds to finance parkway improvements. Although the direct bonding authority for the park board, a first, outraged the city council, it had its desired effect. The parks board's bonding authority was never used because CLIC added parkways to its agenda. From 1972 to 1979, CLIC approved $9 million in bonds for parkway improvements.

The improved funding from the city also reflected a greater commitment on the part of the park board to work with CLIC and to prioritize its requests. Following Brightbill's suggestions, the board significantly improved its planning staff and tried to develop better staff relationships with other agencies, including CLIC. The board also established clearer standards for park acquisition and improvements, which made CLIC's job easier. The board's success at the legislature in 1969 and 1971 was partially due to the ten-year capital improvement plan Ruhe called "Challenge for Leadership." The plan made it easier for policy makers to appreciate what needed to be done and provided context for each year's budget request. In the twelve years Ruhe was superintendent, the board received $36 million in bond funding compared with $6 million in the fourteen years after World War II.

"Those who seek park lands for their own particular ends must look elsewhere to satiate their land hunger. Minneapolis park lands should not be looked upon as land banks upon which others may draw to satisfy a lack of foresightedness in properly anticipating their land requirements."

MINNEAPOLIS BOARD OF PARK COMMISSIONERS

The success of the park board under Ruhe in obtaining funding has to be viewed, however, in the context of government expenditures across the country. There was a large increase in government spending everywhere, owing in part to a booming economy and the Great Society programs of President Lyndon Johnson. In the years Ruhe was superintendent, federal grants to state and local governments across the country increased more than fivefold. Locally, although the park board's budget more than tripled from 1966 to 1978, the park board's budget increased at a *lower* rate than the overall city budget.

New government programs, many associated with the creation of the Department of Housing and Urban Development (HUD) in 1965, made federal grants available for parks and recreation, and the park board pursued them aggressively. From 1966 to early 1969 the park board secured more than $1.6 million in federal grants to acquire, develop or improve ten park properties. Much more would be obtained in subsequent years.

The board achieved all of the above in Ruhe's first five years, and he won the Pugsley Award in the process. And that was only the beginning. The period of Ruhe's superintendence from 1966 to 1978 was the most productive era in Minneapolis parks since the mid-1910s to mid-1920s when Theodore Wirth reshaped the landscape of parks. During Ruhe's years in Minneapolis, the park board acquired most of the new neighborhood parks and playgrounds recommended by Weir and Brightbill, built many of the recreation facilities they had called for, and began to reshape the recreation system to achieve the broader objectives both men advocated. Ruhe himself claimed that he found his greatest satisfaction in expanding neighborhood parks.

Because of the importance Ruhe attached to the development of neighborhood parks, the rest of this chapter is devoted to a brief account of what was accomplished. However, Ruhe's legacy in the Minneapolis park system also extends to how the park board finally addressed issues surrounding the automobile, from the building of freeways to the improvement of parkways. Ruhe was also at the helm when the park board began to develop a greater awareness of what it had to do to enhance its natural resources: clean up its lakes, preserve its trees, and make better use of the central and upper stretches of the Mississippi River. Succeeding chapters tell those stories.

Robert Ruhe came to Minneapolis from Skokie, Illinois, where he had been superintendent of parks. Like Wirth and Doell before him, he had been active in professional park associations. Even before he moved to Minneapolis, he had received a distinguished service award from the American Institute of Park Executives. At age forty-two, the same age as Wirth when he came to Minneapolis, Ruhe had the credentials for a prestigious park job, such as the one in Minneapolis. And it didn't hurt that he was supported for the job by Charles Brightbill. Ruhe had been a disciple of Brightbill even before Brightbill conducted his study of Minneapolis parks.

When Ruhe arrived, he was the first superintendent raised in an era when active use of parks was the norm, and he was also the first park superintendent with a college degree in park and recreation administration. Berry and Wirth had both learned by doing and observing some of the early masters at work, Bossen studied at the University of Wirth, Doell was trained as an engineer, and Moore as an attorney.

Ruhe brought with him the latest theories in recreation, which Brightbill had already introduced to the board a year earlier. The core of that theory of recreation was an expansion of the belief of men like Horace Cleveland that parks helped to "build character." To Cleveland and others of his time, individual "character" was developed in part through communion with nature. Nature helped people identify and understand their place in the world and feel a part of it. Recreation proponents of Ruhe's time believed the same benefits were also obtained—in a more crowded world—through a wide variety of leisure pursuits.

And the language had changed. Instead of "building character," leisure activities helped individuals achieve "self-realization." What mattered most to Ruhe, said Harvey Feldman, the assistant superintendent for recreation hired by Ruhe, "was not what Johnny did to the ball, but what the ball did for Johnny." Recreation wasn't just a ball game; it was leisure time made "meaningful and rewarding," Ruhe wrote. And he took it a step further. It wasn't only the physical development of individuals that was the interest of recreation programs, but the artistic, cultural and intellectual development as well. Recreation programs should be as much for piano players as football players. When Ruhe hired horticulturist Mary Lerman, he told her that recreation was "more than organized sweat." Further, Ruhe claimed that "the assumption that self-directed and spontaneous use of facilities would automatically fulfill our responsibility has proven erroneous." What was required was "leadership," recreation leaders who would help individuals along the path to "human enrichment."

It was a philosophy of recreation, an extension of park and recreation administration into public education, that required much more than beautiful parks. Minneapolis had those in abundance. What the philosophy required was buildings to house programs and leaders to run those programs. That was what Brightbill had recommended, and it was what Ruhe demanded. Ruhe would later claim that the Brightbill Study was the basis of his administration. To achieve the goals of Brightbill, the city's park system needed facilities.

In only twelve years, from 1966 to 1978, the park board built thirty-seven recreation centers and developed fourteen new parks. The new centers ranged from eight "community" centers that included a gymnasium/auditorium to fourteen "recreation shelters" that were designed mostly to serve children's programs and provide warming houses for skaters. The new parks were all acquired in neighborhoods that Weir and Brightbill had targeted as underserved, mostly in the central city.

The park board acquired or developed many of its properties during this time by collaborating with some combination of three partners:

- Schools: While continuing to collaborate with the board of education in developing sites jointly, the park board also relied on the school board for many of its new park sites. As the school board closed smaller neighborhood schools in favor of building larger complexes, partly to achieve racial integration goals, the park board purchased old school sites for parks.

- Housing authorities: The park board developed some parks in conjunction with housing redevelopment and also acquired some park land from housing authorities.

- Nonprofit social and community agencies: The park board cooperated with social agencies to finance, develop or operate facilities. Some of the operating agreements developed with social agencies during this time continue today. Al Wittman said that Ruhe had reservations about park cooperation with social agencies because there were no guarantees as to the longevity of those organizations.

Also of great importance in obtaining funding and cooperation in the development of new parks and buildings was the priority given to neighborhood development by the Minneapolis Planning Commission beginning in the early 1960s. The focus of planners at the city and the park board was on stabilizing neighborhoods that were deteriorating physically or socially, in part to stem the tide of emigration to the greener fields of the suburbs. With the closing of many neighborhood schools in the 1960s

Pearl Park was one of many city parks to get a new recreation center in the 1970s. The designers had a strong sense of geometry. The northern end of the park *(top)*, now soccer fields, was not yet developed. The northern shore of Diamond Lake is at bottom. (Minneapolis Park and Recreation Board)

and 1970s, the only city agency with a presence in almost every neighborhood was the park board.

In 1966 and 1967, the park board's only acquisition was thirteen acres to expand Bryn Mawr Field to replace land taken for highways at The Parade. The only development project was Pearl Park, which along with the renovation of Martin Luther King Park the following year, would be the last park board projects partly funded by neighborhood assessments. The recreation centers built at Pearl and King would be the prototypes for the medium-sized neighborhood centers built at other parks over the next decade.

To meet Ruhe's recreation goals, the next decade saw an enormous amount of activity in the neighborhoods.

1968

Acquisitions:

- Cavell Park. The park board acquired its first abandoned school site, three and one-half acres at Fillmore Street and Thirty-fourth Avenue Northeast. The board purchased the site with money the state paid for land taken for highways. The site would not be developed into a playground until 1975.

- The board also added ten acres to Northeast Athletic Field, and two acres to Van Cleve Park.

Major developments:

- Northeast Pool. A swimming facility east of the river had been one of Weir's highest priorities. Originally named Rosacker Pool for Henry Rosacker, a prominent park commissioner, the pool was transformed in 2003 into Jim Lupient Water Park.

- Matthews Park. The property acquired in the early 1960s was developed into a neighborhood center attached to Seward School as a joint project with the school board and Pillsbury Waite Neighborhood Services. Matthews Park was one of the first parks in the country developed by that combination of partners.

- Bethune Park. Named Grant Park at the time, the park was developed with a building attached to Bethune School to be operated by the Phyllis Wheatley Community Center. That operating agreement has been renewed up to the present day.

- Luxton Park. A neighborhood recreation center was built at the site of the park, which was adjacent to the Glendale housing redevelopment. This project was a carryover from the Moore administration.

- Martin Luther King Park. The playground was redeveloped and a neighborhood recreation center was added.

- The board added ten small play lots for children, some on park property and some on leased land.

1969

Acquisitions: None

Major developments:

- Sibley Park and Phelps Park. Both were developed with a neighborhood recreation center. They were the first development projects initiated by the board under Ruhe's leadership. They were targeted because they were in neighborhoods on the edge of "tipping" into deterioration.

- Northeast Athletic Field. To avoid duplication of facilities with adjacent Putnam School, a recreation center was created by adding multi-use spaces to the school.

- Bryant Square. The board built a new recreation center and improved the playing fields.

1970

Acquisitions: An addition of seven acres to Wirth Park.

Major developments:

- Folwell Park and Van Cleve Park. The first community centers were built, which included gyms and were designed to serve more than the immediate neighborhood. The cost of each of the community centers, along with redevelopment of the surrounding playgrounds, was approximately $500,000.
- Lynnhurst Park. Redevelopment of the playground was begun, with construction of a new community center gym/auditorium attached to Burroughs School scheduled to begin the following year.
- Logan Park. The original and only park board "field house" was demolished, and a new community center was built in 1971.
- Bryn Mawr Park. Considerable work was begun to create a complex of athletic fields as well as a neighborhood park.

1971

Acquisitions:

- Greeley Center. An acre of land was acquired at Tenth Avenue South and East Twenty-seventh Street for the Edward Waite Neighborhood House.

Major developments:

- North Commons. A community center was built and the park redeveloped.
- Powderhorn Park. Redevelopment was begun that would include the addition of a gym/auditorium the next year.
- Keewaydin Park. Redevelopment of the site would include the building of a neighborhood center the next year. The park and school boards considered attaching the recreation center to the school but decided on a freestanding building.

1972

Acquisitions: None

Major developments:

- Beltrami Park. The park was redesigned.
- Linden Hills Park. Another two-year project began that would see the site redesigned, and a neighborhood center built.
- Loring Park. The shelter was once again renovated.

1973

Acquisitions:

- St. Anthony Park. More than five acres at Jefferson Street and Third Avenue Northeast were acquired with housing authority funds for a playground next to the new Webster School. The land for a playground and school had been set aside as part of a housing redevelopment project begun in 1964. The site would be developed as a playground in 1974.
- Whittier Park. A little less than four acres at Grand Avenue South and West Twenty-sixth Street was acquired, partly with grants from a new "Parks in the Cities" program created by the Department of Housing and Urban Development under President Richard Nixon. Al Wittman, the park board's planner at the time, notes that Minneapolis was the only city that applied for funds under the

program. The same program was used to acquire Willard and Mueller parks. Grants for urban parks from the National Park Service also contributed to all three purchases. The park was developed, and a recreation center was built in 1974–75.

- Willard Park. A small park of just over an acre was acquired mostly with federal money at Queen Avenue and Seventeenth Avenue North. The land was developed as a playground the following year.

- Mueller Park. The third park that was acquired with "Parks in the Cities" money. Nearly two acres at Colfax Avenue South and West Twenty-fourth Street were also developed as a playground. Whittier, Willard and Mueller were all in neighborhoods identified by Weir, twenty-nine years earlier, as needing a neighborhood park and playground.

Major developments:

- North Commons. A swimming pool was added to North Commons, and the park was redesigned around the new community center. This was the city's third outdoor pool. North Commons was the only city park with both a community center and a pool.

- Parade Ice Center. Another of Weir's recommendations in 1944 that was finally achieved. The building was completed over two years at a cost of about $850,000.

1974

Acquisitions:

- The only park land added was several acres at North Mississippi Park acquired in a settlement with the highway department over land to be taken for freeway I-94. The swap of land narrowed the park but extended it north along the riverbank.

Major developments:

- Loring Park. The park was redeveloped as a part of a major housing redevelopment along the Loring Greenway.

- Creekview Park. A neighborhood recreation center was built as an addition to Olson Junior High School.

1975

Acquisitions:

- Corcoran Park. The former school site acquired by the park board was in another neighborhood designated in the 1940s for a park. The park, at Nineteenth Avenue South and West Thirty-third Street, is a little over three acres. It was purchased with highway replacement money.

- Victory Park. This playground adjacent to Loring School at Upton Avenue and Forty-fourth Avenue North was first leased from the school board for a park. The original lease was for twenty years.

Major developments:

- Longfellow Park. Following its construction in 1963, the recreation center at Longfellow was the city's showcase facility. With the addition of a gym in 1975, it was upgraded to one of eight community centers.

- Lake Nokomis. A community center was built to the north of the lake.

- Pershing Park. A neighborhood recreation center was built.

- Fuller Park. Development of a playground and park was begun at this former school site of two acres at Harriet Avenue South and West Forty-eighth Street even before it was officially acquired by the park board.

1976

Acquisitions:

- Painter Park. Another former school site of about three acres at Lyndale Avenue South and West Thirty-third Street was acquired from the housing authority. Along with Fuller Park, Painter was purchased with highway replacement money.
- Currie Park. What had once been Sixth Ward Park, originally leased, was enlarged by more than an acre with the help of the Minneapolis Community Development Agency (MCDA), as part of the redevelopment of Cedar-Riverside.

Major developments:

- Farview Park. The park was redesigned, and a recreation center was built.
- Painter Park. The site was developed as a playground, and a shelter was built.
- McRae Park. A recreation center was constructed.
- Stewart Park. The park was redeveloped, and its layout altered to accommodate the construction of a new school.
- Waite Park. A neighborhood recreation center was built.

1977

Acquisitions:

- Fuller Park. Officially acquired by the park board even though improvements had already begun. Along with Corcoran and Painter Parks, this site had been targeted since 1960 as a possible acquisition. A neighborhood recreation center was constructed immediately.
- Hall Park. Six acres of land at Aldrich Avenue and Sixteenth Avenue North was acquired from MCDA.
- East Phillips Park. The board acquired more than six acres at Seventeenth Avenue South and East Twenty-second Street from MCDA. The land included a building leased to the American Indian Movement, which was demolished in 2007 in preparation for the construction of a new community center.

Major developments:

- Armatage Park, Bottineau Park, Webber Park and Corcoran Park. All of the parks were

Berger Fountain in Loring Park. Ben Berger, a park commissioner and onetime owner of the Minneapolis Lakers, donated the Berger Fountain in Loring Park in 1975. It was a copy of a fountain Berger had seen in Australia. The Loring Park site was chosen after the Walker Art Center rejected the fountain for a site at The Parade opposite the museum because it was not an original art work. Al Wittman relates that the fountain's cost was much higher than Berger anticipated, but he donated it anyway due to a macabre stroke of luck. Berger owned several movie theaters, and he reluctantly agreed to run a movie that other theaters didn't want. The movie was *The Exorcist*. Wittman writes that Berger made enough just selling popcorn during the movie's long run to pay for the fountain. (Minneapolis Park and Recreation Board)

developed to include a neighborhood recreation center. Corcoran Park was the only one of the four that had not been previously developed as a playground.

- Lyndale Farmstead and Lake Hiawatha Park. Both sites were redesigned with new recreation shelters.

- Victory Playground. A playground and shelter were developed next to Loring School.

1978

Acquisitions: None.

Major developments:

- Audubon Park. Redesigned, and a neighborhood center was built.

- East Phillips. The site was initially developed as a playground.

- Hall Park. The site was developed as a playground next to Franklin School, and a shelter was added.

- Hiawatha Park School. The park was redeveloped, and a stand-alone neighborhood center was built.

- Webber Park. The old swimming pool was replaced.

In 1978 the aggressive addition of neighborhood parks ended. The park board had succeeded in acquiring a park in nearly every neighborhood targeted by Weir and Brightbill. One of the only places where the board did not succeed was in the neighborhood between Lake Nokomis and Minnehaha Park. The board tried to purchase the site of the former Minnehaha School, but the neighborhood wanted the space for housing instead. A seven-story housing cooperative for seniors was built on that site at Thirty-fifth Avenue South and Fifty-second Street.

During those productive years the park board also developed many of the facilities recommended by Weir and Brightbill. In addition to numerous shelters and recreation buildings, the board created eight community centers, at Van Cleve, Folwell, Logan, Lynnhurst, North Commons, Powderhorn, Longfellow and Nokomis. A ninth community center, planned for Kenwood Park, was held up by community opposition and was finally built on scaled-down plans as an addition to Kenwood School in 1983. From parkways to recreation facilities, the park board often encountered the most opposition to its plans from residents of the lake district neighborhoods that had benefited most from parks.

After 1977, the park board's land acquisition efforts focused on the central and upper banks of the Mississippi River, the last frontier of open or underused space in the city. Only five new neighborhood playgrounds have been added to the system since then, all acquired from the school board.

The success of the park board during the Ruhe administration in acquiring land for neighborhood parks and building recreation and community centers went a long way toward meeting the shortcomings of the park and recreation system identified by both Weir and Brightbill. But it wasn't enough to satisfy recreation experts of the time who believed recreation programs must play a larger role in the city.

In 1977 the park board invited a team of recreation authorities to review the recreation system and make recommendations for improvement. The team, led by Seymour Greben, director of Los Angeles County Parks, issued the most strongly worded criticism ever of the park system.

Greben's team praised the parks *and* facilities, even their distribution within the city, as unsurpassed in the country—a distinct improvement over the assessments of Weir and Brightbill. They added, however, that "there is little or no evidence of similar progress with regard to the matter of recreation programming."

The failure of the park system remained the "overwhelming" emphasis on competitive sports to the exclusion of other types of recreation. While noting the success of the sports program, its rich tradition and wide participation, and extensive efforts to support it through community activity councils, the team concluded that it excluded participation by those "turned off" by sports and it tended to be male-oriented. Greben even raised the issue of whether competitive sports and scorekeeping had a deleterious effect on children.

Despite an effort to hire recreation leaders with more diverse educational backgrounds, Greben concluded that the recreation staff "reflects limited background and interest in the complexity of the community's social environment and problems." Evidence of that lack of concern for the community was partially demonstrated for Greben by the fact that recreation centers were closed on weekends, and they uniformly closed for two weeks in August, when much of the staff took vacations. Greben concluded that a "commitment to change" was not deep within the organization.

Greben also criticized the system sharply for its lack of provisions for what he called "special populations," including seniors, handicapped, racial and ethnic minorities and teens and young adults. Greben cited population statistics that Minneapolis had the largest percentage of senior citizens of any major city in the United States, yet had very little programming for seniors.

Greben recommended that the recreation staff also be expanded with the addition of program specialists in cultural arts and nature and environmental programming. He acknowledged that efforts to expand the staff in those directions over the years had always come up against budget limitations. Even when specialists had been hired, those positions had always been the first to go in the cycles of costs outstripping tax revenues.

Finally, Greben asked for a commitment to playing a more significant role in resolving social problems of the city. "The luxury of non-involvement," he wrote, "is long gone." Recreation programs, he advised, should be community-centered rather than park- or playground-centered.

The Greben Report reflected the thinking of Ruhe. Ruhe's most intense opposition on the park board came from commissioners, such as Leonard Neiman, who didn't like Ruhe's attempts to *de-emphasize* youth sports programs.

The paradox of Greben's advice, however, presented a challenge to the park board then and now. Greben advocated greater awareness of and commitment to each community's needs. And he argued for greater understanding of what a community wanted from its parks. Yet at the same time he advocated curtailing the influence of the neighborhood activity councils that for many years had been the most active in providing support for park programs.

Recreation Activity Councils. In 1971 Robert Ruhe wrote that park recreation activity councils were an inspiration to him and were, he believed, unique among park and recreation departments in the United States. The councils helped organize volunteers, raise funds, purchase equipment and uniforms, hire officials and issue awards for playground activities, most often boys sports in the early days. The first activity council was the Minnehaha Falls Athletic Club organized in 1936 to promote youth sports primarily at Keewaydin Park. More activity councils were organized in the early 1950s, including the Southwest Activities Council (SWAC), which included Linden Hills and Pershing Parks and became a model for other councils that were created through the 1960s. Several SWAC leaders subsequently became park commissioners, from Inez Crimmins in the 1950s to Leonard Neiman to Bob Fine in the 1990s. The councils continue to play an important role in neighborhood recreation programs in the 2000s.

As a result of the Greben Report, the park board developed a Basic Set of Services in 1978 that established park board responsibilities for social, cultural, environmental and physical programming. The Basic Set of Services that evolved from the Greben Report helped define the board's recreation policies for the next twenty years.

Park sports enthusiasts were not the only people who disagreed with Ruhe. Despite the accomplishments of the park board in acquiring neighborhood parks and building recreational facilities, Ruhe—and his style—had many detractors.

As early as the elections for the new smaller park board in the summer of 1969, an anti-Ruhe "Committee to Save Our Parks" succeeded in electing two new commissioners, Dale Gilbert and Louis DeMars. But Ruhe was not one to back off from a fight; he often welcomed it. He did not concern himself with popularity, only getting enough votes on the park board to approve what he wanted.

When Harvey Feldman was interviewed by Ruhe for a position in the recreation department, he was puzzled by a Ruhe question. "Can you count to five?" Ruhe asked him. Feldman says it took a moment for him to realize that Ruhe was talking about park board votes. On a nine-member board, Ruhe needed five votes to carry out his plans. He didn't care about consensus, he cared about getting five commissioners to vote his way. Ruhe was particularly fond of quoting the advice given to the park board in 1886 by Frederick Law Olmsted: that it was not the duty of commissioners to follow public opinion but to anticipate and act in advance of popular perception. To Ruhe, that was the essence of leadership.

Ruhe and his supporters on the park board were, in a sense, the victims of their own successes. In Ruhe's first years as superintendent, the board had been remarkably successful by taking aggressive action. Why would they abandon tactics that had worked so well?

The willingness of Ruhe and the board at the time to challenge the status quo was nowhere more evident than in the fights to prevent freeway encroachment on park land and to renovate parkways.

The emphasis of parkway redesign in the 1970s was on reducing traffic congestion, reducing traffic speed and preserving the parkways for non-motorized use. The pristine paths along Victory Memorial Drive, shown here, were preserved despite park board fears that the drive might be converted into a county highway. The basic design of most parkways has not changed since the 1970s. (Minneapolis Park and Recreation Board)

Chapter Twenty-One

Freeways, Parkways and Public Action

Ruhe's recreation policy created friction, but it was in dealing with automobile traffic—freeways and parkways—that he met his most powerful opposition. In the end, the battles over various roadways contributed to his demise. The look of Minneapolis parks would have been quite different without Ruhe's and the board's determination. If they hadn't fought freeway expansion so stubbornly, Minnehaha Park would have an elevated freeway running through it, the playing fields of Bryn Mawr would be smaller, North Mississippi Park would be barely a sliver, and the city might not have as many playgrounds. Several of the city's newest inner-city playgrounds were purchased with the larger sums of money the board's confrontational policies extracted from the state for taking park land for highways.

It was also during Ruhe's tenure that the city's parkways were significantly redesigned after four decades of "deferred maintenance," which was an optimist's way of saying they weren't maintained at all. In 1971 the board estimated that the cost of deferred maintenance had reached $10 million. When the parkways were finally improved, they had a quite different—and standardized—look, especially around the lakes, where they were narrower, often one-way, and had parking bays on only one side. The parkways also featured separate paths in most places for pedestrians and bicycles—a return to the arrangement of the 1890s around Lake Harriet.

Park board attorney Edward Gearty found an ally in Ruhe for his fight against freeways. Gearty's suggestion that the board challenge the highway department in court didn't win much support during the year it took the board to hire Moore's successor. But once Ruhe was hired, Gearty had a superintendent who relished a good fight for a principle he espoused. When the state highway department issued a new list of proposed park takeovers, still at 148 acres, or 2.4 percent of the park system, Ruhe commented, "If its 2.4 percent for highways and 1.1 percent for someone else and 1.8 percent for someone else, sooner or later this dissipates what was once a pretty magnificent system."

With the board's defiant land policy of 1966, the fight was begun. Over the next few years, the board succeeded in getting cumulative awards for lost land of $2.4 million, instead of the $1.1 million originally offered by the state. The argument used to increase those awards was developed by Gearty, along with consulting attorney Ray Haik and landscape

Edward Gearty left the park board for the state legislature in 1963. Many of the first park commissioners had already served in other public offices in the city or state, but in later years, a seat on the park board came to be viewed more as a stepping-stone to other elected offices. Burton Kingsley was one of the first to use the park board as a platform, when the former head of park police went from park commissioner to state legislator. In 1957, park commissioner P. Kenneth Peterson was elected mayor. Several park commissioners have moved from the park board to the city council, including Richard Kantorowicz, Richard Erdall, Lou DeMars, Kathy Thurber and Dean Zimmermann. Jeffery Spartz went from park commissioner to Hennepin County commissioner. One of those who moved in the other direction was Walt Dziedzic, who served on the city council for twenty one years before he was elected as a park commissioner in 1997.

architect Don Brauer. Their argument was that the land proposed to be taken should not be valued as "vacant" land, which is how the highway department had determined its value, but as irreplaceable parts of a park "system" that had great social value to the city. The proper value of the land, they argued, was what it would cost to replace that land in the city park system.

In all, the park board eventually lost about thirty acres of park land to freeways, most of it at The Parade, but the losses could have been much bigger. They weren't, because in 1966 the park board decided to fight to the bitter end a decision of the state to take twenty acres of Minnehaha Park to make a freeway of Hiawatha Avenue, Highway 55, from downtown to the airport. The park board would not accept the plan to build an elevated freeway between Minnehaha Park and Longfellow Meadow. It proposed instead a freeway route west of Longfellow Lagoon that would have kept the park intact. That route, however, would have required taking out many homes and businesses. That section of the city was home to future mayor Charles Stenvig and future park commissioner Dale Gilbert, both of whom became bitter enemies of Ruhe, in part out of opposition to those plans.

While the case was being contested in court, it generated such national interest that the park board was asked to outline its case at the 1968 convention of the National Park and Recreation Association. The park board lost its challenge to Highway 55 plans in both district court and the state supreme court but decided in 1969 to appeal the decision to the U.S. Supreme Court. The board was optimistic due to new federal transportation legislation in 1968 that restricted the taking of park land for highways. Before the case was heard by the Supreme Court, the court ruled in a related case in Memphis that park land could not be taken for highways, which established a precedent.

In the mid-1960s work began on the freeway between Loring Park and The Parade. In this photo, looking south on Hennepin Avenue, the Walker Art Center and Guthrie Theater are in the background on the left. (Norton and Peel, Minnesota Historical Society)

On the heels of that decision, the park board, city council and state highway department reached a compromise solution on a tunnel design for a freeway through the park. By that time, however, an environmental impact statement was required, and before that statement could be prepared, federal funding for the highway was no longer available. The eventual construction of Highway 55 through the area in 2003 used the tunnel plan conceived earlier, passing over Minnehaha Creek to avoid disruption of the creek bed, but with park land extending over the tunnel. The land over the tunnel was developed into today's Longfellow Garden. The tunnel plan did require the relocation of the Longfellow House closer to Minnehaha Park, which now serves as an information center for the city's scenic byways.

The other major fight between parks and freeways occurred over North Mississippi Park. The highway department originally wanted to take 76 percent of the park's thirty-one acres for I-94, leaving only a sliver of land along the river for a park. The park board argued that the park provided the only access to the river for one hundred thousand people in north Minneapolis and was therefore irreplaceable. Because of the need for an environmental impact statement, which gave the park board a virtual veto over highway plans, Minneapolis mayor Al Hofstede eventually brokered a compromise in 1974 that would have the highway department take only six acres and give the park board fifteen additional acres of river frontage north of the park. The agreement also provided for continuous public access to Shingle Creek under the freeway, instead of putting the creek through a culvert. The need to drop the creek bed to accommodate the freeway resulted in the creation of the city's third waterfall.

With that compromise, the park board's need to defend park land from freeways was essentially over. The thirty acres lost, along with land at The Parade, included parts of Gross Golf Course, Riverside Park, King Park, Perkins Hill, East River Parkway, Bryn Mawr and Wirth Park.

The park system lost only two parks completely to highways. A one-acre play lot called Elwell Field, in the path of I-35 through southeast Minneapolis, was condemned in 1966. Minneapolis also lost one its oldest parks when the board ultimately decided not to oppose condemnation of Wilson Park on Hawthorne Avenue west of downtown for interchanges between I-94 and Highway 12. Originally named Hawthorne Park, it had been purchased by the city council in 1882 and turned over to the first park board. With the demise of Wilson Park, the park board lost not only one of its oldest parks but the name of Eugene Wilson, who had been a mayor, a congressman and a commissioner on the first park board. He had been instrumental in passage of the 1883 Park Act and had been one of

The park board's compromise with the highway department at North Mississippi Park included the creation of a waterfall to lower Shingle Creek *(far right)*, so it could pass under the new I-94 freeway from Webber Park to North Mississippi Park. Instead of the creek flowing through a culvert under the freeway, as original plans had proposed, a trail follows the creek to the river. (2008 *Star Tribune*/Minneapolis-St. Paul)

Charles Loring's allies in acquiring the city's lakeshores. The board dropped opposition to the condemnation of Wilson Park because it had become a little-used park in a neighborhood with declining population.

The park board also lost several triangles at street intersections. One of the most notable was Virginia Triangle at the junction of Lyndale and Hennepin. The triangle was home to a statue of Thomas Lowry, who had owned the street railway company and much of the land in Lowry Hill, and had donated land for The Parade. With the loss of Virginia Triangle, Lowry's statue was moved to Hennepin Avenue and Twenty-fourth Street, where it still stands.

The park board was not as successful defending its own offices. In 1965, the park board was evicted from its offices in the municipal building, victim of the expansion needs of other city agencies. After a long search and consideration of building a headquarters on park property, the board chose to rent offices in the Public Health Building on South Fourth Street. In 1979, the park board lost its space in that building too, and moved to the Flour Exchange a few blocks away.

The park board majority and Robert Ruhe had made some enemies with its recreation policies and with its vigorous opposition to Highway 55, but that was nothing compared to the protests generated by proposals to improve the city's parkways, especially around the lakes.

The parkways had essentially not been improved since they were constructed by Theodore Wirth. When the park board referred to deferred maintenance over the years, it often meant the parkways around the lakes. Wirth even complained in his book written in 1944 that Lake Harriet Parkway in particular needed work, but area residents had always prevented any changes or improvements. And it wasn't that the park board was behind the rest of the city in maintaining roads. Many city streets were still unpaved in the 1960s.

By the time Ruhe arrived, the parkways built for 1910s and 1920s traffic were in a sad state. Before spending the money to simply repave them, however, Ruhe wanted to look at their projected use for the next thirty to fifty years. "Before we spent one penny on pavement," Ruhe told Ben Wright, "we were going to determine what the purpose of the parkways was."

To help identify what should be done with parkways, the board hired Garret Eckbo, a landscape architect from San Francisco, to make suggestions. The choice of Eckbo for the study did not make some in the city happy, because he was the consultant who had recommended the controversial route of Highway 55 around Longfellow Meadow.

In August 1970, Eckbo submitted an initial report to the park board. When the *Minneapolis Star* published maps along with a report on Eckbo's preliminary recommendations, the city erupted. Al Wittman reported that he spent the whole next day answering his phone and listening to vehement objections to the proposals. Over the next month reaction to the plans ran almost unanimously in opposition.

What the public reacted to was Eckbo's suggestion that the lakes had become a "victim of the automobile." To solve that problem, he proposed closing major sections of the lake parkways. Beyond closing parkways, Eckbo proposed a radical redesign of the lakes themselves, building peninsulas and islands to create more usable land around and in the lakes. The public didn't want the shores of their lakes tampered with, perhaps not realizing that those lakeshores were largely already man-made. Letters to the newspaper complained of "outsiders" like Ruhe and Eckbo coming to town to tell Minneapolis how to improve its parks. Ironically, it had been other outsiders, such as Cleveland and Wirth, who had been responsible for the design of the parks that citizens were now protecting from outside interference.

While it was fighting incursions from automobiles, the park board approved a retro transportation project. In 1969, the board approved a proposal from the Minnesota Transportation Museum to restore the streetcar rails near Lake Harriet and operate several vintage streetcars in the park. (Minneapolis Park and Recreation Board)

In the face of heated opposition, the park board distanced itself from Eckbo's preliminary plan. Even Ruhe admitted that pleasure driving was a legitimate form of recreation. In the furor, however, residents of southwest Minneapolis created the Minneapolis Parkways and Lakes Study Committee, which took the position that all the parkways needed was repaving. In its new direction to Eckbo, the board dictated that he was only to consider parkways, not reshaping the lakes, and that parkways would continue to encircle the lakes.

A revised plan from Eckbo suggested creating one-way traffic at some points around the lakes, narrowing the roadways, creating a bicycle Grand Rounds, and providing distinctive paving, curbing, lighting and signage for the parkways. Later in 1971, a Citizens Parkway Committee approved a plan that was similar to Eckbo's final report. The narrowing of the parkways was an aspect of the plan that generated heated opposition. Ruhe accepted the credit or the blame for that idea. He told Ben Wright that the idea for narrowing the parkways to reduce speeds came to him on a drive through rural Iowa. As he approached a narrow underpass beneath a railroad bridge, he said he instinctively slowed down and realized that narrower roads on parkways would have the same effect on drivers.

Opposition to a one-way parkway around Lake Harriet reached a tragic resolution when in May 1972 Betty Malkerson was struck and killed by a bicycle while walking on the new pedestrian/bicycle path around the lake. The next day the board moved the bicycle path to the roadway and separated it from traffic with concrete curbs. To make room for the bicycle path, traffic had to be reduced to one-way.

By the time the parkway was permanently reconstructed in 1977, everyone had become accustomed to one-way traffic.

Most of the parkway reconstruction was completed from 1972 to 1978. While the city provided bonds to pay for the earlier reconstruction, the Metropolitan Council and its Parks and Open Space Commission, created by 1973 legislation and funded by the legislature, provided significant financial support.

In 1973 Ruhe testified at the legislature on the bill to create the Parks and Open Space Commission of the Metropolitan Council. Although the park board largely ignored the Hennepin County Park District while Ruhe was superintendent, in his testimony at the capitol he supported the effort to create a metropolitan parks body. He insisted, however, that the significant role already played by Minneapolis parks in the regional park framework be acknowledged and funded. Ruhe argued that the redevelopment and maintenance of existing parks that met regional needs required attention and funding as much as the acquisition of new parks. Otherwise Minneapolis would be paying for parks for other metro-area residents, while they would not be helping to pay for Minneapolis parks.

The rationale found a receptive audience in the legislature. In the years since, that body has provided considerable financial support to those Minneapolis parks that have been designated "regional" parks. In 1977, the Metropolitan Council designated 80 percent of Minneapolis's park property as regional parks, which would be eligible for funding by the legislature. Through the Metropolitan Council, the legislature would later play a pivotal role in the development by the park board and the city of the central riverfront and upper river.

When Ruhe testified at the capitol, state representatives James Rice of north Minneapolis and John Sarna from northeast were junior members of the house. As they gained seniority in their twenty-plus year legislative careers, and were joined in 1980 by Carl Kroening, a state senator from north Minneapolis, the three wielded considerable influence in the legislature in support of Minneapolis parks, particularly along the river. Noting their influence—and summarizing decades of park history—Brian Rice, James Rice's son, and attorney and lobbyist for the park board since 1984, said, "The legislature has always been the guardian angel of Minneapolis parks."

The last of the lake district parkways to be completed was William Berry Parkway between Lake Calhoun and Lake Harriet. Park board plans to divert Lake Harriet Parkway away from the lakeshore at the pavilion generated the most opposition. Area residents feared that the parkway diversion was prelude to moving the pavilion itself. The other argument was that the new design would put a road through the middle of the park and destroy trees. Lawsuits delayed construction of the parkway until 1978, with park board planners carefully designing the roadway to minimize tree removal.

While Ruhe and his supporters on the board, often only five, won most of the controversial battles of the 1960s and 1970s, those battles generated enough opposition to undermine the authority of Ruhe and the reputation of the park board.

Angry with the park board for obtaining bonding authority from the legislature to rebuild parkways in 1971, the city initially deducted $1.5 million from the board's bonding authority that year, although in the next six years it provided $9 million for parkway reconstruction. Emboldened by dissatisfaction over parkway designs, Mayor Charles Stenvig temporarily blocked the park board's bond program in 1973 and demanded input in park improvement decisions. In 1974, one of the periodic efforts to abolish the park board gained momentum, which brought out park board critics and supporters. Park board president Alden Smith responded by noting "a general feeling that the city council would do better if it were under the park board." Nonetheless, in 1975, Minneapolis voters comfortably passed a charter amendment that reduced the terms of park commissioners from six to four years and gave the mayor veto power over park board decisions, subject to an override by vote of two-thirds of the park board.

Through aggressive pursuit of its goals, the park board and Ruhe accomplished a great deal in the 1960s and 1970s to increase citizens' access to parks and the benefits of recreation—but their tactics also resulted ultimately in a loss of power and independence.

Chapter Twenty-Two

Rise of Conservation

When Horace Cleveland first arrived in Minneapolis, his message to civic leaders was to protect land from development and preserve it for public use. One hundred years later, with considerable land in public hands, the effort shifted to preserving the health of the city's natural assets.

In the 1960s the park board began two efforts to protect those assets. One battle was to protect something it had created—the urban forest—from attack by an invader. The other was to protect the water of its lakes and streams, which had gradually deteriorated with the development of land in the surrounding watersheds.

Protecting trees and preserving water quality were not new challenges for the park board. The board had legal control of the trees along city streets because of the desire of early park leaders to protect trees. Charles Loring had once offered a bounty to neighborhood boys for campaign posters that had been nailed to trees in an effort to stop the practice. "I got two sheriffs, a mayor and ten aldermen," a boy would shout running up to Loring with a fistful of flyers, eager for his reward.

Both Loring and Folwell had urged acquisition of lakes and riverbanks in part to prevent pollution of the water, especially from the runoff from stables and barns. And commissioner Harry Jones asked superintendent William Berry to investigate the dumping of waste into Minnehaha Creek by a sugar beet processor in St. Louis Park in 1902.

Nearly a century later, when public opinion and concern were catching up with the environmental visionaries, the park board's responsibilities for managing public assets continued to evolve. A board that was created to acquire land for parks had grown into a board that provided also for the recreation of citizens. At the same time, however, it was adapting to increasing demands for the management and care of the land it had acquired.

The mayor's budget commission met with legislators for lunch in the summer of 1974 in the restaurant atop the IDS Center in downtown Minneapolis, which offered panoramic views of the city. Don Willeke, a Minneapolis attorney who hosted the meeting, remembers looking out over the expanse of city and thinking, then asking the others, "Do we want to lose that?" Lose what? From the top of the IDS tower it looked like a green carpet. But at street level it was a canopy. This was Minneapolis's urban forest of elm trees.

Don Willeke didn't know anything about trees at the time. Today he can give a guided tour of the park outside his home on Dean Parkway and tell the name and the story of every tree there. He came to be recognized as a national leader among tree preservationists. The wall of his study is covered with awards from many associations of arborists, surrounding the bronze star he won in Vietnam. His admirers and his critics all admit that he played a critical role in getting the city and the state to take unprecedented action to prevent the deforestation of the city. Because, like his bulldogs named for British lords, he was tenacious. So was his enemy, the Dutch elm beetle.

The park board had known for decades that the city's stately elms were vulnerable to attack from pests. Loring acknowledged that in the 1890s when he suggested that the board diversify its plantings in light of eastern cities' problems with elm diseases. Still, the elm was the favorite tree of early planters. Elms grew fast and tall, and they were hardy trees in the climate extremes of the northern prairie. The elm had become a favorite shade tree in the United States because the fibrous wood of the elm made it hard to split for firewood or use in construction. Elms were able to reach their towering heights in New England and implant themselves in the childhood memories

Residents helped the National Guard dispose of felled trees. (Nancy Conroy, Minneapolis Park and Recreation Board)

of the pioneers who moved west because the wood wasn't useful for anything else. Despite evidence of susceptibility to disease, they were planted in parks and along streets nearly to the exclusion of other tree varieties. In a move to economize, the park board purchased nearly ten thousand elms in 1899 to grow in the nursery for future planting around the city. Seventy-five years later some of those cheap elms would prove very expensive as the city battled to save them.

In 1909 the park board lost 9 percent of its elms to the elm borer and tried to save others by applying chemical treatments. Christian Bossen issued another warning about the urban forest of elms in 1942. He noted then that citizens were cooperating in the care of street trees, but they couldn't help much when it came to pests. "Certain pests have been prevalent for two years," he said, "which may result in the wholesale destruction of the large number of fine elms." When the board reestablished its street-tree planting program after World War II, however, nearly all of the ten thousand trees it planted in eight years were elms.

The most dangerous pest, the Dutch elm beetle, had yet to arrive. In 1958, however, park staff were already on the lookout for the beetle. Charles Doell reported that while Dutch elm disease was creeping north and west and had reached Madison, Wisconsin, it hadn't appeared yet in Minneapolis. The

National Guard vehicles helped haul away elm trees cut down in 1976. Thanks to heroic efforts by citizens, corporations, the park board, city and state in fighting Dutch elm disease and replanting the urban forest, Minneapolis remains today a city of trees. (Nancy Conroy, Minneapolis Park and Recreation Board)

first cases of the disease were finally spotted five years later. Three elms in Minnehaha Park and one along West River Parkway were confirmed to have the disease. The trees were immediately removed and disposed of, but the board warned that other cities had already found that, over fifteen years, they had lost most of their elm trees. Even with sanitation, the board reported, the city will lose 1 to 2 percent of its elms a year over a period of years. In retrospect, the board and the city could have lived with those losses, because when the disease hit full force, it was much worse.

The spread of the disease was slow at first, and the park board *was* taking action. Four more diseased trees were found in 1964, all in northeast Minneapolis, which prompted the park board to borrow $150,000 from its land purchase fund for a Dutch elm eradication program. Prudential Insurance Company paid for two hundred thousand brochures about the disease. The brochures were distributed throughout the city by Boy Scouts. In 1965, another nine diseased trees were found. On the recommendation of the state department of agriculture, with approval from the city council, the board used an obscure statute for plant and animal pest control to levy a tax of 0.4 mills to raise $164,000 for a Dutch Elm Disease Control Fund.

Defense against the attack everyone knew was coming gained momentum. In 1966, the city council granted unprecedented authority for the park board to locate and remove diseased trees and wood from private property. In 1967, the park board once again hired a full-time forester, Dave DeVoto, who would become a hero in the city's fight to save its trees. In 1968, even with only twelve new cases of the disease, the board approved a new planting program for five thousand trees a year to begin in 1970. Experience in other cities had shown that losing many, if not all, elms was inevitable, so the sooner the replanting of other shade trees began, the less stark the city would be when the elms died. The park board's successful legislative program in 1969 that raised taxes for park and recreation operations also raised the levy to care for trees and combined the Dutch Elm Control Fund with other park forestry funds.

As the park board hunted for diseased trees and began planting replacements, action in the state legislature gradually gained momentum. In 1971, state representative Tom Berg held the first hearings on the growing problem. In 1973, the Minnesota Shade Tree Advisory Committee was created with representatives of the University of Minnesota, the state, Hennepin and Ramsey counties and the city foresters of St. Paul, Minneapolis and Bloomington. Don Willeke eventually became chairman of that committee. DeVoto and David French from the university taught Willeke about trees, and he coached them on politics and how to speak effectively to legislators and the media.

The park board continued its aggressive campaign to remove dead trees. DeVoto had elms targeted for removal spray-painted with a big red "T," which meant "terminate." As the number of diseased trees mounted, surpassing one thousand for the first time in 1975, the red paint on trees became a constant reminder to the public of the extent of the problem. Losses spiked to more than seven thousand trees in 1976, which prompted action by the legislature and the park board to impose an additional tax to remove dead wood faster. Removing diseased elms was crucial to limiting the spread of the disease, which was carried by beetles that lived under the bark.

With the lobbying efforts of Willeke and DeVoto and leadership in the legislature by Berg and Willeke's law partner, Hubert "Skip" Humphrey III, the state provided funds to assist the city's fight. In 1977 the state appropriated $28.6 million in funds to fight Dutch elm, with about $2.5 million going to Minneapolis to augment city expenditures of more than $7 million to combat the disease.

The enormous sums spent on treating, trimming, and removing trees, and planting new trees was justified, proponents said, because the cost of doing nothing would eventually be greater. Minneapolis had nearly a quarter million elm trees, and the cost of removal was estimated at more than $300 a tree.

Even if no one cared about the city's shading canopy of elms, it made financial sense to try to at least slow the spread to avoid the cost of just cutting down all the dead wood.

Minneapolis's efforts to stop the spread of the disease paid dividends. In the 1977 legislation, St. Paul was given a larger subsidy than Minneapolis. Noting the difference in allocation, Ruhe observed that St. Paul had already lost four times as many elms as Minneapolis. "If higher tree loss is the price for higher subsidy funds," Ruhe said, "that is not a price we are really prepared to pay."

Citizens volunteered for neighborhood elm watches, and the business community took an active role that has probably never been matched. Dayton's adopted Loring Park's elms, Honeywell underwrote costs for care and reforestation of Washburn Fair Oaks Park, and Pillsbury did the same for Elliot Park. First Bank ran an "Elm Watch" hotline for people to report diseased trees and spent nearly a half million dollars promoting the hotline. Even the national guard got involved, committing people and light vehicles to haul away dead wood.

Elmer the Elm Tree in the 1980s. Park board employees dressed as Elmer were on the front lines of the battle to inform the public and solicit cooperation in fighting Dutch elm disease. Elmer was so well received that new characters, Billy Bass and Crystal Clear, were created in the 1990s to help educate children on the importance of water quality in city lakes and streams. (Minneapolis Park and Recreation Board)

The battle was not without its disputes. Willeke appeared at park board meetings at least three times in 1977 to complain of what he considered a lack of urgency in removing diseased trees. The park board said it was taking them down as fast as it could.

By the end of 1977, the death toll for the year was announced at more than thirty thousand elm trees. But due to a citywide effort, led by DeVoto, the worst had passed. In 1978, the park board doubled its budget for fighting the disease. The toll dropped to twenty thousand elms, a number almost matched by new trees planted by the park board that year. From 1977 to 1982, the park board planted more than one hundred thousand trees to replace dead elms. In each succeeding year the number of trees lost continued to drop until it leveled off at a couple thousand a year. The battle to save the city's elms left Minneapolis as one of the few cities in the country with an urban forest of elms. After the worst of it, the city still had more than one hundred thousand elms. More importantly, it had many blocks of different kinds of shade trees already growing.

Dutch elm disease has never gone away, and there have been periodic spikes in the number of elms lost to the disease. Elm trees in the city now number about sixty thousand, but the city is much less reliant on elms for shade. Since aggressive tree planting began to replace elms in the 1970s, the park board has planted more than two hundred thousand trees of various kinds in parks and along city streets. The board planted different species in careful patterns throughout the city to limit the spread of disease and prevent a repeat of the struggle to preserve the city's trees.

The battle to protect Minneapolis's trees was fought against an invader that didn't leave the park board much choice. The other effort to restore and protect a valuable asset, clean water, was a conscious choice.

And it involved changing human behavior, rather than eliminating habitat for an insect invader.

By the mid-1960s, the water quality in city lakes was deteriorating. The watersheds for the lakes and the creeks flowing into them had been nearly completely developed, and most wetlands that acted as natural filters had been filled. In addition the extensive use of fertilizers on urban and suburban lawns had increased runoff of chemicals that increased fertility in the lakes and impaired visual quality of the water.

In 1966, park board engineer Ed Braddock (who had earlier proposed the system of pumping water from the Mississippi River to raise lake levels) asked Ruhe to support the creation of a Minnehaha Creek Watershed District, which would include Lake Minnetonka and its tributaries all the way to the Mississippi River. Ruhe did so, and the board also expressed itself in favor of participating in the new entity.

In 1969, the board passed its first ordinance against water pollution and committed to a study of lake pollution. The next year the city and the park board jointly sponsored the first formal study of water quality in the city's lakes. The Hickok Report for the new Minnehaha Watershed District, in cooperation with the park board, was published in 1970, which provided a baseline for future measurements.

In 1970 the board also hired its first coordinator of environmental education. The position was funded for the first year by environmental activist Goodrich Lowry, grandson of Thomas Lowry. Except for a seven-year hiatus in the mid-1980s due to budget restrictions, the position has continued since then.

The board then commissioned a study of lake water quality by Dr. Joseph Shapiro of the Limnological Research Center at the University of Minnesota. Shapiro noted that the study he conducted "may be unique in the world: rather than being commissioned out of desperation, it is in response to a demand for excellence that befits the history and tradition of the City of Lakes." He noted that the problem in Minneapolis's lakes was purely ecological and not a public health crisis and that in contrast to many urban areas, the city's lakes were not polluted with toxic wastes or human sewage. Further, he said, the lakes were not dying but had an "excess of life from man's point of view." In sum, the concern for the lakes was predominantly aesthetic—excessive algae growth and lack of water clarity. (The goal of cleaning the lakes was quite different from efforts to clean up the Mississippi River some years earlier. Then the goal was to make river water safe for contact with human skin.)

Using the Shapiro study as a beginning, the mayor appointed a Citizens Advisory Committee on Lake Water Quality in 1973. That group issued recommendations in 1975, which became the basis of remedial action for many years. Steps to improve water quality included stopping additional storm water runoff, vacuum-powered street cleaning, and stocking more game fish in city lakes. One of the contributors to pollution in the lakes were rough fish, such as carp, whose eating habits and biological functions contribute to algae growth. More game fish, which eat other fish, would reduce the population of rough fish.

These efforts and organizations were precursors to the Clean Water Partnership in the 1990s that would lead to more aggressive action to improve the aesthetic quality of water in the lakes.

The park board's focus on the urban forest and water quality in the late 1960s and 1970s demonstrated the willingness of the board to adapt its vision of land stewardship, which in the years since has become a central part of the park board's mission. The park board had acknowledged, although not always to everyone's immediate satisfaction, its evolving responsibility for the management of public resources. Speaking to the National Urban Forest Council meeting in Minneapolis in 1993, then president of the city council and soon-to-be-mayor Sharon Sayles-Belton noted that among the reasons for the success of Minneapolis's urban forests was an elected park board with its own funding authority. This allowed, she said, funding of "environmental amenities, such as trees, with less direct confrontation and competition with proponents of other parts of the urban infrastructure."

Apparently tired of the five-to-four board votes he was so committed to winning, including the vote to extend his contract through 1977, Ruhe announced his resignation as superintendent in the summer of 1977. He gave the board a year to find his successor. He claimed that he had accomplished what he wanted in Minneapolis and at the age of fifty-four wanted another challenge before he retired. Indicative of the deep divisions among commissioners at the time, the board took more than the year Ruhe gave them to find his replacement.

Despite criticism of Ruhe's management style, and a board that was sharply divided on many issues, the park board accomplished a great deal while Ruhe was superintendent. Most of all, the park board had achieved a more equitable distribution of parks and facilities throughout the city. Many neighborhoods, especially the least affluent, had neighborhood parks for the first time. And most neighborhoods had facilities to accommodate whatever recreational programs would be determined necessary in future years. The park board had also defended its land vigorously, preventing defacement of park property, especially at Minnehaha Park, that would have been a lasting embarrassment to the city. Al Wittman's assessment of the era was that there was no substitute for land ownership. "You're a power to be reckoned with," Wittman said, "if you own the land."

The successes of the era were often overshadowed by conflicts, but Ruhe's abrasive manner aside, it was a time in history when those conflicts probably would have emerged regardless of who the players were. Throughout Ruhe's term as superintendent, the park board, as well as every other government agency, was learning to deal with a new phenomenon in public life: intense public participation in decision making. Beginning with the civil rights movement and continuing with opposition to the war in Vietnam, the "power of the people" had been clearly established. People had also grown to distrust, or at least challenge, government on all levels.

A demand for public participation and public oversight led to the creation of citizen advisory councils and to the passage of open-meeting laws in the early 1970s that complicated and often slowed the management of public resources. The management of public input became as critical a factor as the management of resources. The transition to in-depth public participation presents

Cross-country skiing. Use of park ice-skating rinks declined 71 percent from 1972 to 1979, causing the park board to close twenty of seventy-eight skating rinks. The decline in skating, however, was partially offset by an increasing interest in cross-country skiing. The board opened four new cross-country ski trails in 1979 and experimented with lighting the old trail at Wirth Park. The board began to provide snowmaking equipment for cross-country ski trails in the winter of 2007–08. (Minneapolis Park and Recreation Board) issues to park boards and superintendents of today and for the next 125 years. Who serves the public interest more effectively: commissioners and staff selected for their expertise and experience, or for their malleability to public opinion? There is no doubt how Ruhe would have answered the question—and that was partly responsible for his departure from Minneapolis parks.

When Ruhe departed, he left two important pieces of unfinished business, which would be addressed by the staff he left in place. Most of the senior staff at the park board had been hired by Ruhe, and most would remain in positions of influence for years after he left. The first issue was recreation. The Greben Report, issued after Ruhe announced his resignation, made it clear that Ruhe's personal goals for the development of a wider recreation program had not been met. The second issue was the development of the riverfront as a recreational resource. These issues would become the predominant focus of the park board over the next twenty-plus years.

Ruhe also left behind a challenge for his successors that arose from his success. During his tenure, the park board had acquired many new properties and built many new facilities at a time of economic prosperity. But once again, at the end of his tenure, the national economy was deteriorating. Inflation was at unprecedented levels on the heels of the oil crisis of the mid-1970s. In addition, the national mood was increasingly tax averse—in fact, government averse. Ruhe left behind a larger and more costly system to operate at a time when the resources to operate it were about to dwindle. In 1978, the city council informed the park board that its budget for the next year was going to have to be trimmed by $400,000. Whoever replaced Ruhe was not going to have an easy time.

The man who was eventually hired as superintendent was no stranger to Minneapolis parks. Charles Spears had been hired by Ruhe in 1970 to manage the revenue-producing operations of the park system. After a few years in Minneapolis, Spears had left to manage the parks of Nashville, but was brought back as superintendent in the fall of 1978.

The park board settled on Spears after a lengthy and contentious search. His southern manners and charm were viewed as the right oil to be spread on the troubled waters Ruhe had left. But Spears and the park board never clicked, and after only two years on the job, Spears was informed that his contract would not be renewed.

During Spears's brief time in office, the board completed the acquisition of another former school site. Marcy Park, just over an acre at Eleventh Avenue and Seventh Street Southeast, was purchased for $175,000 from the school board in 1979.

And although Spears didn't hold the job long, he can still claim that he was superintendent when the city finally achieved what it had been trying to do since 1866: create a park on Nicollet Island.

The banks of the Mississippi River gorge downstream from St. Anthony Falls had been preserved as wild places since the early 1900s. In the 1970s, the park board turned its attention to development of the central riverfront as park land, reclaiming it from its industrial past. (Peter Schmidt, Minneapolis Park and Recreation Board)

Chapter Twenty-Three

Return to the River

October 17, 1987, will be remembered for a long time by many in Minneapolis. The city hadn't seen such excitement in decades. That evening the Minnesota Twins took the field against the St. Louis Cardinals in the Metrodome for the first game of the 1987 World Series. Many baseball fans still recall vividly that Homer Hanky–waving, ear-pounding evening—especially because the Twins won that night and went on to win a dramatic seven-game series.

But an event that would have more lasting impact on the city took place in front of a much smaller and quieter crowd earlier that day only a couple miles from the Metrodome. That afternoon the city dedicated a new section of West River Parkway (now James Rice Memorial Parkway) from Portland Avenue to Plymouth Avenue upriver from downtown. It represented a milestone in the city's and park board's efforts to create a recreational centerpiece along the central riverfront.

This first segment of the river parkway downtown created a ribbon of green along the riverbanks that confirmed the city's commitment to redeveloping the river. It was fraught with possibilities. It wasn't just an isolated access point to a river the city had turned its back on decades before; it opened up the river as no other park had yet been able to do.

The *StarTribune* that day said the new parkway would satisfy a great hunger for greenery and open space in a "clean but sterile" downtown and "should hasten riverfront development." Minnesota Twins

David Fisher, superintendent of parks 1980–98. (Nancy Conroy, Minneapolis Park and Recreation Board)

stars such as Kirby Puckett and Kent Hrbek became folk heroes that fall for their exploits on the baseball field. The heroes of riverfront development, people such as city manager Tommy Thompson, mayor Don Fraser, park commissioners Orvin Olson and Patty Hillmeyer, park superintendent David Fisher and assistant superintendent Al Wittman, were never commemorated on a Wheaties box but left a bigger imprint on the city.

The Mississippi River was the engine of the city's growth and development. And engines are often messy things. The history of redeveloping the riverfront from industrial to recreational use is messy, too. Long gone were the days when unused land could be bought from a farmer or land speculator. Gone too were the days when the park board was one of only a few city agencies managing the development of city resources and amenities with occasional enabling action from the legislature. The redevelopment of the river involved a web of city, state and federal agencies, some with money to contribute, some with interests to protect. But at the center of the effort, uniquely constituted to manage those complex interests, was a park board with a century-long history of meeting the city's evolving needs for open space and recreation.

From the time Fort Snelling was created at the confluence of the Mississippi and the Minnesota rivers and the first community of pioneers settled at St. Anthony Falls, the river had been the heart of the city's growing industry, first lumber, then flour. To serve those industries, river and railroad transportation networks were created, and power was generated.

The river had been the focus of Horace Cleveland's efforts to convince civic leaders to preserve land for parks. But with the exception of his suggestion for a "driving park" on the banks of the river in northeast Minneapolis, he concentrated on the river below the falls with its picturesque steep banks and islands. It was land that was poorly suited for residential or industrial development.

On either side of St. Anthony Falls, however, industry commanded the river. At and above the falls, mills and railroads dominated. Upriver from the industrial sections, the riverbanks were more typical of the rest of the Mississippi River's rolling length, mostly prairie or savanna sloping gradually away from the river. It was not as spectacular as the gorge below the falls and, therefore, less alluring for early park advocates.

The central riverfront received little more than passing mention over the years in park board documents. Not even Nicollet Island had drawn much interest since the defeat of the plan to make it a park in 1866. In 1908 the park board established a committee to meet with Mrs. William Eastman to encourage her to donate a strip of land around Nicollet Island for parks, but nothing came of it.

In 1911, park board president Wilbur Decker recommended that "at some future time" it might be desirable to establish parkways north of the business center along the river. A few years later, Theodore Wirth said that the river north of downtown might be made "similarly attractive" as the riverbanks downstream from the falls, suggesting especially the desirability of a pier or park on Nicollet Island to relieve overcrowding at The Gateway. When Wirth presented plans for Marshall Terrace Park in 1915, which included plans for a beach on the river, he said that "a much larger tract of river frontage will be due that section of the city later on." He added in his reports of both 1918 and 1919 that the city should acquire both banks of the river throughout the city, and suggested that, at least, the park board should landscape both riverbanks, even if the railroads owned the property. But with the focus on developing property already owned by the board, ideas to incorporate the central and upper river into the park system never gained traction. Moreover, the park board's only ventures into downtown—The Gateway and Pioneers Square—had been costly failures.

In 1937, however, the landscape around St. Anthony Falls was primed for change. That year Congress approved the extension of the river's nine-foot navigation channel to the northern limits of the city above the falls. It was the first step in plans to create an upper harbor, which required locks to bypass the falls. The locks were eventually completed in 1963. To create barge access to the locks, two piers had to be removed from the Stone Arch Bridge and replaced with the steel span that defaces the bridge today. As part of the construction of the upper lock, the Army Corps of Engineers leveled some of the old mills on the west riverbank and filled the canal that channeled water to the mills.

In 1967 the city established an Upper Harbor Terminal on land acquired from the state. The city's previous terminal downriver from the falls, at Bohemian Flats below the Washington Avenue Bridge, was subject to flooding and was too small to accommodate the increase in river traffic caused by rising railroad freight rates. By 1979, most of the Washington Avenue Terminal's facilities had moved to the Upper Harbor. The Upper Harbor never became the economic resource the city hoped, in part due to development of both the St. Lawrence Seaway and the interstate highway system at the time the locks were being built. Both projects contributed to reducing barge traffic on the river by offering other alternatives to railroads.

Even before the upper locks were completed, however, the park board began to take notice of the river's park potential. In 1960, a park board report on goals for the board's centennial in 1983 included an estimated expenditure of $1 million to acquire land at Nicollet Island and St. Anthony Falls for a park and historical site.

In the early 1960s, the park board passed a resolution to cooperate with other city agencies to find a solution to developing Nicollet Island as a park. After a 1964 meeting with a citizens' committee representing Nicollet Island, the board noted that it seemed "practical to embellish" the island with replicas of historic homes, bridges and mills. By this time, the river was no longer the center of city commerce, most of the mills were closed, and Nicollet Island's old rows of apartments had become flophouses.

In the early 1970s, the city's view of the river began to change. In 1971, the land around the falls was placed on the National Park Service's list of National Historic Districts. The redevelopment of the riverfront was complicated—and ultimately enhanced—by the history of the area. Historic preservation played a central role on the riverfront as it never had before for the park board.

The possibilities of riverfront development were really laid out for the first time in 1972 with an ambitious report produced by city manager Tommy Thompson entitled *Mississippi/Minneapolis*. A birthday party, however, provided the first funds for the redevelopment of the river as a recreation space. The American Bicentennial Commission had money to fund a big bash for July 4, 1976, but instead of paying for one big two-hundredth birthday party, Congress appropriated funds for many local celebrations around the country. Minneapolis was one of the sites

The central riverfront in 1951 before the upper lock and dam were created west of the falls. The riverfront was used exclusively for industrial purposes. (Minneapolis Public Library, Minneapolis Collection, M4483)

chosen. Dave Sellergren, an attorney doing work for the park board at the time, remembers getting a call from the local organizers of the event seeking help in acquiring land on Nicollet Island for the party. City-owned land on the southern tip of Nicollet Island, acquired and designated in 1944 for use as a public harbor, was subsequently changed officially into Bicentennial Park. Sellergren remembers that as the first real beginning of riverfront development.

The potential of the riverfront as park land and as a tool of economic development triggered the creation in 1976 of the Riverfront Development Coordinating Board (RCDB), a joint effort of the park board, the housing authority and the city council. The objective of the RDCB was to create a development plan that could be presented to the Metropolitan Parks and Open Space Commission (MPOSC, created in 1973) in order to get regional park funding from the legislature.

The RDCB's final report, issued in late 1978, made specific recommendations for nearly every property that has since been acquired and developed.

- West River Parkway. Create a parkway along the west side of the river.

- Boom Island. Develop a nine-acre park with natural indigenous vegetation.

- B. F. Nelson site: Leave as an open field the former industrial site on the east bank between Boom Island and upper Nicollet Island.

- Upper Nicollet Island. Create a historic village to preserve houses and create a community meeting house and plaza for visitor information. Clear trees and vegetation selectively to open views of the river. Preserve Grove Street Flats for housing. Use the existing railroad bridge to Boom Island for a walking and biking path. (Overall the plan was to provide sixty-five dwelling units, but most of those were scheduled to be in multiunit buildings. The report provided for two "outparcels," land not to be included in the regional park: just over six acres each for residential use and for DeLaSalle High School. The "outparcel" for the school included space for an athletic field for both public and school use. Perhaps due to declining enrollment at the school at the time, the report included a provision that if the school ever ceased to operate, the land would become a park.)

- Lower Nicollet Island: Convert the building once owned by the Island Sash and Door Company to a quality restaurant. Create a regional arts and crafts center in the Durkee Atwood building. Retain the recently created amphitheater at Bicentennial Park. Build a bridge to connect the lower island to Lourdes Square on the east bank. Rehabilitate Main Street, including a terminal for trams that would take visitors on excursions.

- Hennepin Islands/Bluff park: Convert the lower dam hydroelectric plant to a museum. Create interpretive materials for the generating plant that would remain. Build walkways to the west end of the island. Develop unique stairways and landings down the bluff. Create a waterfall on the east channel. Connect all this to a rustic lower park that evoked images of Huck Finn.

- Bassett's Creek: Open the mouth of Bassett's Creek for a surrounding park.

The RDCB report reads remarkably like a description of the riverfront today, with the exception

> The Riverfront Development Coordinating Board was chaired by park commissioner Orvin "Ole" Olson. The newest riverfront park at West River Road and Twenty-third Street North, acquired in 2002, was named for Olson. Olson's son, Jon, was elected to the park board in 2002 and served as president of the board from 2004 to 2007. Ole and Jon are the third father-son duo to serve on the park board. The first was John and Alfred Pillsbury, followed by Leonard and Scott Neiman.

of Hennepin Island. Even before the final RDCB plan was approved, the park board approved in 1977 the acquisition of most of the properties listed. The state legislature began funding the acquisition of the properties needed for Central Riverfront Regional Park in 1979 through the MPOSC. Over the next decade, the park board would receive more than $23 million to acquire and develop land in the regional park.

The first parcel of land acquired and developed was Father Hennepin Bluffs in 1977. The initial development of the eighteen acres on the east bluff between the falls and the Stone Arch Bridge was begun in 1979 and dedicated in 1980.

In 1979, the board acquired Main Street and its first holdings on Nicollet Island in two agreements with the city housing authority for $2 million. Included in the deal was Bicentennial Park with its amphitheater. In the 1979 annual report the park board also noted its ongoing efforts to acquire the Island Sash and Door building, which was finally acquired by the park board in 1986. The building was converted into more than the quality restaurant suggested by the RCDB. The old building, which had once been owned by the Salvation Army, was converted into a hotel and restaurant, Nicollet Island Inn, which now operates under a lease from the park board.

By the end of 1980, the park board had also reached agreement—and received legislative approval—to acquire the Durkee Atwood building on lower Nicollet Island. In part because it was still a functioning business, the property was the most expensive acquired by the park board up to that time. The cost of the property and relocating the company was $6.5 million. The building has since been converted into the Nicollet Island Pavilion. At the same time, the legislature approved $3.5 million for the park board to acquire Boom Island. The flurry of acquisitions in 1980 was augmented by a donation from The Pillsbury Company of more than two acres of land between Main Street and Father Hennepin Bluffs, which is now Pillsbury Park.

In a little less than two years after the RDCB final report was issued, the park board made an impressive start on acquiring the land for a central riverfront park.

Although the work of the RCDB was largely completed while Robert Ruhe was superintendent of parks, he was not around to see the land acquired. And with the exception of Main Street and the first parcels of Nicollet Island, neither was his successor, Charles Spears.

After once again conducting a national search, the board turned in 1980 to an inside man, David Fisher, to replace Spears. Fisher had been hired in 1970 by Ruhe and had become assistant superintendent for operations. Fisher had an older connection, however, to a much earlier park administration. As a student at Texas Tech University, he had taken classes from Charles Doell—"I was in awe of Doell," said Fisher—who was a visiting professor at both Michigan State and Texas Tech after his retirement.

Although he was only thirty-five, Fisher was well-known to park commissioners, and he had a good relationship with the labor unions that had considerable influence on park management. Fisher's style was to create and nurture partnerships with other agencies, much more like his teacher, Doell, than his erstwhile boss, Ruhe. Near the end of his eighteen years as superintendent—the longest tenure since Wirth—Fisher wrote that one of the keys to success as a parks administrator is to create partnerships, particularly with organizations that have money.

It was a lesson learned along the river. Fisher's efforts to create relationships with "money" would pay significant dividends over the years, not only on the riverfront but in neighborhood funding of parks, and with the arts community—especially in the creation of the Sculpture Garden.

With Fisher at the helm and Al Wittman, assistant superintendent for planning, doing much of the negotiating with other city, state and federal agencies, development continued along the riverfront. The thorniest issue was what to do about residential property on Nicollet Island. The island had a history of being home to some of the finest residences in the city from the days when William Eastman, William King and others had lived there. (King's erstwhile city house was acquired for the construction of De-LaSalle High School at the turn of the century.) The problem was that those homes were ancient history in Minneapolis terms and most had been destroyed. The few that remained were in serious disrepair. In 1969 the city's renewal plan for the island called for demolishing all residences on the island. But seven years later city consultants called for the preservation of historic structures on the island.

Two of the last commercial buildings on the island, the old carpentry shop and Durkee Atwood building, were preserved. And in 1983 a private developer created condos on a portion of the "outparcel" reserved for residential property by renovating the Grove Street Flats. The park board had meanwhile acquired ownership of the remainder of the island from the city and private owners. Ultimately, the park board and the successor to the housing authority, the Minneapolis Community Development Agency (MCDA), agreed in 1985 to a complex deal that was neither fish nor fowl. The park board would lease residential sites to the MCDA for ninety-nine years, and the MCDA would sublease them to private parties. The subleases for the properties were awarded by lottery for one dollar, but required considerable investment by lottery winners to improve them under very strict limitations. The visions some had of a Tivoli Garden–type amusement park or something along the lines of Colonial Williamsburg on the island would be left to a future generation to pursue.

To get the ball rolling on the west side of the river, where a parkway was the only plan, the city took advantage of the federal Great River Road program that had been created in the 1930s. The only money available was to fund an initial assessment and plan, but that was a start. Much of a Great River Road along the river in the city was already in place from Minnehaha Park to near Riverside Park, thanks to the foresight of Minneapolitans nearly one hundred years earlier. Now, with a focus on river redevelopment, park efforts shifted to extending that road through the city.

The route for the river road was chosen through an extensive "environmental impact" process in the early 1980s with the park board as the lead agency. By the spring of 1984, the route from Plymouth Avenue north of downtown to the then-existing West River Parkway at Riverside Park was selected. The problem then was how to acquire the land and what to do about the fact that the proposed parkway would cross the site of the old mills and tail races, buried for twenty years near the upper lock beside the falls. Historic preservation then had an urgency that surpassed concern for a few historic, but dilapidated, buildings on Nicollet Island.

The result of the history conundrum was resolved by the idea for Mill Ruins Park, which would

The lower end of Nicollet Island had once been heavily industrialized, as seen here in a photo from 1904. By this time the logs were gone from the river, but railroad tracks dominated the west bank of the river. (Minneapolis Public Library, Minneapolis Collection, M4107)

uncover and preserve the historic mill foundations and the canals beneath them. It would be part of a larger development of historic assets coordinated in part by the St. Anthony Falls Heritage Board created by the legislature in 1988 to manage area development from a historical perspective. Historic preservation in the district included the creation of the Mill City Museum by the Minnesota Historical Society. The museum was created in the shell of the former Washburn "A" mill across the parkway from Mill Ruins Park.

The challenge of acquiring land upriver from the falls had a swift resolution. Glacier Park, the real estate subsidiary of Burlington Northern Railroad, owned a lot of land in the city that was no longer needed for track, especially since the downtown railroad depot had been demolished in 1978. (Amtrak, a national passenger rail company, was created in 1972 to provide the service that private railroads could no longer operate profitably, and it located its station in the Midway area of St Paul.) Glacier Park's large landholdings north of downtown included a site that Cowles Media Company, publisher of the *StarTribune,* wanted for a new printing plant. But that land was not zoned for commercial development of that character.

To facilitate the change in zoning for that property, Glacier Park agreed to donate twenty-two acres of its land along the river to the city for development of a park and parkway. The company got a double benefit. Not only would it be able to sell part of its land to Cowles, its remaining property in the area would be greatly enhanced for residential development with a park running past it. The deal was reminiscent of many park board land transactions of years long past: land was donated to the park board with the expectation that adjacent lands would increase in value. That the deal also benefited the city's only surviving daily newspaper was historically just, as the *StarTribune* and its predecessor newspapers had been among the most consistent and reliable park advocates since the creation of the park board.

The donation, valued at $11 million, gave the park board a twenty-two-acre ribbon along the Mississippi, upon which it built the first stretch of the central riverfront parkway from Portland to Plymouth avenues. The donation was similar to many early land donations also in that it came with a condition: the parkway had to be built in two years. To meet that timetable, the MCDA loaned the park board $7 million to be paid back from future open-space grants. When the loan was due, however, the park board pointed out the tremendous development along the parkway since its creation and the significant increase in tax collections by the city because of that development. In essence, the investment by the MCDA had already been paid back many times over, a view that the legislature supported and MCDA ultimately accepted.

The other piece of land required for the first stretch of the central river parkway eliminated the only restaurant on the river below the falls and created a controversy that has not been resolved. Fuji-ya, a Japanese restaurant, overlooked the river north of Portland Avenue. While the park board wanted to take only the restaurant's riverfront parking lot, a court-negotiated settlement resulted in the park board acquiring the entire property for $3.5 million. The portion of that property not used for the parkway, which the park board never really wanted or planned to develop as a park, has been the focus of intense debate since. The park board has investigated sale of the land to real estate developers, which has generated opposition from those who would prefer to see the land remain in public hands. How that land could be used as a park if it were not sold, and who would pay to develop and maintain it, remain to be seen.

The completion of the first stretch of new river parkway is what brought civic leaders together on the riverbank the day the Twins opened the 1987 World Series against the Cardinals. It was the culmination of a very busy year along the river. On Nicollet Island, the Durkee Atwood building was converted

> Benjamin F. Nelson operated a sawmill and then a shingle factory on the site that still bears his name. The company he founded is now based in Shakopee, Minnesota. Nelson was an influential man in early Minneapolis history. He served on the first park board in 1883 as a member of the city council and later as a replacement for one of the original twelve appointed commissioners who resigned. He was later elected to the school board, where he served for many years.

into a pavilion, and both the pavilion and the Nicollet Island Inn were joined to Main Street by the installation of a bridge between the island and the east bank. A span of the old Broadway Avenue Bridge was floated downstream and installed beside the inn on Merriam Street.

That summer the park board also dedicated a new park on the east side of the river and added significantly to its land holdings. In June 1987 the park board dedicated Boom Island as a park. The twenty-acre park just south of the Plymouth Avenue Bridge had been acquired a few years earlier from Carl Bolander and Sons, a construction company, with money from the state legislature. The new park was designed by the grandson of Theodore Wirth, Ted Wirth, a Montana-based landscape architect at the time.

Also in 1987 the park board completed an unexpected deal to acquire what is known as the B. F. Nelson site. The land had been acquired by the state years earlier as the site for a river crossing for I-335, the freeway that was at one time planned to traverse northeast Minneapolis to connect I-35 with I-94.

When the land was acquired, the federal government paid 90 percent of the $5 million cost, with the state paying the rest. Until 1987, the federal government had permitted states to sell land that was no longer needed for freeways without reimbursing the federal government for its share of the purchase price. But the state's transportation department said it had learned that the federal government was about to change its policy and require reimbursement for its investment. Before that change would take effect, MnDOT said it would sell the park board the B. F. Nelson site for the state's investment, which was only 10 percent of the original cost. But the state also had another motive. It needed a bit more park land from The Parade for the construction of I-394 west from downtown. Moreover, it had not been successful in the remediation of some polluted industrial land it had promised the park board as part of the North Mississippi Park freeway agreement in 1974.

The state ultimately sold the B. F. Nelson site to the park board for a little more than $200,000, plus the transfer of The Parade land and the polluted North Mississippi

The riverfront at Boom Island. The entrance from the Mississippi River to the Boom Island Marina is in the foreground. Boom Island, no longer an island, was once where men snared logs floating down the river and sorted them by owner. Each log was stamped with a brand. The channel that once separated the island from the east bank filled in with debris and sawdust. The RCDB at one point considered reestablishing the land as an island. (Nancy Conroy, Minneapolis Park and Recreation Board) land. The site is still awaiting development after environmental remediation.

By the end of that very busy year, enthusiasm and expectations were high for the new parks on both sides of the river. When Boom Island was dedicated, Fisher remarked that he thought it could become the "premier waterfront park in the United States." Park commissioner Naomi Loper said it was the most important new park construction since the parkways were built around the lakes. "This is going to surpass the lakes in beauty and it's going to take the pressure off the lakes," said city council president Alice Rainville of the new parkway on the west side of the river.

The riverfront parks have spurred significant private investment on both sides of the river. Private investment is estimated to exceed $1 billion along the downtown riverfront, primarily in higher-end condominiums. It appears that the public investment in the riverfront has been successful, especially judging it by the standards of previous park acquisitions. The board's investment in park land around the city's lakes, for instance, did not stimulate significant private investment, in some cases, for decades.

The second phase of West River Parkway, the mile-and-a-half link from downtown to the old parkway along the river downstream, began in 1997. That stretch of the parkway was a much more complicated deal as it required the relocation of existing businesses.

The primary occupant of riverfront below the falls was the J. L. Shiely Company, which had acquired a long-term lease on the land for its concrete business in 1969 after the Army Corps of Engineers had completed the construction of the upper lock. The company's lease to the nine-plus-acre site was eventually bought out for $8 million.

The board acquired another ten acres of riverbank downstream from the Shiely property from First Bank. The last hurdle to completing the parkway was acquiring a permanent easement across property owned by Minnegasco. The complication was the cost of cleaning up the land, which had been the site of a Minnegasco plant that converted coal to gas, a process that left the soil surrounding the plant contaminated. The company, the park board and the Minnesota Pollution Control Agency negotiated an agreement that required the company to clean up the site to meet a standard for parks and parkways, a less expensive standard than for commercial or residential use. In return, Minnegasco offered an easement at a price below the land's appraised value and also paid much of the cost of preparing the site for parkway construction.

With the parkway completed in stages as land was acquired, construction of Mill Ruins Park began on the former Shiely site in 2000 and was completed in 2001. Mill Ruins Park was finished in part with a grant from the National Park Service. The proliferation of government agencies with an interest in the river had continued in 1988 with the designation of the Mississippi National River and Recreation Area to be administered by the National Park Service (NPS). Sponsored by St. Paul Congressman Bruce Vento and Senator David Durenberger, the legislation created a role for the NPS in managing river resources and federally owned land along a seventy-two-mile corridor from Anoka, Minnesota, to Prescott, Wisconsin. Senator Durenberger had been involved for many years in park issues in the metropolitan area before his election to the Senate. He had played a central role in the creation of the MPOSC and was a member

> The northern section of West River Parkway was renamed James I. Rice Parkway in 1997 to honor Minneapolis legislator James Rice. Rice, along with legislators Carl Kroening and John Sarna, is credited with passing much of the legislation that enabled state funds to help develop and maintain Minneapolis's regional parks, including the central riverfront. Rice's son, Brian, has been the park board's attorney since 1984.

Mill Ruins Park. The park is an archeological site that incorporates the excavated foundations of nineteenth-century mills and the canals that carried water to power the mills. Its historic features are listed in the National Register of Historic Places. The park offers popular programs of archeological digs to uncover real and planted artifacts. (Minneapolis Park and Recreation Board)

The Stone Arch Bridge that once carried passenger trains into the Minneapolis depot is now a pedestrian and bicycle link across the river. (Minnesota Department of Transportation, © David Larson)

of the MPOSC when the RDCB created its plan for the central riverfront. At that time he was also the chairman of the Hennepin County Park Reserve Board (now Three Rivers Park District), to which he had been appointed by the Minneapolis park board.

What tied the developments on the east and west banks together so splendidly below the falls was essentially another gift from the Burlington Northern Railroad: the Stone Arch Bridge. Constructed the year the park board was created, 1883, the bridge's two tracks had at one time carried more than eighty passenger trains a day into Minneapolis. But by the mid-1970s, passenger service was discontinued, and the bridge was closed. In the 1980s, the railroad offered to donate the bridge to the city, but the city declined because of concerns about the cost of maintaining it. However, in 1989 Hennepin County bought the bridge for $1,001 with the idea that some day it might be used in a light-rail system. However when the state took over responsibility for light-rail developments, at the insistence of Minneapolis legislators James Rice and John Sarna the state also acquired the bridge. With the help of more than $2 million in federal grants for the reuse of historic transportation structures in 1993, the state developed the bridge as a pedestrian and bicycle pathway. At the present time, the state maintains the bridge superstructure, and the park board maintains the surface of the bridge. Interpretive information on the bridge is provided by the St. Anthony Falls Heritage Board.

The construction of the Federal Reserve Bank building on the former railroad depot site just north of Hennepin on the west side of the river in 2000 presented another opportunity to provide historic interpretation of the river and the city. First Bridge Park was established in 2001 between the bank and the Hennepin Bridge to commemorate the history of river bridges at the site. The foundations of earlier bridges were exposed, and interpretive exhibits were developed.

The focus of the park board from the 1970s

through the 1990s was on the development of the central riverfront, but the board also began to look upriver toward an eventual goal of linking the central riverfront parks with North Mississippi Park and extending the Great River Road north on the east side of the river on Marshall Avenue.

Several steps were taken toward those goals:

- Gluek Park: In 1978 the board acquired the three-acre site of the former Gluek Brewery at Marshall Avenue and Nineteenth Avenue Northeast. The property was improved in 1988.

- Sheridan Memorial Park: The first land for what was then called Water Street Park on the former site of the Grain Belt Brewery, just north of the Broadway Bridge, was bought in 1986, and another lot was purchased in 1995. The old foundry on the site was demolished in 1997 when park improvements were begun.

- Edgewater Park: In 1993 the board purchased for about $300,000 another two acres on the river south of Lowry Avenue that had been the site of the old Edgewater Inn. As with Gluek Park and Sheridan Memorial Park, the land for Edgewater Park was purchased with funds from the Legislative Commission on Minnesota Resources, which was created to allocate state proceeds from the Minnesota Lottery.

- Orvin "Ole" Olson Park: The most recent addition to the board's river holdings was the purchase in 2002 of the site of another former restaurant, the Riverview Supper Club, at West River Road and Twenty-third Avenue North.

The shift of focus to the river beginning in the late-1970s is symbolized by the location of the park board's current offices on the west bank of the river north of Broadway. The park board had considered having its own headquarters on park land periodically over the years. As early as 1920, it considered establishing its offices in the Washburn Fair Oaks mansion across from the Minneapolis Institute of Arts. When the board was evicted from City Hall in 1966, it once again considered the possibility of owning its own building but finally chose to rent space in the Public Safety Building. Evicted from that space in 1979, the park board set up most of its offices in rented space in the Flour Exchange near City Hall. In the 1990s the park board moved its offices once again to the Grain Exchange across the street.

Facing a steep increase in the cost of its leased office space in 2002, the board seized an opportunity to resolve its long-standing office problems. The board found an office and warehouse building on the river that was for sale. Guided by board president Bob Fine, an attorney with experience in real estate transactions, the building was purchased and renovated, and in 2003 the park board moved into the first office building that it owned. While the deal was criticized by some as extravagant, the park board no longer paid rent and generated income by renting the ground floor of the building to a catering service. Since that time the board's decision to acquire its own building has been widely praised as a wise investment. One disadvantage of the location is that the park board staff is no longer in close proximity to other city offices downtown. However, park commissioners cite the enormous advantage of having space that is much more accessible to the public, including free parking, which facilitates public participation in board deliberations. And a park has been created on the riverbank in front of park headquarters.

The symbolic importance of the location of the building, however, is inescapable: the administrative center of Minneapolis parks faces the river that remains one of the board's greatest future development challenges.

One of the issues that has not been resolved along the central riverfront is the future of Hennepin

Island. Xcel Energy, which still generates power from the Hennepin Island plant, and the park board have discussed development of the island as a park for more than twenty years. Included in discussions has been the creation of a whitewater recreation park on the east channel of the island, complete with a restored waterfall. Agreement has not been reached on who would pay to develop and maintain a park there.

A partial—and spectacular—resolution was reached in 2007 with the opening of Water Power Park, which permits access to St. Anthony Falls. Walkways past the power plant extend to the mist-cooled edge of the cement-capped falls. The park is owned by Xcel but is operated and maintained in conjunction with the park board. Displays on the history of the falls and the generation of electricity there were developed by the National Park Service.

While many questions about the future of the riverfront remain, one fact is sure: most of the central riverfront land is owned by the park board and preserved for public use. The "inestimable boon" of public ownership cited by Horace Cleveland more than 125 years ago remains true. With considerable land in public hands, the people of the city at least have options for the future.

Also certain is that development of those public resources will involve many more public and private entities than were involved in park development prior to the return to the river. Riverfront development—or redevelopment for public use—is beyond the scope of any one agency. There have been and, of necessity, must be many players in riverfront development. The cost is now too great and interests too many for any one agency of government, or any private interest, to manage it alone. That so many public and private entities have come together to create something that honors history and serves the future shows Minnesota at its best.

In the end, the complexity of riverfront development, only touched upon here, reinforces admiration for the foresight of park advocates over the decades who urged the acquisition of park land in advance of the city's needs.

West River Parkway, Mill Ruins Park and the Stone Arch Bridge in 2004. The Stone Arch Bridge was converted into a pedestrian and bicycle path. The new Guthrie Theater is under construction in the center foreground. (Minneapolis Park and Recreation Board)

Chapter Twenty-Four

Fragmentation

After more than a decade of developing parks along the river, involving intricate arrangements and conditions with myriad agencies, the inevitable occurred. In July 1988 the *StarTribune* ran an article about neighborhood concerns over the poor state of maintenance of Powderhorn Park. The newspaper asked the obvious question: had the park board neglected neighborhood parks to focus on the river?

Al Wittman's answer was no. Neighborhood parks, he said "are the backbone of the system." But Wittman went on to point out that it was easier to get money for the revival of the riverfront than for neighborhood parks.

The early 1980s had been a time once again of retrenchment at the park board—despite river developments. The steep inflation of the 1970s ate away park board budgets already strained by the high cost of removing and replacing dead elms. In addition, the nation entered a recession in the early 1980s that, combined with a nationwide taxpayer revolt and the election at both the national and state level of politicians committed to shrinking government, made public resources scarce. In 1981, the park board saw the belt-tightening coming. Superintendent David Fisher told the *StarTribune* in September of that year that the future "looks pretty grim to us."

As had happened before, during good economic times the park board had responded to increasing public demand for more—land, facilities and programs—only to find on the down cycle that it didn't have the funds to maintain or operate those facilities and programs.

But this time the money crunch was more complex, because the city had changed since the down cycles of previous decades. Minneapolis had fewer people than any time since Theodore Wirth was superintendent (370,000), and the population was considerably more diverse. Neighborhoods had changed too. With the closing of eighteen more public schools in the 1980s, neighborhood parks were the last true community institutions.

Recreation was also in the process of changing. The way people exercised and the importance they gave it began a dramatic shift. "Wellness" and "lifetime fitness" were becoming the catchwords of the health industry. Jogging, bicycling and, later, in-line skating became daily activities for many people. Cross-country skiing enjoyed a similar new popularity. The trend increased the strain of heavy use on the lakes and parkways and also increased demand for maintenance.

The financing of parks also continued to evolve and, like nearly everything else the park board dealt with, become more complex. With the beginning of a state sales tax in 1967—3 percent!—intended to reduce local property taxes, the collection and allocation of tax revenues became more complicated. State government began to play a much larger role in the allocation of resources and introduced a new variable in park funding. The park board had to negotiate with other branches of city government not only for its share of property taxes but for the amount it would get from local government aid passed to the city by the state as sales-tax revenues. (The old mill rate system of determining property taxes was replaced in 1989 by a system known as "tax capacity funding," which remained based on the assessed value of property.)

Against that backdrop of a changing city and changing recreation habits, the park board had largely achieved the goal of having a park within roughly a half mile of every residence in the city. The acquisition of neighborhood parks was essentially completed in the 1970s. The focus of the board since then, in addition to riverfront development, has been on adding to recreational facilities, rather than acquiring land. Two exceptions were in 1983 when the board leased land for a small playground next to Windom School in south Minneapolis and purchased the former site of Jordan Junior High School in north Minneapolis from the school board for Jordan Park.

The park board was not only done acquiring neighborhood parks, but it put the construction of new recreation centers on hold, too. From 1981 to 1991 the board approved only four new buildings in neighborhood parks:

- A new park shelter was built at Kenny Park in 1982.
- The long-delayed Kenwood Community Center was finally supported by the neighborhood and built in 1983.
- The open shelter at Harrison Park was enclosed in 1984.
- A shelter was built at the newly acquired Jordan Park in 1984.

Other than those four buildings, the park board's building projects were limited to those that were paid for by someone other than the park board or the city. River developments and the new Lake Harriet Bandstand in 1986 were partially paid for by the Metropolitan Council, and the Sculpture Garden and Cowles Conservatory in 1987 and 1988 were paid for with private funds raised by the Walker Art Center.

The issue of maintaining parks was complicated by the poor state of the park board's maintenance facilities themselves. The park board's primary maintenance center at Lyndale Farmstead was constructed in 1922 when Theodore Wirth was still not done reshaping Minneapolis parks. It had been built when the city was still emerging from horse-and-buggy days and before the days of "deferred maintenance" that reached into the millions of dollars.

With state funding focused on the river in the 1980s, the Metropolitan Council did not approve a $1.5 million grant to complete construction of the new central maintenance facility. The park board needed a loan from the city to complete the facility in 1987. To get that loan, the board had to forego neighborhood park improvements for two years, Wittman explained at the time. In 1992, the Metropolitan Council reimbursed the board for the $1.5 million, bringing its total contribution to the project to nearly $3 million. The money was then spent to build new gyms at Farview and Luxton parks.

The board made two important additions in 1988 to its facilities at two former school buildings: the gym of former Central High School, and the gym and pool of former Phillips Junior High. The board acquired the Central gym to provide another neighborhood facility in an area that the park board had for many years targeted for a playground. In the 1990s, the park board acquired adjacent residential property, some from the MCDA, to expand the gym site into a playground as well.

Another school property converted to a recreation center was Phillips Junior High School at East Twenty-fourth Street and Seventeenth Avenue South. The former school offered the benefit of not only two gyms but a swimming pool. The operation of the Phillips gym and pool was a collaborative effort of the park board, the Boys and Girls Clubs, the YMCA, which operated a day-care center at the site, and Pillsbury United Communities. The $1.5 million improvement to the site—the most ever spent on a recreation center by the park board until then—was funded by city and federal grants and the McKnight, Bush and Minneapolis foundations. The participation of nonprofit foundations marked one of the first developments of park facilities with private funds.

The other major development of a recreation facility in 1988 was the addition of an ice arena to The Parade. With the demolition of the Minneapolis Auditorium to make way for a new convention center, Minneapolis high schools lost the ice arena where they played most of their hockey games. To replace that lost venue, the board built a new 1,400-seat arena at The Parade adjacent to the 1973 ice rinks. The arena opened in 1989 with a skating exhibition by former Olympic champion Dorothy Hamill.

The park board also expanded Currie Park in 1992 and took ownership of the new Coyle Community Center built and operated on the expanded site by Pillsbury United Communities. One of the original Pillsbury settlement houses had been located on the site before the board acquired the land in 1941.

The most significant addition of outdoor athletic space to the park system since the 1970s began in 1992 when the park board entered into a seven-year lease with the Minnesota Department of Natural Resources for land at Fort Snelling State Park. The initial lease covered nearly fifty acres, which included a nine-hole golf course. When the original lease expired in 1999, the board reached agreement with the state to add fifty acres to the lease and extend it for thirty years. In addition, the park board purchased seventeen acres. The new land was converted into tournament-quality playing fields. The complex contains seven soccer fields, two baseball fields, and three softball fields. It was dedicated in 2003 as the Leonard Neiman Sports Complex. The complex includes an indoor tennis center developed with a gift of $5 million from the Fred Wells Foundation.

During the difficult years of the early 1980s, when park operating budgets were so tight that welcome mats were removed from recreation centers, the park board continued to provide new recreation facilities in neighborhoods in any way it could. At the same time, however, parks in the city continued to evolve. Over its first hundred years, the board had changed from a preserver of open space in advance of development to a rehabilitator of abandoned industrial space along the river. It had gone from providing skating rinks and concert bands to running active recreation programs and constructing facilities to house them. But nowhere was the transformation of park

Lake Harriet Bandstand. A new Lake Harriet Bandstand was built in 1986. Designed by Milo Thompson, the bandstand was reoriented to provide a lake view for the audience. A refectory matching the fanciful design was built next to the bandstand in 1989. A picnic shelter *(far left)* was added in 2007. (Peter Schmidt, Minneapolis Park and Recreation Board)

management more obvious than in the development that resulted from a phone call on David Fisher's second day on the job as park superintendent in 1981.

David Fisher got a phone call from a man he had never met, but agreed to have lunch with. That lunch launched a unique project that would help create a remarkable park space and a new image for the city. A few other cities have lakes, and many others have redeveloped riverfronts but none has what was begun that day. Fisher's lunch date was with Martin Friedman, director of the Walker Art Center, a progressive and renowned center for modern art, music and film. Friedman wanted to discuss what the Walker and the park board could do together to develop the land opposite the Walker.

After the construction of I-94 had narrowed the park and cut it off from Loring Park, the board stopped planting the Kenwood Garden in 1967. Since that time, the space had been an open grass field with softball fields at the northern end. The Walker and the park board had held discussions since the late 1960s about what could be done there, and the space had been used for temporary sculpture exhibits. In the wake of the Greben Report in 1977, the park

Peace Garden. The Rock Garden at Lyndale Park, originally built by Louis Boeglin in 1929, was overgrown with oaks and abandoned during the lean years of the mid-1940s. Theodore Wirth noted in 1934 that it was the most popular of all park gardens because it was the coolest during a very hot summer. The garden was rediscovered in 1981 during the cleanup after a tornado blew down many of the trees. Horticulturist Mary Lerman convinced her bosses to use the money they saved when she was on maternity leave for the birth of her daughter Harriet in 1983 to begin renovation of the garden. As residents saw the work unfold, many donated money toward revival of the garden, which was designed by Betty Ann Addison. The garden was eventually transformed into the "Peace Garden" after donations of rock from the nuclear bomb sites of Hiroshima and Nagasaki, Japan. A "Peace Pole" in the garden was a gift from Chiba, Japan, to Minneapolis Mayor Don Fraser, which he donated to the garden. The "Spirit of Peace" sculpture was dedicated October 25, 2006. (Minneapolis Park and Recreation Board)

board wanted to expand non-sports recreation, but with the departure of Ruhe in 1978 and the arrival of a new administration, nothing had materialized.

But Fisher and Friedman both saw the possibilities. Their lunch meeting eventually led to the creation of a highly praised public space, the Minneapolis Sculpture Garden. Friedman would later call his collaboration with the park board to create that garden "one of the best I've ever been involved in."

The result of that collaboration is a seven-and-a-half-acre garden of sculptures, connected to Loring Park with a pedestrian bridge that is a sculpture itself. The garden also features the Cowles Conservatory, designed, in part, to serve as a walkway from The Parade parking lot to the Walker and Guthrie Theater. The Sculpture Garden was opened to a delighted public in 1988.

Creating the Sculpture Garden required collaboration with practically as many partners as riverfront development, and was another lesson for Fisher in the advantages of partnering with organizations that had money. On the riverfront it was the MCDA and the legislature through the Metropolitan Parks and Open Space Commission. At the Sculpture Garden, it was with the Walker, which had a prodigious ability to raise money through foundations and individual patrons of the arts, and federal and state agencies.

The project was initiated with a grant of $2.3 million from the McKnight Foundation. Once the project was off the ground, Friedman lined up other donors: Frederick Weisman contributed more than a million dollars for the sculptural centerpiece of the garden, *Spoon Bridge and Cherry,* a fountain created by the husband and wife team of Claes Oldenburg and Coosje van Bruggen; Sage and John Cowles gave another million for the conservatory; the family of Irene Hixon Whitney gave $800,000 for the bridge designed by Siah Armajani; Kenneth and Judy Dayton gave more than a million for art purchases; and Regis Corporation pledged $350,000 for plant displays at the conservatory. More foundation contributors added to the list: the Dayton Hudson Foundation, Bush Foundation and Kresge Foundation together added another million dollars to development funds.

The park board and the Walker were also joined by a third partner, the University of Minnesota, which agreed to manage the conservatory as part of its landscape arboretum program. The downside of operating partnerships was learned by the park board when the University eventually withdrew from participation, leaving the park board with the responsibility—and expense—of maintaining the conservatory.

The collaboration worked from Fisher's perspective because it put the responsibility for acquiring sculpture in the hands of a respected arts institution. That avoided, he said, the prospect of anyone wanting to install a "car bumper sculpture" made by a nephew.

The Sculpture Garden, called "gloriously serene and strong" by the *New York Times,* has become one of the symbols of the city and stands as an example of the creative use of park land. The garden was such a success—the first requests to hold weddings in the garden began coming in before it was finished—that it was expanded in 1990 by removing another softball field. The costs of that expansion were paid by

The Minneapolis Sculpture Garden as seen looking north from the Walker Art Center. The garden, designed by Edward Larrabee Barnes, was developed in two stages. The popularity of the initial garden, which ended at the row of trees beyond the famous *Spoon Bridge and Cherry,* led to the removal of another softball field, and the addition of another "courtyard" of sculptures. (Walker Art Center)

Cowles Conservatory, designed by Michael Van Valkenburg, under construction in 1986. The center courtyard houses Frank Gehry's marvelous *Standing Fish* sculpture surrounded by palm trees. The original palms had to be replaced—with the help of a Teen Teamworks crew—because they grew through the glass ceiling. (Minneapolis Park and Recreation Board)

the Walker, mostly through a gift from the family of N. Bud Grossman.

The history of the park board is replete with examples of the changing notion of parks and how they should be used. The Sculpture Garden is one of the shining examples. That square of land had undergone several transformations in park history, from open space to garden to softball fields to a sophisticated yet remarkably accessible art space. The continuously evolving public perception of parks is also apparent in the management of park land—and water—beginning in the 1970s.

The board's venture in the 1970s into water quality management evolved into a much more sophisticated and visible water quality program through the Clean Water Partnership in 1994. By the 1990s the board was collaborating with four watershed districts to improve water quality in lakes, river and streams. Those efforts have led to a steady improvement in water quality and heightened public awareness of what can be done to improve water quality.

Al Wittman gives much of the credit for environmental programs at the park board to some of the first commissioners who took an intense interest in the environment, such as Walter Bratt and Naomi Loper. They were followed in 1989 by Annie Young and later by Dean Zimmermann, who were elected partly due to their commitment to preserving nature and protecting parks and lakes from overdevelopment.

Their campaigns were stimulated in part by a controversy in 1988 that was not of the park board's making. (The controversy might have been avoided if the park board had listened to Charles Loring and Theodore Wirth in 1912 when they insisted that the park board acquire the land across Lake Street from the Lake Calhoun beach to prevent development there.) Plans to build a residential tower in 1988 next to the Calhoun Beach Club across from the lake incited heated opposition and eventually resulted in a city ordinance that limited the height of buildings adjacent to lakes. It also sparked interest in preserving the environments of lakes and parks. Even sailors on Lake Calhoun got involved, by arguing that tall buildings around the lake would divert wind from the lake surface.

The efforts to protect water quality combined with attempts to restore lost landscapes—and save maintenance costs—led in the mid-1990s to a new program in park management. From 1994 to 1997 forty-five park sites were converted from mowed lawns to prairie grasses and wildflowers or allowed to revert to their natural state. In 1996, the park board cited not only the environmental benefits but annual savings in maintenance costs of fewer park lawns. One hundred years earlier when the park board didn't have the money to mow park grass, it sold the hay that resulted. This time, it converted some areas to native vegetation that would pay longer-term returns in cost savings, ecological diversity, and cleaner lake water.

Remnant prairies were protected along West River Parkway, Minnehaha Park and the western edge of Wirth Park. Parts of Boom Island, Powderhorn Park, Ridgway Parkway, North Mississippi and Cedar Lake Trail were seeded with prairie grasses and wildflowers, and the Nokomis Naturescape Garden was created. In addition, old wetlands, which had once been so zealously filled, were re-created. The first was at Cedar Meadows, southwest of Cedar Lake in 1996. That was followed by similar efforts on the southwest shores of Lake Calhoun and Lake Nokomis. The Lake Calhoun neighborhoods that had once battled in court to stop the filling of the lakeside wetlands now argued that the wetlands shouldn't be re-created because the land had historical significance. The wetlands near the lakes not only restored native vegetation but reestablished the wetlands as filters for the lakes. In addition, parts of the shoreline of nearly every lake were allowed to grow naturally instead of being manicured up to the water's edge.

Along with the restoration of native grasses and wildflowers to parks came a sustained and ongoing effort to rid the parks of invasive plant species.

In the mid-1980s the park board began efforts to remove purple loosestrife—a reedy marsh plant—and buckthorn—a prolific scrub tree—from parks. The first efforts to remove invaders focused on the bog and wildflower garden at Wirth Park. Buckthorn removal was an important element in the restoration of the Quaking Bog through the mid-1980s. The campaign to remove those species and others from public and private property in the city has since involved thousands of people combing park hillsides, lakeshores and the banks of the Mississippi to pluck the fast-growing invaders before they crowd out native plants.

The harmful effects of invasive species in city lakes became an issue in 1989 with the first reports of Eurasian milfoil in Lake of the Isles. Milfoil—a fast-growing aquatic plant that chokes lakes and absorbs oxygen when it dies and rots—has now spread to all city lakes. In the absence of any natural way to curtail milfoil growth, it is now harvested in parts of the lakes through a permit from the Minnesota Department of Natural Resources.

Mary Lerman, park horticulturist since 1976, points to climate change in the past thirty years as a significant factor in the growth of invasive species. Climate change has also had an impact, she said, on park maintenance—and expense. Warmer winters mean that more harmful insects survive. Less snow cover results in more damage to plants. More severe storms in summer and winter damage more trees. Warmer temperatures throughout the year have altered the type of trees, shrubs and flowers the park board has planted.

The success of the park board in managing change through the 1980s was recognized in 1989 when the park board won the Gold Medal Award at the National Park and Recreation Congress. The award praised the board's efforts along the river, the creation of the Sculpture Garden, and innovations in youth programs. At the time, Fisher attributed the success of the park system, in part, to the park board acting as a neighborhood-based social service agency. "I viewed myself as a social worker who happened to be in charge of land," Fisher said of the time. The management of parks had changed more than a little from the days of Charles Loring and Theodore Wirth.

In the mid-1980s, the park board had branched into social service programs to meet the changing needs of the city's population. Building on the recreational philosophy of Robert Ruhe, Harvey Feldman and his successor as assistant superintendent for recreation, Mary Merrill Anderson, and following the suggestions of the Greben Report, the park board began a number of programs to provide social services.

The first of the programs was Teen Teamworks. Beginning in 1986, the program provided summer jobs to teens referred by other agencies. (The park board had run a similar teen-employment program in 1965–66.) The teens worked on park projects, supervised by park personnel, and also spent time in education programs. Fisher said he viewed the program more as an education program than a jobs program. Its value, he said, was that if it could make kids care about themselves, they would care about their city. Although the program was initiated with private grants, the program has been supported for most of its twenty-one-year history by state funding, too.

The second program inaugurated in the 1980s was Recreation Plus, which provided scheduled after-school supervision at parks for children of working parents. Children are bused directly from their schools in the afternoon to park recreation centers, where they participate in supervised activities as well as unstructured play. The program was inaugurated in sixteen neighborhood recreation centers and has since expanded to provide similar supervised recreation during summer weekdays.

In 1991, Youthline Outreach Mentorship Program was created to provide leadership experiences, skills development and mentor relationships to teens. The program has served thousands of teens annually in year-round and summer programs.

The park board also has continued working

A hiker enjoys the solitude of the Quaking Bog in Wirth Park. A floating walkway passes through the tamarack bog. Extensive efforts, begun in the 1980s, to remove buckthorn and other invasive plant species led to the preservation of the city's only remaining bog. (2008 *Star Tribune*/Minneapolis-St. Paul)

relationships with social service agencies that operate from park board facilities, including Boys and Girls Clubs at Phillips and Phelps parks, Pillsbury United Communities at Currie Park, and the Phyllis Wheatley Center at Bethune Park.

The park board made one of its most unusual purchases in the early 1990s. Way back in the second decade of the century, the park board had closed a couple dozen saloons when it condemned land downtown for The Gateway, and it had closed a few "resorts" of ill repute around Keegan's (Wirth) Lake about the same time. But in 1992, the Phillips neighborhood asked the park board to go a step further—to buy a liquor store. The unusual request came as part of a new process of funding neighborhood improvements that began in 1990.

The Neighborhood Revitalization Program (NRP) was created in 1990 by the city and the state legislature as a way to give neighborhoods more input in development decisions. The program was created to provide $20 million a year for twenty years to be distributed among eighty-one neighborhoods to spend on public improvements. Part of the goal of the program was to redirect "jurisdictional budgets," meaning the funds of city organizations like the park board, into projects selected by community organizations.

Fisher said the park board was confident in the funding it would receive under the NRP because "when people have a choice, they choose parks." Neighborhoods chose parks in large measure due to a pent-up demand for improved neighborhood recreation facilities. The wave of recreation centers built in the 1970s had created center-envy in neighborhoods that didn't get a center then, and the board simply didn't have the money to build more in the 1980s. With the inauguration of the NRP in 1991, many neighborhoods chose to contribute to park board efforts to upgrade or replace the recreation centers in their parks.

Since NRP funding began, neighborhoods have spent $18 million on park improvements. As a result of the 1970s building boom and neighborhood funding in the 1990s, the park board nearly quadrupled the size, in square feet, of its recreation buildings. The board also updated many play lots for younger children, including many wading pools, with NRP funds.

NRP funds have been used for a wide variety of park projects. While tree planting along streets and in parks has been the most frequently chosen expenditure by neighborhood committees, more money has been spent on building or improving recreational facilities and programs. The largest single NRP expenditure for parks was $1.8 million to enlarge Whittier Park. The second largest was to renovate Loring Park.

And that's how the park board came to buy a liquor store. The store was one of two private properties that still remained in Peavey Park at Franklin and Chicago avenues. The liquor store on the edge of a park was viewed as a nuisance and worse by area residents, and they requested that the board buy those last two lots to expand the park. At a cost of nearly $500,000, the park board did—and tore down the liquor store.

In every corner of the city neighborhoods allocated NRP funds to supplement park board funding for parks and recreation.

- Many neighborhoods near lakes contributed funds to shoreline restoration and wetland projects. Both Seward and Longfellow neighborhoods on the west bank of the river contributed to restoration of the riverbanks and protection of a remnant prairie.

- Five neighborhoods near Lake Harriet contributed to "Spiff the Biff," a project to rehabilitate the Harry Wild Jones–designed women's bathroom near the Lake Harriet Pavilion.

- Waite Park neighborhood paid to extend the Recreation Plus program for child care to the Waite Park recreation center.

- Four neighborhoods used NRP funds to install air-conditioning in their recreation centers. (Only sixteen of the city's forty-nine recreation centers are air-conditioned.)

- Longfellow neighborhood contributed money to build a new recreation center at Brackett Park.

- One of the most notable successes of the NRP in parks was the revitalization of Loring Park.

With close cooperation from the neighborhood and Friends of Loring Park, a neighborhood nonprofit organization, the park gave one of the city's oldest parks an extensive makeover. Loring Pond was drained in 1997, and a protective liner was placed in the bottom to prevent seepage. The shoreline was reseeded with native vegetation, and a new Garden of the Seasons was created. An aeration system was added to the pond in 1998. In the later stages of the renovation plan the shelter donated by Charles Loring in 1906 was renovated and expanded into a community arts center.

Park board staff took a slide show from neighborhood meeting to neighborhood meeting to give community organizations ideas of what they could do. It was an empowering program in many respects; people deciding for themselves how the city should spend money in neighborhoods. As the NRP program nears the end of its original funding mandate, however, others have concerns about the effect of the program. The process, some say, has weakened contacts among city agencies. Rather than city planners from various agencies working together to prioritize or coordinate plans, they were off at neighborhood meetings competing for dollars. The other concern is an old one that harkens to the battles the Ruhe-era board fought: how does a city and a park board balance the views of its professional staff—who should bring a citywide view, historical perspective and years of experience—with the views of neighborhood activists who may have more parochial, shorter-term viewpoints and no experience in addressing a particular type of construction or programming challenge?

There is no doubt that many NRP initiatives have proved very successful and have provided a forum for new voices and ideas. There is also no doubt that some NRP projects would not have been high on priority lists if citywide needs and challenges were taken into account.

Whatever the ultimate assessment of the NRP program, the fragmented funding of parks that is represented by the NRP process will remain a part of park board life. Director of planning for the park board in 2007, Judd Rietkerk, said the key to developing parks is for planners to follow the strings attached to every project and see if any of those strings are connected to money. The park board, now as ever, can't develop all the parks and make all the improvements it, or anyone else, would like. Whether it's getting money from the WPA for park improvements and recreation supervisors, HUD for inner-city park land, the legislature for river developments, Walker Art Center for an art park, or NRP for new facilities, the basic principles of paying for parks have changed little. The history of Minneapolis parks demonstrates that an extensive park system can survive, barely, on property tax receipts but cannot move forward without additional funding. That is the price of magnificent parks—however people choose to use them.

One of the best examples of collaboration between the park board and citizens in creatively seizing park opportunities began in the late 1980s. When word got out that Glacier Park, the Burlington Northern subsidiary, was planning to sell land along its tracks north of Cedar Lake, area citizens became concerned that private development would destroy the wild habitat of the lake. Residents created a committee to Save Cedar Lake Park, which had an aim not much different than the Board of Trade had in 1883 when it drafted the first Park Act: people saw attractive open land and wanted to preserve it for public use.

The park board was sympathetic to the goals of Save Cedar Lake Park and pledged support for their efforts, but simply had no money for the proj-

A path beside West River Parkway cleared for winter use. The path and adjacent parkway are part of the Grand Rounds, more than fifty miles each of trails and parkways, which was designated in 1998 as the first urban National Scenic Byway. Legislation sponsored by Minnesota Congressman Jim Oberstar in 1996 led to the designation of American Road and National Scenic Byways. The Grand Rounds were presented as a candidate in 1997. Following the official designation, the park board developed a Grand Rounds Interpretive Master Plan, which established criteria for all signs and kiosks along the route. The Grand Rounds, foreseen by William Folwell in 1891 as a citywide treasure, meander through parks and past creeks, lakes and river, revealing Minneapolis's greatest beauty preserved by more than a century of park visionaries. (2008 *Star Tribune*/Minneapolis-St. Paul)

ect. Through private and state funding, the organization raised the money to purchase forty-three acres of land, which it turned over to the park board. With the help of federal government transportation funds, part of the acquired land was converted into the Cedar Lake Trail, a bicycle trail that extends from the city's western boundary to downtown.

It was the first in a web of new trails—some not owned but maintained by the park board—that follow old railroad beds west from the city center past the lakes or through Wirth Park to the suburbs. Similar trails have extended north along both sides of the Mississippi River and beside Shingle Creek.

Citizen involvement in the Cedar Lake Park and Trail was one of the first and most successful examples of activism in the development of park amenities. A proliferating number of nonprofit organizations in the years since have focused on protection of natural resources in and out of parks. The degree of public participation and interest in parks is what sets Minneapolis apart from many other cities. It has made the job of the park board both more difficult and more rewarding: every decision is scrutinized, but at least park commissioners know that what they are doing matters to a lot of people.

The 1980s and 1990s will be remembered as a time when a great deal was accomplished by the park board amid great change. Certainly some of the credit must go to mayors, especially Don Fraser and Sharon Sayles-Belton, who were friendly to parks. The park board was a central player in riverfront development and created a unique art space in the Sculpture Garden. Many new recreation facilities were developed. The board became a more integral player in addressing the city's social needs. And the board began to recognize its environmental responsibilities and incorporate them into its management of resources. But most importantly, it was a time when new partners were needed—and found—to pay for park improvements and acquisitions. City, state and federal funds were needed, but so was money from neighborhood councils, nonprofit foundations and citizen-action groups. Partnering with money—Fisher's phrase—had become a reality of park management.

In one of his last acts as superintendent in early 1999, Fisher initiated a new position of assistant superintendent for development to place a greater emphasis on generating nontax revenues. Fisher recruited Minneapolis city budget director Don Siggelkow to fill the new post and to create a more formal structure for pursuing new sources of funding through concessions, partnerships and donations. One result of that effort was the creation of The Foundation for Minneapolis Parks in 2003, the publisher of this book, to provide a vehicle for individuals, foundations and businesses to perpetuate a rich tradition of private philanthropy in support of Minneapolis parks.

Longfellow House in Minnehaha Park now serves as an information center for the Grand Rounds. The house was moved to its present location and renovated in 2002 when Highway 55 was finally expanded. The highway, behind the house in this photo, which proved so contentious in the 1960s, ultimately followed a modified tunnel plan. To avoid endangering Minnehaha Creek, the highway passes over the creek, but a land bridge was created over the highway. That land bridge is now the site of Longfellow Garden, one of three gardens at Minnehaha Park. The Song of Hiawatha Garden, which includes part of Longfellow's famous poem inscribed in stone, was created in 1994 on the site of the former parking lot and overlook east of Minnehaha Falls. At that time, the Pergola Garden was also created south of the falls. (Peter Schmidt, Minneapolis Park and Recreation Board)

Flocks of ducks and geese appear to fly through the interior of the Carl Kroening Interpretive Center in North Mississippi Park. The center, which opened in 2002, is operated in partnership with Three Rivers Park District. Kroening was a Minneapolis legislator who was instrumental in acquiring state funding for park development, especially along the river. (Peter Schmidt, Minneapolis Park and Recreation Board)

Chapter Twenty-Five

What Endures

The most recent chapter in Minneapolis park history illustrates how much parks have changed as the city, its people and their lifestyles have changed. Yet it also demonstrates what has remained constant—and how solid a foundation was built 125 years ago.

The central role of recreation in park operations was given a strong endorsement when Fisher's successor was chosen. For the first time, someone from the recreation side of park administration was chosen as superintendent of parks. Mary Merrill Anderson was not only the first recreation professional to become superintendent, she was also the first woman and the first African American superintendent.

Merrill Anderson had been at the center of efforts to create programs at recreation centers that met community needs, such as Rec Plus and Youthline. She knew her community. She had grown up in the city and attended Central High School. When she graduated from the University of Minnesota in 1972—she was the third superintendent, along with Doell and Moore, who attended the U of M—she joined the recreation department as a supervisor at Powderhorn Park. There she caught the attention of Harvey Feldman as a supervisor who was not cut from the old competitive sports cloth, and after five years in the field, she was appointed training coordinator for the recreation staff, then manager of recreation center programs. When Feldman was moved to assistant superintendent for administration and secretary to the board in 1987, Merrill Anderson was appointed to the top recreation job.

> Theodore Wirth's contributions to Minneapolis parks were commemorated in the summer of 2004 when bronze statues of Wirth surrounded by children were installed in front of the Wirth Park Chalet. The statues were a gift of the Minneapolis Parks Legacy Society.

The hiring of a superintendent from the recreation side of park management reflected a renewed emphasis on recreation programs and facilities that followed the election of Walt Dziedzic, Bob Fine and Ed Solomon to the board in 1997. Each of them had developed an interest in parks in part through their involvement with youth sports programs. They joined long-time recreation advocate Scott Neiman on the board to provide a new focus on park recreation programs. Merrill Anderson's "playing for life" recreation philosophy and her emphasis on programs for children and youth meshed with the board's new composition, resulting in a commitment to upgrade the quality of park recreation facilities and programs.

The park board's agenda also included further riverfront development, the NRP process of updating recreation centers and neighborhood parks, efforts to recreate wetlands and defend prairie remnants, and negotiations to determine the future of the board's lease at Fort Snelling. Each of these ongoing projects was advanced.

- Ground was broken for Mill Ruins Park, which opened in 2002.

- The Carl W. Kroening Interpretive Center was built at North Mississippi Park and dedicated in 2002.

- A patch of available land on the upper river, now Olson Park, was acquired, also in 2002.

- The Fort Snelling lease was extended in 2000 for thirty years to encompass more land, 17 more acres were purchased and the Leonard Neiman Sports Complex was opened in 2003. At the time the Neiman complex was created the park board also planned to develop two other sites as tournament-quality playing fields: Northeast Park and Bryn Mawr. However, funding was only available for one complex and the board chose to develop the Fort Snelling site. The decision was criticized at the time, and since, because the complex is too far from the neighborhoods that most needed the fields. The complex now hosts nearly 2,500 games a year in a variety of sports.

- The relocated Longfellow House reopened as an information and interpretive center for the park system and the Grand Rounds National Scenic Byway.

One of the most important developments at the park board during Merrill Anderson's tenure as superintendent was the acquisition, at her suggestion, of the new headquarters for the park board along the river, which was renovated and opened in 2003.

In 2003, the park board also completed a swap of land with the Metropolitan Airports Commission. The park board traded eight acres of the land it owned at the airport for ownership of twelve acres and a long term lease for another twenty eight acres

Mary Merrill Anderson became the first female and first African American park superintendent in 1999. The first African American elected to the park board was Rochelle Berry Graves in 1994. The first African American to serve on the park board, however, was Richard Hall in 1968. He was appointed by Mayor Arthur Naftalin to fill the ex-officio seat designated for the mayor at that time. Hall lost his bid for an at-large seat on the board in 1969. In 1973 he was appointed as a park board representative to the Hennepin County Reserve Park District board. The second African American elected as a park commissioner was Ed Solomon, who had been appointed to fill a vacant seat in 1996 before running for the office the following year. Merrill Anderson added to her list of pioneering achievements in 2005 when she became the first former park superintendent elected to the park board.

of land, partially wetland, northwest of the intersection of Highway 62 and Cedar Avenue. In 2004 that park was named Edward Solomon Park in honor of the president of the board in 2001–02, who was also a volunteer coach for many years at McRae Park.

Efforts to solidify park board funding also reached a critical point at the turn of the millennium. The park board and city reached agreement on a "service redesign" that had been discussed for some time. The agreement shifted some maintenance responsibilities between the city and the park board. In essence the city took responsibility for maintaining everything "black," meaning roads, and the park board assumed responsibility for "green," or trees and lawns, reducing duplication of services and resulting in savings to both city government and the park board. The agreement also codified relationships between city and park police.

The park board also reached a new capital funding agreement with the city. The park board had approved a referendum asking for an increase in property taxes for parks, but the measure was vetoed by Mayor Sharon Sayles-Belton. Instead of a referendum, Sayles-Belton negotiated an increase in capital funding from the city for the park board.

The capital funding agreement didn't last long. In 2003, a new mayor and city council rescinded the agreement and returned park board funding to previous levels. Not only did the city cut park funding, but it submitted a bill to the park board for $800,000 as a surcharge for administrative services from the city. The funding dispute with the city council and mayor was exacerbated when the state cut funding to local governments. It was a double whammy—and both remain subjects of political debate.

The other major development in recreation facilities in the early 2000s relied on funding once again from a nonprofit foundation. In 2003 the former Rosacker Pool in Northeast Park was extensively upgraded and converted into a water park and renamed Jim Lupient Water Park. The renovation and an endowment for teaching kids to swim were provided by a gift from the Jim Lupient Foundation.

On the environmental front, in cooperation with the Minnehaha Creek Watershed District the park board completed restoration of wetlands at Lake Calhoun in 2000 and broke ground for a new wetlands project at Lake Nokomis. In 2001, the park board also began a new program to map all park vegetation with a Geographic Information System.

> The park board devoted park land to an entirely new use in 2000 when the first dog parks were opened at Franklin Terrace (Riverside Park) and Lake of the Isles. Three more dog parks, officially called "Off-leash Recreation Areas," have been added at Minnehaha Park, Columbia Park and Loring Park.

The park board developed two water parks, one at North Commons *(shown here)* and the Jim Lupient Water Park at Northeast Park. The former Rosacker Pool at Northeast Park was renovated and renamed Jim Lupient Water Park in 2003 following a gift from the Jim Lupient Foundation for renovation and programming at the pool. (Peter Schmidt, Minneapolis Park and Recreation Board)

A collaboration between the recreation division and the environmental operations division in 1999 resulted in a popular program of environmental education. The "neighborhood naturalist" program is designed to help city children appreciate the nature that surrounds them, not only in parks, but in their own yards and neighborhoods. More than forty recreation centers participate in the program, which in 2007 included activities and presentations on nature art, insect invasions and a program entitled "skull, bones and scat" that studied the animals of the city.

Support for the development of bicycle trails, mostly in old railroad track beds, also continued in the early 2000s. The pioneering collaboration on the Cedar Lake Trail was closely followed by the development of the Kenilworth Trail in 1998. Additional trails developed since include the Fort Snelling Trail (2002), the Forty-ninth Avenue North Corridor (2003), the Luce Line Trail (2005), and the Fridley Water Trail and Loring Bikeway Trail (2006).

In the recreation sports programs, changes followed societal trends. Youth sports participation increased significantly—nearly 50 percent—from the mid-1990s. Following an initiative begun in the early 1990s to get more girls involved in playground sports programs, girls participation in youth sports increased sharply. Adult participation in organized sports, however, saw a trend in the opposite direction. From more than 830 adult softball teams registered in men's, women's and co-rec play in 1996, the number dropped to 600 by 2001, a decline of nearly 30 percent.

The participation of adults in nearly all organized sports declined sharply, with the exception of soccer, which saw renewed participation, in part due to the popularity of the game among new immigrants from Africa and Latin America, the fastest-growing segment of the city's population. An adult soccer league began play in 2003, eighty years after Theodore Wirth had noted declining interest in the sport.

After nearly five years on the job, Merrill Anderson announced her intention to retire at the end of 2003. Once again, the park board initiated a national search for a replacement and once again had a difficult time choosing a candidate. Unlike earlier efforts to hire a new superintendent, however, partisan politics were no longer an issue. No Republican-endorsed candidate for park commissioner had won election since the early 1990s, reflecting the trend across the city to elect only candidates endorsed by some combination of labor, the DFL and the Green

In 2003, the park police took on a new role by providing sixteen school liaison officers. The officers are assigned to schools during the school year and work in neighborhood parks in the summer. While the park police have not played a central role in this book, that is a tribute to their success—and the unique structure of a dedicated park police force. Public safety has rarely been an issue throughout the history of Minneapolis parks. Parks in the city, over the decades, have been perceived as safe places. Of course there have been exceptions, which the park police have addressed, such as an increased presence in Peavey Park to curtail drug dealing. Parks comprise 16 percent of the city's area but account for only 2.5 percent of the city's reported crime. One of the strongest supporters of a dedicated park police force is a man who has experience in the matter, Walt Dziedzic, a park commissioner as of this writing, who was a career Minneapolis police officer and served on the city council for twenty years before he was elected to the park board. "Our parks are safe because we can put our own officers in them," he said. "The two things we can never do away with are an independent park board and an independent park police force." Combining the park police with the city police force has often been mentioned as a way for the park board to cut costs, but park leaders since the 1880s have argued that park police play a unique role in park safety that would be lost if policing parks were a part of regular police responsibilities. A dedicated park police force helps to ensure that park security issues have the highest priority.

Party. As had happened in 1980 when David Fisher was hired, some leading candidates withdrew from the process, apparently uneasy with working for an elected park board that could be contentious.

With the withdrawal of candidates and Merrill Anderson's last day of work looming, park commissioners considered for the job a man already well known to park professionals in Minnesota, Jon Gurban. Gurban was executive director of the Minnesota Recreation and Park Association, a statewide association for enhancing parks and developing park professionals, which had been renting the former superintendent's house at Lyndale Farmstead for offices since Fisher had moved out of the house in 1997.

Without Gurban applying for the job, or becoming part of the formal selection process, he was hired as interim superintendent for one year. Gurban was, like Merrill Anderson, a Minneapolis native. He had grown up near Lake Harriet and attended Southwest High School. Gurban was the first Minneapolis native hired as superintendent who had not spent his entire career within the Minneapolis park system. He had worked in the park systems of Vancouver, British Columbia, Apple Valley, Minnesota, and Estes Park, Colorado, before returning home to work for the MRPA.

The process of Gurban's hiring angered some critics of the park board, and, in retrospect, commissioners who supported hiring him conceded that a more formal process of appointing him as interim superintendent might have avoided controversy. The interim tag was removed from Gurban's title in 2004, and his contract has since been extended into 2010.

Merrill Anderson was not the only employee of the park board to retire in 2003. Forty park employees accepted early retirement that year as the board attempted to cut costs. Many of the positions were not filled.

In the four years since Gurban stepped into the job, the board's emphasis has not diverged significantly. The most important addition to park board inventory was an indoor ice arena in 2005. The Edi-

Jon Gurban, superintendent of parks since 2004, was the captain of the 1967 Southwest High School basketball team. Pictured with Gurban is coach Walt Williams. (Jon Gurban)

son Ice Arena on Central Avenue Northeast, which had been built with privately raised funds to support hockey in northeast Minneapolis, was purchased by the park board for about a third of its original cost and was renamed Northeast Ice Arena.

The board's most recent initiative to redevelop recreation space was at The Parade, which, as always, generated some neighborhood opposition. Artificial turf was installed on one of the fields to make it a more valuable multiuse space and reduce maintenance costs. One of the long-running challenges of the park board has been to maintain the quality of

> The many efforts to expand recreation programming beyond sports included Art in the Parks. The cooperative program with the Minneapolis Institute of Arts, which began in 1993, was expanded to forty-seven parks in 2001 to introduce children to art and artists. In the same year, computer labs were installed at five recreation centers.

> The rounds of golf played at park board courses declined through the 1990s and into the 2000s. From a peak in the late 1980s of more than 300,000 rounds, before the Fort Snelling course was added, the number had dropped to 240,000 in 2006. Even at that, however, fees from golf generated more than one million dollars in net income for the park system. Park courses began an outreach and teaching effort in 2001 to appeal to more prospective golfers. Encouraged by a turnout of more than 2,200 kids for a 1999 appearance by Tiger Woods at Hiawatha Golf Course sponsored by the Fairway Foundation and Minnesota Minority Junior Golf Foundation, the park board inaugurated a First Tee program for children in 2001.

multiuse fields. From the original designs of many playgrounds by Theodore Wirth, nearly all were intended for use as skating rinks and ball fields—not a combination that makes for easy maintenance. With the increasing popularity of soccer, which punishes grass, especially in wet fall conditions, park playing fields are often in poor condition. The creation of dedicated high-quality grass fields at the Neiman complex relieved some of the pressure but didn't resolve the issue for most neighborhood parks. That fact that many of those fields were originally constructed on filled lowlands—the least desirable, therefore the cheapest land to acquire for parks—doesn't make maintenance easier. (Neighborhood skating rinks have dropped from a high of near eighty in the 1960s to thirty in 2007, but the process of flooding playing fields for rinks still makes it hard to maintain grass on many park fields.) Artificial turf playing fields in some locations may provide a compromise solution at selected fields.

The demand for playing fields in neighborhoods has also changed. "It used to be that the board allocated money for ten baseball fields, then decided where to put them," said Gurban. "Now some neighborhoods don't want a baseball field, they want a soccer field or more gardens instead. Each neighborhood has different needs." The same is true with tennis courts; some neighborhoods want their tennis courts improved, others want them removed.

Partly due to the increasing divergence of park needs across the city, Gurban implemented a reorganization of park staff in 2005 that placed park management closer to the neighborhoods. The park system was divided into three management districts that have considerable autonomy across park functions. Instead of the old "silo" system of managing parks through recreation, forestry, maintenance, planning and other functions, which were controlled centrally over the years, each district was given resources to manage all those functions on a district basis.

The park board's efforts to meet diverging and emerging needs was demonstrated by the facilities provided for "new" sports.

- Skate parks. In 2004, skate parks were opened at Armatage, Creekview and Elliot parks. There are now skate facilities with rails and ramps in six parks.

- Off-road bicycling. In 2004, the park board also introduced pilot off-road cycling trails in Wirth Park, and the following year designated nearly four and one-half miles of trail for the purpose.

- Lacrosse and cricket. The park board also saw an increasing interest in lacrosse and cricket, the latter interest spurred by immigrants from India, Pakistan and the Caribbean.

- Snowboarding. Improvements at the Wirth Park winter recreation area provide a better experience for a greater variety of snow sports.

In a changing city with more poor and more rich, more young and more old, and more immigrants from both the suburbs and other countries, the challenges of meeting neighborhood needs have changed, and the challenges of meeting citywide needs have become more complex. Not every neighborhood wants or needs everything, and the park board can't afford to provide everything to every neighborhood. Michael Schmidt, general manager of park operations in 2007, summarized those challenges when he said, "We have the money to do anything, but not the money to do everything. The time when softball, tennis and ice-skating were enough for each neighborhood are gone. Everyone in the city defines parks as something different."

In the late 1990s, even before Fisher retired, the park board began to consider a new survey of the park system to establish priorities for the future, something along the lines of the Weir or Brightbill studies, the latter of which took place in 1965. In the 1999 annual report board president Bob Fine urged the creation of a new "vision of the future" and Merrill Anderson reported that the board's work plan for the coming year included development of a comprehensive park and recreation master plan with "citizen involvement." Following steps to develop internal resources for the review process and the hiring of a consultant to advise the board during Merrill Anderson's tenure, the park board launched a comprehensive review of the park system under the direction of Jon Gurban in 2005.

The striking difference with earlier survey efforts was the degree of "citizen involvement," which clearly reflected the historical trend of increasing public participation in the design and operation of park facilities. Instead of asking outside experts to review the park system and make recommendations, the park board went directly to the citizens of Minneapolis for input.

Following the course recommended by Charles Loring to George Brackett in 1883 at the time they were campaigning for votes to approve the Park Act, the creation of a new comprehensive plan avoided "exciting localities." It did not address the specifics of park locations or improvements, which Weir and Brightbill had done, but focused instead on the qualities people wanted in their park system. The only exception was an explicit recognition of the need to provide more park amenities in the north and northeast neighborhoods.

The comprehensive plan was approved by the board in October 2007, following extensive public input from questionnaires mailed to more than 170,000 Minneapolis households, focus groups, phone surveys and public input sessions at many park locations.

While the board now focuses on implementation steps, the plan established "vision themes" that distilled nearly 150 years of thinking and debate over parks in the city. The plan addressed:

- Land and resource stewardship to preserve, protect and develop natural assets, as well as "sustainable" management practices.

> Following the trend in the private sector to outsource services and reduce fixed costs, the park board leased space at the Lake Calhoun refectory for the Tin Fish restaurant to provide food service in 2003. That was followed by a similar arrangement at the Minnehaha Park refectory for Sea Salt restaurant in 2005. The board also granted bike- and boat-rental concessions at Minnehaha Park, Lake Calhoun and Lake Nokomis. The debate over whether the park board should grant concessions on park property had its roots in 1887, when the board first considered the question of boat rentals at Lake Harriet. Theodore Wirth, who opposed granting concessions, and Jon Gurban, who favors them one hundred years later, used almost identical words to explain their positions: We want to create the best experience possible for people visiting our parks. To Wirth, that meant controlling every aspect of service in parks; to Gurban, that means assigning the provision of those services to people with experience and expertise. It is the history of Minneapolis parks in a nutshell: same goal, different times, different strategies.

Youth sports remain a popular program for thousands of children at city parks. (Minneapolis Park and Recreation Board)

- Recreation opportunities to inspire personal growth and health, as well as a sense of community.
- An equitable distribution of park and recreation resources throughout the city that could be supported economically, now and in the future.
- Parks that shape city character and meet diverse community needs, while providing safe places to play, celebrate, contemplate and recreate.

"Create a sense of place and a sense of belonging."

JON GURBAN

The park board and city residents who participated in the comprehensive plan process had learned well the lessons of Minneapolis park history—and reaffirmed the wisdom of those who, with such great foresight, had created the park system and managed its evolution. Nearly 125 years earlier the first park board committed itself to preserving land for the edification of all, had spread the first four parks around the city, and had adopted as its motto: Health and Beauty. Park founders, as park advocates of today, saw the value of parks to all residents of the city individually and collectively. And always the focus on the future.

What is remarkable today about Minneapolis parks is that the motivation and the structure of the first park board continue to provide a clear direction. The motivation was to acquire land and preserve it for future use. In land ownership there is permanence. "We are still rooted in the land," said Al Wittman, "The pioneers set the pattern: get the land, adapt as you go on."

But the structure of the first park board provided another advantage that is still enjoyed today: responsiveness. A park board elected directly by the people has had to adapt to public perception and demand on only one important issue: parks and how they are used. And that's the key to the success of a park system that remains at the core of city life. The ownership of land—and the remarkable bodies of water within it—and an independent elected body devoted solely to its acquisition, maintenance and use elevated parks to a place of prominence in Minneapolis life that is matched in few other places. Those core facts of the city's history have led to myriad places within the city with which people for decades have established a personal connection every bit as vivid as Charles Loring's connection to a stretch of creek that to him was a "New England picture in a prairie frame."

When Gurban presented his 2008 work plan to the park board on September 27, 2007, he concluded with two goals born of the work of nearly 150 years of park planning. Ultimately, he said, the goal of Minneapolis parks was to create "a sense of place and a sense of belonging." Those were fitting—and consistent—goals for the parks that have largely come to define the city and millions of people who have lived in it since parks were created.

But perhaps Gurban left out something in that succinct summary. Earlier in 2007, the park board and Xcel Energy had opened the newest park in the city, Water Power Park. In the new park, still owned by Xcel, but operated by the park board, one can walk to the edge of St. Anthony Falls. It is a falls that has been used, abused and modified by man. Yet the power of the falling water, however altered over a concrete apron from its original form, has the capacity still to inspire a sense of wonder.

The immutable torrent so close at hand is a reminder that the creation of parks and the definition of their use is not done. It inspires the hope that this newest park will one day be expanded into a larger Hennepin Island Park, that the city will continue to improve on its magnificent system of parks and give a gift to the future that has been given to it by the past.

Along with that hope comes a profound admiration for those who once saw the possibility of parks and pursued those visions. Charles Loring, William Folwell and Horace Cleveland. Theodore Wirth, Eloise Butler, Clifford Booth and Alice Dietz. Maude Armatage and Francis Gross. And a litany of latter-day heroes.

Those and many others have changed the landscape of Minneapolis, and no doubt our children will continue its transformation to meet their needs. Guided by a nobler spirit and an appreciative eye, they will learn and relearn the need to preserve, protect and promote what is best in our world—and what is best in us.

Park Commissioners and Superintendents 1883–2008

Elected and Appointed Commissioners

Adin C. Austin, March 1883–April 1886

Daniel Bassett, March 1883–January 1889

George A. Brackett, March 1883–April 1887

Samuel Chute, March 1883–April 1885 (R)

Judson N. Cross, March 1883–April 1884

William W. Eastman, March 1883–April 1884

Andrew C. Haugan, March 1883–October 1883 (R),
　　January 1889–January 1895

Charles M. Loring, March 1883–January 1891,
　　January 1893–January 1894 (R),
　　January 1904– January 1907

Dorilus Morrison, March 1883–April 1887

Benjamin F. Nelson, October 1883–April 1884

John C. Oswald, March 1883–September 1889 (R)

John S. Pillsbury, March 1883–April 1886

Eugene M. Wilson, March 1883–January 1889,
　　August 1889–April 1890 (D)

Matthew Bredemus, April 1884–April 1885

John R. Everhard, April 1884–April 19, l884 (R)

Charles A. Nimocks, April 1884–May 1886 (R),
　　January 1907–January 1913

Byron Sutherland, April 1884–January 1889

Charles Johnson, April l885–January 1889

William S. King, April 1885–April 1887

Andrew J. Boardman, April 1886–January 1893

Baldwin Brown, April 1886–January 1889,
　　January 1891–August 1895 (D)

P. J. E. Clementson, April 1887–January 1889

Joseph Ingenhutt, April 1887–January 1891

Samuel A. March, April 1887–January 1891

A. H. Mitchell, April 1887–January 1891

A. E. Allen, January 1889–January 1893

Z. Demules, January 1889–January 1893

William W. Folwell, January 1889–January 1907

Jesse E. Northrup, January 1889–January 1895,
　　April 1900–January 1901,
　　January 1903–April 1913 (R)

J. Arthur Ridgway, January 1889–January 1895,
　　February 1895–January 1897 (R)

Herman J. Dahn, January 1891–January 1897

(A) = Appointed　　(D) = Died　　(R) = Resigned

231

Commissioners

James W. Lawrence, April 1891–January 1893

Patrick Ryan, January 1891–January 1897

Jacob Stoft, January 1891–January 1899,
  April 29, 1922–October 10, 1925(D)

Abraham S. Adams, January 1893–January 1905

Harry W. Jones, January 1893–January 1905

Wallace G. Nye, January 1893–January 1899

Chelsea J. Rockwood, January 1893–January 1895 (R)

Portius C. Deming, January 1895–January 1899 (R),
  November 1909–January 1919

Samuel Hunter, January 1895–January 1901

Frank G. McMillan, December 1895–January 1897

Charles H. Woods, January 1895–April 1899 (D)

Geo. T. D. Baxter, January 1897–January 1903

Chas J. Johnson, May 1897–January 1903

N. P. Peterson, January 1897–March 1897 (D)

Fred L. Smith, January 1897–January 1909

Joseph C. Young, January 1897–January 1903

Edward M. Bartlett, January 1899–February 1899 (D)

Howard M. DeLaittre, March 1899–January 1905

John S. Dodge, January 1899–January 1905

Wyman Elliot, January 1899–January 1901

John S. Bradstreet, January 1901–January 1907

Eder H. Moulton, January 1901–January 1907

James W. Raymond, January 1901–July 1903 (R)

Paul D. Boutell, January 1903–May 26, 1914 (D)

Daniel W. Jones, January 1903–January 1909

John W. Allan, January 1905–January 1917

Wilbur F. Decker, January 1905–January 1917

Chas. O. Johnson, January 1905–May 27, 1910 (R)

Edmund J. Phelps, January 1905–October 12, 1923 (D)

William McMillan, January 1907–January 1913

Milton O. Nelson, January 1907–October 4, 1909 (R)

Carl F. E. Peterson, January 1907–January 1913

Fred W. Nye, January 1909–December 2, 1912 (R)

Thomas Voegeli, January 1909–January 1915

Francis A. Gross, May 27, 1910–January 1911,
  December 2, 1912–July 1921,
  March 17, 1926–July 1, 1933,
  July 5, 1933–July 1949

Harry B. Cramer, January 1911–January 1917,
  June 19, 1918–March 4, 1926 (D)

Joseph Allen, January 1913–January 1919

William H. Bovey, January 1913–January 1919,
  December 1919–July 1933

David P. Jones, January 1913–January 1919

Alexander A. McRae, April 1, 1913–July 1921,
  September 14, 1934–May 2, 1944 (D)

Robert E. Fisher, January 1915–August 1919

Leo B. Harris, January 1915–June 19, 1918 (R)

William A. Anderson, January 1917–December 1919 (R)

Burton L. Kingsley, January 1917–January 21, 1931(R)

Phelps Wyman, January 1917–September 17, 1924 (R)

Arthur C. Andrews, January 1919–July 5, 1933 (R)

Robert R. Bertch, January 1919–July 1925

James R. Hartzell, January 1919–July 1925

William Lohff, December 1919–July 1923,
  September 30, 1925–July 1927

Washington Yale, January 1919–August 28, 1944 (D)

Maude D. Armatage, July 1921–June 1951

Thomas G. Winter, July 1921–September 16, 1925 (R)

Emil S. Youngdahl, July 1923–April 6, 1927 (R)

Horace A. Gray, November 28, 1924–November 5, 1930 (D)

(A) = Appointed   (D) = Died   (R) = Resigned

Commissioners

Thomas Beauchaine, July 1925–July 1931

Alfred T. Oberg, July 1925–January 11, 1926 (D)

Alfred F. Pillsbury, October 1925–July 1935,
 July 7, 1937–August 21, 1946 (R)

Lucian C. Miller, January 20, 1926–July 26, 1941 (D)

Goodman B. Sigurdson, June 15, 1927–July 1929

John H. Jepson, July 1927–August 25, 1935 (D)

Joseph J. Oys, July 1929–March 18, 1935 (R)

Joseph A. Wojciak, July 1931–July 1949

Clinton L. Stacy, December 2, 1931–July 1947

Anthony W. Ingenhutt, January 20, 1932–July 1935

B. B. Sheffield, July 1933–September 8, 1934 (D)

Harold R. Ward, July 1933–June 21, 1939

Walter P. Quist, March 8, 1935–July 1959

Edward A. Chalgren, July 1935–December 19, 1954 (D)

Edwin A. Hendricks, July 1935–July 7, 1937 (R)

Paul C. Johnson, July 1937–July 1957

Henry G. Knight, July 1939–July 1945,
 July 1949–November 1952 (D)

Thos. F. McCarthy, August 20, 1941–July 1949,
 January 4, 1950–February 1953 (R)

Harold H. Tearse, June 7, 1944–June 1951

Paul C. LaBlant, November 1944–February 29, 1948 (D)

Clifford C. Peterson, July 1945–December 1950 (R)

Edwin F. Kelley, August 21, 1946–July 7, 1947,
 January 1, 1949–March 24, 1957 (D)

Leonard A. Johnson, July 21, 1947–December 31, 1948 (R)

Dr. Roy E. Peterson, July 21, 1947–July 7, l965

Claude E. Petersen, December 2, 1948–February 16, 1955 (R),
 March 2, 1955–January 8, l958 (R)

Daniel B. Paulsen, July 1949–December 21, 1949 (R),
 July 1955–July 1961

Theo. A. Tomaszewski, July 1949–July 1955

Edward J. Grimes, July 1951–September 1952 (D)

Edwin L. Haislet, July 1951–July 1957

Harry C. Rosacker, July 1951–July 1973 (D)

Viggo Rasmussen, January 1953–July 1955

Peter Skurdalsvold, February 1953–July 1955

Clifford C. Sommer, January 1953–December 31, 1954 (R)

W. James Johnston, Jr., January 1955–July 1955

J. Richard Johansen, February 1955–April 1959 (R)

Richard Kantorowicz, July 1955–July 1961

Glen K. Morrill, Jr., July 1955–July 1967

P. Kenneth Peterson, July 1955–July 1957 (R)

Earl A. Arneson, July 1957–November 1961 (R)

George Todd, July 1957–July 1963

Arnold E. Hagland, December 1957–July 1967

Lorna L. Phillips, December 1957–July 1967

Inez Crimmins, April 1958–July 1, 1963

Alexander Gallus, July 1959–July 1973

Edward J. Gearty, July 1959–July 1963

Earl J. McGovern, July 1961–August 1962 (D)

Stephan Romanowski, July 1961–July 1969

Arthur B. Johnson, June 19, 1963–February 16, 1965 (D)

Edwin Rapacz, June 19, 1963–July 1969

Benjamin Berger, July 1963–January 2, 1976

Richard Erdall, July 1963–January 18, 1967

Robert G. Malmquist, July 1963–July 1967

Beverly Smerling, July 1963–July 1969

Walter S. Carpenter, July 1965–July 1971

Warren A. Finberg, July 1965–July 1969

George Bauman, July 1967–July 1969

(A) = Appointed   (D) = Died   (R) = Resigned

Commissioners and Superintendents

John Bergford, Jr., July 1967–July 1969

William I. Holbrook, July 1967–December 1989

David N. Kienitz, July 1967–July 1969

Leonard Neiman, July 1967–January 3, 1978

Louis G. DeMars, July 1969–July 1971

Dale W. Gilbert, July 1969–August 2, 1996 (D)

James Nelson, July 1969–July 1973

W. W. Bednarczyk, July 1971–January 2, 1974 (R)

Alden C. Smith, July 1971–December 31, 1981

Daniel K. Peterson, November 21, 1973–January 2, 1976

Patricia Hillmeyer, January 2, 1974–January 1, 1998

Jeffrey R. Spartz, January 2, 1974–January 3, 1977

Orvin L. Olson, January 16, 1974–January 4, l978

Nancy Anderson, January 2, 1976–December 1989

G. Rolf Svendsen, January 2, 1976–January 3, 1978

Walter Bratt, July 6, 1977–January 3, 1994 (A)

Thomas Baker, January 3, 1978–January 1, 1998,
June 20, 2001–January 1, 2002 (A)

Naomi Loper, January 3, 1978–January 3, 1994

Sherman Malkerson, January 3, 1978–December 31, 1981

Patricia D. Baker, January 1, 1982–January 1, 1997 (D)

Scott Neiman, January 1, 1982–January 1, 2002

Kathryn Thurber, January 2, 1990–January 3, 1994 (R)

Annie Young, January 2, 1990–Present

Rochelle Berry Graves, January 3, 1994–January 1, 2006

George Puzak, January 3, 1994–January 2, 1998

Dean Zimmermann, January 3, 1994–January 1, 2002

Edward C. Solomon,
November 6, 1996 (A)–December 12, 2002 (D)

Vivian Mason, March 5, 1997 (A)–January 1, 2006

Ernie Belton, January 2, 1998–June 13, 2001 (R)

Walt Dziedzic, January 2, 1998 to Present

Bob Fine, January 2, 1998 to Present

John Erwin, January 2, 2002–January 1, 2006

Marie Hauser, January 2, 2002–January 1, 2006

Jon C. Olson, January 2, 2002–Present

Carol Kummer, March 5, 2003 (A)–Present

Mary Merrill Anderson, January 3, 2006–Present

Tracy Nordstrom, January 3, 2006–Present

Tom Nordyke, January 3, 2006–Present

Scott Vreeland, January 3, 2006–Present

Superintendents of Parks And Recreation

William M. Berry, April 1884–December 4, 1905 (R)

Theodore Wirth, January 1, 1906–November 30, 1935

C. A. Bossen, November 30, 1935–August 28, 1945

Chas. E. Doell, August 28, 1945–May 8, 1959

Howard I. Moore, May 28, 1959–January 1, 1966 (R)

Robert Ruhe, January 3, 1966–July 15, 1978 (R)

Del Green (acting superintendent),
July 15, 1978–October 2, 1978

Charles R. Spears, October 2, 1978–August 15, 1980 (R)

Del Green (acting superintendent)
August 15, 1980–April 1, 1981

David L. Fisher, April 1, 1981–January 5, 1999

Mary Merrill Anderson, March 1, 1999–December 31, 2003

Jon Gurban,
Interim Supt. January 1, 2004–December 31, 2004,
Superintendent January 1, 2005–Present

(A) = Appointed   (D) = Died   (R) = Resigned

Selected Sources

Anfinson, John. *River of History: A Historic Resources Study of the Mississippi National River and Recreation Area.* National Park Service and U.S. Army Corps of Engineers, 2003.

Atwater, Isaac. *History of the City of Minneapolis.* New York: Munsell and Company, 1893.

Balcom, Tom. "4600 Fremont: A House History." Unpublished, 1985.

Benidt, Bruce Weir. *The Library Book: Centennial History of the Minneapolis Public Library.* Minneapolis: Minneapolis Public Library and Information Center, 1984.

Brackett, George A. Papers (correspondence and legal documents). Minnesota Historical Society, St. Paul.

Brightbill, Charles, and Associates. *Parks and Recreation in Minneapolis.* Chicago: University of Illinois, 1965.

———. *Record of Achievement: 1965 Park Study.* Minneapolis Park and Recreation Board, 1969.

Bromley, Edward. *Minneapolis, Portrait of the Past.* Minneapolis: Voyageur Press, 1890.

Cleveland, Horace. *Landscape Architecture, As Applied to the Wants of the West.* Introduction by Daniel J. Nadenicek and Lance M. Neckar. Boston: University of Massachusetts Press, 2002.

———. *Suggestions for a System of Parks and Parkways for the City of Minneapolis.* First Annual Report of the Minneapolis Board of Park Commissioners, 1884.

———. *Outline Plan of a Park System for the City of St. Paul.* St. Paul: 1885.

———. *Park Systems of St. Paul and Minneapolis.* An address delivered May 10, 1887, St. Paul.

———. *The Aesthetic Development of the United Cities of St. Paul and Minneapolis.* Minneapolis: A. C. Bausman, 1888.

———. Letters, N 197. Northwest Architectural Archives, University of Minnesota Libraries.

Doell, Charles, and Gerald Fitzgerald. *A Brief History of Parks and Recreation in the United States.* Chicago: The Athletic Institute, 1954.

Doell, Charles, and Felix K. Dhainin. "A System of Parks for Hennepin County," Hennepin County Park Reserve District, 1958.

Folwell, William Watts. *A History of Minnesota.* 4 vols. St. Paul: Minnesota Historical Society, 1921–30.

———. *William Watts Folwell: The Autobiography and Letters of a Pioneer of Culture.* Ed. Solomon J. Buck. Minneapolis: University of Minnesota Press, 1933.

———, and Family. Papers (letters, especially from William M. R. French, Horace W. S. Cleveland, and Charles M. Loring, and on park matters; also notes for *A History of Minnesota*). Minnesota Historical Society, St. Paul.

———. Papers (correspondence). University of Minnesota Archives.

Greben, Seymour. *The Role of the Recreation Division in the Minneapolis Recreation Delivery System.* Minneapolis Park and Recreation Board, 1977.

Haglund, Karl. "Rural Tastes, Rectangular Ideas, and the Skirmishes of H. W. S. Cleveland." *Landscape Architecture,* January 1976.

Hickok, Eugene A., and Associates. *Water Quality and*

Biological Investigation of the City of Minneapolis Lakes. Minneapolis: Minneapolis Park and Recreation Board, 1969–70.

Hilmer, Paul. *Breaking New Ground, Building Strong Lives: 140 Years of Youth Work with the Minneapolis YMCA, 1866–2006.* Minneapolis: YMCA of Metropolitan Minneapolis, 2006.

Hudson, Horace, ed. *A Half Century of Minneapolis.* Minneapolis: Hudson Publishing Company, 1908.

Lanegran, David, and Ernest Sandeen. *The Lake District of Minneapolis.* Minneapolis: University of Minnesota Press, 1979.

Linden Hills History Study Group. *Down at the Lake.* Minneapolis, 2001.

Loring, Charles. "History of the Parks and Public Grounds of Minneapolis," *Collections of the Minnesota Historical Society.* Vol. 15. Minnesota Historical Society, 1912.

———. "Vistas of Fifty Years," *Compendium of History and Biography of Minnesota and Hennepin County,* 1914.

———. Report of the Commissioners for the State Park of Minnehaha, 1888.

———. Scrapbooks (mostly undated newspaper clips and excerpts of handwritten journal entries). Minnesota Historical Society, St. Paul.

Marcley, Jessie. *The Minneapolis City Charter 1856–1925.* Bureau for Research in Government. Minneapolis: University of Minnesota, 1925.

Minneapolis, Department of Planning and Development. *Mississippi/Minneapolis,* 1972.

Minneapolis Park and Recreation Board. Annual Reports, 1883–2006.

———. Proceedings, 1883–1980.

———. "Possible Areas of Encroachment on the Minneapolis Park System," 1960.

———. "Operation 'Century of Parks' 1883–1983," 1960.

———. "Disposal and Replacement of Park Lands," 1963.

———. "Challenge for Leadership," Legislative Program 1969–1979, 1971 Supplement, 1971.

———. "Central Riverfront Open Space Master Plan," 1978.

———. "West River Parkway, Final Environmental Impact Statement," 1983.

———. "Citizens Advisory Committee on Regional Parks," 1983.

———. *Minneapolis Lakes and Parks: Proceedings of a Special Session.* North American Lakes Management Society International Symposium on Lake, Reservoir and Watershed Management, 1997.

———. "Above the Falls Master Plan," 1999.

———. "Comprehensive Plan," 2007.

Nadenicek, Daniel Joseph. "Emerson's Aesthetic and Natural Design: A Theoretical Foundation for the Work of Horace William Shaler Cleveland." In *Nature and Ideology, Natural Garden Design in the Twentieth Century,* ed. Joachim Wolschkee-Bulmahn. Washington, D.C.: Dumbarton Oaks, 1997.

Neckar, Lance M. "Fast-tracking Culture and Landscape: Horace William Shaler Cleveland and the Garden in the Midwest." In *Regional Garden Design in the United States,* ed. Therese O'Malley and Marc Treib. Washington, D.C.: Dumbarton Oaks, 1995.

Nimocks, Charles. *An Early History of the Minneapolis Parks from 1857 to 1883.* Minneapolis: Minneapolis Board of Park Commissioners, 1910.

Olmsted and Associates. Papers. Library of Congress.

Olmsted, Frederick Law. Papers. Library of Congress.

Riess, Steven. *City Games: The Evolution of American Urban Society and the Rise of Sports.* Chicago: University of Illinois Press, 1989.

Shapiro, Joseph. *Water Quality in Minneapolis Lakes.* Minneapolis: Minneapolis Park and Recreation Board, 1973.

Shutter, Marion Daniel. *Gateway to the Northwest, History of Minneapolis.* Chicago: Clarke Publishing Company, 1923.

———. *In Memoriam: Hon. Charles Loring, Father of the Minneapolis Park System.* Memorial address delivered March 21, 1922, and Report by the Board of Park Commissioners. Minneapolis: Syndicate Printing Company, 1922.

Shutter, Marion Daniel, and John S. McLain, ed. *Progressive Men of Minnesota: Biographical Sketches and Portraits of the Leaders in Business, Politics.* Minneapolis: Minneapolis Journal, 1897.

Thornley, Stewart. *Baseball in Minnesota: The Definitive History.* St, Paul: Minnesota Historical Society Press, 2006.

Tishler, William H., ed., *Midwestern Landscape Architecture.* Chicago: University of Illinois Press, 2000.

Tishler, William H., and Virginia S. Luckhardt. "H. W. S.

Cleveland, Pioneer Landscape Architect to the Upper Midwest," *Minnesota History* 49, 7, Minnesota Historical Society, 1985.

Weir, Liebert H. *Recreation Survey: Minneapolis, Minnesota*. Minneapolis Park and Recreation Board, 1944.

Windom, William, and Family Papers (correspondence with Charles Loring). Minnesota Historical Society, St. Paul.

Wirth, Theodore. *Minneapolis Park System 1883–1944: Retrospective Glimpses into the History of the Board of Park Commissioners of Minneapolis, Minnesota and the City's Park, Parkway and Playground System.* Minneapolis, 1945.

———. Letters, unpublished. Minneapolis Parks Legacy Society and Minneapolis Park and Recreation Board archives.

Wittman, Albert. *Writing in Progress: The Minneapolis Park and Recreation System 1945–2000.* Unpublished, 2000.

Wright, C. Ben. *Minneapolis Parks and Recreation: A History of the Park and Recreation Board, 1944–1978.* Unpublished, 1980.

Interviews (2007)

Sara Aplikowski, Catherine Beck, Peter Beck, Joan Berthiaume, Walter Dziedzic, Harvey Feldman, Bob Fine, David Fisher, Jon Gurban, Marc Holtey, Carol Kummer, Mary Maguire Lerman, Dick Mammen, Mary Merrill Anderson, Tom Nordyke, Jon Olson, MaryLynn Pulscher, Brian Rice, Judd Rietkerk, Jennifer Ringold, Michael Schmidt, David Sellergren, Don Siggelkow, Liz Van Zomeren, Scott Vreeland, Don Willeke, Ted Wirth, Albert Wittman, Dick Yates, Annie Young.

Index

*page numbers in italic refer to illustrations

Addison, Betty Ann, 212
American Institute of Park Executives, 163, 174
American Legion, 116, 144
American Park and Outdoor Art Association (APOAA), 67–68, 71, 76
Ames, Alfred, 18, 23
Anderson, Mary Merrill, 215, 221–22, *222*, 224–25
Anderson, Nancy, 102
Armajani, Siah, 213
Armatage, Maude, x, *100, 101,* 100–2, 155–56, 228
Armatage Park, 101, 156, 179–80, 226
Armour & Company, 117
Armour Golf Course. *See* Francis Gross Golf Course
Army Corps of Engineers, 199, 205
Arneson, Earl, 168–69
Atwater, Isaac, 19, 23
Audubon Park, 93, 100, 126, 155, 158, 180
Austin, Adin, 21

Baker Park, 166
Barnes, Edward Larrabee, 213
Barnes Park, 50
Barton, A. B., 33, 54
Bassett, Daniel, 21, 37
Bassett's Creek, 90, 94, 112, 144, 148, 160, 161, 200
beaches and swimming, 127–29, 145
Beard, Henry, 32–33, 36, 48
Beard's Plaisance, 33, 110
Belton, Ernie, 222
Beltrami Park, 92–93, *93,* 177
Berg, Tom, 191
Berger Fountain, Loring Park, 179, *179*
Berry, Frank, 121, *121,* 123, 127, 132–34
Berry, William Morse, 33–34, *34,* 53, 55–56, 65–66, 68, 72, 74, 76, 174, 189

Berthe, A. E., engineer, 113
Bethune Park, 176, 216
bicycles and bicycling, 40, 66–67, 219, 223–24, 226
Boardman, Andrew, 22, 27–28, 46, 51
Boeglin, Louis, 81–82, 212
Bohannon Park, 148, 156, 158
Boom Island, 200–201, 204–5, *204*
Booth, Clifford T., 121–27, *121,* 228
Bossen, Christian, 81, 141, 146–47, *146,* 149–52, *151,* 164, 174, 190
Bossen Field, 155
Bossen's Lane, 152
Bottineau Park, 95, *137,* 179–80
Bovey, William, 112, 118
Boys and Girls Clubs, 211, 216
Brackett, George, x, 11–14, *12,* 19, 21–22, 39–40, 42, 44–46, 53–54, 64, 93, 116
Brackett Field, 96, 136, 160, 217
Braddock, Ed, 161, 193
Bratt, Walter, 214
Brauer, Don, 183–84
Brightbill, Charles, 169–70, 173–75, 180–81, 226–27
Brown, Henry, 46, 48, 54, 69, 101
Brown, Susan, 68–69
Brownie Lake, 90, 109, 160, 162–63, *162*
Bryant Square, 77, 107, 127, 134, 160, 177
Bryn Mawr Park, 85, 94, 134, 148, 176, 177, 183, 185, 222
Burlington Northern Railroad, 203, 206, 218
Butler, Eloise, 82, *82,* 148, 228. *See also* Eloise Butler Wildflower Garden
Butler, Henry, 48

Camden Park. *See* Webber Park
Capital Long-range Improvement Commission (CLIC), 157, 158–59, 169, 173

Carl W. Kroening Interpretive Center, 220–21, *220*
Carlson, Arne, 184
Cavell Park, 176
Cedar Avenue Field, 95
Cedar Lake, 35, 36, 38, 75, 77, 90, 105–20, 109, 113, 149, *149,* 159, 214, 218
Central High School, 210–11, 221
Central Park (Minneapolis). *See* Loring Park
Central Park (New York City), 5, 6, 12, 27, 41, 90
Central Riverfront Regional Park, 201
Chute, Richard, 19, 77
Chute, Samuel, 27
Civilian Conservation Corps (CCC), 112
Clarke, F. A., 100
Clean Water Partnership, 193
Cleveland, Horace William Shaler, x, 1–9, *4,* 11–13, 15–18, 20, 24–34, 35–36, 39, 41–44, 46, 49–52, 56, 60, 62, 65, 67–70, 71–72, 77, 85, 138–39, 159, 174, 187, 189, 198, 208, 228
    quoted, 3–4, 31–32, 41
Cleveland, Maryann (Dwinel), 5, 17, 33, 71
Cleveland, Ralph, 33, 50, 71
Clinton Park, 96
Columbia Park, 51, *56,* 95, 98, 117, 129, 155, 164, 168, 223; golf course, 110, 122, 134–35
Committee to Save Our Parks, 182
community sings, 131, *131,* 145, 161
Corcoran Park, 178, 179–80
Cornelius Amory Pugsley Award, 146, 166, 171, 174
Cowles, Sage and John, 213
Cowles Conservatory, 210, 212–13, *213*
Coyle Community Center, 211
Creekview Park, 178, 226
Crimmins, Inez, 101–2, *101,* 181
Crone, Martha, 148, *148*

Index

Cross, Judson, 21
Currie Park, 148–49, 179, 211, 216

Dayton, George, 62
Dayton, Kenneth and Judy, 213
Dayton Hudson Foundation, 213
Dayton's, 192
Dean, Joseph, 38
Dean Parkway, 38, 90, 109, 115, 190
Decker, Wilbur, 85, 95–96, 126, 198
DeLaSalle High School, 200, 202
Dell Park, 110
DeMars, Louis, 182, 184
Deming Heights, 117
Depression. *See* Great Depression
DeVoto, Dave, 191–92
Dhainin, Felix, 166, 167
Diamond Lake, 100, 102, 112–13, 148, 175, *175*
Dickman Park, 155, 161
Dietz, Alice, 132, 134, 136, 144, 145, 153, 228
DNR. *See* Minnesota Department of Natural Resources
Doell, Charles, 113, 131, 137, 146, 151–53, *151, 157, 157*, 159–61, 163–67, 174, 190, 201, 221
Dunwoody, William, 42, 77
Durenberger, David, 205–6
Dutch Elm Disease Control Fund, 191
Dziedzic, Walt, 158, 184, 221, 224

East Phillips Park, 179, 180
East River flats, 57
East River Parkway, 95, 185
Eastman, William, 12–13, 17, 19, 21, 90, 202
Eastman, William, Mrs., 198
Eckbo, Garret, 186–87
Edgewater Park, 207
Edison Ice Arena, 225
Edward Waite Neighborhood House, 177
Ellingsen, Chris, 143
Elliot, Jacob, Dr., 29, 49
Elliot Park, 29, 33, 97, 154, 192, 226
Eloise Butler Wildflower Garden, x, 82, 148, *148*. *See also* Butler, Eloise
Elwell Field, 148–49, 158, 159, 163, 185
Elwell Law, 133–34, 173
Erdall, Richard, 184

Fair Oaks, 14, 94, *94,* 207. *See also* Washburn Fair Oaks Park
Farview Park, 26, 29–30, *29,* 32, 40, 61, 66, 69, 78, 95–96, 123, 179, 210
Fairway Foundation, 226
Father Hennepin Bluffs, 200–201
Feldman, Harvey, 174, 182, 215, 221
Fine, Bob, 181, 207, 221, 226
First Bank, 192, 205
First Bridge Park, 206
Fisher, David, 197–98, *197,* 201–2, 205, 209, 212–13, 215, 219, 224, 226
Fletcher, Loren, 7, 12, 13, 16, 19, 20, 116
Fogg, Joseph, 48

Folwell, William Watts, x, 1–3, 7–9, *8, 9,* 11, 15, 18, 24, 26, 30, 47–51, 54–57, 61–62, 61–64, 65, 67–72, 79, 81, *116,* 125, 138, 147, 165, 189, 218, 228
  quoted, 62, 68, 69, 165
Folwell Park, 95–96, 131, 136, 155, 177, 180
Ford Dam, 97, *97,* 106
Fort Snelling, 29, 102, 159, 198, 221, 222
Fort Snelling golf course, 211, 226
Foundation for Minneapolis Parks, 219
fountains, 50, 56, 90, 91, *91,* 157, 179, *179*
Fox, William, 136
Francis Gross Golf Course, 117, 122, 135, 136, 153, 170, *170,* 185
Franklin Cooperative Creamery, 143
Franklin Steele Square, 18, 27
Fraser, Don, 198, 212, 219
freeways and highways, and park land sales, 162–64, 167–68, 172, 183–87, 220
French, David, 191
French, William, 18, 52, 71
Friedman, Martin, 164, 212, 213
Fruen, Arthur, 148
Fuji-ya, Japanese restaurant, 203
Fuller Park, 178, 179

Gale, Samuel, 8, 19, 46
Garden of the Seasons, Loring Park, 217
gardens, 77, 84, 169, 212, 217, 220. *See also* flowers; specific gardens
Gateway, The, 13, 19, 89–92, *91, 92,* 147, 198, 216
Gearty, Edward, 168, 183–84
General Mills, 145, 158, 171
Gilbert, Dale, 182, 184
Glacier Park, 203, 218
Glendale Park, tennis court, 66
Glenwood Housing Redevelopment, 159
Glenwood-Inglewood Company, 148
Glenwood Park. *See* Theodore Wirth Park
Glueck Park, 207
Godward, A. C., 113
golf and golf courses, 122, 134–36, 170, *170,* 226. *See also* Francis Gross Golf Course; Fort Snelling golf course; Hiawatha Golf Course; Meadowbrook Golf Course, Columbia Park
Grand Rounds, parkways encircling city, ix, 3, 25–27, 49, 73, 88, 93, 95, 115, 116–17, 118, 166, 187, 218, 220, 222. *See also* parkways
Graves, Rochelle Berry, 222
Great Depression, 53–57, 101, 104, 118, 119, 141–44, 146–47, 147–48, 153, 155
Great River Road, 202, 207
Greben, Seymour, 180–82
Greben Report, 180–82, 195, 212, 215
Green, John, 35, 37
Gross, Francis, x, 90, 111, 145–47, 149–50, 153–54, *154,* 157, *157,* 166, 228
Gross Golf Course. *See* Francis Gross Golf Course

Grossman, N. Bud and Arlene, 214
Gulick, Luther, Dr., 121, 123
Gurban, Jon, 224–28, *225;* quoted, 228
Guthrie Theater, 160, 184, 208, *208,* 212

Haik, Ray, 183–84
Hall Park, 179, 180
Hall, Richard, 222
Harrison Park, 159, 210
Haugan, Andrew, 21, 55
Hawthorne Park. *See* Wilson Park
Heffelfinger, Frank, 157
Hennepin Avenue, parkway, 36, 48, 49
Hennepin County, independent park district, 165, 166, 188, 206
Hennepin Island, 200–201, 208, 228
Hiawatha Golf Course, 122, 134–35, 226
highways and freeways, and park land sales, 162–64, 167–68, 172, 183–87, 220
Hill, James J., 20, 92
Hillmeyer, Patricia, 102, 198
Hi-View Park, 155, 168
Hofstede, Al, 185
Holiday, Lucille, 131
Holmes Park, 159
Holt Motor Company, 145
Honeywell, 168, 192
horse racing, on frozen lakes, 40, 68, *68*
horseshoes, 137
Housing and Urban Development Department (HUD), 173, 177–78, 218
Howe, Mary, 149
Hoyer, Eric, 157
HUD. *See* Housing and Urban Development Department
Humphrey, Hubert, 151, 157, *157,* 168, *168*
Humphrey, Hubert "Skip," III, 191

ice hockey, 122, 130
ice skating rinks, 39–40, 66, 122, 129–30, 145, 194
Interlachen Park. *See* William Berry Park
Island Sash and Door Company, 200–201

Jackson Square, 77, 107, 124, 126
James I. Rice Memorial Parkway, 197, 205
Jim Lupient Foundation, 223
Jim Lupient Water Park, 176, 223
Johnson, Charles O., 83
Johnson, Elsa, 102
Johnson, H. A., 136
Johnson, Lyndon, 168, *168,* 173
Jones, David, 111
Jones, Harry Wild, 61, 63, 66, 67, 189, 217
Jones, Robert "Fish," 64, 99–100
Jordan Park, 210

Kantorowicz, Richard, 169, 184
Keegan's Lake. *See* Wirth Lake
Keewaydin Park, 100, 155, 160, 177, 181
Kenilworth Lagoon, 109
Kenny Park, 156, 210

Index

Kenwood (Boulevard) Parkway, 35, 36, 38–39, 49, 51, 57, 66
Kenwood Gardens, 169, *169*, 212
Kenwood Park, 88, 104, 125, 180, 210
King, William S. (Colonel), ix, 7, 10, 14–15, *14*, 19–20, 22–23, 31–33, 36, 48, 75, 89, 92, 93, 202; quoted, 23, 31
King Park. *See* Martin Luther King Park
King's Highway, 14, 115
Kingsley, Burton, 83–84, *83*, 184
kittenball, forerunner of softball, 133
Knights of Labor, 22
Kroening, Carl W., 188, 205, 220–21

Lake Amelia. *See* Lake Nokomis
Lake Calhoun, x, 18, 25, 30, *38*, 40, 88–89, 104, 107–18, 125, 139, 149, 214, 223
    beaches and bathhouses, 61, 128–29, *128*, *129*, 158
    boat rentals, 59, 60, 129, 227
    channel, 37, *37*, 75, 77, 108, 109, *109*, 149, *149*, 167, *167*
    parkway, 26, 33, 36, 38, *38*, 48, 188
Lake Harriet, x, *10*, 25, 30, 48, 96, 104–13, 125, 160
    bandstands and pavilions, 59, *59*, 60, *60*, 61–63, *61*, *62*, *63*, 83, 96, 129, 131, 165, 210, 211, *211*, 217
    boat rentals, 31, *31*, 59–60, *59*, 129, 131, 160, 227
    music in park, 130–31, 145, 156, 165
    parkway, 32–33, 36–39, 42, 48, 139, 186–88
    William King's land, 14, 15, 32–33, 48
    See also Lyndale Rose Garden; Thomas Sadler Roberts Bird Sanctuary
Lake Harriet streetcar line, 48, *48*, 60, 187
Lake Hiawatha, x, 35, 89–90, 98, 112, 122, 125, 134–35, 148, 156, 180. *See also* Hiawatha Golf Course
lake levels, in chain of lakes, 160–61, 168
Lake Nokomis, x, 57, 77, 88–89, 109–13, 125, 180, 214, 223
    beaches and bathhouses, 128
Lake of the Isles, x, 30, 36, *36*, 78, 88–89, 104–13, 139, 215
    channel, 37, *37*, 75, 77, 108–9, *109*, 149, *167*
    dredging and filling, 38–39, 51–52, *52*, 105–6, 108–9
    park and parkway, 35–38, 49, 57, 160
Lake Pollution Control Fund, 173
Lake Street, boulevard, 30–31
Lakewood Cemetery, 7, 14–15, 30, 33, 48, 71–72, 116, 159
Landscape Architecture as Applied to the Wants of the West (Cleveland), 2
Lathrop, Harold, 113
Legislative Commission on Minnesota Resources, 207
Leighton, B. G., 136
Leonard Neiman Sports Complex, 211, 222
Lerman, Mary, 174, 212, 215

Lewis, Anna B., 92
Lewis, Henry, 43
Linden Hills (Boulevard) Parkway, 33, 48
Linden Hills Park, 96, 107, 110, 136, 139, 177, 181
"Little Falls, The" (Lewis, 1854), 43, *43*
Logan Park, 26, 28, 29–30, 32, 40, 131, *131*, 144, 152
    field house and community center, 122, 124, *126*, 126–27, 132, 134, 138–39, 143, 177, 180, 217
    playground, 78, *78*, 121, *122*, 123
Long John's Pond, 77
Longfellow, Henry Wadsworth, 4, 5, 99
Longfellow Field, 95–96, 98, 117, 126–27, 132
Longfellow Garden, 185, 220
Longfellow House, 99–100, 185, 220, *220*, 222
Longfellow Lagoon, 184
Longfellow Meadow, 64, 99, *99*, 184, 187
Longfellow Park, 96, 98, 169, 178, 180
Loper, Naomi, 102, 205, 214
Loring, Charles Morgridge, ix, x, 1–3, 6–9, *6*, 11–19, 21–23, 27, 29, 31–42, 44, 47–54, 56, 60, 63, 65–69, 71, 76, 79, 91, 112, *116*, 138, 147, 154, 186, 189, 228
    quoted, 37, 52, 53, 60
Loring, Emily (Crossman), 6, 54, 71
Loring, Florence (Barton), 54, 67, 68–69, 91
Loring Cascade, man-made waterfall, 112
Loring Park, 14, 27–30, 32–33, 35–36, 40, 44, 50, 61, 67, 69, 73, 137, 152, 160, 164, 184, 217
    expansions and maintenance, 54–55, 75, 78, 217
    gardens, 169, 212, 217
    parkway, 37–38, 51
    shelter and warming house, 1907, 79, *79*, 177, 217
    skating rink, 40, *40*, 66
Loring Pond, 27–28, *28*, 40, *40*, 70, 79, *79*, 140, *140*, 217
Lowry, Goodrich, 193
Lowry, Thomas, 13, 36, 42, 46, 49, 51, 59, 60, 75, 77, 91, 92, 193; statue, 186
Lowry Hill, 36, 38, 42, 157, 186
Lowry Park (Mt. Curve Triangle), 97
Luxton Park, 95–96, 127, 159, 176, 210
Lyndale Farm/Farmstead, 14, 48, 75, 92, 144, 146, 159, 180, 210, 224
Lyndale Park, 14, 30, 48, 51, 57, 212, *212*
    fountain, 91, 157, *157*
    playground pageants, 131–32, *132*
Lyndale Rose Garden, 76, 77, *77*
Lynnhurst Park, 96, 136–37, 139, 160, 177, 180

Malkerson, Betty, 187
Manning, Warren, 77
Maple Hill Cemetery, 92, *93*. *See also* Beltrami Park
Marcy Park, 195
Marshall Terrace Park, 95–96, 198
Martin Luther King Park, 95, 136, 145, 152, 155, 158, 168, 176, 185

Matthews Park, 98, 159, 167, 176
McNair, William W. (Mac), 7, 8, 12, 23, 36, 38
McRae Park, 155, 158, 179, 222
Meadowbrook Golf Course, 122, 135, *135*, 136, 153, 170
Mendenhall, Richard, 13–14, 36, 93
Merriman, Orlando, 11, 21
Merritt, James, 32
Metropolitan Airports Commission (MAC), 102–4, 166, 222
Metropolitan Council, 165, 166, 188, 210, 218
Metropolitan Parks and Open Spaces Commission (MPOSC), 188, 200–201, 204–6, 213
Mill City Museum, 203
Mill Ruins Park, 202–3, 205–6, *206*, 208, *208*, 221
Miller, Lucian, 138
Minneapolis Board of Park Commissioners, 2, 3, 16, 18, 25–34, 95–96, 147–49, 173
    annual reports, xi, 39, 52, 54, 60, 61, 62, 67, 72 , 91, 103, 125, 134
    created (1883), 20–24, x
    and economic decline, 53–57
    first meeting, 1883, 27
    Folwell, president, 1895–1902, 55, 69
    lakes, focus on, 1880s, 35–42
    Loring, first president, 27, 51
    motto, 27, 227
    recreation program, begins, 121
    river, focus on, 1905, 72
    See also Minneapolis Park and Recreation Board
Minneapolis Board of Trade, 16–17, 19–22, 28, 44, 142, 218
Minneapolis Community Development Agency (MCDA), 179, 202, 203, 211, 213
Minneapolis Housing Authority, 159
Minneapolis Improvement League, 68, 125
Minneapolis Improvement Society, 15
Minneapolis Institute of Arts (MIA), 13–14, 36, 54, 93–94, *93*, 207, 225
Minneapolis Municipal Airport, 102–4
Minneapolis Park and Recreation Board, x, 39, 169, 172, 227. *See also* Minneapolis Board of Park Commissioners
Minneapolis park system, maps, viii, 26, 80, 114
Minneapolis Parks Legacy Society, 221
Minneapolis Planning Commission, 175
Minneapolis Sculpture Garden, 84, 88, 148, 169, 201, 210, 212–15, *213*, 219
Minneapolis Society of Fine Arts, 3, 41, 42, 44, 94
Minneapolis Woman's Club, 82, 125
Minnehaha Creek, *42*, 72, 135, 144, 166, 189
    highway construction, 172, 183–85, 220
    and lake levels, 152, 160, 168
    park, 26, 46, 63
    parkway, 35–36, 38, 42, 48, 139
Minnehaha Creek Watershed District, 193, 223

Index

Minnehaha Falls, 5, 29, 43–47, 54, 64, 168, *168*
    photo kiosk, 50, 63–64
Minnehaha Falls Athletic Club, 181
Minnehaha Park, 16, 26, 33, 43–47, 64, 78, 124, 159, 168, 180, 227, 214
    bicycle path, 66–67
    highway plans, 172, 183–85, 220
    refectory, 63, 158, 160
Minnehaha Parkway, 35–36, 38, 42, 51, 56, 57, 66, 89
Minnehikers, hiking club, 136
Minnesota Audubon Society, 150
Minnesota Department of Natural Resources, 211, 215
Minnesota Historical Society, 3, 203
Minnesota Minority Junior Golf Foundation, 226
Minnesota Pollution Control Agency (MPCA), 205
Minnesota Shade Tree Advisory Committee, 191
Minnesota Transportation Museum, 187
Mississippi River, x, 15, *199*
    gorge, 97, 196, *196*
    parklands, 35, 51, 72, 165, 174, 180, 196, 197–208
MnDOT (Minnesota Department of Transportation), 204
Moore, Howard, 167–71, *167*, 174, 176, 183, 221
Morris Baker Foundation, 166
Morrison, Clinton, 13, 46, 93
Morrison, Dorilus, 7, 12–15, *13*, 19, 21–22, 38, 93, 97
Mt. Curve Triangle (Lowry Park), 97
Mud Lake. *See* Lake Hiawatha
Mueller Park, 177–78
Murphy, Edward, 12, 16, 49
Murphy Square, 12, 16, 27, 33, 40, 168
music, in parks, 59, 130–31, 144–45, 156

Naftalin, Arthur, 169, 222
National Guard, 190, *190*;
National Guard Armory, 84, *84*, 148
National Park and Recreation Association, 184
National Park Service (NPS), 81, 178, 199, 205, 208, 221
National Public Links Championship (golf), 135, 170
National Recreation Association (NRA), 141, 142
National Register of Historic Places, 206
National Scenic Byway, 218, 222
Neighborhood Revitalization Program (NRP), 216–18, 221
Neiman, Leonard, 181, 200, 211
Neiman, Scott, 200, 221
Nelson, Benjamin F., 200, 204–5
Nelson, Dorothea, 134, 136–38
Nicollet Island, *xii*, 11–13, 42, 195, 198–204, *202*
Nicollet Park. *See* Martin Luther King Park
Nokomis Naturescape Garden, 214

North Commons, 88, *88*, 123–25, *124*, 127, 132, 136, 138, 152, 177–78, 180, 223
North Mississippi Park, 155, 178, 183, 185, *185*, 207, 220–21
Northeast Athletic Field Park, 142, 149, 176, 222, 223
Northeast Ice Arena, 225
Northeast Pool, 176
Northrup, Jesse, xi, 89, 91, 134
Nutter, Frank, Jr., 113

Oak Lake Park, 147
Oak Lake Park Improvement Association, 41, 147
Oberhoffer, Emil, 63
Oberstar, Jim, 218
Odell, Clinton, 148
off-road cycling, 226
Olmsted, Frederick Law, 4, 5–6, 9, 15–16, 52, 60, 68, 71, 76, 77, 182
Olson, Jon, 200
Olson, Orvin "Ole," 198, 200, 207
Olympics, Winter. *See* Winter Olympics
Orvin "Ole" Olson Park, 207, 222
Oswald, John, 21, 94

pageants, playground, 1916–1941, 132
Painter Park, 179
Panic of 1893, 55, 56
Parade, The, 75, 77, 158, 179, 186, 225
    as amateur sports and recreation park, 122, 126, 133, 142
    land sales, 164, 168, 176, 184, 185, 204
    playgrounds and sports fields, 124, 126, 127, 133, 142
Parade Ice Center, 178
Parade Stadium, 157–58, *158*, 160–61
Parent-Teacher Association (PTA), 152, 155
Park Act of 1883, 152, 185–86, 218, 227
Parks in the Cities program, 177–78
parkways, 36, 40, 48–49, 114, 115, 182, 186–88.
    See also specific parkways
Peace Garden, 212, *212*
Pearl Park, 100, 102, 148, 175–76, *175*
Peavey, Frank, 50, 96
Peavey Fountain, 50, *50*
Peavey Park, 96, 154–55, 158, 161, 217, 224
Pergola Garden, 220
Perkins Hill Park, 155, 185
Pershing Park, 96, 100–101, 139, 160, 178, 181
Peterson, P. Kenneth, 101, 184
Phelps, Edmund, 84–85, 91, 146
Phelps Park, 96, 136, 176, 216
Phillips, Lorna, 101–2, *101*
Phillips neighborhood, 216, 219
Phyllis Wheatley Community Center, 176, 216
Pillsbury, Alfred F., 142, *142*, 144, 146, 200
Pillsbury, George, 19, 142
Pillsbury, John S., 8, 14, 21, 142, 200
Pillsbury Company, 192, 201
Pillsbury Park, 201

Pillsbury settlement houses, 148–49, 211
Pillsbury United Communities, 211, 216
Pillsbury Waite Neighborhood Services, 176
Pioneers Square, 147, 149, 198
Playground Association of America (PAA), 121–22
playground pageants, 1916–1941, 131–32, *132*, 134, 144–45, 149
playgrounds, 51–52, 67–69, 78, 107, 121–27, 132–34, 136–38, 142, 146, 153, 155–56, 158–59, 225
police, park force, 39, 66, 83, *83*, 224
polio, and playground attendance, 156
postwar progress, 151–62
Powderhorn Lake, 31, 48, 51, 56, 111, 112, 126, 180
Powderhorn Park, 42, 97, 177, 221
    design and implementation, 56
    playground, summer program, 123
    recreation center, 160, 169
    toboggan and sled tracks, 130
Pratt, Robert, 68
Prudential Insurance Company, 163–64, 191
PTA. *See* Parent-Teacher Association
Public Playgrounds Association, 68
Pugsley Award. *See* Cornelius Amory Pugsley Award
Pulscher, MaryLynn, 105
Purcell, William Gray, 115

Quaking Bog, Wirth Park, x, 215, 216, *216*
Quist, Walter, 75, 158

Rainville, Alice, 205
Raymond, Karl, 121, *121*, 123, 136, 137, 142
Recreation Activity Councils, 181
recreation and sports, in parks, 39, 40–41, 51–52, 57, 59–64, 65–70, 152, 209, 221–26, 228
    active service vs. ornamentation, 137, 138, 143
    evaluation of, 141–50
    philosophy, 169, 174–75
Recreation Plus, 215, 217, 221
Reeve, Charles, 32
regional parks, 166, 188, 205
Regis Corporation, 213
Rice Lake. *See* Lake Hiawatha
Rice, Brian, 188, 205
Rice, James I., 188, 205, 206
Richard Chute Square, 77
Ridgway, James Arthur, 81, 84, 90, 131
Ridgway Parkway, 117, 168
Rietkerk, Judd, 218
Riverfront Development Coordinating Board (RDCB), 200–201, 204, 205–6
Riverside Park, 29–30, 33, 38, 40–41, 69, 78, 98, 104, 121, 131, 168, 185, 202, 223
Rober, Lewis, 133
Roberts, Thomas Sadler, 150; *See also* Thomas Sadler Roberts Bird Sanctuary
Rockwood, Chelsea J., 84–85

Rosacker, Henry, 168, 176
Rosacker Pool, 176, 223
Ruhe, Robert, 171–82, *171,* 183–84, 186, 188, 192, 194–95, 201, 212, 215, 217
Ryan, Patrick, 55, 57, 69

St. Anthony, city, merged with Minneapolis, 1, 11,
St. Anthony Boulevard, 95, 117
St. Anthony Falls, 228
    mills and milling, 3, 7
    nearby dam and reservoir, 97
    park, 198, 199, 208
    river gorge, 97, 196, *196*
St. Anthony Falls Heritage Board, 203, 206
St. Anthony Park, 177
St. Mark's Episcopal Cathedral, 27, 28
Sandy Lake, 51, 110
sanitary sewer system, 166
Saratoga Park, 47
Sarna, John, 188, 205, 206
Sayles-Belton, Sharon, 193–94, 219, 222
Schmidt, Michael, 226
schools, and parks, 155–56, 175
Sea Salt restaurant, Minnehaha Park, 227
Sellergren, Dave, 200
Seward neighborhood, 159, 167, 176, 217
Shapiro, Joseph, 193
Sheridan Memorial Park, 207
Shiely (J. L.) Company, 205
Shingle Creek, 90, 106, 127–28, 154, 156, 161, 166, 168, 185, *185*
Shutter, Marion, Rev., 116, 125
Sibley Park, 96, 136, 176
Siggelkow, Don, 219
Simonds, O. C., 71
skate/skateboarding parks, 226
Smerling, Beverly, 101–2
Smith, Alden, 188
snowboarding, 226
softball, 133
Solomon, Ed, 221, 222
Song of Hiawatha Garden, 220
Southwest Activities Council (SWAC), 181
Spears, Charles, 195, 201
speed-skating, 130, 145, 167
Spirit of Peace sculpture, 212
sports and recreation. *See* recreation and sports
Spring Lake, 42, 104, 112
StarTribune, 197–98, 203, 209
Steele, Franklin, 18, 27, 49
Stenvig, Charles, mayor, 184, 188
Stevens, John, 40
Stevens Square, 88, 97, 125–26
Stewart, D. D., 95
Stewart Park, 95, 100, 126, 127, 155, 158, 179
Stinson, James, 33
Stone Arch Bridge, 20, *20,* 201, 206, *206,* 208, *208*

Suggestions for a System of Parks and Parkways for the City of Minneapolis (Cleveland, 1883), 2, 25–26, *26,* 31–32, 33, 43
Sumner Field, 94–95, 126, 127, 136
swimming and beaches, 127–29, 145. *See also* specific beaches, lakes, pools

Teen Teamworks, 213, 215
tennis courts, 40, 66, 126, 133, 158, 171
Theodore Wirth Park, x, 47–48, 71, 73, 77, 87–88, 130, 134, 144, 146, 148–149, 158, 162–163, 185, 214–216, 226
    chalet, golf clubhouse and warming house, 130, 134–35, *135,* 221
    golf course, 122, 130, 134–35, 165, 170
    skiing and ski-jumping, 130, *130,* 194, *194*
    See also Eloise Butler Wildflower Garden; Wirth, Theodore
Thomas Sadler Roberts Bird Sanctuary, x, 112, 139, 150, 152
Thompson, Milo, 211
Thompson, Tommy, 198, 199
Three Rivers Park District, 206, 220
Tin Fish restaurant, Lake Calhoun, 227
Todd, George, 168–69
Todd Park, 148
Tower Hill, 88
Tree Preservation and Reforestation Fund, 172
trees and tree planting, 34, 35, 39, 57, 189–94, *190, 192*
Turnblad, Swan, 54–55

Upper Harbor Terminal, 199

Van Cleve Park, 48, 66, *66,* 126, 176, 177, 180; playground and fields, 50, 67, 123, 136
Van Valkenburg, Michael, 213
Vaux, Calvert, 5, 15
Vento, Bruce, 205
Victory Memorial Drive, 95, 115–17, *115, 117,* 182, *182*
Victory Playground, 178, 180
Villa Rosa, Morrison home, 93
Virginia Triangle, 186
Voegeli, Thomas, 90

Waite, Edward, 156, 177
Waite Park, 155–56, 157, 179, 217
Walker Art Center, 164, 179, 184, 210, 212–14, 218
Washburn, William, 13, 14, 36, 94
Washburn Fair Oaks Park, 14, 94, 97, 104, 192. *See also* Fair Oaks
Water Power Park, 208, 228
Webber, Charles and Mary, 106, 127
Webber Park, 77, 90, 93, 95, 117, 126, 154, 179–80, 185; community center and library, 106, 127, 158

Webber Pool, 106–7, *107,* 127–28, 180
Weir, Liebert, 133, 141–46, 150, 152–56, 158, 160–61, 166, 169–70, 174–76, 178, 180–81, 226–27
Weisman, Frederick, 213
Wells, Fred, 211
Wells, Henry, 21, 27, 28
West River Parkway, 70, *70,* 197, 200, 202, 205, 208, *208,* 214, 218, *218*
West River Road, 107, 200, 207
West, John, 22
Whitney, Irene Hixon, 213
Whittier Park, 177–78, 217
Willard Park, 177–78
Willeke, Don, 189–90, 191–92
William Berry Park, 48, 60, 62, 111
William Berry Parkway, 188
William Bros. Boiler Works, 200
Wilson, Eugene (Gene), 7, 22–23, 46, 185; quoted, 22
Wilson Park, 18, 27, 185–86
Windom, William, 53
Windom Park, 42, 50
Winter Olympics, 130, 145, 167
Wirth, Theodore, x, 6, 25, *34, 74, 76,* 98, *151, 157,* 187
    burial, 159
    as earth mover, 105–20
    as man of action, 73–80
    as man of his time, 87–104
    as man of structure, 81–85
    and rise of recreation, 121–40
    and river development, 198, 201
    superintendent of parks, 1906-35, 54, 69, 74, 121, 139, 146, 151, 166, 170–71, 174, 186, 209, 227, 228
    See also Theodore Wirth Park
Wirth Lake, 27, 77, 87–88, 90, 112, 128, 149, 216
Wirth Park. *See* Theodore Wirth Park
Wittman, Al, 171, 177–78, 179, 187, 194, 198, 201–2, 209, 210, 214, 227–28
Wold-Chamberlain airfield, 102
Women's Welfare League, 94
Works Progress Administration (WPA), 144, 145–46, 149, 153, 218
World War I, 94, 102, 116, 134, 149
World War II, 101, 145–46, 149, 167, 173, 190
WPA. *See* Works Progress Administration
Wright, Ben, 157, 167, 186, 187

Xcel Energy, 208, 228

YMCA, 121, 123, 125, 126, 127, 211
Young, Annie, 214
Youthline Outreach Mentorship Program, 215–16, 221

Zimmermann, Dean, 184, 214
zoos, 64, 99–100